Nassau William Senior, M. C. M. Simpson

Conversations with M. Thiers, M. Guizot, and other distinguished Persons, during the Second Empire

Vol. II

Nassau William Senior, M. C. M. Simpson

Conversations with M. Thiers, M. Guizot, and other distinguished Persons, during the Second Empire
Vol. II

ISBN/EAN: 9783337166540

Printed in Europe, USA, Canada, Australia, Japan

Cover: Foto ©ninafisch / pixelio.de

More available books at **www.hansebooks.com**

CONVERSATIONS

WITH

M. THIERS, M. GUIZOT,

AND OTHER DISTINGUISHED PERSONS,

DURING THE SECOND EMPIRE.

BY THE LATE

NASSAU WILLIAM SENIOR,

MASTER IN CHANCERY, PROFESSOR OF POLITICAL ECONOMY,
MEMBER CORRESPONDANT DE L'INSTITUT DE FRANCE, ETC.
AUTHOR OF
"A TREATISE ON POLITICAL ECONOMY," "BIOGRAPHICAL SKETCHES," "ESSAYS ON FICTION,"
"HISTORICAL AND PHILOSOPHICAL ESSAYS,"
"JOURNALS KEPT IN TURKEY AND GREECE," "JOURNALS KEPT IN IRELAND,"
"JOURNALS KEPT IN FRANCE AND ITALY,"
"CORRESPONDENCE AND CONVERSATIONS WITH ALEXIS DE TOCQUEVILLE," ETC.

EDITED BY HIS DAUGHTER,

M. C. M. SIMPSON.

IN TWO VOLUMES.

VOL. II.

LONDON:
HURST AND BLACKETT, PUBLISHERS,
13, GREAT MARLBOROUGH STREET.
1878.

All rights reserved.

Ballantyne Press
BALLANTYNE AND HANSON, EDINBURGH
CHANDOS STREET, LONDON

CONTENTS

OF

THE SECOND VOLUME.

1855.

March 2nd.
CONVERSATION WITH THIERS.
England a naval, France a military power 1
English officers are gentlemen 2

March 3rd.
CONVERSATION WITH THIERS.
Death of Emperor Nicholas 2
Doubts as to its being natural 3

CONVERSATION WITH MANIN.
Allows his conversations to be published 3
Fears the desertion of Victor Emmanuel 4
Poland is Russia's vulnerable point 4
Hopes for Italy 4
Misery of the French army in the Crimea 5
Louis Napoleon becoming unpopular 5

March 4th.
CONVERSATION WITH MOHL.
Profuse expenditure of the Court 6
Louis Napoleon impatient of restraint 6

CONVERSATION WITH MÉRIMÉE.
Emperor's proposed journey to the Crimea 6
Peace depends on the fall of Sebastopol 6
Mismanagement of the siege 7
Death of Nicholas too opportune to be natural 8

CONVERSATION WITH CIRCOURT AND CHRZANOWSKI.
Levée en masse enough to account for Nicholas' death . . 8

Excellence of English army	9
Wickedness of allowing it to starve	9
Mismanagement of attack and defence	10
Tactics of Lord Raglan and Duke of Wellington	10
Inkerman a soldier's battle	11
Dense masses of the Russians	11
Inactivity of the French	12
Turks should not be at Eupatoria	12
Want of horses	13
Probability of pestilence	13
Indecision of Generals	14
Inexperience in war	15
Army of Austria	16

May 18th.

The Institut	17
Coup d'État aimed at its independence	18
Deputation to the Emperor	19
He modifies his demands	19
Wolowski is elected	20

May 20th.

CONVERSATION WITH GRIMBLOT.

War has become unpopular	20
Ignorance and incapacity of Louis Napoleon	21
Inaccessibility to argument	21
Mismanagement of war	22
Enormous fortunes and expenditure of the Court	22
Envy and hatred occasioned by them	22
'Maison nette'	22
Abuses of power	23
Interference with justice	23
Arrest of Grassot	24
Arrest of a Professor	24
Admonition of Jules Simon	24
People are exiled or 'interné'	24
Badness of Louis Napoleon's instruments	25
Attempt of Pianori	25
The 'peuple' love military glory	26

May 22nd.

CONVERSATION WITH RÉMUSAT.

Louis Napoleon's friends and ministers eager for peace	27
They attempt to hamper the war	27

CONTENTS. vii

	PAGE
Enormous tribute of men	28
Result of Conscription in the time of Napoleon	28
Deterioration of 'physique'	29
Demands of Austria	29
Louis Napoleon has lost the prestige of success	29
Is shaken by Pianori's attempt	29

May 23rd.
CONVERSATION WITH CIRCOURT AND MANIN.
Influence of the Pope greater without temporal power . . 30
Ancient colonisation of Africa 31
Polytheism is tolerant 32
Superior effect of Christianity on conduct 32
Ancient amalgamation of races 33

May 25th.
CONVERSATION WITH DUC DE BROGLIE.
Expensiveness of Algeria 34
Difficulties in the Crimea 34

CONVERSATION WITH AUGUSTE CHEVALIER.
The Crédit Mobilier 35
Expensiveness of living in Paris 35

May 30th.
CONVERSATION WITH MANIN AND RÉMUSAT.
Alfieri's tragedies 36
Our reception of Louis Napoleon 36
Causes of his popularity in England 37
Persigny's antecedents 37

May 31st.
CONVERSATION WITH RÉMUSAT.
Prospects of the English Alliance 38
The Empire required a war 39
French love for conquest 39
Louis Napoleon is grateful to England 40
He has no keeping in his mind 40

CONVERSATION WITH LABAUME.
Attempt of Pianori 41
Endeavour to hush it up 41
Difficulty of obtaining verdicts from juries 41
Long interrogation of prisoners 42

CONVERSATION WITH CHRZANOWSKI.
Armies in the Crimea 42
Corruption and decay of Russia 42
Tyranny and influence of the Crown 43
Reckless waste of life in Russian army 43
Frequency of 'sorties' 44
Russian Generals 45
Intermixture of German officers 45
Blunders of Menschikoff 46
Blunders of the allies 48
They did not stick to rules 48
Mortality in the French army 50
Plans of Chrzanowski 50
Want of unity among the generals 51
Peace has been always expected 53
Importance of good supplies 54
Marches of ancient armies 54
Marches of Napoleon 55
Importance of the Mamelon 55
Futile negotiations 56

CONVERSATION WITH MANIN AND ARRIVABENE.
Russia considers Austria a traitor 56
Incongruous materials of her army 57
German leaning to Prussia 58

June 7th.
CONVERSATION WITH MADAME CORNU.
Joseph's letters 58
Louis Napoleon jealous of his uncle 58
He should have been a poet 59
Character of Jérôme 59
Fête at the Hôtel de Ville 59

November 1st.
CONVERSATION WITH AUGUSTE CHEVALIER.
Louis Napoleon anxious for peace 61
His motives 61
His socialistic theories 61
His expenses 61
His ministers 61

November 2nd.
CONVERSATION WITH CHRZANOWSKI.
Character of Pelissier 62

	PAGE
Inactivity after the fall of Sebastopol	62
The Russian army demoralised	63
Dispersion of English troops	63
Anxiety for Kars	64
Lessons taught by the siege	64
To adhere to the rules of war	64
French capture of the 'Malakoff'	65
English failure at the Redan	65
What Russia and the allies should do	65
Austrian and Russian treatment of conquest	69

1856.

May 9th.

CONVERSATION WITH DUC DE BROGLIE.

Paris has lost its charm	71
Dignified attitude of the malcontents	71

CONVERSATION WITH MÉRIMÉE.

Orloff at the Congress	71
Was ordered to contest, but not to insist	72
Blunders of Walewski	72
Hostility between Russia and Austria	72
Tripartite treaty	72

CONVERSATION WITH MONTALEMBERT.

English House of Commons	73
Mischievousness of the Puritans	74

May 12th.

CONVERSATION WITH CIRCOURT AND ELLICE.

State of religion in France	74
Sacrifice of two bishops	75
Substitution of Roman for Gallican liturgy	76
Louis Napoleon hates Austria	77
Austria has mismanaged her affairs	77
Cavour is not ill-satisfied	78

May 13th.

BREAKFAST AT SENIOR'S.

Montalembert's book on England	79
Arrests of insignificant people	79
Secrecy of proceedings	80
Conduct of individuals cannot be predicted	80
Tripartite treaty	81
Complaint against Belgium	81

CONVERSATION WITH MADAME CORNU.

	PAGE
War favourable to Louis Napoleon	81
French 'peuple' would applaud the ruin of the 'agiotage'.	82
Danger of ennui to the French	82
Finesse of Orloff	82
Wishes to separate England from France	82

May 17th.
CONVERSATION WITH MANIN.

Proposed to become a teacher	83
He cannot attend except to politics	83
Italians should not remain quiet	83
Austria cannot reform herself	83
Every Italian movement has done good	84
Italy cannot be a confederation	85
She must be under one head	85
Hopes and prospects of Italy	86

May 18th.
CONVERSATION WITH MONTALEMBERT.

Louis Napoleon's treatment of Belgium	87
Freedom of Belgian press	87
A press should be entirely free	87
English freedom of press beneficial at home	87
But mischievous abroad	87
Only our blunders are known abroad	88
Folly of Walewski	88
Law of Entail in England	89

May 19th.
CONVERSATION WITH COUSIN.

Palmerston's opposition to Suez Canal	90
Sortie against Belgium	91

CONVERSATION WITH THIERS.

Folly of English opposition to Suez Canal	91
The Congress	91
The tripartite treaty	92

May 20th.
CONVERSATION WITH COUSIN.

Extension of French territory	92
Fortifications of Paris	93
Danger from the populace in a siege	93
France must rectify her northern frontier	93

CONTENTS. xi

	PAGE
And send King Leopold to Constantinople	93
Belgium does not wish to be French	94
The Rhine as a frontier	94
Annexation of Savoy and Nice	94
Exchange of Malta for Algiers	95
English sympathy with Italy	95
Algiers an encumbrance	96

CONVERSATION WITH CHRZANOWSKI.

French marshals	96
Criticisms of Thiers	96
Blücher and Sir John Moore	97
Duke of Wellington	98
Blunders in the Crimea	98
Defence of Sebastopol	99
Expenditure of men and ammunition	99
Russian and Prussian Poland	100
Stimulant of Russian soldiers	100
Polish troops in Austria	101

1857.

April 10th.

Dulness of Paris	103
Subjects of conversation	103

April 11th.
CONVERSATION WITH THIERS.

Emperor's compliment on his history	103
Duke of Wellington	103
Position of Louis Napoleon improved	104
Length of usurpations in France	104
Madame de Castiglione	104

April 15th.

Habits of the Emperor	105
He wears no coat of mail	106

April 17th.

| Russians hate Austria | 106 |

April 18th.
CONVERSATION WITH CHRZANOWSKI.

Motives of Russian soldiers	106
They hate the Germans	107

	PAGE
Bad Government of Russian Poland	107
The Emperor Nicholas	108
The defence of Sebastopol	108
Horrible condition of the Russian hospitals	108
Raw meat as a diet	109

CONVERSATION WITH DUSSARD.

Ruin of the Fusion	109
(Letters of the Duc de Nemours)	109
Chances of Bonapartes in 1833 and 1834	110
Louis Napoleon in private life	110
Mistakes in public affairs	111
Confidence is *not* restored	112
Alterations in the tariff	112
Loans	113
Name of Bonaparte no longer a spell	114

DINNER AT CIRCOURT'S.

Extravagance in dress	114
Workmen neglect Sunday	115
Workman does not save	115
Women earn their own subsistence	115
Dispute between the Emperor and Bishop of Moulins	115
Pope's great almoner	116

April 23rd.
CONVERSATION WITH CHRZANOWSKI.

Criticism of Napoleon's Russian campaign	116
In the first place he intended only a demonstration	118
French army died of want and fatigue	121
Napoleon always wasted his soldiers	121
Consequently his army at last consisted of conscripts	122
Thiers did not know this	122
Jobez praises the good sense of the Constituent Assembly	122
Chrzanowski on courage in the field of battle	123
Circourt on Lamartine and his difficulties	123

April 24th.
CONVERSATION WITH MANIN.

French protection of the Pope	125
Romans detest priestly rule	125
Rome alone can be capital of Italy	125

		PAGE
Opposition of Pope Gregory to railroads		126
Ideas *will* travel by them		126
Differences between Manin and Montanelli		127
Subscription for arming Alessandria		127
Manin at first warned by the Police		128
The Emperor allows him to go on		128

CONVERSATION WITH MONTANELLI.

Union of Italy impossible at present	128
Position of Naples	129
Opinion of Mazzini	129
Fine dresses at the Embassy	130
The chief expense in Paris	130
Society in the Faubourg St. Germain	130

April 26th.
CONVERSATION WITH DUMON.

Emperor's position stronger	131
Effect of colossal and sudden fortunes	131
Crédit Mobilier	131
Development of avarice and vanity	131
A crisis might sweep away the Empire	131
Villemain reads aloud	132

April 28th.

Tourguénieff agrees in the weakness of Nicholas	132
He should have roused the Sclavonic populations	132

May 1st.

Chrzanowski thinks the Principalities must fall under the influence of Russia	133
Manin thinks them dangerous to Austria	133
Rémusat says Austria's only real friend is England	134

CONVERSATION WITH MONTANELLI ON HIS TRAGEDY.

France the only country where the acting is good	134
Badness of Ristori's supporters	134
Montanelli hampered by their badness	134
Prosaic atmosphere of Paris	135
Ristori best in comedy	135

CONVERSATION WITH MONTALEMBERT.

Censure of the Bishop of Moulins	135
Censure and suspension of newspapers	136

Immaterial for a monthly journal 136
Religion unpopular with the Liberal party 137
In consequence of the behaviour of the Church 137
Its self-abasement and apostacy 137
Church can be free only when the people is free 138

May 2nd.
Smallness of Parisian rooms 138

May 6th.
CONVERSATION WITH CORCELLE.
Colonisation with 'honnêtes gens' 139
St. Arnaud's principles of Government 139
Algiers an expensive opera-box 139
Madame Cornu 139
The Gipsy's prophecy 140

May 7th.
Preparation for First Communion 140

May 8th.
CONVERSATION WITH MÉRIMÉE.
'Jeux innocents' at Villeneuve 141
Activity of the Emperor 141
Attempts on his life 141
He is a Fatalist 142
Courage of the Empress 142
Emperor will wear no secret armour 142
Irregular habits of exertion 143
Charm of manners and conversation 143
Prospects of the dynasty 143
Message to Thiers 143

CONVERSATION WITH LAMARTINE.
Voltaire and Rousseau 144
Richelieu and the Academy 144
Academy gave social power to literature 144
Tocqueville's 'Ancien Régime' 145
Revolution a revolt against mental slavery 145
So it enlisted the sympathies of Europe 146
In 1789 and 1848, all was hope and trust 146
In 1791 and 1849, disappointment, mistrust, and despondency 146
The country was terrified by the 'Rouges' 147

May 9th.
CONVERSATION WITH RIVET.
  Present indifference to Parliamentary Government . . . 147
  Desire for wealth 147
  The 'Siècle' the tool of Fould 147
  Will Cavaignac take the oath 148
  Such an oath not binding 148
  Scruples of honour 149
  A candidate must formally present himself 149
  The ballot no protection 150
  How the Government influences electors 150
  Consequences of the return of Cavaignac 151

  Dumon on the Spanish marriages 151

  Why Cousin will not go out of France 152

May 10th.
CONVERSATION WITH THIERS.
  He would increase duties on foreign coal 153
  Maritime wars will be coal wars 153

May 11th.
CONVERSATION WITH MÉRIMÉE.
  New military system 154
  Evils of French marriages 154
  'Mariages d'inclination, de convenance, de terreur' . . . 155
  Unmarried women have no position 155
  Definition of a 'gentilhomme' 155

May 14th.
DINNER AT ST. GERMAIN 156

CONVERSATION WITH MÉRIMÉE.
  Emperor more liberal than his entourage 156
  Right in excluding Republicans from Corps Législatif . . 156
  Game played by him while President 156
  Intriguers should be excluded 157
  Nothing permanent in France 157
  Expectations as to Spain 157
  Montpensier an improving landlord 157
  Unpopular in Spain as in Ireland 157
  Position of Spanish Grandees 158
  Dependants eat up their fortunes 158
  Centralisation an enemy to Republicanism 159
  France would not consent to be inglorious 159

1858.

	PAGE
The 'Attentat'	160
Loi de sûreté générale	160

March 3rd.
CONVERSATION WITH COUSIN.
Principal object of his life 161
Disturbed by public affairs 161
Effect of the 'attentat' at first good 162
He was urged to violence and lost his head 162
Adheres to alliance with England 162
Military addresses 162
Stupidity of Walewski 162
Palmerston threw the despatch upon the table 162
Military addresses sanctioned by the Emperor 163
Violence of the law of public safety 163
Thiers 'illustre et national' 163
Honourable conduct of Chevalier and MacMahon . . . 163
Satisfaction of Montalembert 164

March 6th.
Courage of the Emperor for the first three days 164
Urged to violence by his 'entourage' 165
Empress an enthusiast 165
They both wish to pardon Orsini 165
A usurper like the prince in the ' Arabian Nights' . . . 165
Morny's dislike of England 165
Billault's disgrace 165
Conspiracy was European 166

CONVERSATION WITH BLANCHARD.
The plot was French 167
Arrests under the new law of public safety 168
The principle was numerical 168
Some will be exiled 168
England will exercise no surveillance over them 169
The professional class will furnish most exiles 169
They will be ruined 169
Publication of Orsini's letter 170
Unaccountability of Emperor's behaviour 170
Recall of exiled generals 170
Marshal Vaillant 170

CONTENTS.

March 7th.
CONVERSATION WITH RÉMUSAT.
Calmness of Emperor at first 171
Pietri and the police. 171
Unnatural excitability of Louis Napoleon 171
His only friends the peasant and the priest 172
Orsini is interesting 172
Empress has gained in public estimation 172

Story of Espinasse in 1851 173
Inflammability of bombs 174
Emperor has ceased to believe in his star 174
Police at Lady Cowley's ball 175

March 8th.
BREAKFAST AT THE DUC DE BROGLIE'S.
Philosophy of Bentham. 176
Rejection of utility as basis of morals 176
Bentham's political economy 176

CONVERSATION WITH MOHL.
Unpopularity of Louis Napoleon among the working classes 177
Some day the discontent will explode 177

CONVERSATION WITH GUIZOT.
Dismissal of Lord Palmerston 177
Evils of parliamentary government 177
Balance in its favour 177

CONVERSATION WITH MADAME ——.
Exasperation of the French against England 178
Their envy and jealousy 178
Speech of Jules Favre 178
His difficulties and the ground he assumed 179
Speech of Chaix d'Est-Ange 179
Jules Favre's peroration 180
Orsini's letter 180
Quotation from the 'Gerusalemme' 181
Motives for publishing the letter 181
Louis Napoleon's conduct inexplicable 181
Ferocity of the Imperialists 181

April 16th.
Marochetti's château 182
He expects it will be burnt in a Rouge revolution . . 183
Absence of fine trees 183

VOL. II.

CONTENTS.

April 17th.
CONVERSATION WITH COUSIN.
Chances of war with England 184
Louis Napoleon's conduct is senseless 184
English to blame about Dr. Bernard 184
Emperor has lost his prestige 184
France wants a dictator 184
All business is at a stand 185

April 18th.
CONVERSATION WITH THIERS.
Want of confidence is returning 185
Savings are hoarded 185
There will be great distress 185
Relations with Austria 185
Orsini's letters 186
Relations with England 186
Suez Canal 187
Perim 187
Louis Napoleon after the 'attentat' 188
Thiers 'illustre et national' 188
Law of public safety 188
Threat against England 188
English laws more repressive of aliens than French . . . 188
Bernard ought not to have been acquitted 189
A war with England would ruin Louis Napoleon . . . 189
Thiers' advice to England 190

CONVERSATION WITH DUCHÂTEL.
First effects of the attentat 190
Spoilt by Louis Napoleon's subsequent conduct 190
Insults to England 190
Law of public safety 190
He was already absolute 191
Conduct of England unfriendly 191
Fresh plots 191

CONVERSATION WITH GUIZOT AND CORCELLE.
Destruction of old Paris 192
Society in old times 192
Madame de Houdetot 193
English do not understand conversation 194
Thomas à Becket at Val Richer 194
The Trappists 194

	PAGE
Motives for their retirement	194
Regrets of a Carthusian	195

April 22nd.
CONVERSATION WITH DUMON.

Deficit in the budget	195
War the most expensive of luxuries	165
Crimean war did good only to Louis Napoleon	196
He has no aggressive intentions	196
Only a navy of use against England	196
Increase of indirect taxes	197
Extravagance of the upper classes	197
New loan for public improvements	197
Haussman offends the Corps Législatif	198

April 27th.
CONVERSATION WITH GRIMBLOT.

Emperor attached to the English alliance	198
He is as grateful as he is vindictive	198
His head was turned by the 'attentat'	198
He is looking forward to another war	198
Orsini ought to have been pardoned	200
His enormous popularity in Italy	201
Louis Napoleon intends a war for Italy	201
His procrastination	201

April 29th.
CONVERSATION WITH CHRZANOWSKI.

Conduct of absolute monarchs cannot be predicted	202
Education in Russia	202
Notables in Russia	202
Register of census	202
Emperor Nicholas	203
His generalship to overwhelm by numbers	203
Rejoicing at his death	204
Russia and Austria could ruin each other	204
An alliance between France and Russia a mistake	205
State of Russian army	205
Improvements in arms	206
Indian mutiny	206
Dangers in India	207

April 30th.
CONVERSATION WITH LORD COWLEY.

Effect of the 'attentat' on Louis Napoleon	207

Execution of the 'loi des suspects' 208

May 1st.
CONVERSATION WITH WOLOWSKI.
Execution of the 'loi des suspects' 208
Louis Napoleon is 'ébranlé' 209

May 3rd.
BREAKFAST AT BUFFET'S.
Prefects ordered to arrest a minimum 209
Arrest in the Charente 209
Arrest of an 'armateur' 210
Arrest of a physician 211
Unhealthiness of Lambressa 211
Arrest of a woman 211
Arrest of a barber 212

May 7th.
CONVERSATION WITH MADAME CORNU.
Louis Napoleon had two fixed ideas, to be emperor of
  France and liberator of Italy 212
Opinion of Ceruschi, his history 213
Furious passions of Louis Napoleon 214
'Loi des suspects' long prepared 214
He did not wish to insult England 215
Alliance has received a shock 216
Harsh execution of 'loi des suspects' 216
Prince Napoleon vainly tries to interfere . . . 216
Emperor every day more intolerant of resistance . . . 217

May 11th.
Tampering with the elections 217

CONVERSATION WITH CHRZANOWSKI.
Mr. Senior's Turkish journal 218
Ruin of Turkey owing to the diplomatists 218
Internal disorders of Russia 219
The principalities 219

1859.

April 24th.
CONVERSATION WITH COUSIN.
Savoy would like to be French 221
Unpopularity of the war 221
France does not sympathise with Italy 222

The war is the work of the Carbonari 222

April 25th.
CONVERSATION WITH GUIZOT.
Unpopularity of the war in the provinces 223
Want of preparation 223

CONVERSATION WITH THIERS.
Complaints of the British cabinet 224
Conduct of Austria 225
Insincerity of English government 225
Dangerous position of French army 226

CONVERSATION WITH CORCELLE.
Real motives of Louis Napoleon 226
Position of the French clergy 227

April 28th.
CONVERSATION WITH MADAME CORNU.
Louis Napoleon delighted with the war 227
Thinks he has great military genius 228
Satisfaction of the Carbonari 228
Negotiations with Austria 228
He hates Piedmont 228
Russian alliance 229
War not unpopular in the lower classes 229
The soldiers think that Piedmont is the enemy . . . 230

Russian disbelief in the alliance with France 230
Letter from Madame Arconati 231

April 30th.
CONVERSATION WITH CHRZANOWSKI.
Cause of Austria's delay 232
Piedmontese fortresses 232
Russian fortresses 233
Austrian army inferior to the French 233
French soldier is overloaded 233
Pillaging soldiers worth nothing 234
Louis Napoleon will not give Lombardy to Piedmont . . 234
Russian alliance 235
Improvidence of Louis Napoleon 236
In war everything depends on time 236

May 1st.
CONVERSATION WITH DUMON.
Five millions added to the debt since 1848 237

War essentially revolutionary 237
Wishes of the Republicans. 237

Debate in the Corps Législatif on the loan for the war . . 238

CONVERSATION WITH THIERS.
Opponents of Louis Napoleon wish France to fail . . . 240
England has been hostile to Austria . . . . . . : 240
What England will allow Celui-ci to do 241
Palmerston will never sacrifice England 241
England has guaranteed the independence of Turkey . . 241

May 3rd.
CONVERSATION WITH MÉRIMÉE.
War unpopular in the 'salons' 242
Emperor despises the 'salons'. 242
His speech to Hübner 242
Conduct of Austria 243
Importance of Louis Napoleon's utterances 243
Thiers' memorial against the war. 243
The Emperor a fatalist 244
He and the Empress are delighted with the war . . . 244
His strongest motive hatred of Austria 244
His second motive desire for military glory 245
Danger of Russia becoming a Mediterranean power . . . 246
Evil of Russian aggrandisement 247

CONVERSATION WITH DE WITT.
Politics of the peasantry are socialistic 247
Condition of the upper classes. 248
Difference of living in Paris 248

Delight of the Princess Belgiojoso with the war . . . 248

May 5th.
Sadness of the Duc de Broglie 248
The Duc de Chartres in the Sardinian army 249

May 6th.
BREAKFAST AT SENIOR'S.
Biographical prejudices. 249
Louis Napoleon did not succeed in London 250
He is a copyist 250
Cardinal Mezzofante's head 251

CONVERSATION WITH A——.
Emperor must dazzle 251

He is anxious for peace 251
Plans for Italy 252
He is vacillating and irresolute 253
Why Sebastopol was not taken earlier 253
St. Arnaud and the coup d'état 253
Interference of England 254
English public men 254
Louis Napoleon dreads war with England 254
'Les deux larrons' 255
Addresses of the colonels 256
England should make preparations for defence . . . 256

CONVERSATION WITH LAFITTE.
Faith of the Comtists 257
They desire an absolute dictator 257
Do not care for freedom 257
Dislike constitutional government 258
Wishes of the Communists 260
No religion among the working classes 260

CONVERSATION WITH A LEGITIMIST.
Dislikes constitutional government 261
Wishes for an absolute King 261
Similarity of views with those of the Comtists . . . 261

May 8th.
CONVERSATION WITH MADAME CORNU.
Louis Napoleon has resumed his fatalism 262
Answer to the Italians in 1848 263
Desire for posthumous fame 263
Does not distinguish between right and wrong . . . 263
He lives in the future 264
Success of the loan 264

May 10th.
CONVERSATION WITH CHRZANOWSKI.
Some delay necessary 265
Giulay and Hesse 265
Presence of the two Emperors 266
Improvement in arms 267
Causes of Austrian failure 268
Vaillant's dismissal 268
Official rank the only aristocracy left 269

CONTENTS.

May 15th.
CONVERSATION WITH TOURGÉNIEFF.
Treatment after Alexander's death 270
Horrors of a recruitment in Russia 271
Lord's power over his serfs 271
Distribution of land 272
Miserable cultivation 272
Russian bureaucracy and nobles 273
The serf question 274

May 18th.
BREAKFAST AT SENIOR'S.
Patriotism of Madame Ristori 275
The Venetian Republic 276
General hypocrisy 276
Devotee at Palermo 276
Interruptions at St. Roch 277
Compliment to Massillon 277
Mirrha 277
Proposals to the Pope 278
England and France should have come forward in 1848 . 279

CONVERSATION WITH COUSIN.
Palmerston a thorough Englishman 279
Popularity in Paris 280

CONVERSATION WITH THIERS.
Giulay has probably made way for Hesse 280
Loss of opportunities 280
French have no pontoons 281

DINNER AT THE MOHLS'.
Villemain president of republic of letters 281
Mary Stuart and Elizabeth 282
Henry VIII. and Nero 282
Villemain cannot understand England's policy 282
Constantinople should be a free commercial city 283
English constituency already too democratic 283

1860.

May 6th.
CONVERSATION WITH DUSSARD.
Estate in the Pyrenees 286
Injustice of legal decisions 286

CONTENTS. XXV

	PAGE
Italian war favourable to Louis Napoleon	287
French dazzled by success	287
Popularity of loans	287
The high rate of wages	287
He must make another war	288
Louis Napoleon in England	288
His prophetic utterances	289
Military fever is spreading in France	290

CONVERSATION AT MADAME MOHL'S.
Madame Récamier	291
Her habits of life	292
Her dignity	292
Her salon	292
Châteaubriand	293
Prince Augustus of Prussia	293
Relation to her husband	294
Devotion of her friends	294
Letters	295
Story of Ampère	295
French delighted with the annexation	295
Desire another war	295
French intrigues in Germany	295
Commercial treaty unpopular	296
Supposed to be a sop to England	297
Louis Napoleon's position is strengthened	297
Disposition of the clergy	298

CONVERSATION WITH CHRZANOWSKI.
Want of military skill in the war	298
The soldiers did everything, the generals nothing	298
French surprised at Solferino	299
Enormous slaughter at Solferino	300
Piedmontese army ill-led	300
Victor Emmanuel depends on the French	301
'La Vérité sur la Russie'	301
Internal condition of Russia	301
Religion in Russia	302

DINNER AT THE BOURKES'.
Effect of solitary confinement	303
Condition of Papal army	303
Receptions at Thouvenel's and Marshal Randon's	304

May 11*th*.
CONVERSATION WITH MONTALEMBERT.
England is inclining to Democracy 306
This will lead to centralisation and autocracy 306
Public men gagged by fear of the *Times* and their electors. 306
Foreign policy of England 307
Danger of universal suffrage to determine nationalities . 307
Effect of the dissolvent principles in Europe 308
Will England permit Ireland to secede? 308
Prejudices of the uneducated 308
Always under the influence of a single idea 309
Creation of Italian Kingdom injurious to France . . . 309
English desire to deprive the Pope of his territory . . . 309
Protestant bigotry 310
Sympathies with Garibaldi 310
He disapproves the annexation of Savoy 311
And in such matters of national suffrage 311
Interest takes the place of patriotism 312
Priests distrust Louis Napoleon 312
Feeling in the Rhenish provinces 312
War for the natural frontiers 313
Louis Napoleon despotic and socialistic 314

May 12*th*.
CONVERSATION WITH CHEVALIER.
History of the commercial treaty 314

May 13*th*.
CONVERSATION WITH MADAME CORNU.
Emperor is writing a history of Julius Cæsar 316
Is quite absorbed in it 316

May 14*th*.
Breakfast at the Mohls' 316
Louis Napoleon's new studies 316
Story of M. de la Ville Marqué 317
Dissolution of the Breton Archæological Society . . . 318
Persecution of an editor 319
Restrictions on industry in Germany 319
Prussia a vast Trades Union 319
She cannot reduce her army 320

May 18*th*.
CONVERSATION WITH GUIZOT.
Mischief of the violation of treaties 320

CONTENTS. xxvii

And transfer of States 320
Conduct of England 320
Value attached by Louis Napoleon to the English alliance. 321
He fears Cavour 321
His danger from assassination increased by the Peace . . 322
He desires to return home 322

May 19th.
CONVERSATION WITH THIERS.
All parties prepared for the annexation of Belgium and
    Rhenish Prussia 323
Louis Napoleon behaved well in Italy 323
The ' Zouaves' compared with the ' Ironsides' 324
Zouaves are impracticable in peace 324
They never live to grow old 325
Excellence of French army 325
Dangers of the Prussian system 326
Thiers' Protectionist principles 327
Opinion on Gladstone's budget 328
Annexation of Savoy has made the Emperor stronger . . 328
Napoleon might have succeeded in 1815 329
Conduct of Marmont 329

May 20th.
CONVERSATION WITH DUC DE BROGLIE.
Admiration of Garibaldi 329
Compared with William III. 329
Russian demonstration against Turkey 330
Attempt to upset Treaty of 1856 330
Gladstone's budget 330
Treaty between France and England 330
Evils of direct taxation 331
Of loans 332

May 21st.
A wedding and a funeral 333

CONVERSATION WITH MALLAC.
France is resolved to have the Rhine 334
Dangers of a military democracy 334

CONVERSATION WITH MADAME CORNU AND TROUVÉ CHAUVEL.
Things in Italy going too fast for the Emperor 334
Signs of Dutch blood 334

No doubt of his legitimacy 335
Louis Napoleon as a child 335
Delight in fine scenery 336
He has great self-command 336
His letters to Madame Cornu 336
Escape from Ham 337
Believes himself to be providential 337
His behaviour as a Deputy in 1848 338
Relations between him and the Assembly 338
Cavaignac might have saved the Republic 338
Thiers in 1849 339
Excitement in Rhenish provinces 339
They will not become French 339
Preparations for war 339

May 22nd.
CONVERSATION WITH THIERS.
Dislikes public speaking 340
Ignorance of the Constituent Assembly 340
Astonished that the Republic did not bring prosperity . . 340
Duties of a Government are preventive 341
Thiers' love of justice 341
Turkey must be kept together 341
Treaty between the two Emperors 341
Patriotism of Napoleon 342
His nephew has none 342

May 28th.
CONVERSATION WITH MÉRIMÉE.
Attachment of Louis Napoleon to old friends 342
History must decide as to his public merits 342
Disbelieves in the influence of individuals 343

CONVERSATION WITH MONTALEMBERT.
Turkey will fall in pieces 343
England should be prepared with a policy 343

CONVERSATION WITH MADAME RISTORI.
Applause necessary to an artist 344
A 'claque' worse than silence 344

CONTENTS.

May 29th.
Ristori takes leave of the Parisian public 345
Her acting in comedy 345
In tragedy far surpassed by Mrs. Siddons 345

May 31st.
CONVERSATION WITH VEFYC EFFENDI.
Climates of Teheran and Bagdad 346
Delightful but exhausting 346
Eastern and Western life 347
Despotism of society 347
English diplomatists in the East 348
Eastern fatalism 349
French are resolved on annexing Belgium and Rhenish provinces 349
Greeks are not better off for their independence . . . 349
Their commerce is fraudulent 350

June 1st.
CONVERSATION WITH BEAUMONT.
Letters of Tocqueville 350
Second volume of the 'Ancien Régime' 351
Beaumont will not publish it 351
Charm of Tocqueville's conversation 352
His religious opinions 352

June 2nd.
CONVERSATION WITH BEAUMONT AND AMPÈRE.
Roman Government changed for the worse 353
Jealous control over MSS. 353
Pope depends on the French troops 353
Lamoricière's attachment to the Pope 354
Development of religious feeling in France 354
A young man of fortune has become a Jesuit 354
Decline of religion in Rome 355
Italians are soberly enthusiastic 355
Emperor is liked in the provinces 355
Hated in Paris 355
Unpopularity of England 355
No country is greater that it believes itself to be . . 356

CONTENTS.

August 25th.
CONVERSATION WITH ROSSINI.
Misery and Exasperation of Venice 356
Hatred against Louis Napoleon 356
Helplessness of the Grand Duke of Tuscany 357

CONVERSATION WITH CHRZANOWSKI.
Present impotence of Russia 357
Her home dangers 358
Louis Napoleon wise in making peace 358
The French soldier is critical 358
Mischief of picked regiments 359
Louis Napoleon must have retired 359
Blunders on both sides 359
If he had stayed it would have been a parallel to his uncle's Russian campaign 360
Pedantry of the Austrian army 361
Jealousy of its generals 361
French generals far superior 361

August 26th.
CONVERSATION WITH BEAUMONT.
Will publish nothing unfinished of Tocqueville's 362
Letters should be arranged chronologically 363
Letters to Kergorlay and Stoffels 363
Tocqueville's view of democracy 364

CONVERSATION WITH THIERS.
Louis Napoleon more peaceful 365
Fears the results of a war 365
Especially of a maritime war 365
Peace will give liberty to France 366
He gained enormously by Magenta and Solferino . . . 366
Piedmont took the bit into her mouth 367
He was disgusted with actual war 367
Napoleon was indifferent to its horrors 368
The enemies of Italy 368
Defences of Venice 368
Louis Napoleon would like to carry out the treaty . . . 369
Mazzini, Garibaldi, and Cavour 369

August 28th.
Val Richer 369

Description of the place 369
Life at Val Richer 371

August 29th.
CONVERSATION WITH GUIZOT.
Believes that the Emperor wishes for peace 372
Would like a successful war 372
Prefers to enjoy himself 372
His conversation is uninteresting 372
His manners exceedingly good 372
Annexation of Savoy 372
Italy will never be united 372
Difficulty of making a new kingdom 373
Evils of direct universal suffrage 373
Revolutions are relentlessly logical 373

August 30th.
CONVERSATION WITH GUIZOT.
Lawless colony 374
Life of the curé of St. Roque 374
Sale of the Bible prohibited 375
Mistaken persecution of the Jansenists 376
Good effects of the Puritans in England 376
Ultramontanism produced by the revolution and the concordat 376
Peasantry indifferent to religion 377
Château of La Roque 377

August 31st.
CONVERSATION WITH GUIZOT AND DE WITT.
Characters of English statesmen 378
Wisdom of Lord Aberdeen 378
Warlike preparations a substitute for war 379
France likes war 379
Character of Palmerston 379
Defence of Palmerston 380
Till 1848 revolution was associated with reform 381
Refugees prefer France to England 381
Question of asylum 381
Inconvenience of an alien act 382
Addresses of colonels in 1858 382
Conspirators in Spain in 1830 382

September 1st.

CONVERSATION WITH GUIZOT AND DE WITT.

Gifts and faults of Lamartine 383
King David as a prefect 383
Paucity of children in higher classes 383
Effects of lowering the suffrage in England 384
Democracy bad for foreign policy 384
Bulwarks against France 385
The 'Revue Rétrospective' 386
The letters favourable to the writers 386

September 2nd.

CONVERSATIONS WITH GUIZOT AND DE WITT.

Sermons of Bourdaloue and Massillon 387
The 'Ami de la Réligion' 387
Espinasse and the Duc d'Aumale 388
Louis Philippe in 1848 389
Political conduct of Thiers 389
Thiers as a speaker 389
Louis Philippe an admirable 'causeur' 390
Queen Christina 390
The King of Würtemburg 390
Statesmanship of Metternich and the Duke of Wellington . 391
French generals 392
Foreign orders of M. Guizot 392
Pictures at Val Richer 393

CONVERSATION WITH GUIZOT.

Hebrew poetry 393
Egyptian civilization 393
Greek poetry 394
Italian poetry 394
Macaulay's knowledge of literature 394
Helen of Troy 394
Goethe 395
English novels 395
English painters and architects 395
English actors 395
Madame Viardot's 'Orfeo' 395
Rachel 395
Madame Ristori 396
Quotation from Molière 396

September 3rd.
Village school 397

CONVERSATION WITH GUIZOT.
Difference between agricultural and manufacturing villages 397
Conscription in France 398
Algiers a drain 398
Future of Constantinople 398
It should be Greek 399
Ionian Islands 399
Countries like to govern themselves 399

CONVERSATIONS.

1855.

[Mr. Senior's next visit to Paris was at the close of the winter during which our soldiers underwent such terrible hardships in the siege of Sebastopol.

The account of their sufferings aroused so much indignation in England that Lord Aberdeen resigned, and a new Administration was formed under Lord Palmerston.

Mr. Senior's journal begins with a very interesting conversation with Tocqueville, which has already been published.]—Ed.

Friday, March 2nd.—After Tocqueville left us I called on Thiers and found him walking in his garden, though it is scarcely more than a week since he broke his arm in two places.

Thiers.—I refused to take to my bed, and I think that I thus escaped fever, though I suffer much pain.

Things have turned out much as I expected. You have failed from deficient military organisation, and I doubt whether great improvement is within your reach. You can scarcely bear, or rather you will not bear, the expense of being permanently a great military as well as a great naval power. But no nation does well what it does not do habitually. Your attempts to improvise an army will fail, like ours to improvise a fleet.

Besides our long experience in war, we have an advantage possessed by no other people in the world, except the Swiss, and they are too poor and too few to make war out of their own country; we have a warlike bourgeoisie. Our middle classes have the pride and spirit and vigour and military ardour of an aristocracy, and the numbers of a people. We do not feel therefore the miseries of war as you do, for ours are diffused while yours are concentrated. We have lost in the East twice as many officers, more indeed than twice as many, as you have, but the loss is spread over millions of families. Your loss is divided among thousands; our loss is repaired as soon as it is incurred, for the material out of which we make our officers is inexhaustible. You take yours from an aristocracy; I admit that it is the largest as well as one of the best in the world, but the largest aristocracy can never form more than a small minority of a nation. A few years of war on a great scale would put all your Lords and Commons into mourning.

By this time the garden, which Thiers uses as his reception-room, began to fill. All Paris, he tells me, comes to condole with him on his accident or to congratulate him on his recovery. He dwelt with some pleasure on a message from the Emperor. So I left him.

Saturday, March 3rd.—I went to Thiers and found him with his ladies and a large circle, standing before the fire discussing the great event of Nicholas' death.

Louis Napoleon is at Boulogne. The Empress first received the news, and sent it on to Morny. The funds have risen ten per cent., and all other investments in proportion. Great fortunes must have been made and lost this morning. The Court and the ministers are said to have been speculating for a fall, relying on the bad effect of the Crimean journey.*

---

* Louis Napoleon's proposed visit to the seat of war.—ED.

Thiers believes the death to have been natural, and the previous illness to have been concealed. He thinks Alexander, the probable successor, a man of judgment and knowledge.

The general opinion however seemed to be that Nicholas' apoplexy was of the kind to which Czars are subject; but whether it were the work of the landlords, irritated by the sacrifices of the war; or of the Muscovite party, enraged by the acceptance of the four points; or of the friends of the heir, eager to profit by a new reign, no one had the materials for an opinion.

From Thiers I went to Manin. An Italian, to whom I was a stranger, was sitting with him. After he had given me, in August, permission to print his conversations,* I sent to him a copy of them, with a request that he would erase, modify, or add, as he thought proper.

Receiving no answer, I wrote to him in November to say that if I heard nothing I should use the manuscript in its actual state. Still no answer, and accordingly I sent it to the press without omitting or adding a word. To-day he said to me:

Manin.—I suppose that you understood my silence?

Senior.—What I inferred was that you saw nothing to object to, but did not wish to commit yourself by an express admission of the accuracy of all the details.

Manin.—Exactly so. There are some omissions, but I have no doubt that I said all that you have attributed to me. The only expression of which a bad use may be made is that of my acquiescence in a kingdom of Italy. When I was willing to take the King of Sardinia as our Sovereign he had not become the ally of Austria. His desertion of our cause makes me dispirited as well as angry. The

---

* In an article on the State of the Continent in 1854 which Mr. Senior contributed to the *North British Review.*—ED.

death of Nicholas is an *immediate* blessing to all Europe, excepting to us. Whether it will *ultimately* be a benefit even to the rest of Europe is a question. The peace which probably will follow will leave Russia not much weaker than the war found her. Poland, not the Crimea, is her vulnerable point. If the war continues she will probably be attacked there by a united French and Austrian army, and may perhaps be driven beyond the Vistula. But you and the French are so sick of the war that you will be ready to catch at peace on any terms, and Heaven knows how long it may be before it will again be possible to create a coalition against Russia, or how soon some of those who are now her enemies may become her accomplices.

Only two suppositions give any hope for Italy. One is a war between France and Austria; this would lead to our immediate emancipation. The other is a war in which Austria should be the ally of France against Russia, and which should continue long enough to shake all existing treaties and political prejudices, and to produce a revision of the map of Europe; a revision under which Austria may be induced to change her Italian possessions for territory on the right bank of the Danube. The first supposition is now out of the question, so far as in these times any event can be said to be out of the question. The other supposition appears now to be almost equally improbable. In the meantime it is the duty of the Italian patriots to remain quiet, to be patient if they cannot be resigned. Any movement would do pure mischief. It would produce great immediate suffering, uncompensated by any rational expectation of future benefit.

Italian.—I had a letter a few days ago from a French officer who has just reached the Crimea from Algiers. It is written in a tone of despondency. 'I have seen,' he says, 'much misery and disease in Algeria, but nothing comparable to what I find here. I can compare it only to the retreat from Moscow. We are so broken down by sickness and privations that, so far from attempting an assault, I do not believe that we can resist one. Unless the Russians are as much reduced as we are, their next attack will be successful.

Senior.—What was the date?

Italian.—Recent; later than the 10th of February.

The last person whom I saw was Duvergier. I asked what had been the effect of the war on Louis Napoleon's popularity.

Duvergier.—At first, while all was smiling, it did him good. But that has been worse than undone during the last four months. Though we have no newspaper correspondents we have letters from the army, and their contents are terrible. I do not believe that there is the difference you suppose between your state and ours. So far as you have had more to do in proportion to your numbers, and as your people are less able to shift for themselves, you have suffered more, but our commissariat has not been much better than yours, and our sickness has been frightful. On the whole, the campaign has been disastrous.

Sunday, March 4th.—I called on the Mohls. We talked of Louis Napoleon's present position.

Mohl.—It has not altered materially since you left us in May; so far as it has changed it is for the worse. The war is admitted to have been grievously mismanaged. The expenditure becomes every day more and more profuse—It is supposed to have amounted during the last year to ninety millions sterling—and he has forced the principal cities into equal extravagance. The revenues of Paris are mortgaged for years. The prefect who had long and well administered them was turned out to take in Haussmann, a tool of the Court, who calls himself indeed the Emperor's sous-préfet. But even he remonstrates, and some still more flexible instrument is to be substituted. Louis Napoleon cannot submit even to the slight restraints which the existing laws impose on him. He is constantly attempting little coups d'état about trifles, often unsuccessfully. The forms or the delays of office are interposed and the thing gets forgotten.

I then went to Mérimée's. We talked of the journey to the Crimea.

Mérimée.—I had some conversation about it a few days ago with the Emperor, and more with the Empress, and as we spoke in Spanish, it was free. The motive urged by them both in favour of it was that Canrobert refuses to act on his own judgment or to incur any responsibility, and that it is impossible to send him orders from hence on matters of importance, as at least a fortnight must elapse between the state of things when our last news left the Crimea and the state of things when the order, founded on that news, gets to the Crimea. The Emperor thinks that by being on the spot he can enable, or perhaps force, his generals to act.

Senior.—Do you believe that the dismantling Sebastopol is among our demands?

Mérimée.—I do; and therefore I believe that while Sebastopol stands peace is impossible, and also that if it fall peace will follow immediately. We cannot require the Czar himself to destroy fortifications which we cannot subdue, but if we have destroyed them there will be nothing very offensive in our requiring them not to be rebuilt.

Senior.—But is Sebastopol takeable by the army that we have before it? The capture of the walls of Saragossa did not give you the town, and the houses of Sebastopol are at least as defensible as those of Saragossa.

Mérimée.—Yes; but it is very differently garrisoned. We have before us regular Russian troops, who will fight only so long as the rules of the game require them; as soon as they have a right to consider themselves beaten they will yield. Suchet had driven into Saragossa the guerillas of all the country; they were far more numerous than the besieging army, and they hung up every inhabitant who refused to join in the defence. This is what enabled them to make their war to the knife. I have seen General Niel, who has just returned from the Crimea. He complains of gross mismanagement.

'We might,' he says, ' have taken the southern side the day that we approached it. It was protected only by a wall on which, as we have ascertained, only twelve guns were then mounted. A French and an English division were the first that came in sight of it. The English, which was Brown's, for some time showed no intention to encamp, and our people were convinced that they intended, as soon as it was dark, to make a dash and get in. Our general desired that the motions of the English should be carefully watched, in order that, when they moved, we might move too, and get in with them. But it seems that the English, like our own people, had no orders, and would not act without orders, so *that* opportunity was lost.

' Another was offered to us on the 5th of November. While you were fighting at Inkerman, and engaging the attention of the bulk of the Russians, the remainder attacked us, were repulsed, and were followed up to the walls. General de Lourmel was killed in the gate. If he had been supported we must have got in, for the whole garrison had been engaged in the sortie and was flying in disorder. But General Forey, who was in command, recalled his troops under an apprehension that they might be wanted at Inkerman. So this second opportunity was lost as the first had been.'

Senior.—What do you hear of Nicholas' death?

Mérimée.—We do not think that he was strangled. For some days the Russian minister at St. Petersburg had sent home reports that he was suffering from influenza, and was carelessly exposing himself to the cold, which has been as unusually intense there as it has been here. But he may have been poisoned, and the 'levée en masse' was enough to render the Russian proprietors desperate. Wherever it is applied it is confiscation, for the value of a Russian estate depends on its serfs, and a serf once made a soldier never returns to his master. The chances against so opportune a death having been natural are enormous. The chances against its having been artificial do not appear to me great.

Circourt and Chrzanowski drank tea with us. Circourt, who has lived much in Russia and through his wife is a Russian proprietor, leans to the opinion that Nicholas was poisoned.

Circourt.—What was called the 'levée en masse' was quite enough to account for it. It was one of the wild freaks into which Nicholas's impatience of resistance has lately been driving him. It is a levy of two and a half per cent. on the whole population, *i.e.*, of about twelve per cent. on the population capable, as respects age, of military service. It will produce three hundred thousand men. Each of these men is worth at least 100*l.* to his owner; so that this is a tax of about thirty millions sterling on the landlords. But this is not the worst. The serfs are generally hostile to their masters; sixty or seventy landlords are murdered every year by their peasants. Siberia and the knout are liberally administered, but they cannot repress the vengeance of the serfs. There will be an interval between the time when these men are freed from the control of their masters and that at which they are incorporated in regiments. There is no saying what mischief they may do in that interval. My strong suspicion is that Nicholas' death was the means adopted to avert these calamities.

Chrzanowski is indignant at the management of the war.
Chrzanowski.—Such an army as England sent out perhaps never existed before. With such an army 'on aurait pu faire des merveilles.' Every man was worth his weight in gold. It was an army which could not have been made in fifteen years; which cannot be replaced in fifteen years. England will feel the loss of it during all the rest of our lives. And to think that such soldiers should have been starved to death only six miles from their supplies, and by the richest nation in the world! 'C'est incroyable; c'est inouï; c'est-ce qui jamais n'est arrivé depuis que le monde existe.'

In every army there may be maladministration, especially at the beginning of a war; but the worst that is feared is that a bad 'ordonnateur en chef' (commissary general) pays fifty per cent. more than he need. But that men should be allowed to starve because food cannot be carried six miles; that they should be frozen because it was not foreseen that it would be cold in winter; that they should be without fuel, with forests before them and coal mines behind them; that this should be going on for week after week and month after month; that their general should be so utterly indifferent to the fate of his men, and those *such* men, as to be sometimes for a fortnight, sometimes for a month, without examining with his own eyes the state of his troops, and of his magazines, and of his communications; that this should happen in the nineteenth century, and that the persons who have been guilty of this inconceivable 'légèreté, paresse, insouciance et cruauté,' should be an English Government, and an English general, is what posterity will refuse to credit. I cannot bear to talk of it; I cannot bear to think of it.

Senior.—How do you estimate the strategic events of the campaign?

Chrzanowski.—I think that on every side—on the part of the Russians, on the part of the English, and on the part of the French—it was worthy of Turks or of Chinese. Menschikoff is a clever man; that is, a clever courtier; but he never before commanded six men. He is a smart child learning his business. At the Alma he ought to have destroyed the allied army. The French were to attack his left, and the English, by a flank movement, to turn his right. They attempted precisely what the Russians attempted at Austerlitz. If he had done as Napoleon did, as any man with military experience would have done; if he had attacked your weak centre, he would have broken through it, cut your army into two parts, and destroyed one of them.

Senior.—After we had changed our plan and attacked their front, instead of trying to turn it, what do you think of Lord Raglan's conduct?

Chrzanowski.—I think that he made too much use of the bayonet. You use that weapon powerfully, but you do not possess with it the enormous superiority that belongs to your fire. There is nothing in the world equal to the fire of the English, and nothing worse than the fire of the Russians. Lord Wellington, who knew how precious is an English soldier; who cared only for the real, not for the apparent; who never paid for a success a life more than was necessary, seldom used the bayonet. His line let a French column approach; at a certain distance the flank companies advanced a little, a concentrated fire was poured on the head of the column, and in a quarter of an hour it turned. You had lost perhaps sixty men, and the French three hundred. With the bayonet it might have been done in five minutes, and there are occasions in which it may be worth while to sacrifice hundreds of lives to save ten minutes, but they are few. I fear that you are borrowing a little of the vanity and love of display of your allies, and I am sorry for it. The calm, quiet, business-like intrepidity of the Duke's army was ten times better than all the *élan* and impetuosity of the French.

Then it was monstrous that you should have let the Russians retreat unmolested. You did not deserve a victory, for you did not know how to use one. If they had been properly followed up they would have been destroyed. Their cavalry was worthless. A few shells kept it off. You need not have cared for it. Of course you could not catch their guns as they galloped off, but at the first defile, where they had to pass one by one, they were at your mercy.

I am not sufficiently informed to say whether, if you had not wasted two days on the field of battle, you could have entered the north side of Sebastopol with the flying Russians, but there seems to be no doubt whatever that you could have entered on the south; in fact, all the works that you are now attacking have been erected since you were first at Balaclava.

I see that your newspapers call Inkerman the soldiers' battle. It certainly was not a general's battle. Each side managed it equally ill; and each being equally unskilful, the bravest prevailed. *You* were surprised for want of vigilance and for want of field-works, of which the youngest ensign ought to have seen the necessity. The Russians were brought against you as if Menschikoff had intended them to be destroyed. They came up in masses so dense that not a ball or a bullet could miss them, and so narrow that they could not fire effectually. Menschikoff managed to make his numbers a cause of defeat, and when they were repulsed they fled in such a panic that they broke down the bridges behind them, and had consequently two days' march before they could get back to the town.

As for the French, after they had repulsed the sortie of the garrison, they left General de Lourmel and his men, who had actually entered the place, unsupported; and during the next two days, while the garrison consisted of not four thousand men, demoralised by defeat—when the Russian army in consequence of the destruction of the bridges was more than a day's march off, they remained totally inactive while success was actually in their grasp.

On the 5th, 6th, and 7th of November Sebastopol was yours if you chose to take it. But there is a degree of incapacity which cannot be assisted even by fortune.

Another inconceivable folly is your sending the Turkish army to Eupatoria. The first rule of war is that the different corps should support one another. They must sometimes be separated in order to subsist, but they ought always to be able to unite in order to fight. You have voluntarily broken your force into two, and let the Russians be between them. You have no communication by land, and keep up none regularly by sea. You should have steamers continually plying between your camp and Eupatoria. If the Russians are not as much broken down and as incapable of exertion as you are, those Turks at Eupatoria are a *pâture* for them to devour.

Senior.—What would you have done with them?

Chrzanowski.—What would I have done with them? Had you too many men to man your trenches and keep up your communications before Sebastopol? Why did you let Liprandi occupy the woods within a mile or two of your camp, cutting off your supplies, threatening you with a surprise, and depriving you of fuel? Of course, only because you had not men enough to drive him off. Why did you not employ these Turks for that purpose, or in taking your places while you did so yourselves? Joined to your army they might have done something, at Eupatoria they are useless.

Senior.—I have no right to express a military opinion, but it seems to me that if we sent the Piedmontese contingent and a further French force to Eupatoria, such a combined army might advance against the Russians at Simferopol and invest the north of Sebastopol.

Chrzanowski.—Certainly; but you cannot do that without horses. An army by the seaside can be supplied by its fleet, but you cannot march inland without the means of transport, and they are not to be found in the Crimea. They must be carried thither; you cannot advance on Simferopol without twenty thousand horses, and you have none. It will take three months to get them there, and this campaign will be decided in six weeks. In war almost all depends on the calculation of time.

It is impossible that the allied army can remain in its present camp during the month of April. If it does, it remains there for ever. There are there, loosely concealed under a foot of earth, the bodies of 20,000 French, 15,000 English, and 6000 Turks, besides Russians, and besides more than 2000 horses and mules, some buried, some lying as they fell, and besides, all the sources of disease that accumulate when 60,000 men occupy one encampment for four months. As soon as the warm weather comes there will be a pestilence from which not a man will escape. And there are only two directions in which they can move: they can assault Sebastopol, take it, and encamp on the other side; or they may drive off the Russians to their right, and encamp to the north-east of Balaclava. But if they take the latter step they must either abandon all their works and heavy artillery, and in fact give up the ground which has been gained at the expense of 50,000 lives, or they must leave 20,000 men to hold them, and expose those 20,000 men to the fever. The situation is almost a desperate one, but I believe that the boldest plan is the least dangerous. I would make the assault.

Senior.—At what amount do you estimate our allied force?

Chrzanowski.—From 50,000 to 60,000, of which not 10,000 are English. I doubt whether the Russians are so numerous; I cannot account for their long inactivity, while you were almost defenceless from disease and discouragement, except by supposing that their sufferings have almost equalled yours. A glorious opportunity was lost when they made that strong reconnaissance on Eupatoria. Sebastopol must have been left very bare. The rarest of all qualities is the willingness to incur responsibility. One cannot wonder that a man who never before faced a civilized enemy does not possess it.

Circourt.—There is a third course, and I think it probable that it will be adopted. We may propose an armistice to the new Emperor while the negotiations are going on, and move our whole army to the east of Balaclava, leaving our works and trenches protected by the armistice. If that is not done I believe that Louis Napoleon will proceed to the Crimea. It seems that his presence is absolutely necessary to make the generals act with decision.

I do not wonder, my dear Senior, that you are impatient to change this climate for that of Africa, yet I almost think that in your place I should wait a couple of days, for in a couple of days the matter ought to be decided. It ought, indeed, to be decided to-morrow; and I believe that the only question is between the Emperor's journey and the armistice. We hear of mutinous cries, and I am not surprised by them. I had a letter the other day from one of our officers; the average loss, he says, from the fire of the town is one hundred and fifty men a day. This is not the sort of campaign that suits the French soldier. I wonder that he has borne it so long. It is natural that he should cry for Lamoricière or Changarnier.

Chrzanowski.—We have no evidence that Changarnier or Lamoricière would have done better. All their experience has been against mobs and Arabs. The great deficiency however is not in the Crimea; it is in Paris and in London; perhaps the error began at Biarritz. You have forgotten what sort of a thing a war is. You think that it may be made 'en plaisantant.' You do not know that it consists in seizing opportunities. In April you might have had Sebastopol;* there were not 12,000 men in the place; no Russian reinforcements could reach it for five or six weeks. You were not expected there; you might have carried it by a coup de main. Instead of that you kept telling the Russians for four months that you were going there; you gave them time to prepare fortifications, armies, and reserves; and at last you landed in the autumn, when the unhealthy season was beginning, and the winter was to follow. You landed without horses, and, as respects the English, without tents; you began your attack before you had prepared your communications with your supplies, and you went carelessly, blindly, blundering on, until your army was starved to death, as if it had been a horde of savages.

Senior.—Lord Lansdowne surprised me just before I left London by estimating the Austrian army, exclusively of the troops in Italy which cannot be moved, at not more

---

* It is well-known now that this was not Lord Raglan's fault.—Ed.

than 200,000 men, and as inferior in number to the Russians opposed to them on the Polish and Hungarian frontier.

Chrzanowski.—I believe that the Austrian army is not much more numerous than Lord Lansdowne supposes it to be; but he is mistaken in thinking that it is inferior in number to the Russians before it. It *is* inferior, but it is in quality. The Russian Imperial Guard is there, and some of the best divisions of the Russian army. The Austrians are wise in asking for French co-operation.

Monday, March 5th.—We left Paris early this morning for Algiers.

Friday, May 18th.—We returned to Paris yesterday, having spent the interval between the 4th March and the 17th of May in Algeria, in the journey thither, and in our return. The ten weeks of our absence have produced little change. The days indeed are longer, but the weather is little warmer. We have returned to fires, greatcoats, and umbrellas, of which we had almost forgotten the use. Paris is still in a state of demolition or reconstruction. Nearly the same politics seem to be talked; in short, we might fancy that we had not moved.

Ampère breakfasted with us. He related to us the event of the week, the coup d'état aimed at the Institut. The Institut consists of five academies:—

L'Académie Française,
L'Académie des Inscriptions et Belles-Lettres,
L'Académie des Sciences,
L'Académie des Beaux-Arts,
L'Académie des Sciences, Morales et Politiques.*

The number of members in the Académie des Sciences Morales et Politiques, was confined by the ordonnance of Louis Philippe, which re-created it after its abolition by Napoleon, to thirty. In this academy there is a vacancy, and the principal candidates are Say, Lavergne, Reynouard, and Wolowski. Say is the favourite. To prevent his election an imperial decree has been issued, raising the number of members to forty by the nomination of ten new academicians. Who they are nobody chooses to recollect, except that among them is M. Cormenin. The others are second-rate politicians, belonging to the Imperialist faction.

Another imperial decree has vested in the Minister of Public Instruction the right—

First. To designate the members forming the different

---

* It was of this Academy that Mr. Senior was a membre correspondant.—ED.

VOL. II.   C

committees, into which the Institut divides itself, for the despatch of business.

Second. To designate the office-bearers in the Institut.

Third. To appoint its subordinate officers.

Fourth. To give the tickets which admit to its public sittings.

Against this second decree the Institut has protested, and having by prescription the right to an audience from the Sovereign, a deputation, consisting of the Duc de Noailles, M. Villemain, and the Bishop of Orleans, is to have an interview with Louis Napoleon to-day.

Ampère.—We have agreed not to submit. I wished for a general resignation, but the majority prefer a passive resistance; therefore,

First. We shall not serve on any committees for which the Government may designate us.

Second. We shall not accept the offices to which it may appoint us.

Third. We shall not employ the subordinate officers whom it may give to us.

Fourth. We shall not attend the public sittings for which it may give tickets.

Senior.—What is the motive of this decree?

Ampère.—Its first motive is Louis Napoleon's hatred of independence. The Institut was almost the only independent body left in France.

Senior.—But if the Emperor can by decree add to the members of one of your academies, what is your independence?

Ampère.—The 'Académie des Sciences Morales et Politiques,' is of much later creation than the others. It has always been considered as rather a political than a literary institution, and its numbers and its duties have been frequently changed by the Government for the time being. We do not consider an addition to its numbers a precedent implying a right to add to any of the other academies. We do not therefore protest against the first decree. Besides his dislike of our independence, he is offended by the selection of works to which we have given prizes. He knows that all our leading men are hostile to him, and believes that while we appoint our committees and office-bearers we shall be able to show our hostility.

We spent the evening at Madame Mohl's, and heard the result of the audience. Mérimée was with the Emperor just before. Louis Napoleon said to him, ' Je vais voir vos amis et mes ennemis.'

The Duc de Noailles began by expressing his regret that an attempt should have been made to destroy the independence of the most illustrious literary institution in the world.

Louis Napoleon of course disclaimed any such intention. ' But,' he said, ' you must admit that in your recent elections and in the selection of works for prizes you have shown a decided hostility to my Government.'

It was now the turn of the deputation to disclaim. The Bishop of Orleans assured the Emperor that the Institut was devoted to him, and defended the election of Berryer and the prize given to Simon's book on moral philosophy— the things most complained of—by the obvious superiority of the man and of the book to any other candidates.

The conference ended by the Emperor expressing his intention to have the decree so modified as to leave no just subject of complaint.

Mohl.—It is obvious that he is frightened. In attacking the Institut he attacked the national vanity. We have always boasted that from the time of Richelieu it has been independent. It is said that Fortoul, the Minister of Public Instruction, who signed the decree, is to resign.

Senior.—Fortoul is himself an academician, and ought to have known better the feelings of his colleagues.

Mohl.—He is an academician, but he seldom comes among us, and he does wisely. He bought his seat by a profuse distribution of patronage; out of the twenty-nine who voted at his election eighteen had been promoted by him.

Saturday, May 19th.—We called on the Dunoyers. While we were sitting with Madame Dunoyer, Dunoyer came from the Institut. He told us the result of the election.

Dunoyer.—The election is over; Wolowski, the candidate whom the Government least feared, has been elected, by the votes of the new members. Say's friends, whose votes, if the Academy had not been swamped, would have given him a large majority, abstained from voting. Six of them were absent and ten put blank papers into the balloting-box.

Sunday, May 20th.—Grimblot breakfasted with us yesterday, and took a walk with me to-day. I will throw together the substance of two long conversations.

Senior.—Has your great man gained or lost since we talked on French politics last year?

Grimblot.—He has lost ground, and he is losing ground every day. He is in a position of great, almost unexampled, difficulty. The war which is the essential characteristic of his Government, is opposed to the wishes and to the interests of every one round him. He has not an adviser who sympathises with his feelings; he has not an instrument who is not an unwilling one. 'La paix à tout prix' is the earnest desire of all those on whom he relies to conduct the war.

The only party that approves of his policy is the old Opposition—Tocqueville, Thiers, Rémusat, and the different nuances of the Gauche; but they are deeply hostile to his Government. They abhor him as a usurper, as the destroyer of constitutional liberty, and as the creator and upholder of a violent and corrupt despotism. The Royalist parties sympathise with Russia and hate the English alliance; the bourgeoisie wishes for nothing but material prosperity. A Sovereign who wishes to carry on so vast an enterprise as a great and distant war against the wishes of his Court, of his ministers, and of his people, must have not only the inflexible will, but the energy, the knowledge, the diligence, and the genius of Napoleon. Our Emperor has only the will. He wants industry, and what is incurable, he wants capacity. When we were together in England I saw much of him. We have walked for hours in the Green Park. His range of ideas is narrow, and there is always one which preoccupies him for the time and shuts out the others. He never sees each side of a question. He learns little from his own meditations, for he does not balance opposite arguments; he learns nothing from conversation, for he never listens. While you are talking his mind is intent on its own course of ideas, and if he perceives that you differ from him, he only pities you. The consequence is that he knows nothing of administration; he knows nothing of the details by which the business of the world is carried on. Even as a conspirator, which is his forte, he failed in Italy, he failed at Strasburg, he failed at Boulogne, and if he succeeded in Paris it was because the details were managed for him by clever, zealous adherents.

Until the war his task was easy. Under our centralised system France governs itself. When the war began he had for the first time to contend with the difficulties of execution. As far as we can judge, in the darkness in which we are kept, he has lamentably failed. His campaign has been ill-planned and ill-managed. With an enormous expenditure of money and, of life no results have been obtained; greater exertions seem to be necessary, and it seems difficult even to keep up those that we are making. The deficit is known to be great, though no one can tell how great. A third loan will soon be wanted. Austria will not join us unless we can assist her with 200,000 men. ' *You* are fighting,' she says to us, ' for power. If we fight it will be for existence. We will not run so tremendous a risk unless we can see clearly our way to success, and for this purpose we think 200,000 French troops necessary.' Well, after reducing our garrisons, including that of Paris, to their lowest numbers, we can spare only 120,000.

His Government is as odious at home as it is unfortunate abroad. The fear of the Rouges, which was its support, has subsided. We now despise them perhaps as unreasonably as three years ago we feared them. We want back our tribune, our press, and our journals. I passed the winter near Toulouse; all my neighbours were indignant at their loss of local power and at the arbitrariness of the imperial authorities.

The immense and rapid fortunes that have been made by corruption and favouritism, and the insolence with which they are enjoyed, excite against the Court, and against all that belong to it, a mixture of envy, contempt, and hatred. I have heard sober moderate men say that we must have three weeks of anarchy ' pour faire maison nette.'

Senior.—What is the meaning of ' maison nette ?'

Grimblot.—It means the ruin, the pillage, the exile, perhaps the death, of all those who since 1848 have made fortunes at the public expense; of all those who have abused power or have assisted others to abuse it; it means the unbounded gratification of revenge, and, what is a stronger passion in France, of envy.

Senior.—You talk of the abuses of power. Tell me some of them.

Grimblot.—The first and greatest is the disregard of the national will, or rather, the care taken that the nation shall not express a will. You cannot mention a single portion of Louis Napoleon's policy, a single act of his Government, which has been suggested or modified by the public opinion of France; we feel that we are the helpless slaves of an individual will. He has persuaded us, or forced us, to place our destinies in his hands; to confide all that we value to his wisdom, his knowledge, his activity, and his good intentions; and we find that none of them are to be trusted. We find that he is selfish, rash, ignorant, and indolent.

Senior.—You are dealing in generalities. Come to particulars.

Grimblot.—One of the first that occurs to me is his interference with the course of justice. Even in suits between man and man the decisions of the tribunals are known to be influenced by the Court. The suit between the heirs of Lusignan and the heirs of Cayla is an instance. The former are anti-Napoleonists—the La Fayettes, Rémusat, and Guizot, through his first wife; the latter are the Prince and Princess de Craon, strong Imperialists.

The right of the Lusignans is clear. The claim made against them by Madame de Cayla, and carried on by her representatives, the Craons, has, however, succeeded. The administration of criminal justice is of course still worse. I will tell you things that have occurred within the last couple of months to acquaintances of my own.

One was Grassot, the comic actor. He was breakfasting in a coffee-house, thought himself ill-attended, and said,

'Mais c'est ici comme à Sebastopol, on ne peut rien prendre.' He was arrested and detained in prison some days. If he had not been a favourite with the public he might have been kept for weeks.

Another friend of mine, Morin, a professor in one of our large colleges, is suspected, with truth, of liberal opinions. A couple of months ago the police entered his lodgings and ransacked his papers. They found nothing except a packet tied up and lettered 'Bernard.' This they took away. Morin went to breakfast at his coffee-house, where he met me and told me the story with much amusement. 'They think,' he said, 'that they have got something about Bernard the Republican; they are some Latin memoranda about St. Bernard. Ils seront bien attrapés.' But when he returned he was met by a commissaire de police, who took him to the prison of the prefecture, where he was kept *au secret* for six weeks. At the end of that time he was released. He complained, and the only apology was, that they had released him as soon as they had found time to look into the packet found in his lodgings.

Simon, the author of the work crowned by the Institut, was sent for the other day by the police, and admonished to be more careful as to the language used in his house. You will find in our salons much more reserve than there was last year. I am struck by it on my return from the country; and the conversation in the guinguettes, and other resorts of those who cannot appeal to the public, is watched and punished more severely than ever.

Senior.—Do the deportations to Cayenne and your other colonies continue?

Grimblot.—No; they are too expensive and too notorious. People are exiled or 'internés'—that is to say, ordered to leave the country, or to leave their homes and reside elsewhere under the surveillance of the police.

Others are arrested whenever an émeute is feared, and not let out till the danger has passed. A mark is set against the names of others, and they are excluded from the public service or from promotion, and refused the permission which a Frenchman has to ask for half the things that he wishes to do.

I do not know where I should end if I were to tell you all the ways in which power is abused.

Another source of the unpopularity of Louis Napoleon is the badness of the instruments whom he selects. Vaillant is a good engineer, but he is not an administrator, and he hates the English alliance. Ducos is a loss. He was not brilliant, but he was energetic. His Baltic fleet was a very bad one, but it was marvellous that he got up one of any kind. How Walewski, a mere man of pleasure, hating work, hating to read, and unable to write, will get through the business of the Foreign Office, I cannot guess, unless it be by giving it up to his subordinates. Louis Napoleon wants the first talent of a Sovereign, a knowledge of human nature.

Senior.—You must admit that he has shown great knowledge of the feelings of the French people.

Grimblot.—I admit no such thing. He has certain fixed ideas as to the wishes of the French people, which from time to time coincide with the truth, just as a clock which stands still is twice in the twenty-four hours exactly right. But he cannot follow the movements of public opinion. You will find that every day he will wander further and further from the course which it indicates.

Senior.—What would have followed if Pianori's* pistol had been well aimed?

Grimblot.—Perhaps scenes like the worst in our history;

---

* Pianori attempted to shoot the Emperor on April 29, 1855, by twice firing at him with a double-barrelled pistol. Pianori was executed on the 14th May.—ED.

all the anger, resentment, indignation, envy, and other malevolent passions which have been accumulating since 1848, would have burst out. We might have had 'maison nette.' I have often been asked by English people whether he will be faithful to the alliance. I have no doubt that he will. Not from any feelings of honour, or fidelity, or honesty, for he is not affected by them. He has no moral sense; he does not, in the English sense of the words, know right from wrong; but because all his passions are on your side, you have flattered him as much as the Russians have tried to humiliate him. If his talents and industry were equal to his courage and his obstinacy, I should have no fear. And it is possible that some good may come even out of the violence of his character.

It is possible that when other resources fail, when he cannot raise men by the legal conscription, or money by ordinary loans, he may throw himself on the people and attack Russia with the immense means which the feelings of France, when really excited, can supply.

Senior.—But what can he get by appealing to the people? You tell me that the war is unpopular; that the desire is for 'la paix à tout prix.'

Grimblot.—The war is unpopular among the higher classes and the bourgeoisie, but not among the people. Its pecuniary losses do not fall on them; they are not 'actionnaires' or speculators. Ever since it began the price of their produce and of their labour has been rising. They have not the cynical indifference of their superiors to the honour and to the military glory of France. They might be roused now, as their grandfathers were in 1793; but it must be by revolutionary measures, and I believe Louis Napoleon to be capable of employing them.

I have given this conversation fully, because Grimblot is

a man of great sagacity and experience, and singularly moderate. He is connected with many parties, is an intimate friend of Rémusat's, and was secretary of legation to Walewski, and afterwards to Persigny.

Last year his opinions were more favourable to the permanence of this Government than those of most of my friends. It is not likely therefore that they are now peculiarly unfavourable.

Tuesday, May 22nd.—Grimblot breakfasted with us, and I gave to him for correction my report of our conversation. I called on M. de Rémusat. We talked of the war.

Rémusat.—I think that you are wrong in giving as you do to Louis Napoleon the lead in its management. You are right in relying on his good faith and on his courage, but not in trusting to his capacity. He has neither knowledge nor industry, and therefore cannot possess administrative talent. And he is ill-seconded. All his friends and all his ministers, his war ministers not excepted, are eager for peace. They do not encourage him in the preparations which are necessary for a long war. I doubt whether they would regret if they found that we were unable to make one. They exaggerate difficulties instead of providing the means of overcoming them. They have persuaded him that it is impossible to increase our taxation, and that the war therefore must be carried on by loans. He may try another of the same kind as the last, but of course such a system must come to an end; and perhaps they would not be sorry if it did so. They have persuaded him that he must confine himself within the conscription of the current year, which does not give more than 150,000 men, and that either to anticipate the conscription of a future year, or to require those who have encountered the ballot in a past year to submit to it again, would depopularise the war and even the Government. These two restrictions render it impossible to exert our utmost strength.

Senior.—One hundred and fifty thousand a year seems to be an enormous tribute of men.

Rémusat.—It *is* enormous. But you must recollect in the first place that we have not, what you have, the drain of a large annual emigration. And in the second place, that the stations of our garrisons are generally so healthy, and their food, clothing, and lodging are so good, that the great bulk of those who enter the service in their twenty-first year live to return to their families at the end of the seventh, or even before, for they seldom serve for more than six years.

During Napoleon's wars we perceived a gradual diminution in the size and strength of our conscripts. We were forced to make a slight reduction in the height required in them. This was accounted for by the circumstance that the strongest and healthiest being taken, the weakest were left as breeders; and we trusted that with the peace, the old stature of the French would be recovered. Peace came, but was followed by no such improvement. During forty years, in which the conscription did not affect more than one in a hundred of the population, the diminution of stature has continued slowly but perceptibly, and yet during all that time the lower classes have been better fed, clothed, and lodged, than they ever were before. I explain the fact by this very prosperity. My solution is, that until the Revolution the condition of the peasantry was so deplorable that all the weaklier infants died. There was a constant elimination of bad breeders. The existing race consisted of the strongest sons of the strongest sons of the strongest sons of families who had been struggling with hardships for centuries. Now, under the influence of increased prosperity and civilization, almost all live and propagate. The existing generation is the offspring of the bad breeders as well as of the good ones.

Senior.—Still, the conscription must have something to do with its deterioration. You cannot condemn every year to a six years' celibacy 40,000 of your best men without affecting the quality of your stock.

Rémusat.—To a certain degree that must be true, and I admit that that is a motive for trying rather to enlist foreigners than to increase our conscription.

Senior.—To return to the war. The change of generals seems to be an improvement.

Rémusat.—I hope so, though Canrobert is a good man. We are told that he was much put out by the electric telegraph. It is not easy to manage large operations when every minute you may have an order, or a suggestion, or a warning, or a counter-order from your master, who is 3000 miles off. It is said that Pelissier made a condition that the wires should be cut. I have great reliance on his courage, his experience in actual fighting, and his resources. What I fear is his temper. Happily he has a thorough gentleman to deal with in Lord Raglan.

Senior.—Do you believe that Austria demanded an auxiliary force of 200,000 men?

Rémusat.—If she did it must have been for the purpose of interposing between herself and war an impracticable condition. She well knows that we have not such a force to spare.

Senior.—Do you think Louis Napoleon stronger or weaker than he was a year ago?

Rémusat.—Weaker; he has lost the prestige of success. He has shown administrative incapacity. And this attempted assassination has shaken him. Pianori is supposed to be one of a band, in which case it is likely to be repeated. It has brought strongly before our eyes the instability of a power depending on a single head, and on a head the object of so much fanatical hatred. The waiters on Providence are thinking what would have been their fate if the shot had taken effect.

Wednesday, May 23rd.—Payne, Circourt, Manin, and Rémusat breakfasted with us. Dunoyer and Madame Mohl came in while we were at table.

Circourt showed us letters from French officers in Rome, expressing a strong wish to be removed to some other service, lest they should be employed in the odious task of repressing an insurrection. These letters represent the unpopularity of the Pope, and the hatred of the ecclesiastical Government as increasing every day. When he appears in public the Romans get out of his way. A superstition has grown up that to meet him is unlucky.

Circourt and Manin expressed their conviction that it is necessary to the permanence and the good working of the spiritual power of the Pope that he should be deprived of his temporal power.

Circourt.—The unlearned cannot believe him to be infallible in the things which they do not understand, when they see that he is constantly blundering in the matters of which they are good judges. 'Whenever,' they say, 'we can test the correctness of his judgment he goes wrong. We suspect therefore that he goes wrong where we cannot test it.' In order to be venerated as a theologian he ought to be nothing else. To talk oracularly about heaven he ought never to meddle with earth. He ought never to quit the inaccessible, impenetrable clouds of dogmatism. If Narses* and his successors, instead of retreating to Ravenna, had resided in Rome, we should have heard

---

* In the time of Narses and his successors as exarchs of Ravenna, there was only one Emperor who governed the East, and who governed the West through the exarch.

nothing of the temporal Papacy. The Bishop of Rome would have been kept under by a western Emperor just as the Patriarch of Constantinople was by the eastern Emperor. On the other hand, if the eastern Emperor had resided at Adrianople, it is probable that, like the Pope, the Patriarch might have become independent. In the absence of the Emperor he would have become the greatest man in Constantinople, as the Pope became in Rome. The power of the Pope in temporal affairs is exercised as illegally as it was acquired. His weapons are all revolutionary. He enforces his decrees by insurrections. It is by encouraging resistance to lawful authority that he has attempted to prevent the Piedmontese from exercising in their own country the rights of an independent nation. I cannot believe that such a constantly acting cause of disaffection, disturbance, and revolt, will long be suffered to exist. I cannot but hope that we shall see the Pope relieved from all his temporal duties, and confined to the interpretation of texts and the definition of dogmas. In that capacity I am ready to acknowledge his supremacy.

We talked of the ancient colonisation of Africa.

Circourt.—It is evident that Phœnicia, Greece, and Rome, each impressed on Africa her own nationality. They implanted there a Phœnician, a Greek, and a Roman population. On the other hand, Spain, after persevering for three hundred years in attempts to establish herself on the African soil, has seen her possessions there dwindle down to a single garrison; and France, after a quarter of a century of war and expenditure, has not succeeded in fixing in a country almost as large as France more than a few thousand families of French colonists. To what causes is the ill-success of Spain and of France to be attributed? I believe that the great cause is the difference as to religious belief between ancient and modern Europe and ancient and modern Africa.

Polytheism was naturally tolerant. It admitted the existence of an indefinite number of deities, and the worshipper of one class, though he resented any insult offered to his own gods, saw nothing objectionable in the reverence shown to any others; in fact, he was willing to join in it.

Senior.—Gibbon, in his antithetic style, remarks that the people thought all religions equally true, the philosopher equally false, and the statesman equally useful.

Circourt.—Well, experience has shown that the philosopher and the statesman were as much mistaken as the people. We now know not only that there is a true religion, but that in proportion as the faith of a nation approaches that truth, its welfare and its civilization improve; that a Mussulman is superior to a Pagan, a Jew to a Mussulman, and a Christian to a Jew. Perhaps indeed I might go further. But though I admit the vast, the infinite blessings conferred on man by Christianity, I can enter into the feelings of the Roman persecutors. In those times I should have been a persecutor myself. They saw religion, which had been a neutral ground, a matter of inheritance or of education, or perhaps of caprice, which every man had been allowed to retain or to adopt without interference, made a source of fierce animosity. A new sect arose which considered their gods as evil spirits, and the worship of them as a sin, who hated the poetry, the feasts, the amusements, and almost all the pleasures by which this life is sweetened, and devoted the whole human race, except their co-religionists, to eternal misery in another life. *We* are accustomed to religious intolerance. All existing sects, the Mussulman and the Jew, as well as the Christian, believe their own peculiar belief to be essential to salvation. But to a Roman such a theory was new. It shocked him as mischievous as well as absurd, and it was natural that he should endeavour to extirpate it.

To return however to ancient Africa. The religious antipathies which separate the Christian conquerors from their Mussulman subjects did not then exist. There was not, as there is now, a bar which rendered the amalgamation of the European and the African impossible; and I believe that to a considerable extent it took place. Africa could not have been the richest province in the empire; the Roman Carthage could not have rivalled Rome herself and Alexandria; hundreds of large cities could not have been scattered not only along the coasts but among the mountains and the plains of the interior—African learning, African theology, and African refinement could not have been illustrious for centuries—if the Greek and the Roman had not been widely grafted on the rude Libyan and Getulian stock.

Rémusat.—May not the European element have been rather substituted for the African than mixed with it? May not the Greeks and Romans have formed a nation apart, unconnected with the aborigines, as the English have done in America?

Circourt.—I think not. The English have taken the place of the American Indians, because the latter have fled or died before them. The Africans do neither. They are sufficiently civilized to maintain their ground against the white man. And they appear to have enjoyed a higher civilization in ancient times. Juba and Jugurtha were treated by the Romans as their equals—not with the almost unconscious feeling of superiority with which we look down on Abd-el-kader and his Khalifs. The second Juba is said to have been honoured with a statue by the Athenians. I believe that the only race under which Africa has been really civilized was a mixed race.

Friday, May 25th.—I called on the Duc de Broglie. He asked me what I heard in Algeria as to an exportation from thence of sugar, cotton, and cochineal.

Senior.—I saw a cochineal insect in the Jardin d'Essai, but heard nothing of sugar or cotton.

Duc de Broglie.—Unless Africa can supply us with tropical productions, it will be of little value. We have grain and forage and cattle of our own. The supplies which we have drawn this year for the Crimea have been of use, but it is an exceptional case.

Senior.—It is valuable to you as a great military position; but I do not believe that for many years it will be anything else.

Duc de Broglie.—Then it has cost us, and still costs us, more than it is worth.

We talked of Louis Napoleon.

Duc de Broglie.—He has lost ground since you were with us last year. He has shown what we can least tolerate, incapacity. He has shown that he knows neither how to administer himself nor how to choose persons who can administer for him. We can bear the loss of liberty; we are anxious for repose. We should submit easily to be deprived of the management of our own affairs provided they were well managed for us; but we are indignant when the man who has violently seized the helm runs the ship among the breakers.

We have now in the Crimea as large an army as we can feed, and as good an army as France can produce. If we cannot beat the Russians now, I do not see how we are ever to do so. Our difficulty is that we cannot leave the coast. We have not, and I do not believe that we can get, the 30,000 draft animals that are necessary to enable us to follow the Russians if they move thirty miles inland.

They have only to place this interval between themselves and us and they are safe. Louis Napoleon's presence would not have diminished this difficulty; it might have been useful in giving decision to Canrobert, but it would only embarrass Pelissier.

Auguste Chevalier drank tea with us. I asked him about the Crédit Mobilier.

Chevalier.—It is a trust company on the largest scale, and with almost discretionary powers. It acts as borrower for those who wish only to lend their money, and as speculator for those who wish to employ it. It borrows at from four to five per cent., and purchases shares, commodities, properties, everything, in short, which for the time being is to be bought advantageously. Its shareholders are dealers in every kind of investment. In the hands of such a man as Perreire, and of such associates and subordinates as Perreire selects, they are safe. It has been very profitable to me, but a few months of mismanagement might ruin it. One of the causes of its great success has been the rise of prices, which has been continuous ever since it was established. Little more than a year ago I bought my house for 300,000 francs; I am now offered for it 500,000. Living has become so dear in Paris that many persons are quitting it, and still more shorten their time of residence here. Some Gascon friends of mine brought with them their country servants. The first time the cook went to the market she returned in the utmost indignation. The people, she said, were laughing at her for being a provincial. They asked twenty francs for a fowl, and five for a bunch of asparagus. They cannot persuade her to go to market again. She says she will not go to be made fun of.

The war, the Exposition, the shortness of the last harvest, the inclemency of the winter, may all have something to do with this rise; but it is so general that I attribute it mainly to Californian and Australian gold; and, as I said before, it is very favourable to a company of speculators. But it exposes the Government to difficulties. It increases its expenses, and our new dynasty is not strong enough to increase its taxation. We shall have borrowed in a year and a half 50,000,000*l.* sterling. Our debt is now about half as large as yours.

Wednesday, May 30th.—Manin, Kergorlay, Lord Fitzwilliam, Mr. Thompson, Prince Butera and his second son, and Lord Ashburton, breakfasted with us, and Madame Mohl, Rémusat, and Wolerych Whitmore came before we rose. Manin and Butera spoke with enthusiasm of Ristori, one of an Italian company who are acting tragedies and comedies. In Alfieri's 'Myrrha' she converted an almost disgusting part into a seductive one.

Senior.—Do Alfieri's tragedies act well?

Manin.—Better than they read. When you read them you feel that they are not an imitation of Nature, but an imitation of Sophocles; a copy of a copy. As the characters are few, they can be well acted, and a good actor supplies the naturalness which Alfieri, who had passion without imagination, could not give.

I found Manin, like the French, attributing our good reception of Louis Napoleon to our fears.

Senior.—The educated classes might well be afraid of him, as every one is afraid of a man who has no fears and no scruples; but the mob are not politicians. They shouted for him as they shouted for Soult, and as they will shout for Henry V. if he visits us after his restoration, merely as a strange phenomenon, as a sight which gratifies their curiosity.

Manin.—The mob are not politicians, but the signal to

applaud was given to them by those who were, and they obeyed it instinctively, just as they would have instinctively hissed if the example had been set. I have known a column of soldiers burst out into a laugh, and when I asked why I have been told, 'le *lustig* est là-bas.' He had amused those who heard him, and those who did not hear the joke still passed on the laugh. You would have stood higher in the estimation of Europe if you had not abused him as long as you thought him weak, and fawned on him as soon as your relative positions were reversed. Your flattery began with your disasters in the Crimea, and it has kept pace with your ill-success. If you are driven from before Sebastopol you will adore him.

Ashburton.—On the contrary, we shall curse him. What the mob worshipped in him was success, and he is united to us by one of the strongest of ties, a common enemy. Next to his throne, Nicholas and Alexander are the sources of his popularity.

We talked of Canrobert and Pelissier.

Rémusat.—Pelissier is the most eminent of our African generals, excepting those in Belgium, and he is senior to Canrobert; but Canrobert was in Paris at the time of the coup d'état, and was useful. Pelissier, as was the case generally with the army in Africa, received the news coldly; he was out of favour at the time of Canrobert's appointment.

It is said that Canrobert saw his own letter of resignation first in the *Moniteur;* that the one which he wrote was long and exculpatory, and expressed merely a wish to continue with the army, not a request for Pelissier's division, and that he has refused the command which has been offered to him.

Senior.—Do you know the antecedents of Persigny?

Rémusat.—Certainly. His father, whose name was Fialin, was a huissier in a small provincial court of justice near St. Etienne. Young Fialin disliked his father's profession, and entered the army and rose to the rank of corporal; he left it not very creditably, went to Switzerland, and offered his services to Louis Napoleon; he accompanied his master to Strasburg and to Boulogne, where he was arrested and sentenced to imprisonment; he is married to a pleasing woman, niece of Edgar Ney, and has acquired the manners of the world; he is pecuniarily honest, which is rare in this Court; he is devoted to Louis Napoleon, and he is not without talent. These are his merits; but he has no real education or knowledge.

Senior.—How did he become Persigny?

Rémusat.—His father once had a cottage and a field to which he gave that name; he sold them while his son was still Fialin. The assumption of the name was an odd piece of impudence.

Thursday, May 31st.—Rémusat paid me a long visit. We talked of the prospects of the English alliance.

Rémusat.—You will always find the most cordial friend in a Government which does not rest on divine right. Henri V.'s Government may be friendly to you, and if Thiers is its minister it will be so; but I will not answer for it under Molé or Berryer; it will be your friend only accidentally. A Government founded on the will of the people is your friend naturally; it fraternises with you, as the offspring of a common parent. A Legitimist Government has something to overcome before it accepts you.

Senior.—And yet the Imperial Government, though founded on universal suffrage, was at first hostile to us.

Rémusat.—The Imperial Government required a war. No inferior excitement could compensate for the loss of liberty. The indignation which the coup d'état excited in England, the violence of your press, and the old rivalry of the two countries might perhaps have drawn the storm upon you if Nicholas had not offered Louis Napoleon a quarrel in which justice, generosity, and policy, were all on his side, and in which he could reckon on you as an ally. I believe that he accepted this war far more readily than you did, far more readily than it would have been accepted by an established Government. I believe that he might have had an honourable peace, and that he did not wish for one; but I do not think, as some of my friends do, that it was with an 'arrière-pensée' of conquest. I believe that at present he sincerely bounds his wishes to the maintenance of the European equilibrium; but if the war lasts long, if he is forced to call on France for painful sacrifices, if he has to increase our taxation, and make an extraordinary conscription, he may find it, or he may think it, necessary to offer us a bribe, or at least an indemnity, and that can be only an extension of territory. From the beginning of the reign of Louis XIV. down to the end of that of Napoleon, that is, for one hundred and fifty years, the object of all our wars has been conquest; it is our only test of success. A war for the preservation of Turkey, a war for the freedom of the Black Sea, or of the navigation of the Danube, even a war for the sake of European civilization are things which the bulk of the French people cannot appreciate, cannot even understand; they call such things abstractions. Really to excite them you must offer them something immediate, something visible and tangible: a new province, a new fund for taxation, a new field for the conscription, something that would require prefects, maires, and débits de tabac.

But the determination to add to our Empire does not necessarily imply a quarrel with you. I know that you will not allow us to seize Belgium, but we may take Mayence, or Rhenish Prussia, or Savoy; and if he thinks that he *can*—that is to say, if he sees another way by which his purposes may be as well effected—he *will* avoid a war with England. He is grateful for the asylum which you afforded to him in his exile; he is grateful for your ready recognition of him as Emperor, when Russia was rude and Austria was scarcely civil. The praises of your press please his vanity, and your reception of him intoxicated him with delight. You are the only people that have treated him as a Sovereign; but he has no scruples, no moral sense; he does not know the meaning of the words right and wrong; he will act purely according to what he believes to be his interest for the time being, and, if he believes that his glory or his power will be best promoted by invading Belgium, or by invading England, he will act on that belief without the slightest compunction. One of the many unfortunate results of the campaign of 1854 is, that he fancies, and the opinion is general in France, that you are utterly at his mercy; that the English power is a phantom, a bubble which the first touch will dissipate. The deference, whatever may be its amount, with which he treats you, you must accept as an act of great condescension.

He has one quality which makes it peculiarly difficult to predict his conduct—he has no keeping in his mind; he cannot appreciate according to their respective values the objects of his desires; the immediate wish which for the time being possesses him, swallows up all the others. At one time he thought of nothing but the finishing of the Louvre and the embellishment of Paris; then he was anxious for a royal bride. I have no doubt that his visit to England excluded all other ideas for weeks. The failure of this Exposition has given him quite as much annoyance as the failure of the Crimean campaign.

I dined with Auguste Chevalier, and sat next to M. Charles de Labaume, the Avocat-Général. We talked of Pianori.

Labaume.—There is little doubt that he was the agent of Mazzini, Ledru Rollin, and the others who form the revolutionary committee in London. He went to England a few weeks before he made the attempt in rags and penniless; he returned well dressed, with three pistols, and a dagger, and money. Who, except that committee, could have thus supplied him? If the crime had been committed in the Bois de Boulogne, or in any little frequented place, I have no doubt that the thing would have been hushed up, as previous attempts have been. But its publicity made the trial unavoidable; the Emperor wished the whole matter to be over, and the man to be executed in a week; this was done, but it was a mistake; during that period he preserved his strength of body and of mind, and resisted all our attempts to extort from him evidence as to his accomplices. But if he had been kept 'au secret, sur une diète modeste,' until his bodily and mental force was reduced, he would have come out quite tame, and by holding out to him hopes of the Emperor's clemency we should have induced him perhaps to make a full confession, almost certainly to give us valuable information.

Senior.—What is your guess as to the immediate consequences if he had succeeded?

Labaume.—I think that King Jérôme would have been acknowledged by the army as Emperor, that the Republicans would have made a war of barricades, and that they would have been beaten.

He talked of the difficulty of obtaining a conviction from a jury.

Labaume.—If they were not allowed to find ' circonstances

atténuantes' they would always acquit ; they cannot resist the solicitations of the friends of the accused.

Senior.—But how do they become exposed to them ?

Labaume.—They become exposed to them whenever a trial lasts more than one day; and as we interrogate the prisoner, and admit much evidence which you exclude, our trials often last a week.

Friday, June 1st.—General Chrzanowski* and Lord Ashburton breakfasted with us. I asked Chrzanowski as to the force of the armies in the Crimea.

Chrzanowski.—The English, French, and Piedmontese, together with the Turks who are available, amount to little more than one hundred and twenty thousand men. The Russian, including those who are on their march, and so near that they may be considered as having joined the main body, consists of ten divisions of infantry and four of cavalry. Notwithstanding that the infantry division should be sixteen thousand men each, the two armies may be considered as nearly equal in numerical strength. The allied army is morally inferior to that which fought on the Alma. That army consisted of old troops, and, as respects the French, of picked troops. They had injured the regiments left behind by forming corps d'élite. Still, morally it is enormously superior to the Russian army; more so, relatively, than it was at the Alma, because the Russian army is greatly inferior to what it was.

In general the whole administration of Russia, civil as well as military, is in a state of corruption and decay. It has been going down ever since the time of Catherine. Its rise and its fall are a repetition of the history of many an

---

* This conversation was corrected and annotated by General Chrzanowski, sometimes in English, sometimes in French—hence an occasional peculiarity in the style.—ED.

Asiatic empire. Everything is sacrificed to what are supposed to be the personal interests of the Czar. He wishes all around him to be perfectly subservient, and for that purpose, in the first place, to be poor. It is the system of the Court to encourage extravagant expenditure, and to reward those who have ruined themselves by giving them places, which being ill-paid, are valuable only as a means of robbery. An honest employé in Russia would be dismissed. He would interrupt the hierarchy of plunder. His salary perhaps is a 1000 roubles, he spends several thousand; and besides, he has to give 2000 to his immediate superior, who has to give 4000 to *his* superior, who has to give 10,000 to the favourite who protects him. The man with 1000 roubles takes 200 or 300 from each of his subordinates; they each fleece those below them, and thus the apparently modest salaries of the Russian administrators are swelled to an amount which you would think decent in England.

This gives to the Court, too, another means of influence. No account between the Crown and a subject is ever finally closed. A man may be sent to Siberia charged with embezzlement committed forty years before. For instance, Paskewitsch, when colonel, must have done as others did. If he were to offend the new Emperor, all his honours and his age would not protect him from ruin. Not only the lives and fortunes, but the characters of all who have ever acted in the public service are at the mercy of the Sovereign.

As respects the military power of the empire, the result is, that the soldier who has to bear this vast superstructure of fraud is ill-fed and ill-attended to. Of the great convoys of provisions which you see from the heights entering Sebastopol, half are probably uneatable. The average annual mortality in the Russian army in peace is ten per cent. You may fancy what it is in war, and how rapidly a couple of campaigns must destroy the old troops, and occasion the ranks to be filled with new levies. The Russian conscriptions during the last two years have amounted to about 34 per 1000 souls. In Russia the males only are counted, and a census is seldom taken oftener than about every twenty-five years. From census to census, the population of each village is considered as unaltered.

Supposing the male population of Russia giving recruits to amount to 25,000,000, 34 per 1000 amounts to nearly 800,000. Deducting about 120,000 soldiers who served fifteen years, supposing frauds and evasions as well as the ordinary mortality of recruits to have diminished the actual levy, still about 450,000 men have been raised, so that the new levies must constitute nearly half of their troops in the Crimea. To these general causes must be added the manner in which the Russians have carried on the defence of Sebastopol, and which must ruin an army. Their system has been that of constant sorties in large bodies, sometimes 3000 or 4000, consisting in great part of volunteers. In the first place, a sortie ought not to consist of more than from 50 to 200 men. A larger number can scarcely escape detection, is at night unmanageable, and occasions losses never in proportion with the gain obtained. In the second place, the abstraction of the volunteers, like the creation of corps d'élite, destroys the muscles and nerves of an army. Of an average regiment not three per cent. are really brave, and fifty per cent. would run away if they could; forty-seven per cent. would not run, but they lose their presence of mind; and if they do not serve long enough for doing it well mechanically, they fire wildly, load with the ball before the powder, or leave the ramrod in the gun and do not hear, or do not understand, the word of command.

It is the three per cent. who preserve their courage and their coolness that keep up, and direct, and manage, and give the *élan* to the others. Deprive a regiment of this small vivifying principle in order to make corps d'élite, or volunteers who perish, and you leave it an inert mass.

The Russians have done this to so mad an excess that their army in the Crimea, I think, cannot venture to deploy. If they were to form in line, half would run. They are forced to attack, and even to stand, in columns, where they can put their least bad men at the sides and behind, and those within are kept together by pressure; but this deprives them of much of their power of action, and subjects them to frightful destruction. If they are properly attacked they will deteriorate every day. An army does not remain stationary. It gets better or it gets worse, and when it is in the state to which the Russians are now reduced, it falls more and more rapidly as its losses increase.

Senior.—What do you think of their present generals?

Chrzanowski.—Gortschakoff has every military quality, with one exception. He is brave, he has studied the theory of war, he has seen its practice, he is intelligent, he is everything, except being decided. His irresolution and his fear of responsibility amount to a mental disease, besides his health his bad. He may plan wisely, but he will never execute. A campaign between Gortchakoff and Canrobert would resemble one of the battles of the Italian *condottieri*. They will stand squaring at one another for months, without either of them venturing to strike. Liprandi is a good general of division, but nothing more. Ostensacken is a charlatan. I used to see him, Lutheran as he is, in the Russian churches, singing among the priests, to please the Emperor. He is unpopular too as being a German. The intermixture of German officers is one of the weak points in the Russian army. They are generally poor and economical. The Russian officers, almost all noble, and all expensive, relying on their own Court influence, look down on them, disobey and insult them.

The Russians, however, are better commanded than they were. Menschikoff, though brave and intelligent, was so ignorant that his whole campaign was a series of blunders.

He has had opportunities to have driven you into the sea, or at least to have seriously injured you; but these opportunities were thrown away on him. In the beginning he was in a very delicate situation, and did not perceive it. He was unable to oppose your landing, and he has had a very inferior force to fight his battle. This delicate situation he transformed into a desperate one, not knowing that a defence of a position depends upon reserves. He placed his troops behind the Alma in two lines, without any reserve. When he was menaced in the flank, and a gap was made in his lines, he had nothing to stop it with, and after three hours' fighting, he ran away without looking behind. He was saved from destruction as he was not pursued immediately, and the allies followed him only on the third day. The first business of a general is to find out what the enemy is doing. Neither the Russians nor the allies seem to have thought of this, having lost sight of each other after the battle. You went east and he went north; if he had set out two hours later, you would have caught him at Mackenzie's farm without seeking him; or perhaps he would have caught you, for you would have been surprised, just as his rear was. The two armies were playing at blind-man's buff. Nothing again could have been more absurd than his battle of Balaclava, after he was joined by reinforcements and possessed a superiority. He had at least 40,000 men at his disposition; you had only some poor redoubts, some bad Turks, and a few English regiments. If he had attacked you with 40,000, using 15,000 to attack Balaclava, disposing other 15,000 against the reinforcements which could come from the main camp, and for overpowering one after another single battalions descending the heights, having besides 10,000 in reserve to support the one or other part, he must have driven you over the cliffs, and beaten the supporting troops from the camp. Instead of that, he employed only 15,000 men. Soldiers in war are like capital in commerce, one cannot have too many of them. One need not spend them, but one ought always to make use of them.

As it was, using only a part of his force, he was obliged to desist from the attack of Balaclava, and to retreat, being menaced in the flank by troops coming from the camp. Your cavalry charge obtained a success which could not have been expected, and if everything had been prepared to follow it up instantly, the Russians might have been destroyed. But as no means were taken for it beforehand, that charge has been justly blamed; it was an heroic execution of an absurd conception.

Pour la bataille d'Inkerman Menschikoff a à la vérité employé toutes ses forces, mais il ne savait pas en faire usage. Sur une espace très-resserrée il a entassé toutes ses troupes en colonnes, par bataillons, les unes sur les autres, de manière qu'elles s'empêchaient mutuellement d'agir. Le feu des alliés faisant un ravage affreux dans cette masse informe, après quatre heures de boucherie elle était obligée de se replier en désordre derrière la Tchernaya. Aurait-il deployé sur deux lignes autant de bataillons que comportait l'espace, destiné quelques autres bataillons pour garantir les flancs de ces lignes, et gardé le reste en réserve hors de partie, il aurait eu de quoi changer plus que quatre fois sa première ligne. L'infanterie de la division Lipraudi devait aussi faire partie de cette réserve, et devant Balaclava la cavalerie seule, avec son artillerie à cheval, était suffisante pour faire des démonstrations et du bruit. Y laisser aussi l'infanterie c'était s'occuper du soin de rendre la victoire décisive avant de l'avoir remportée. Les troupes anglaises, qui, s'étant laissé surprendre, n'ont pas engagé l'affaire avec tout l'ordre désirable, n'auraient pas pu résister aux efforts victorieux des troupes fraîches, et les secours partiels de la division Bosquet auraient tout au plus servi à prolonger un peu leur résistance, si l'attaque des Russes aurait été convenablement arrangée. Après avoir battu l'armée anglaise, Menschikoff tombant sur l'armée française par le flanc, n'aurait eu à faire qu'à une division après l'autre et un succès décisif n'était pas impossible. Toujours est-il que l'armée alliée ne s'est encore trouvée dans une position aussi critique comme pendant cette journée.

Dans l'attaque d'Eupatoria, Menschikoff avait de nouveau des forces insuffisantes et il a seulement tâté sur un point les Turcs. Au lieu d'arriver avec deux divisions d'infanterie il devait arriver avec cinq, et faire à la fois plusieurs attaques franches. Il ne risquait rien, car dans le cas improbable, que toutes ses attaques eussent échoué, il se couvrait de sa cavalerie. Ce dernier échec fit voir à l'Empereur Nicolas que l'apprentissage de Menschikoff pour être général en chef, ne pouvait pas réussir, et il le rappela.

Senior.—You have criticised the Russians. What do you think of the allied siege of Sebastopol?

Chrzanowski.—I think ' qu'on s'est trop écarté des principes reçus.' The success of an attack depends on the besiegers having a superiority of fire over the besieged. To obtain this a small portion of the fortress, generally a salient angle, is selected for attack. A gun requires about ten mètres— two for itself, and eight for those who are to work it. On a face of 800 mètres therefore only eighty guns can be used. But the attacking party may direct on that face more than double the number of guns by placing them not only in front but at the sides, and thus obtain on one particular point the required superiority of fire. When the French took Dantzig they found in it 4000 guns. They had not 300, but on the precise point attacked they were greatly superior.

Now the allies, instead of selecting a portion, have thought fit to attack nearly the whole southern semicircle. The necessary consequence has been that, instead of being superior, they have not even been equal. For the first time in military history the fire of the besieged has been more powerful than that of the besieger.

Another discrepancy to the rules was the distance at which you opened your trenches. The distance usually adopted ranges between 350 mètres, which is unusually near, to 600, which is unusually distant. A dark night is chosen when the wind blows from the place, and if the first, or the second, or the third night be not favourable, the besieger waits for a fourth.

You opened yours at the distance of 1200 mètres, or about 1300 yards, nearly three-quarters of a mile. You thus imposed on yourselves three months of useless labour, three months of useless expense, and three months of unnecessary sickness. Again, as to this Mamelon, of which so much has been said, you had it for three months staring you in the face, and never saw its value. A man with the eye of a general would have seen its importance as he galloped by it for the first time.

If you want more military blunders I could give them to you, but these are enough.

Senior.—When we talked in the beginning of March of the prospects of the campaign, you believed that it might be decided in six weeks. You thought that the allies could not remain in their camp before Sebastopol after the middle of April; that to escape from the pestilence which the warm weather would bring with it they must assault the town or

desert their works and march to the north-east of Balaclava.
It does not seem that any of these events have taken place.

Chrzanowski.—The assault certainly has not taken place, but in a certain degree each of the two other events has occurred. The French acknowledge a loss of 5000 men a month; that is, at the rate of 60,000 a year. This approaches to a pestilence. I admit, however, that the exertions of the allies in applying disinfecting materials have been more successful than I expected; and they have partially shifted their quarters. They have extended themselves to the Tchernaya and beyond it.

Senior.—What would you do if you were in Pelissier's place?

Chrzanowski.—My object being to drive the Russians out of the Crimea, two things must be done—Sebastopol taken and the Russian army beaten. As the allied army is not strong enough to undertake seriously the two operations at once, they must be done in succession. There is no choice: to keep in check (contenir) the Russian army and assault the southern part of Sebastopol, or to keep in check the garrison and attack the army. Each course, as is always the case in war, has its own inherent disadvantages. Taking the first: the assault might fail, 10,000 men or more might be lost, and the rest demoralised, rendering offensive operations impossible. Taking the second course, at least 10,000 men less would be brought into the battle, and the prospects of success diminished. For deciding what is preferable, I ought to see Sebastopol with my own eyes. At all events I would begin by establishing three or four bridges upon the Tchernaya, and cover them with entrenchments, establishing batteries on the left bank to protect these entrenchments. Having found that the assault had little chance of success, I would march to attack the Russian army. I do not believe that it is near Simferopol, or even about Baktchi-Serai. At such a distance it could not prevent our investing Sebastopol. I should expect to find it near the town, covering the road to Baktchi-Serai. It would be necessary to leave 30,000 men before Sebastopol to protect my works and camp. I should march on the Russians with 70,000, placing 20,000 between the two posts as a reserve.

If the Russians sent from their main body reinforcements into the town, I should make the 20,000 men join the covering force. If they did not, I should make them join my main body. I believe that I should thus have a force sufficient to beat the Russians; they would not be numerically superior, they are morally inferior, and though they have a much larger cavalry, the ground between Sebastopol and Simferopol is ill-suited to cavalry. There is no place where more than a couple of thousand could be employed.

I am sure that if the allies were commanded by a man of experience and enterprise all this might be done. But for great operations unity of command is required, and there are four independent generals of four different nations. The decisions are taken by a council of war; a good instrument for doing nothing. To this moment not one of the generals has shown such an incontestable superiority in moral qualities and knowledge that the others could submit themselves willingly to his direction. Bosquet has given proofs of his vigilance and activity; Brown is good in actual fighting, but we have not seen that he is more; Pelissier has the reputation of an enterprising man, but he wants experience of moving and putting in action great bodies of troops, and it is hardly possible that he should be well obeyed.

How this experience is wanted on both sides is very visible; all the 'tâtonnement' with such brave men as are generally the chiefs of the allied army, all the faults committed, derive in greater part from it; they are trying to learn their business while they are practising it.

At the battle of the Alma the Turkish division was forgotten. It was posted in vineyards, and from that time until the battle was over received no orders. In this battle, too, you did not have your cavalry; it was left behind. On the other hand, you wasted it absurdly and uselessly at Balaclava; you made up for not using it when you ought to have used it by using it when you ought not. Thirty thousand Turks were placed at Eupatoria who could do nothing, and were exposed to be crushed by the Russians, whose force amounted to 50,000.

The Russians found that they were beaten at Balaclava because they were too few. Therefore at Inkerman they heaped man upon man and column upon column, and were beaten because they were too many. They resolved not to repeat that error, and attacked Eupatoria with two divisions instead of five, and were beaten again because they were too few.

I do not understand your want of the means of naval transport. You tell me that when you left Algiers three thousand horses and mules were there, and had been there for some weeks, waiting for English ships to take them to the Black Sea. In the Peninsular war, when you had all the ports of the Continent to blockade, and carried on your commerce by means of only your own ships, and when you had no steam, you never were in want of transports. Now, in the second year of the war, when you ought to have discovered all your requirements and provided against them, your operations are constantly impeded for want of shipping. Why do you not employ your men-of-war as transports? Now that the Russian fleet is sunk or imprisoned, and all the sailors killed, you cannot require large fleets in the Black Sea. A ship of the line of two thousand five hundred tons, with her guns and ammunition taken out, and with only enough sailors to navigate her, could well carry two thousand soldiers. A man, with his effects, food, and water, does not weigh a ton. She might be towed by a steamer. Again, such a ship could carry, instead of men, 2000 tons of rations, or 4,800,000 pounds, which would be more than enough to feed 100,000 men for a fortnight. England and France have the strength of giants, but seem to be afraid to put it out.

Senior.—What would you do with the force at Eupatoria?

Chrzanowski.—Bring it back as soon as you can to your main body; that is your best remedy for uselessly detaching it. As soon as you seriously advance against the Russians they will have too much to do to attack Eupatoria; you need not leave there more than a small garrison.

Senior.—How do you account for our not having attacked Kertch before?

Chrzanowski.—The solution of that question must be political; it cannot be military. According to all the rules of war you ought to have occupied it a year ago. To say that you wanted men is no excuse; the Turks that have been lying uselessly at Eupatoria might have been sent thither; they would have been safe at that distance from the Russians. The solution, I repeat, must be political; you have never ventured to attack Russia seriously; you have been always afraid of embittering the quarrel, of diminishing the chances of peace. I am not sure that even now you are altogether free from that influence.

The value of your success at Kertch depends on the state of the provisions of the Russian army in the Crimea. If they have food and forage for four weeks, the loss of the magazines at Kertch and the interruption of further supplies from that quarter will not force them to leave the Crimea. In four weeks, by stripping all the country to the north of

Perekop, they will obtain supplies which will enable them to remain in the Crimea until a great battle has decided whether you or they are to be masters there. The country will be ruined, but the soldiers and horses will be fed. But if they have provisions for only a week or a fortnight, or even for only three weeks, they must retreat in order to meet their supplies; their army requires at least seven hundred waggon loads of food for men and horses every day. If the Austrians cease to menace them, and thereby enable them to bring against you their force from Poland, the difficulty, probably an insuperable one, of feeding more men and horses will be the only cause limiting their numbers. In some respects you are much better off than they are. A ship can carry more than a thousand waggons can. While you keep close to the sea you can feed an indefinite number of men; but you cannot move inland; you have an excellent base of operations, but you are tied to it.

Senior.—I have often wondered at the long marches of the armies of antiquity without magazines or great means of transport.

Chrzanowski.—To feed an army on a march is comparatively easy. Supposing it to march ten miles a day, and to strip the country for five miles on each side of its march, the infantry collecting all that is near, and the cavalry foraging at a greater distance, you can take every day all that is to be found within a hundred square miles of new country. Now there is no waste so great as that of war. The green crops are trodden down; the grain is thrown in heaps on the ground before the horses; you see all round you careless or wilful destruction. But wasteful as an army on march is, still a hundred square miles will in most countries afford a day's food and forage to seventy thousand men and twenty thousand horses, and armies seldom march in much larger bodies. A very numerous army advances upon three or more parallel roads extending the front thirty or more miles; and as seldom good parallel roads can be found, a great part of the army must march upon small and bad ones. Napoleon generally marched without magazines and with a small amount of provisions; he relied on what he could find on his road. It is when an army is stationary, or has to march through a barbarous country, that it becomes difficult to feed it.

Senior.—Do you attach much importance to the capture of the Mamelon?

Chrzanowski.—The Mamelon is eight hundred mètres from the place; it ought to have been in the rear of your first parallel. I am glad to see that you are paying more attention to the rules of war. You are making your attacks converge; but I do not perfectly understand the importance which you attach to getting possession of the south of the town, while the north, which appears to command it, remains untouched. This was one of the reasons why I said that I could not decide without seeing Sebastopol whether the assault of the town, or the attack of the Russian army, ought to be the first operation. It is difficult to suppose that you have employed eight months in besieging a place which you cannot hold when you have got it; and yet the inference which I draw from the plans and descriptions of the fortifications is, that the south cannot be held against the master of the north. There seems, he added, to be a fatality that defeats the resistance of the west against Russia. You make what look to be immense exertions; you spend money like water. Each of these bombardments costs in powder and shot, including the expense of conveying them to your batteries, ten millions of francs a day. This war has cost England and France already sixty millions sterling. But you are always negotiating while you are fighting, and always hope to frighten Russia into peace, instead of resolving to beat her down.

Senior.—Napoleon went to work with her decidedly.

Chrzanowski.—No; he, too, was negotiating. What but negotiations led him to waste a fortnight at Wilna, and after two irretrievable months in Moscow? Russia always gains by time; a barbarous country is not affected by loss of men, or even of money, as a civilized one is. Taxes, conscriptions, requisitions, and devastation are submitted to in Russia as the cold and snow are submitted to. Her rough rude capital is quickly replaced, and she has always the resource of bankruptcy. You cannot really weaken her but by dismembering her, and that you have not courage to attempt, or even to propose to yourselves as your object.

Wednesday, June 6th.—Manin and Arrivabene breakfasted with us.

Manin.—I hear from all my friends who have relations with Russia, that the resentment there against Austria is far fiercer than that against England or France. She is considered rather as a rebel and a traitor than as a mere enemy. Whatever be the result of the war she will have to pay.

Senior.—But to whom is she to pay? Who is to force her to pay?

Manin.—The conqueror, whoever it may be; she is no longer a great power. Her peculiar strength, her obstinate vitality, is gone. She owed it to her federal origin. The different nations that had coalesced under her sceptre were proud of their respective nationalities, and attached to her as their common protector. They provided her with new armies and new treasures as fast as she wasted what she had. She was constantly defeated, constantly bankrupt, but never without men or without money. These very nationalities which saved her she has attempted to destroy. She has attempted to fuse them into one Austrian empire. She has failed. Instead of fusion she has produced repulsion. We may regret the present development of exclusively national feelings. We may be sorry to see a tendency to constitute Governments rather on moral and ethnological, than on territorial principles, to see a language or a dialect form a frontier, instead of a river or a mountain. The passive resignation with which dissimilar and even hostile races consented to be grouped together, and kindred ones to be separated, was convenient. It gave facilities to the system of exchanges, arrondissements, and indemnities, by which the balance of power was maintained. But our regrets are useless. The peoples are taking these matters out of the hands of the diplomatists. And Austria, which was the 'mauvais idéal' of that system which was constructed without regard to nationalities, and kept together only by favouring and respecting them, falls to pieces as soon as her rash, ignorant, young Emperor attempts to trample on them. Her German, Polish, Sclavonic, Magyar, and Roman elements are separating from one another; they are crystallising according to their peculiar chemical affinities into hostile nations. Her cohesion rests on her army, which a single campaign may destroy. Nor is that army to be blindly relied on. Some portions of it are Italians, with all the Italian hate of the German. Others consist of the Hungarian Honveds, or National Guards, whom, after the subjugation of Hungary, she forced as a punishment to serve in the line. They are far superior in knowledge and fortune to the ordinary privates, and have exercised over them an influence very unfavourable to Austria. I do not believe that even the German part of the population wishes to remain Austrian. It naturally leans to the centre of German intelligence, literature, constitutional freedom, and industry, Prussia. As soon as that throne is occupied by a man of sense and spirit, the German provinces will look towards him as their natural Sovereign. You must recollect that I have always maintained that she will not engage in this war, because she loses Hungary if she attacks Russia, and Italy if she attacks France. And if she remains neutral, I think that she probably will lose both. Louis Napoleon and Alexander are quite capable of terminating the war by an amicable partition of Austria. Think, too, of the ruin which her armed neutrality brings with it. Her army alone costs more than her whole revenue. Already, in peace, she is reduced to revolutionary expedients. When did a great nation, or any nation before, sell to foreigners all her railroads? Her loan was in the first place a forced one—you were required voluntarily to supply a certain sum fixed by the Government according to your supposed means; and, secondly, it was raised on false pretences. A solemn promise was given that it should be employed in redeeming the national paper, then at thirty per cent. discount. It was not so employed, and that paper is at a lower discount than ever, lower than our Venetian paper was during the siege.

Thursday, June 7th.—I went to breakfast with the Mohls, and met there Madame Cornu, the early friend of Louis Napoleon. Joseph's letters were mentioned, and some one expressed surprise at Louis Napoleon's having allowed a work so injurious to the moral character of his uncle to appear.

Madame Cornu.—I doubt whether, supposing him to have moral sense sufficient to perceive the immorality of Napoleon's letters, he would have thought *that* an objection to their publication. He is beginning to be jealous of his uncle. He hopes to become his rival. At first he was satisfied to be Augustus; now he wishes to be also Cæsar.

He has mistaken his vocation. He aspires to be a statesman, perhaps to be a soldier. What nature intended him for was a poet. He has an inventive, original, and powerful imagination, which, under proper training, would have produced something great.

Senior.—Is his taste good?

Madame Cornu.—He cannot tolerate French poetry. He is insensible to Racine; but he delights in Shakspeare, and Goethe, and Schiller. The great, the strange, and the tragic suit his wild and somewhat vague habits of thought and his melancholy temperament. Of the fine arts the only one that interests him is architecture, probably from the vastness of its products. He hates music, and does not understand painting or sculpture. Among the mistakes which the public makes with respect to that family, one of the greatest is the treating Jerôme as an unimportant member of it. Jerôme has as much courage and as much ambition as Louis Napoleon himself. His ambition, however, is less selfish, for it looks towards his heir. He idolises Plon-Plon; and in the improbable event of his surviving Louis Napoleon, and succeeding to the crown, he will endeavour to hand it over to his son. But he will not without a struggle let it be worn by a Bourbon or broken by a Republic. He will fight, and fight desperately, for the rights of the Bonapartes. The enemies of that family ought to pray that he may die before his nephew.

In the evening Mérimée persuaded us to go to an enormous fête at the Hôtel de Ville by promising to use his privilege as Senator to take us in and out without delay or trouble. We drove straight to the gate facing the river, and found the vast court behind it covered with a roof about seventy feet above us, lighted with thousands of gas-burners in ground glass, with a mountain of flowers in the centre, and bright dashing fountains at the corners. All the windows that look into it were crowded tier over tier with guests gazing at the strange splendours above them and beneath them. Mérimée's acquaintance with the building enabled him to take us over the whole without returning on our steps. Everywhere, even in the garrets, we found crowds. I can well believe what we were told, that eight thousand persons were present. The historical associations of the building are not those of festivity. In one of the ball-rooms Robespierre lay mangled until he was summoned to trial and execution. From the windows of another Coffinhal and Lebas jumped, and were dashed to pieces on the pavement. We had refreshments in the room in which the Provisional Government of 1848 was besieged by the mob, and in the doorway at which we entered Lamartine stood when his mere courage and eloquence repulsed the Red Republicans. Among the eight thousand guests I did not recognise a single face that I had ever seen before.

We returned to London on the 13th.

[Mr. Senior passed through Paris again in November, on his way to Egypt. Sebastopol had fallen in September, but the allied armies were still in the Crimea.—ED.]

Monday, November 1st.—We have been in Paris for two days, but have been so occupied in preparations for our Egyptian journey, and in making the acquaintance of our future fellow-travellers, that there has been little conversation worth recording. We dined to-day with Auguste Chevalier; there was only a family party.

Chevalier believes the Emperor to be anxious for peace on many grounds.

First. Because the war is unpopular, and the English alliance equally so, as tending to prolong it. French vanity was interested in taking Sebastopol, but now that is done, the war is supposed to be carried on merely for English objects, the preservation of India, and the annihilation of Russia as a naval power.

Secondly. Because he fears the creation of a great military reputation, which he might find a dangerous rival. He could not, like the Sovereigns by the grace of God, feel secure if there were another man in France whom the people, or even the army, might prefer to himself. He certainly wished to accept the Austrian propositions, and rejected them not, as he desires to be believed, because they were at first ill-explained to him, but because we—that is to say, the heads of the English Cabinet—privately let him know that we disapproved of them.

I asked if he was likely to turn his head to financial and economical improvement; to greater freedom of trade, for example.

Chevalier.—I fear not. He has little knowledge on those subjects, and as he is very indolent and very conceited, is not likely to acquire much; besides which, his uncle was a violent, blind protectionist, and he professes to worship ' les idées Napoléoniennes.' He has strange notions as to doing good to the people by giving them employment and giving them money. So far as he has theories, they are socialist. I am alarmed at our financial state. We are carrying on a necessarily expensive war in the most expensive way; we are rebuilding Paris and many of our provincial towns, and we have had a bad harvest. Our funds have fallen twenty-five per cent., while yours have fallen only ten. His only tolerable ministers were Persigny and Drouyn de Lhuys. One has resigned; the other is absent. I believe, however, that Persigny will be recalled. He is more wanted in Paris than in London. The rest are mere valets.

I have seen Thiers twice, but only for a few minutes each time, and he was full of nothing but the conclusion of his history, which is passing through the press, and requires great labour. 'Je fais mon style,' he said, ' sur les épreuves.' He, too, expects peace.

Tuesday, November 2nd.—Lord Lansdowne, General Fox, Colonel Rawlinson, Arthur Russell, and General Chrzanowski breakfasted with us. Chrzanowski had much to say, and out-stayed the others. Much of the following conversation occurred when we were alone.

We asked him what he thought of Pelissier.

Chrzanowski.—I believe him to be a brave, intelligent general of division, but I see no marks of the higher military qualities. I put the management of the siege out of the question, and judge him neither by his early failure nor by his subsequent success. A general-in-chief may show talent or incapacity in undertaking or in omitting such an operation. Lord Wellington's attacks on Ciudad Rodrigo and Badajos were masterpieces of military boldness and intelligence, but when once the siege has begun the actual details are managed by others. The engineers are responsible for the approaches and for deciding that the breach is impracticable. The generals of division and of brigade, and the colonels, conduct the assault; the commander-in-chief has little to do except to see that his men are well lodged and fed, and well covered against any relieving army. It is only when his army is in the field that he shows his ability. Pelissier has shown none.

The Russian army is either equal or inferior in force to that of the allies. If it be inferior, how is the lethargy of the allies for the two months that have followed the capture of Sebastopol, the most important two months of the war, to be explained? Nothing is truer than Napoleon's favourite aphorism, that in war 'le moral est tout.' The defeat at the Tchernaya, the destruction by the bombardment, and the loss during the assault, must have utterly demoralised the Russian army. If it was inferior in numerical force to that of the allies, why was no advantage taken of its demoralised state? Why have the allies gone to sleep for two months while it has been reunited and reinvigorated? The only excuse is that it was *not* inferior numerically; that it was too strong to be attacked even after so great a disaster. But in that case what madness it was in Pelissier, in the face of an army which on the supposition was not much inferior in number to his own, to disperse his forces in all directions; to detach 6000 men, some to Kinburn, some to Kertch, some to Batoum, and a little army to Eupatoria? I do not believe that there are now 70,000 of the allies before the Russians. If the Russians have in the Crimea 100,000 men (and considering the stake they are playing for it is monstrous if they have not), I see no military obstacle which can prevent their breaking through your lines and re-entering Sebastopol.

To disperse an army in the face of an enemy is a calamity when it is necessary, and a crime if it can be avoided. In this case it was totally unnecessary. You had not the excuse of having a long line to guard, or of requiring supplies from an extensive country. You were supplied from your fleet, and you had not ten miles to watch, nor had you any great objects to gain. You have detached 20,000 men to Batoum merely to make a demonstration; Kars cannot be succoured from thence; there are only paths across the mountains, impassable by artillery, and, what is worse, inhabited by a Christian population which has been oppressed and robbed by the Turks for centuries. So is the force at Eupatoria. It is not strong enough to attack the Russians or to penetrate to their rear.

It is a mere demonstration; you think that it will frighten them; but as they, in their concentrated position, are probably much stronger than any one of your separate bodies, they will laugh at your demonstrations. All that I see in Pelissier's conduct is mere 'tâtonnement.' He seems to have no plan, or if he has one, to be afraid to follow it up.

I am very anxious for the brave defenders of Kars. It is too late now to march to their relief by the direct Erzeroum road, and, as I have already said, it cannot be reached from Batoum. Mouravieff may be forced by cold and want of provisions to retire; but if he does so he will lay waste all the country round, and I do not see how the garrison can escape famine.

The conversation turned on the siege.

Chrzanowski.—The great lesson taught by it is the importance of adhering to the established rules of scientific war. From the beginning to the end you violated them most audaciously, and on every occasion you have been punished. You began by besieging a large and strong fortress without investing it, though a relieving army was at its gates. You opened your trenches twelve hundred yards from the outworks instead of five hundred or six hundred. You attacked the whole line of works instead of concentrating your fire on a portion, and it was not until you had wasted your efforts and your armies for a whole year that you thought of turning to account your maritime superiority and crushing the Russian defences with thirteen inch shells. No fortress can withstand for more than fifteen days the vertical fire of one hundred of the largest mortars, but it is seldom that any fortress can be exposed to such a fire—as to transport them, with their ammunition, any distance by land would require fifteen thousand horses.

At Sebastopol you were attacking a maritime fortress,

and you were masters of the sea. Therefore you could use these dreadful weapons, and as soon as you had recourse to them, the Russians lost, under what they well called a 'feu infernal,' from fifteen hundred to two thousand men a day. A garrison thus attacked, especially if the sap of the besiegers has reached the counterscarp, is between the two dangers. If it remains in its defences, it is destroyed; if it retires behind them, they are exposed to be carried by a rush. The fire suddenly ceases, the besiegers throw themselves into the ditch, scramble up the wall, and have lodged themselves within the works before the garrison has time to repel them.

It was thus that the French took the Malakoff, and thus you would have taken and kept the Redan, if, like the French, you had carried your approaches up to the ditch. But you stopped some hundreds of yards short of it, and you ceased your firing some minutes before you made your assault. The Russians therefore had time to return to their works, they were able to fire on your troops and to weaken and demoralise them as they were crossing the glacis, and, as your first advance was unsupported, the Russians were in sufficient force at the gorge of the work to drive you out before you had protected yourselves in it. The French succeeded because, at last, they followed the rules of the art of war; you failed because you continued to the very end to disregard them.

Senior.—What would you do if you were Gortsckakoff?

Chrzanowski.—It would depend first on my strength. If I had 100,000 men—and, as I said before, the Russians have been incredibly remiss if he has not got them—I would drive your army, weakened as it is by your imprudent detachments, into the sea; if I were not strong enough to do this, my conduct would be governed in the first place by my ultimate object. If that were to obtain a peace before next spring, I would keep my position; I should lose in the next winter 30,000 men, you would lose 20,000, but the possession of the Crimea would enable me to obtain better terms, and the loss of 30,000 is less important to the Russians than that of 20,000 to the allies.

But if I were not thinking of an early peace, if my country intended to continue the war until it could be ended triumphantly, I would retire at once from the Crimea to the Cherson country, beyond the Isthmus. Thither you could not follow me. I could recruit, and clothe, and discipline my army; restore its numbers, its 'physique,' and its 'moral,' and attack you next spring with two hundred thousand men, fresh and vigorous. I should leave behind me thirty thousand Cossacks to harass you, who would retire when you advanced, and return as you retired, and keep you in continual disquiet. You would pass an uncomfortable winter in the Crimea, ill-lodged and ill-fed, at an immense expense, and I should attack you next spring with a great chance of success.

Senior.—What would you do if you commanded the allies?

Chrzanowski.—Their game, which was a very fine one, has been so spoilt that it would be difficult to repair it. If the season were less advanced I would call in the detachments and attack the Russians. I fear, however, that we are too near the winter, and that you have nothing to do but to keep your ground and prepare large reinforcements for the fierce struggle that awaits you in the spring. But I would not send those reinforcements to winter in the Crimea. They will do no good there, and they will suffer much. I would prepare them in England and France and send them out in ships of the line, screws, or towed by steamers, only a fortnight before they were wanted. Your

Black Sea fleet has nothing else to do; let it be armed en flûte and carry fifty thousand men at once.

One thing you should do at once, without a moment's delay. You should utterly destroy all the fortifications, docks, and even houses of Sebastopol. That is to say, unless you are prepared for five or six years of war, for nothing less than five or six years of continued disastrous war will force the Russians to cede the Crimea. If you make peace next year, or the year after, or even the year after that, you will have to restore the Crimea, and you will have to give back Sebastopol in the state in which the preliminaries of peace find it. *Now*, you can do what you like; as soon as you negotiate your hands will be tied.

Another thing of the utmost importance is to provide huts for your men. I hear that a great part of them are still under tents. Those that are left so will die this year as they died last year, and neither your military resources nor your military reputation can bear the loss of another army.

Senior.—You have told us what you would do if you commanded the Russian army, and if you commanded the allied army, what would you do if you were the Autocrat himself?

Chrzanowski.—If I had been the Autocrat, I hope that I should not have contented myself with resting on the defensive, for the defensive leads to nothing, and sooner or later must fail. The enemy keeps repeating his attacks, and sooner or later comes one that succeeds.

I would begin by requiring the active co-operation of Austria. If she refused, I would attack her. The Austrian army is not a mere militia like what is called the Russian army. It is an army, but it is an imperfect one. The men are enlisted for eight years, but return to their homes at the end of the first four, and are not called out again except on an emergency. When they are recalled they come back with the feelings of the provinces to which they belong.

When these provinces are loyal, the recalled old soldiers and the new recruits are also loyal. Now that the violent abolition of all the ancient local institutions has rendered almost all the Austrian provinces disaffected, the army, except the portion of it which has acquired an esprit de corps by three or four years of an uninterrupted service, is equally disaffected. Men are such fools, that if Russia were to attack Austria with revolutionary weapons, if she were to come forward as she did in 1813, as the restorer of constitutional freedom, she would be believed as she was then; all the Magyars, the Croats, the Servians, the Dalmatians, and the Italians would join her.

The old vivaciousness of Austria depended on the loyalty of the different nations who form her empire, and supplied her with fresh armies after every defeat. Now she depends on a single army. An army is a very fragile machine. It takes years to form it, but it can be broken to pieces in a day as that of Prussia was at Jena. And if this existing army of Austria is destroyed where can she find a new one? If Russia were to enter Hungary a month hence she would overrun it before France could send any assistance. Austria thinks that if she has got the Principalities by finessing, that she has made friends of the whole world. She is mistaken; the whole world has found her out. You hate her, France hates her, the rest of Germany hates her; all her subjects with few exceptions hate her, and Russia hates her more bitterly than anybody else does. She has served the Russian cause, but not frankly or cordially or effectually. She has refused to pay the immense debt of gratitude which she incurred in 1849, and as to the Principalities she has succeeded in making even the Russians regretted.

I have correspondents in Jassy and Bucharest. They tell

me that nothing has so prepared the Moldavians and Wallachians for incorporation with Russia as their experience of Austrian rule. The pressure of Russia is heavy, but gradual. It is a screw, slowly turned. The Austrians are brutal and impatient; they use not a screw, but a mallet; they insult while they rob. Russia consolidates her conquests; the subjects of Russia are always impatient, always on the brink of an insurrection. Though I cannot perceive the precise way in which it will happen, I feel convinced that Austria is the power which will suffer most by the war, if it continues long enough to become European, instead of being a mere duel in the Crimea.

1856.

[THE winter of 1855-6, spent by Mr. Senior in Egypt, was one of great hardship to the French troops before Sebastopol. They are said to have suffered almost as much in this second winter as the English had done during the first; disease thinned their ranks. Louis Napoleon began to feel a strain on the resources of the country, the war became increasingly unpopular, and he was now as anxious to end it as he had been to begin it.

England, on the other hand, had by this time learned to use her strength, and it was for her interest to prolong the war until the power of Russia should be thoroughly broken, but the Emperor of the French prevailed; Russia was only too happy to put an end to hostilities, negotiations were entered into, a Congress met in Paris, and peace was concluded on the 30th of March, 1856.—ED.]

Paris, Thursday, May 9th, 1856.—From the 3rd of November, 1855, the day on which the previous page of this journal was written, until the 10th of April, 1856, our history is recorded in my Egyptian and Maltese journals. We left Malta on the 11th of April, reached Marseilles on the 13th, Nismes on the 14th, Montpelier on the 15th, and Paris on the 19th. On the 20th I left Paris for London, remained in London till the day before yesterday, and then returned to Paris.

I find Paris unusually empty. Guizot, the Rémusats, Corcelles, Beaumont, Grimblot, and Buffet are absent. Thiers and Tocqueville are immersed in proof-sheets. Montalembert goes to-morrow, so does the Duc de Broglie.

Lady Holland and Lady Cowley have ceased to receive. Poor Faucher we have lost, and we are losing Say; he is slowly sinking under palsy.

I saw the Duc de Broglie this morning.

Duc de Broglie.—Our society is in an uncomfortable state. A few persons formerly hostile have been brought together by having a common enemy, as, for instance, Thiers and Montalembert; but the tendency in general is more and more to separate into small cliques. People do not like to talk except among intimate friends, for they do not know how long the present toleration of freedom of speech in our salons may last. Nor are our subjects of conversation agreeable. Paris has lost its charm. Nothing but this unusually severe weather has detained us so long, and as it seems to be a little improved we shall all fly to the country and try to forget public affairs in the management of our fields and of our cattle.

Senior.—Has Celui-ci gained any adherents since we met last year?

Broglie.—As neither I nor any of my friends ever go to his Court I cannot say who frequent it; but I do not believe that either his absolute power, or his unbounded patronage, or his successful war, or all of them together, have obtained for him the countenance of one single respectable person. We have been called a nation of place-hunters, but the conduct of the good society of Paris ever since the coup d'état has been dignified and honourable.

From the Duke's I went to Mérimée's.

Mérimée.—You will be amused by gossip about the Congress, and I can tell some which I believe to be true.

When Orloff came the first person that he saw was the Emperor.*

---

* Louis Napoleon.—Ed.

'I am very sorry,' said Orloff, 'that this mission has been given to me, for I am no diplomatist, and I know that I have none but enemies to meet in the Congress. Under such circumstances I throw myself on your Majesty's protection, being well convinced that you are a generous enemy, if you still are an enemy, and that you do not wish Russia to be seriously injured or humiliated, and to enable you to protect me I will tell you what are my instructions. They are to *contest* everything, but to *insist* on nothing. Peace is absolutely necessary to us. I trust in your magnanimity that you will not force us to buy it too dearly.'

And in fact, on one or two occasions on which questions as to which the Congress could not agree were referred to the Emperor as umpire, he decided in favour of Russia.

Senior.—How did Walewski manage it?

Mérimée.—What Walewski did himself was pitiable; his historical and geographical blunders would make an amusing volume. But he saw the Emperor twice a day and took from him his instructions; and then all his papers, all that could be read instead of being spoken, were drawn up for him. Next to him the person most laughed at was Manteuffel.

Senior.—What seemed to be the feeling between Austria and Russia?

Mérimée.—Bitterly hostile. Orloff speaks openly of Austria as the most treacherous, the most cowardly, the most malignant of enemies. Poor Buol was very unhappy. He was browbeaten by Cavour, insulted by Orloff, and countenanced by no one. It was to escape from this isolation, and perhaps to revenge himself on Russia, that he imagined this tripartite treaty. *We* could not object to it. It covers our most exposed frontier. *You* were glad to have a treaty which makes it a *casus belli* if we seize Egypt.

Senior.—Is it true that as soon as the great treaty had

been agreed upon, the Emperor said, 'Maintenant je vais commencer à embellir Paris?'

Mérimée.—It is bien trouvé, and I daresay that it is true.

I spent the evening at Montalembert's.

Montalembert.—I wished very much for you a few days ago. We had a delightful réunion at Berryer's. Cousin, Broglie, Villemain, and Thiers were there. Thiers above all others, above even himself, was charming. The slavery of the press was talked of, and somebody ventured to palliate it by alluding to the scurrilities of the journals of the Republic. 'C'était horrible,' said Thiers, 'mais pour moi, j'aime mieux être gouverné par des honnêtes gens qu'on traite comme des voleurs, que par des voleurs qu'on traite en honnêtes gens.' I would have given anything to have had it all recorded.

Senior.—I have been spending a fortnight in England, after six months' absence. What struck me most was the childishness of English politics. I found the House of Commons engaged for days in discussing the Maynooth grant, then for a week deliberating whether the band of the Horse Guards ought to play on Sundays in the Kensington Gardens; before that it had decided that the local duties on ships entering Liverpool and Hull were the property of the corporations of those towns, and, as such, free from the jurisdiction of Parliament. The subjects and the mode of treating of them seemed to me only worthy of a vestry meeting. Now I come to Paris and read your book, and I find that, instead of children or vestrymen, our members of Parliament are awful senators, the magnanimous rulers of a grand high-minded people.

Montalembert.—Distance perhaps lent enchantment to the view, and contrast still more; but I agree with you that the conduct of your House of Commons would disgust one, if anything could disgust one, with representative government. As a Catholic, however, I do not complain of it. The Puritans are our best friends.

If we can suppose a man hesitating between the two religions, the conduct of the Protestant party would decide him. What I fear is that your stupid ascetics are making religion itself unpopular among the masses. It is very dangerous to tell a labouring man that religion forbids him to amuse himself on his only holiday.

Those who have the leisure and the means of inquiring find out that it is only a sect, and only the most narrow-minded of that sect, that believe in such an absurd prohibition. But the ignorant will believe that all Christianity is opposed to innocent relaxation, and on that supposition will infer that a religion which leads to such consequences must be false. I do not believe that the Christianity of London has more deadly enemies than Mr. Robert Spooner and Lord Robert Grosvenor.

Senior.—They do not care about that. Their piety is selfish. They wish to go to heaven, and do not care at whose expense. ' *Liberavi animam meam*,' says the bigot. ' I have spoken and voted for the fourth commandment. I hope that no harm will come of it to others, and I am sure that good will come to me.'

Monday, May 12th.—Edward Ellice, Michel Chevalier, Kergorlay, and Circourt breakfasted with us. We talked of the state of religion in France.

Circourt.—The higher classes are rather careless than sceptical. In general they no more think of studying the evidences of Christianity than they do those of Mahometanism. The women accept it and the men reject it without examination. The lower classes are irreligious and intolerant. Before 1848 the Duchess of Orleans passed me one

Sunday on her way to the Protestant chapel. Some masons were at work in the street. One of them said, 'There goes the Duchess to her prêche.' 'It is a scandal,' said the other; 'it ought not to be suffered. Why cannot she go to Mass like the rest of us?' And yet he had not the least scruple in profaning the Sunday, though he objected to her keeping it as a Protestant. As for Celui-ci, outwardly the clergy are on their knees to him. They deify him as no Byzantine Emperor was deified; but in their hearts they hate him as a Socialist and as a usurper. And he at bottom hates as well as despises them. Strip him to his skin and you will find under all his robes an Italian refugee, detesting the Pope and all that belongs to Popery, except its capability of being made an instrument of tyranny. But as far as he has any religion he is a Catholic, and, like most Catholics, thinks more about the Madonna than our Saviour, or, if he thinks of Jesus Christ, thinks of Him as the Bambino.

Senior.—I hear that he and the Pope have each sacrificed a Bishop to the other; that the Pope has degraded a Legitimist, and the Emperor a Gallican.

Circourt.—It is true; they were the Bishop of Luçon and the Bishop of Pamiers. The Bishop of Luçon was a Vendéan peasant, just able to read and write bad French, but not understanding a word of his Breviary, full of honest prejudices against all that was revolutionary, and of course against the Bonapartes, and worshipping Henry V. and right divine. The Bishop of Pamiers was an excellent man, learned and pious, and a strong Gallican. Louis Napoleon asked for the removal of the Bishop of Luçon. Pio Nono consented on condition that the Bishop of Pamiers should be given up to *him*.

The Pope sent a message to the Bishop of Luçon requesting him to visit Rome. The Bishop was received by

Antonelli, and informed that his presence was required for the purpose of signing a paper, produced to him for the first time, and containing a resignation of his see. He asked if he was to starve. 'Oh, no,' said the Cardinal; ' you are to have a good pension, and to be kept here and employed on the index.' He submitted, and is now exercising his judgment and knowledge as to the books which may be safely read by the faithful.

The Bishop of Pamiers was summoned too, but, suspecting treachery, refused to move. A few weeks ago a person called on him, and showed to him a letter from the Pope commanding him to resign, and a Bull appointing the bearer administrator of his diocese. The Bishop refused compliance. The intruder assembled the ecclesiastics of the town, who, like almost all the French clergy, are Ultramontane, and was acknowledged by them as their spiritual superior.

A few days after the prefect occupied the palace with a body of gendarmerie, seized the Bishop, and informed him that he was to be kept in arrest, without any communication with the outer world, until he signed his resignation. The poor Bishop had no taste for martyrdom, and so he signed.

Yesterday I met one of the few Liberal priests of my acquaintance returning from Church. He was in great distress. ' I have been hearing,' he said, ' a mandement of the Archbishop, by which, in the whole diocese of Paris, the Roman liturgy is substituted for the Gallican.'

Senior.—Is the difference between them great?

Circourt.—Enormous. The Gallican liturgy is not a pure kind of worship, but it is a tolerable one; some parts of it are excellent, and there are few that are very objectionable. The Roman liturgy assumed its present form in the fifteenth century, when the Council of Trent was stereotyping the abuses that during fourteen hundred years had been encrusting Christianity. It is full of the most childish legends, absurdities, and indecencies. Fourteen dioceses retained last week the Gallican liturgy; the most important of them was Paris. Now it has fallen into the grasp of Rome.

We are relapsing into paganism, and the next swing of the pendulum will throw us back into Atheism; we are unfit for Protestantism or any other faith founded on proof and conviction. It is almost admitted among us that Christianity is an affair not of reasoning but of feeling, which in fact degrades it into a superstition.

Next to our master's hatred of the Pope is his hatred of Austria. I believe that she is the first whom he intends to break or to bend, but he must have time. The public treasury is exhausted, the local treasuries are not much fuller. In two years the city of Paris has spent more than two millions in giving to its inhabitants bread under its natural price.

Senior.—But if he hates Austria, why did he enter into this second treaty with her? An alliance, though only for an especial purpose, denotes at least goodwill.

Circourt.—There were several motives. He is essentially a conspirator, and may have made this treaty as a blind. Besides, it completes the rupture between Austria and Russia. Orloff is wild about it, and certainly it is a most strange proceeding, when, only a week before, a solemn treaty had been made to which all the five Powers were parties, which stipulated that no one of them should take separately any hostile measures against Turkey.

Ellice.—Austria is supposed to have played her game well; but, in fact, she has mismanaged it lamentably. She has not got the Principalities. She has mortally offended Russia and Prussia. I expect to see England reunited to

Prussia. The alliance between the royal families is to take place. If Austria goes on persecuting the Protestants, a religious anti-Austrian feeling will show itself. Saxony will join it. The Protestantism of England will become ungovernable. An Italian insurrection may arise which Austria may be unable to put down, and France unwilling.

Circourt.—Cavour is not ill-satisfied with the results of the Congress. ' J'ai été entendu,' he said to me, ' quoique je n'ai pas été écouté.' The ministers were thoroughly bored, not so much by the labours of the morning as by those of the evening. Every day they had to endure a great official dinner, of always the same persons, always ranged in the same order. When they dined at the Tuileries, Louis Napoleon used in the evening to take some one by the arm, lead him into an adjoining room and talk to him *tête-à-tête*, sometimes for an hour. In one of these conversations with Cavour, the Emperor said to him, ' I wish Piedmont to do two things, one is to keep up her army.' ' That we should do,' answered Cavour. ' The other,' said the Emperor, ' is to make up her difference with Rome.' ' That,' replied Cavour, ' your Majesty and the Austrian empire have rendered impossible. You have so prostrated yourselves before Rome that she has become absolutely unreasonable. She will listen to no terms which as a weak nation, anxious to remain an independent one, we can offer. Austria may be strong enough to allow her clergy to be virtually the subjects and the instruments of a foreign Sovereign ; *we* are not. Her present instruments, too, are such as the Pope delights in ; ours are such as he detests. If we were to accept the Austrian concordat there would be in every parish a conspirator against constitutional government. We could not punish nor even prosecute.'

Wednesday, May 13th.—Ed. Ellice, Duvergier de Hauranne, Lanjuinais, and Barthélemy St. Hilaire breakfasted with us. We talked of Montalembert's book on England.*

Senior.—In some respects it is almost self-refuted. He describes France as subject to a grinding despotism; a despotism under which nothing can be told, nothing can be denied; into which no light penetrates except what is admitted by the despot himself. Yet he publishes a bitter attack on that despotism: such an attack as could not be published in Russia, in Naples, in Tuscany, in Rome, in Austria, or even in Prussia, and publishes it not only without danger, but without alarm. Future historians will find it difficult to reconcile the publication of Montalembert's book with its contents.

Duvergier.—It is true that books as distinguished from periodicals enjoy considerable liberty. But to publish with safety such a book as that it was necessary to be Montalembert, or at least to be a man who could not be trampled on without exciting outcries in the salons of Paris. If an obscure or an unpopular man had published that book he would be now on his way to Cayenne. It is the same as to conversation. *We* can talk freely because we are known, and because we are in Paris. But if a set of provincials had talked as we are talking, and had been reported, or if we were to talk in this way at Orleans, we might soon find ourselves breaking stones in Algeria.

A few weeks ago two hundred persons were arrested one night in Reims. Monsieur Derodet, an advocate of celebrity, a native of Reims, had to see the prefect of the Department of the Marine. The prefect said to him, 'You must be very much obliged to me in Reims; I have rid you of all your worst characters.' 'You have relieved us,' answered Derodet, 'of some bad people, but I miss some

---

* The book alluded to is called 'De l'Avenir Politique de l'Angleterre.'—Ed.

respectable ones.' 'Of course,' said the prefect, 'when these large measures are used, some mistakes are made; I am going to send back fifty who ought not to be taken.' 'And what,' said Derodet, 'has been done with the others? Quand est-ce qu'ils seront jugés?' 'Ils ne seront pas jugés,' replied the prefect. 'Nous ne voulons pas les faire juger.' 'What, then,' said Derodet, 'is to be done with them?' 'Cela,' replied the prefect, 'c'est mon secret. Personne ne le sait, personne ne le saura.'

Ellice.—We as Englishmen have nothing to do with the internal government of France, unless, like that of Naples, it should become dangerous to her neighbours; and with the exception of this escapade against the Belgian press the Emperor's foreign policy has been admirable. Clarendon stood alone in the Congress, or supported only by Cavour. He relied on Louis Napoleon and never found himself deserted or deceived.

Lanjuinais.—I trust that your caution has not been relaxed by his good conduct. I trust that you are on your guard against a spring from the tiger who now appears to be so affectionate.

Ellice.—Of course, though we trust in him we keep our powder dry.

Duvergier.—One can almost always foresee what will be the conduct of a nation, sometimes what will be that of an Assembly, but seldom that of what will be that of an individual.

Senior.—And an individual who is not restrained by the ordinary checks, by shame, or by self-respect, or by honour, or even by fear.

Duvergier.—As to fear, I do not believe that he is peculiarly insensible to it. He is sometimes rash, but he is not remarkably intrepid. Those who were with him on the morning of the coup d'état represent him as anxious and nervous, and before it he was irresolute, and planned it and altered it, and put it off, and put it off, and was at last impelled to action by men of firmer nerves.

Ellice.—I never saw foreign affairs so complicated or so perplexed. This tripartite treaty unsettles everything. Cavour thought himself safe in the sympathy of England and France in his attack on Austria, now he finds that they are the allies of Austria.

St. Hilaire.—I hope that England feels that Belgium and Piedmont are her outposts, and that she will not suffer them to be driven in.

Lanjuinais.—The real complaint against Belgium is that the Belgian jurors are so timid that up to the present time it has been found impossible to obtain from them a single conviction against the press. They are afraid to expose themselves to attack: the law therefore which Belgium passed some time ago, at the request of Napoleon, by which, on the complaint of a foreign minister that his Government had been libelled, the Belgian Government is bound to prosecute, is illusory.

I hear that it is proposed to assemble for such trials a special jury from a higher class of men and from different provinces. Such a law may be passed without altering the constitution, and may perhaps be effectual.

Thursday, May 15*th.*—I called on Madame Cornu. We talked of Louis Napoleon.

Madame Cornu.—I believe that war is more favourable to Celui-ci than peace.

Those who know the French only superficially are deceived by the outcries which war excites among those who suffer from it, and by the terror with which the speculators predict a crisis in the Bourse.

If there had been a crisis, it would have effected only

a comparatively small number of persons, very much disliked, very much despised, who appear to be powerful only because some of the Emperor's favourites are among them. If the whole *agiotage* of Paris were ruined the public would clap. As to those who have to furnish conscripts and pay a little more in taxes or in the purchase of substitutes, they complain, but they are amused and interested by what is going on.

The French are really most to be feared when they are silent, for it shows 'qu'ils s'ennuient, et quand le peuple s'ennuie il est capable de tout.' If we have a bad harvest and vintage, and appearances are threatening, there will be danger unless he can find something new in Italy or on the Rhine to amuse us.

I know Orloff well. 'Il est très-fin.' His description of himself as a soldier, not a diplomatist, was a trick. He is little of a soldier, but a finished diplomatist.

The object of Russia is to separate Louis Napoleon from England. It is said that Orloff early in his mission obtained from Louis Napoleon some assurances which were afterwards found inconvenient. One was that no Polish questions should be discussed in the Congress. But in return Alexander promised to make certain changes in the administration of the kingdom of Poland at Napoleon's request.

Saturday, May 17th.—Manin called on me.

I received in Cairo a letter from him, in which he asked me if I thought that he could maintain himself as a teacher in London. In my answer I said that so many persons immeasurably his inferiors in talent, knowledge, and reputation did só, that I could not doubt his success; but that he might have a few months to wait. I asked him now if he had given up that scheme.

Manin.—I have. There is so much that is exciting and

so much that is painful in the present state of Italian politics that I should not be able to attend to my business.

It has always been so with me. When I was at the bar political matters were constantly diverting my attention from legal ones. I tried to prevent it. I said to myself that my duty to my clients was a definite engagement, which, when once I had contracted it, I had no right to neglect, though in the hope of being useful to Venice or to Italy. 'Mais c'était plus fort que moi.' I never could be a good advocate when there was a political crisis. Besides that, I am ill; my brain is surcharged with blood. A good deal has been taken from me, and the sort of crown of hot iron, which seemed to crush and burn my head, is cooled and lightened. But the disease though palliated is not removed, and I fear the east winds and heavy atmosphere of London. The climate of Paris is not good, but it is better than yours, especially to the irritable nerves and lungs of an Italian. Here, too, I have more influence than I could have in London, and I hope that that influence may be usefully exerted.

I utterly differ from my English friends who say, like Lord John Russell, that the Italians ought to remain quiet; that they will obtain their object by waiting for the reforms which public opinion and her own interests will extort from Austria. In the first place, Austria will never reform; she cannot, for every reform would be used against her. Every Italian whom she employs is a conspirator against her. All the money and property that she leaves in our hands form part of our insurrectionary capital. If she were to allow us liberty of speech, we should use it to curse; if we were allowed to print, we should libel her. Her misgovernment has been so long, and so stupid, and so irritating, that its effects are irremediable. She cannot afford to improve. She is like a man who has accustomed himself to arsenic, he must die as soon as he leaves it off. But, in the second place, our object is not to reform Austria, but to expel her. It may be an absurd object or an impracticable object; but, wise or silly, attainable or unattainable, it is our object. I do not defend it; I only state it. And you must admit that it is not to be attained by sitting still.

Senior.—Certainly not by sitting still for ever; but there may be times when action may be inopportune, when it may only keep you back.

Manin.—Of course there may; but I could prove to you that every movement which we have made up to the present time has done good; that is to say, good to the cause, not to the individuals who took part in it. In the present state of Italy a political life cannot be a happy one. A public man has to endure shame and remorse if he serves the despots; or chains, or poverty, or exile if he serves his country.

I never deceive my friends by hopes of happiness or of fame, or even, as far as they are concerned, of success. I expect ultimate success, but generations may perish in obtaining it.

Senior.—By success you mean independence?

Manin.—By success I mean not merely independence, but unity; and by unity I mean a single political organ, be it a Monarch, or a Senate, or a Congress, with power to direct against the common enemy the force of the whole Italian nation.

Senior.—I suppose that you require unity only as a security for independence. If the Italians, though divided into a dozen sovereign States, without any central authority, could be certain that they would be allowed to manage their own affairs without being subject to foreign intervention or being in danger of foreign conquest, you would be satisfied?

Manin.—' Pour satisfait, non; pour content, oui.' Your

supposition is, however, an impossible one. Italy, if divided into a dozen or half a dozen, or even a couple of separate States, would be torn to pieces by civil war, and sooner or later be subjugated by foreign wars.

There is no safety for us against France, or against Austria, or against one another, unless we are one. It has always been so; it will always be so. But give us independence and unity, and I do not care under what form. My theoretical prejudices are in favour of Republican institutions. I believe them to be the institutions under which the human race is susceptible of the highest improvement, and they have the advantage that you may unite several Republics in one federation, as we see in the United States; whereas a confederation of Monarchs becomes a conspiracy of Kings against their people as we see in the German Bund.

Senior.—Might you not have a confederation in which some members should be Republics and others Monarchies?

Manin.—I think not; it would perish by a civil war. The Republican portion would drive away the Monarchs, or the Monarchs seize the Republics. If we are to have a Monarch he must be the King of all Italy. I am perfectly ready, I am eager, to accept the King of Sardinia as such. I refused to join in an attempt to put Murat on the Neapolitan throne, not because a Murat dynasty would not be much better than a Bourbon one, but because the establishment of the house of Murat in Naples and the house of Savoy in Turin would render Italian unity impossible. So I should refuse to join in any attempt to give Lombardy or Venice to Piedmont on the supposition that it was to be a final arrangement. I will not support the King of Sardinia to be a greater King than he is *in* Italy. I *will* support him in every attempt to be *the* King *of* Italy. I will desert him as soon as he engages in any treaty by which he recognises the state of things which it is his mission to destroy;

as soon as he engages in any compact with the irreconcilable enemies of Italy, Austria, and the Pope; as soon as he ceases to be the nucleus around which the fabric of Italian unity is to crystallise itself; as soon as he allows any other nucleus of unity to arise; as soon, in short, as he shows that he is not ready to risk the crown of Piedmont in order to gain that of Italy.

Piedmont must act; she cannot stand where she is. Austria and the Pope will undermine and destroy her.

Senior.—But how can she act? She is no match for Austria. That experiment has been tried twice.

Manin.—Supported by France, she is more than a match for Austria; supported by the whole Liberal party in Italy, she is more than a match for Austria. Whenever Austria is seriously attacked three-fourths of the inhabitants of her heterogeneous, disorganised, disaffected empire will join the invader. The best friends of Austria, and therefore the worst enemies to Italian unity, are the Piedmontese party and the Mazzini party. The Piedmontese party prefers to Italy the aggrandisement of Piedmont. The Mazzinists prefer to Italy the extension of democracy. The Piedmontese party, in order to add Lombardy and Venice to Piedmont, would leave Tuscany, the Roman States, and Naples enslaved. The Mazzinists, in order to destroy a Monarchy, would make an enemy of the most powerful and the most Liberal State in Italy. I trust that the really patriotic men in each party, and among them Mazzini and Cavour, will give up their subordinate objects, and join to make one national party with independence and unity on its banner. And I believe with such a party we could beat Austria, though we were unassisted by you.

Sunday, May 18*th.*—Montalembert called on me to-day on his return from Belgium.

Montalembert.—Louis Napoleon, as respects Belgium, has not behaved with his usual discretion. Twice he has betrayed himself too soon, first, when just after the coup d'état, he signed the decree annexing Belgium to France, and the other day during the Congress.

He has put Europe, and particularly Belgium, on its guard, and has excited a national feeling among the Belgians which will make it difficult to obtain from the Chambers even the changes in the law of libel, which the constitution allows.

The Belgians tell us that though governed by a foreigner and a Protestant, and divided into hostile factions, religious as well as political, they have not found it necessary during twenty-six years to tighten the curb on their press.

The fact is, a press is mischievous only where it is partially and irregularly free. Just as a draught gives you a cold, while even a storm in the open-air is innocuous. If the press were free in France for a fortnight only in every year there would be an annual revolution. So the perfect freedom of the Belgian press does no harm in Belgium, but the Belgian papers circulated in France, where the native press is gagged, are certainly dangerous. They are eagerly read, they are not answered, they are believed, and in the general absence of information they are supposed to indicate even more than they tell. So your free press does no harm in England, or, to speak more correctly, atones for the harm it does by doing ten times or ten thousand times as much good. But abroad it does you harm. Your newpapers and your public men think only of the English public. They denounce and they exaggerate everything that is wrong in your institutions and in your conduct, and by doing so they get it corrected. But abroad all these exaggerations are believed, and no one hears of the correction.

On the other hand no one reveals, at least no one reveals fully, the errors, deficiencies, and crimes of the Continental Governments. Last year your newspapers told us that your Crimean army was destroyed by cold and hunger, within seven miles of abundant supplies. All the Continent repeated with delight that the English are impotent on land.

This year you have one of the finest and most efficient armies in Europe. No one knows it. This year the French army suffered as much as yours did last year. No one knows it. My French and Belgian friends are boiling over with indignation against me for speaking well of the English, who, they say, systematically torture to death their subjects in India, in order to extort a revenue. I tell them that it was the crime of native officials; that as soon as it was discovered it was denounced and repressed, and the perpetrators punished, and I tell them that if such a thing had occurred, as without doubt it would have occurred, in the distant dependencies of an absolute Government, it would never have been denounced, and probably never have been corrected. They will not listen to such excuses; they point to your Radical newspapers and try to believe that torture is a fiscal instrument in India as regularly employed as it is in a Turkish pashalic.

What adds to the folly of Walewski's sortie is, that the Imperial Government has never used the remedy which the Belgian Chambers invented for it, and put into its hands. A law was made, at our request, by which the Belgian Government is bound to prosecute every publication which we designate as dangerous to France. We thanked the Belgians for their law, and expressed ourselves perfectly satisfied with it. But it has never been applied. We say that we should not get a conviction. How can we know that, unless we prosecute? What Louis Napoleon wants is that the Belgian Government should take the initiative and select for prosecution of its own accord whatever it thinks ought not to be published. This the Belgians refuse to do. Walewski, who is a weak, vain, presumptuous man, and like all weak men, afraid of the press, was nearly getting into a similar scrape in England. He wanted to make a formal complaint to the English Government of the excesses of the English press, and was restrained with difficulty by his colleagues. Since that time he has been hostile to England in general, and to the Liberal party in particular. During the Congress he always tried to defeat Clarendon, and was kept in order only through the Emperor. I am told that Clarendon complained to the Emperor that Russia had three representatives at the Congress—Walewski, Orloff, and Brunnow, and that Austria had three—Bourqueney, Buol, and Hübner, and that France was left without a voice or a vote.

We talked of his last book, and I told him he was mistaken in supposing that the power of defeating entails is recent. When I explained to him that for four hundred years our law of entail has not materially differed from the present law in France, and that during all that time the father and son concurrently, or, in the absence of a joint action of father and son, the son alone, after his father's death, have been able to dispose absolutely of all entailed property, he could scarcely reconcile such a state of the law with the permanence of English families.

Montalembert.—There cannot be a more remarkable example of the aristocratic and territorial instincts of your proprietors, especially when we recollect the numerousness of your children. With us the few old families that remain rich do so because they do not keep up their numbers. With your number of children all our great families would have become poor in two or three generations, even if economists, and ruined by a single spendthrift. Dukes of Buckingham with us would be the rule rather than the exception.

Monday, May 19*th.*—After breakfast I spent a couple of hours with Cousin.

Cousin.—You have been in England since you left Egypt. What is the news as to our canal? Will Palmerston let us have it? You must stay a few weeks in Paris to estimate the irritation which your opposition to it excites. We consider Palmerston's conduct as a proof that his hatred of France is unabated, and the acquiescence of the rest of your Cabinet as a proof that, now we are no longer necessary to you, now that we have destroyed for you the maritime power of Russia, you are indifferent to our friendship. I am most anxious that this stupid subject of dispute should be removed. Louis Napoleon professes to be anxious that you should allow the Sultan to give his consent; but I doubt whether he is sincere. I am not sure that he is not pleased at seeing the Parisians occupied by something besides his own doings, especially as it promotes the national dislike of England. Now that the war is over we want an object. He tries to give us one by launching us into enormous speculations. He is trying to make us English, to give us a taste for great and hazardous undertakings, leading to great gains, great losses, profuse expenditure, and sudden fortunes and failures. Such things suit *you;* they do not suit *us.* We like the petty commerce of commission and detail; we prefer domestic manufactures to factories; we like to grow moderately rich by small profits, small expenditure, and constant accumulation. We hate the 'nouveaux riches,' and scarcely wish to be among them. The progress for which we wish is political progress; not *within,* for that we are satisfied to oscillate, and shall be most happy if in 1860 we find ourselves where we were in 1820; but *without*. I believe that our master's sortie against Belgium was a pilot balloon. He wished to see what amount of opposition he had to fear from you and from Belgium, and how far we should support him. He has found the two former greater than he expected. I am not sure that he is dissatisfied with the last.

I spent the evening at Thiers'. He, too, attacked me about the Suez Canal.

Thiers.—Do entreat your public men to overrule their ill-conditioned colleague. I told you a year ago the mischief you were doing; but I do not think that you believed me. You may find too late that I was right.

I repeated to him Ellice's opinion that the Indian commerce of England would not use the canal.

Thiers.—I have heard that from Ellice himself; but I differ from him. I agree with him, indeed, that your sailing vessels will not use the canal; but I believe that in a few years hence you will have no purely sailing vessels, except for the small coasting trade. Every large ship will have propellers to be employed occasionally, and sails for ordinary use. The Mediterranean and the Red Sea are very navigable. I believe that the canal will be useful, and particularly to you; but whatever be the real merits of the scheme, for God's sake let it be tried. Do not treat us like children, and say, 'We know better what is good for you than you do for yourselves. You shall not make your canal, because you would lose money by it.'

Senior.—What did you hear about the Congress?

Thiers.—I heard that Clarendon was very good and was the best, and that Walewski was very bad and was the worst.

Senior.—Can you tell me the real history of the tripartite treaty?

Thiers.—I can. There was an old engagement between the three Powers, entered into last spring, that if they succeeded in the war they would unite to force Russia to perform any conditions to which she might submit. This engagement had been allowed to sleep. I will not say that it was forgotten; but no one seemed disposed to revert to it. But after the twenty-second protocol, when Piedmont was allowed to threaten Austria, and neither England nor France defended her, Buol got alarmed. He feared that Austria might be left exposed to the vengeance of Russia on the north and east, and to that of the Italian Liberals on the south. An alliance with France and England, though only for a single specified purpose, at least would relieve Austria from the appearance of insulation. She would be able to talk of the two greatest Powers in Europe as her allies, and would thus acquire a moral force which might save her from attack. He recalled therefore the old engagement to the recollection of Clarendon and Louis Napoleon, and summoned them to fulfil it. I do not believe that either of them was pleased. But the engagement was formal, and its performance, though open to misconstruction, and intended by Austria to be misconstrued, was attended by some advantages, though different ones to France and to England. So both your Government and ours complied.

Wednesday, May 20th.—I called on Cousin at the Sorbonne. He recurred to the subject on which we talked the day before yesterday, the plans of Louis Napoleon and the wishes of France.

Cousin.—No Frenchman can be satisfied with the present state of France. We are still confined within the limits to which we were reduced when we were a conquered people, when Europe, in a blind spirit of vengeance, thought that she could not trample us down too deeply. We are still without a northern frontier; Prussia is only three days' march from Paris.

Senior.—That was a situation of danger when Paris was an open town; but now all the conditions are changed. Paris, fortified and defended by her inhabitants, is impregnable.

Cousin.—Paris unfortified, but defended by her inhabitants, could have resisted in 1814. You can never depend on the resistance of a great capital, or of any town, of which the inhabitants are more than a match for the garrison. It is seldom they are so *exaltés* as to bear long the miseries of a siege. But we feel not only the insecurity of Paris, but the loss of fellow-countrymen, speaking our language, and resembling us in character, to whom we were united in the last century—whom we kept at the Peace of Amiens. We have never acquiesced in that loss; even I, a retired philosopher, feel injured and degraded by it. How can you expect it to be tolerated by a Napoleon; by a man who is now the arbiter of Europe, who can give victory to the side which he supports, who by joining you can crush Russia, and by joining Russia, and dispensing, as he then would do, with the assistance of Austria, could crush Prussia and you. We must, in the language of the protocols, 'rectify' our northern frontier. We do not want Antwerp or Ostend. You may make them free ports; but we must have Liége, and Hainault, and Brabant. We could easily find indemnities for Leopold. Turkey is dead. Her European provinces must be governed by a Christian. There is spoil enough in them for everybody. We could carve out for him a kingdom much larger, finer, and more populous than his mushroom of Belgium. He might have Constantinople instead of Brussels.

Senior.—Are we to return to the brutalities of the first Empire? Are we to parcel out populations without reference to their wishes?

Cousin.—God forbid. I assume the Belgians to be willing to become again a portion of the great French Empire instead of being a weak independent Principality.

Senior.—I believe your assumption to be utterly false; the Belgians are now the most prosperous and the freest people on the Continent. Indeed, they and the Dutch and the Piedmontese are the only free Continental nations. There exists now in Belgium as strong a national feeling as in France.

Cousin.—Then we must look elsewhere. There is Mayence and Rhenish Bavaria. Will you let us take them?

Senior.—Sooner than any part of Belgium.

Cousin.—I think then that you would be wrong. I believe that our possession of Mayence and the intervening district would be more dangerous to Europe than our possession of the part of Belgium which I covet. Mayence establishes us in the centre of Germany. It menaces Prussia and all the smaller States. Savoy, of course, we shall have. Since Piedmont has become Italianised, the Savoyards, who detest the Italians, and are French in habits, manners, and language, have become anxious to become so in government. Their clergy, who are fanatically Ultramontane, are revolted by the quarrel of the Piedmontese with the Pope. They are preaching disaffection and holding up Louis Napoleon, the dutiful Son of the Church, against its irreligious enemy. In annexing Savoy the people will be with us, and I am not sure that we could not obtain the acquiescence of the Government. To obtain Lombardy and Venice through our assistance, and to purchase that assistance with Savoy, was for many years the dream of Charles Albert. The minds of all are prepared for it. Savoy gives little revenue to Piedmont, and adds little to her commerce; it is useful to her only as furnishing her best soldiers. This advantage is not to be despised, but the acquisition of the great, populous, and rich plain of the Po would be an ample indemnity. There is another exchange too I should like to make. I wish that you would give us Malta for Algeria. As harbours and fortified positions, Oran, Algiers, and Philippeville would be more valuable to you than Malta. They are nearer to you, and they lie on the route to Alexandria. You would colonise Algiers and make it a source of revenue. To us it is merely a most expensive military position. Malta is just what we want, a mere fortress and port. We should manage the people better than you do. We should associate with them, and we agree with them in religion.

Senior.—Is it true that Napoleon said he would rather give Constantinople to Russia than Malta to England?

Cousin.—I believe it is true.

Senior.—*Fas est et ab hoste doceri.*

Cousin.—Well, if you are to retain Malta, I wish you would keep the Maltese press and the Maltese intriguers in better order. You are so strong that you do not fear yourselves any harm from the Maltese incendiaries, and you are so unscrupulous that you do not care what harm they do to others. I believe, in fact, that you sympathise with them.

Senior.—I own that I should not be sorry to get rid of the Pope and of the King of Naples.

Cousin.—Nor should I. I am a very *mince* Catholic, and I forget the Pope in the tyrant. If Murat were presentable I believe that we should put him on the Neapolitan throne and give you Sicily.

Senior.—We would not take it.

Cousin.—Not avowedly; not if you had the trouble and responsibility of managing that perverse childish people.

But you would not be sorry to make a Portugal of it—to put there a puppet who should do all the disagreeable business for you, and let you enjoy the influence and the trade. As to Austria, it is said that she has been sounded, and that she has answered that she cannot openly countenance any attack on King Ferdinand, but that she will not quarrel with his deposition when it has become a fait accompli. But to return to Algeria. I wish that we were quit of it. In peace it is a mere encumbrance; in war, at least in a war against you, the only war that would be formidable to us, it is a source of danger. A country which is not mistress of the sea ought not to have outlying possessions. You would intercept our communications, raise the country against us, and wear out our army.

Senior.—It has at least given you good soldiers for the Crimean war.

Cousin.—Good privates and good regimental officers, but that is all. When the time of trial came we found that we had no generals; and our engineers and artillery, of which we were proud, were very inferior to yours. War against barbarians is not a good school. There are no opportunities of practising the scientific parts of the art, and troops accustomed to easy victory are surprised and perhaps disheartened by the obstinate resistance of a civilised enemy.

Tuesday, May 20*th.*—Chrzanowski dined with us. We talked of the French marshals.

Chrzanowski.—The best was Masséna; next to him I put Soult.

Senior.—Thiers maintains that Soult, though a good administrator, was a bad general.

Chrzanowski.—When a soldier reads the military criticisms of Thiers, he sees that a very clever man is writing about what he does not understand. Masséna, Soult, St. Cyr, and Davoust were the best of Napoleon's lieutenants. Perhaps the most skilful was St. Cyr, but his selfishness and jealousy made him unfit to act with any but subordinates. In the invasion of Russia I served in a corps of the grande armée, commanded by Oudinot. We were marching up the left bank of the Dwina, between Dunabourg and Witepski; before us was Wittgenstein. Napoleon not trusting to the skill of Oudinot, put St. Cyr by his side as an adviser. Oudinot consulted St. Cyr as to all his orders, and obtained from him nothing but silent acquiescence. They were not skilful, and we were beaten and had to retreat. Oudinot was wounded and gave up the command to St. Cyr. St. Cyr thereupon instantly altered all his predecessor's arrangements, beat Wittgenstein, and cleared the road to Witepski.

Senior.—Where do you put Blücher?

Chrzanowski.—Not high scientifically, very high morally. And his admirable moral qualities did instead of intellectual ones, for they enabled him to use the intellect and knowledge of Gneisenau. All that he required was to have four squadrons attached to his person to charge with. The rest he left to Gneisenau. When Gneisenau's arrangements were criticised, as is always the case at headquarters, Blücher did not commit himself to defend them at the risk of being persuaded to alter them. The only answer that he made was, 'My orders have been given;' and the only question he put to Gneisenau was, 'Are my four squadrons ready?' Above them all I put Sir John Moore. His retreat was a masterpiece of skill and courage. He had a weak army, a difficult country, dreadful weather, and was followed with superior forces by Ney and Napoleon, two of the most dangerous pursuers that a general could have. And when he had reached the coast he turned, beat the enemy, and embarked without leaving a man or a gun. No one portion of any campaign of the Duke of Wellington's equals this retreat.

Senior.—Where do you put the Duke?

Chrzanowski.—Above all the French marshals. But he wanted rapidity of movement. He introduced into your army a most unfortunate practice which has ever since destroyed half the advantage of all your victories, that of remaining a day on the field of battle, instead of following up the enemy. He did so at Vimeira, though, indeed, that was not his fault; he did so at Talavera; he did so at Busaco; he did so at Salamanca; he did so at Vittoria; and if it had not been for Blücher he would have done so at Waterloo. He would have taken up his position at La Belle Alliance, the French would have rallied five miles farther, and the campaign would have recommenced. It was this precedent I suppose that kept you inactive at the Alma* and at Inkerman. At the Alma you said that you had no cavalry, and that you feared the Russian cavalry, which was still unbroken. But the conduct of that cavalry showed how little it was to be dreaded. If it contented itself with making mere demonstrations before the infantry was in flight, it is not probable that it would have done more afterwards. The Russians were thoroughly demoralised. Their retreat was a rout. The false news of your having entered Sebastopol with them, which was spread after the battle, was merely anticipating what ought to have taken place, and would have taken place if the allied army had been commanded by any average general. After such a defeat an army is utterly dispirited. During every half-hour of its flight, if it is unpursued, it recovers some of its courage, but if it is followed up it loses not only its courage, but its presence of mind. It is a flock of sheep, and if it

---

* It is well known now that St. Arnaud would not stir.—ED.

enters a fortress it communicates its terror to the garrison.

Senior.—I hear that Todleben is a man of inventive genius, and that the defence of Sebastopol will improve the art of war.

Chrzanowski.—That is a mistake; there was nothing new in the fortifying or in the defence of Sebastopol. The attack, indeed, was made after an original fashion, and may improve the art of war as a warning. All that the arming and the defence of Sebastopol show is what may be done if you are not stinted in time, in supplies, or in men. But when will such an occasion recur. No fortress ever before had a garrison of forty thousand men constantly renewed. No fortress was ever before attacked from a distance of twelve hundred mètres, and therefore allowed three months time to improve its defences. No fortress was ever so supplied. A thousand charges for each gun is considered an enormous provision. It is three times as great as is usual. Three shots can be fired from a gun every two minutes. Supposing therefore a battery to be fired with the greatest rapidity, it would exhaust its whole ammunition in six hundred and sixty-seven minutes or about eleven hours. In general, instead of ninety times an hour, a gun is fired only twenty times. But the fire from Sebastopol was sometimes continued at its utmost rapidity for many hours. No fortress could do so unless it possessed, as I said before, unlimited resources. However, as respects the Russian garrison and the engineers, the defence was admirable; as respects the relieving army, it was detestable. If it had established itself in force at Liprandi's position, on your flank, you must either have withdrawn from the attack or have been cut off from Balaclava. But had I been the Czar I would have made no Crimean campaign; I would have left Sebastopol to its fate. Its fate from the beginning was certain; it was not worth while to spend 300,000 men in order to retard its fall for a year, or even in order to destroy 150,000 of the allies. You could not have advanced beyond. I would have gone straight to Vienna; if Austria refused to join me I should have crushed her before France could come to her assistance.

Senior.—Has much progress been made in Russianising the kingdom of Poland?

Chrzanowski.—Not much as yet, but if the Russians take pains and treat the people well they may succeed in doing so. The Prussians are Germanising quickly the province of Posen. The Government lends money at a low interest to the Prussians who wish to purchase in Posen, and in no long time the bulk of the land will be owned by Prussians. In the meantime the hostility of the Poles has occasioned a new set of evils to Russia. In order to weaken Poland, the Russians have taken from thence for the last twenty-five years a double conscription. The Poles being better educated and more intelligent than the Russians, become in general 'sous-officiers.' Probably half the 'sous-officiers' in the Russian army are Poles. These men all wish their fellow-soldiers to be beaten. As for the Russian private, having no feeling of honour or hope of advancement, he is driven on by only three stimulants—plunder, blows, and brandy. There was none of the first in the late war, so the other two were profusely applied. A large portion of those who fought at Inkerman were drunk. Such treatment may sometimes succeed, but unless a drunken column carries everything before it by its first rush, it is lost. A curious use was made by the Austrians of their Polish regiments in 1848. When Windischgrätz attacked the revolutionists in Vienna, his German and his Italian regiments turned down the muzzles of their guns and refused to advance. Then he ordered up the Poles, whereupon their officers, though Austrians, appealed to their national hatred of the Viennese. 'Come on,' they said, 'let these Germans see what Poles are made of.' The same thing occurred at Dresden. It was the Polish troops who suppressed the insurrection when the Germans refused to act.

[Tocqueville joined the party in the evening. The very interesting conversation which followed is published in the Tocqueville volumes. On the next day Mr. Senior returned to London. He visited Paris again in the following spring. The eleven months which elapsed were comparatively uneventful.—ED.]

1857.

Paris, Hôtel Bedford, Thursday, April 9th.—We reached this place last night. The Tocquevilles are in our hotel. I went to them in the evening. Tocqueville asked me how long I intended to remain. Four weeks, I answered.

Tocqueville.—I do not think that you will be able to do so. Paris has become so dull that no one will voluntarily spend a month here. The change which five years have produced is marvellous. We have lost our interest not only in public affairs but in all serious matters.

Senior.—You will return then to the social habits of Louis Quinze. You were as despotically governed then as you are now, and yet the salons of Madame Geoffrin and Madame du Deffand were amusing.

Tocqueville.—We may do so in time, but that time is to come. At present we talk of nothing but the Bourse. The conversation of our salons resembles more that of the time of Law than that of the time of Marmontel.

I spent this evening at Lamartine's. There were few people there, and the conversation was certainly dull enough to justify Tocqueville's fears.

Friday, April 10th.—I called on Lord and Lady Holland. They confirmed Tocqueville's description of the general dulness of Parisian society, and admitted that the staple subject was the Bourse, but not that it was the only one.

Lady Holland.—We talk also of Mr. Home, the American clairvoyant, who has so much struck the Empress, and, indeed, the Emperor too, by his revelations, that he has been sent to America to bring to us his sister, who has still more lucidity than he, and they are to be Clairvoyant- and Clairvoyante-in-Ordinary to their Majesties. Then we talk also of our great Italian beauty, Madame de Castiglione.

Senior.—What do you say of Falloux's reception ?*

Lady Holland.—We say that the only good mot that it produced was the Emperor's, when Falloux was presented to him, 'C'est le désordre qui nous a uni. Je suis fâché que l'ordre nous ait séparés.' Falloux's speech was meant as an explosion of legitimacy, but missed fire. It was as cold as ice.

Senior.—Brifaut consulted Patin as to his reply. 'Il fallait patiner,' said Mérimée, 'pour aller sur la glace.'

Saturday, April 11th.—I spent the morning with Thiers. We talked of his history. He repeated the Emperor's allusion to him as a 'historien illustre et national' in the speech from the throne, and asked how we liked the last volume, the fifteenth. I said that the fourteenth delighted us as a grand tragic picture, slowly unrolled, but that we had not had time yet to read the fifteenth.

Thiers.—I have tried to be impartial to Lord Wellington. I have read the whole of his letters and despatches. About three-fourths of them were translated in Belgium; the remainder I had translated for me. They have raised him very high in my estimation. He belongs to the order of generals and statesmen immediately below Alexander, Cæsar, and Napoleon.

Senior.—Do you put him on a level with Turenne ?

Thiers.—A little below him in his knowledge of war, much above him in his knowledge of men and politics. The perspicacity with which he divined the state of our military

---

* As a member of the Institut.—Ed.

councils, with which he foresaw our faults, and how far with sixty thousand men he could safely venture among three hundred thousand; the apparent audacity of his advances, and their real safeness—depending not on military grounds, but on the jealousies, dissensions, and disobedience of our generals—make the story of his latter campaigns almost a romance. Without doubt he did not press his successes; he did not, like Napoleon, abuse his victories, or even use them. He was a man of sense rather than of genius; and when we see what sense can do, and what genius can do, one is inclined to prefer the former. In the degree in which Wellington possessed it, it is not only the safer, but perhaps the rarer quality. Then his uniform good fortune—unless we suppose good fortune to be a quality in itself—must have been the result of wonderful sagacity in discovering *indicia* of failure or success unperceived by others, perhaps rather felt than reasoned out by himself.

The conversation passed to France.

Thiers.—Celui-ci is firmer than when we parted last year. He has shown, what is very rare, moderation in power. ' Il sait reculer,' a knowledge not possessed by his uncle.

Senior.—Will his power last as long as his life?

Thiers.—No; unless his life is cut short suddenly. But it will last longer than I expected when it began.

Senior.—Aristotle gives seventy years as the longest duration of a usurped despotic power.

Thiers.—No such usurpation will last in France half that time, or a quarter of that time.

I dined with Lord Holland, and met Guizot, St. Jachimo of Naples, and the Count and Countess Castiglione. I thought her wonderfully beautiful, more so than when I saw her last year at Holland House. She is a Louis-

Quinze beauty: tall, round, well-formed, with large dark eyes, long eyelashes, straight eyebrows, a clear white complexion, and a mouth which, as I saw it, always smiling, was charming. She sat in the evening, filling with her crinoline a whole sofa, to receive and certainly to enjoy the homage of all around her.

Guizot was delightful, and the dinner remarkably pleasant, but the conversation contained little of journal matter. That substance is generally deposited by têtes-à-tête or trios. What is amusing to hear is often difficult to remember and impossible to record.

[Some very interesting conversations on the following days have already been published in the Tocqueville volumes—the initial Z indicates M. Guizot.—ED.]

Wednesday, April 15*th.*—I dined with the L——s, and met there Mr. Evans, the Emperor's dentist, who sees him every day. He denies the indolence attributed to the Emperor.

Evans.—He rises at seven, takes a cold bath, a cup of coffee and a roll, and immediately afterwards sits down to work in his dressing-gown. This lasts till about nine, when he dresses and receives his ministers, and works with them till eleven. At eleven he goes to the Empress, and they breakfast. From about twelve to two he works or gives audiences; and at two, whatever be the weather, he drives out or rides till four. From four till dinner-time he works again, and after dinner sometimes returns to his work until late in the night. I found him two or three mornings ago with a headache. His candles were on his table burnt down to the sockets, and he admitted that he had been writing until three in the morning. The average time which he devotes to business cannot be less than ten hours a day, of which seven or eight are passed with the pen in his hand.

Senior.—We are told that he wears under his waistcoat a coat of mail.

Evans.—Nonsense; he takes no precautions. The police take some for him, but not by his orders, perhaps scarcely by his wish.

Friday, April 17th.—I dined with the Wolowskis, and met there a Polish party. Among them was Branitski, one of the great family of that name. I alluded to the inferiority of the Russian soldiers in the Crimea.

Branitski.—That is because 'on n'a pas su faire vibrer le vrai fibre.'

Senior.—What is the 'vrai fibre?' Is it not antipathy to the Roman Catholics and Protestants?

Branitski.—No; that passion is extinct among the higher classes; and as the officers do not feel it they cannot communicate it to their men. Their really strong passion is hatred of the Germans. If Austria had entered frankly into the war, you would have seen its effects. A Russian army would have been in Vienna before a French one. Even we Poles, much as we hate the Russians, hate the Germans still more.

Saturday, April 18th.—Chrzanowski and Dussard breakfasted with us. I repeated my conversation with Branitski.

Chrzanowski.*—It is true that no fibre in the heart of the Russian soldier was touched, but it was because there was none to touch. 'Dans la présente composition de l'armée russe il est impossible d'inventer un principe moral pour cette armée. Il ne lui reste pour tout mobile que le bâton avant l'action, et l'eau de vie pendant l'action. Ce qui fait que le soldat russe est une brute militaire.'

---

* The conversations with General Chrzanowski were corrected by him, and the passages in French inserted by him.—N. W. SENIOR.

Senior.—Do you believe in the hatred of the Germans, ascribed by Branitski to the Russians and Poles?

Chrzanowski.—I do; though I doubt whether it goes so far among the Poles as to make them prefer the Russians. Russians as well as Germans are oppressors. Russian Poland is worse governed than Posen or Galicia. All the three parts of Poland are indeed administered by foreigners ignorant of the language and habits of the people, but in addition to these defects the Russians are thieves; the Germans, though brutal, are honest. The Germans observe the forms and generally the substance of the law. The Russians disregard both. What disgusts the higher classes in Prussian Poland is the systematic attempt to Germanise the country. Whenever land is to be sold the Government will lend a German at two per cent. money to buy it. The Poles, who are accustomed to invest at five per cent., cannot compete with such a bidder, and about one-fourth of the land has passed into the hands of the Germans.

Senior.—This would in time produce a state of things like that in Ireland—a landed proprietary differing in race and religion from the actual cultivators of the soil.

Chrzanowski.—No; the purchasers become in most cases the actual cultivators. Property is much subdivided, and the German peasant is a purchaser as well as the German noble.

Senior.—What do you hear of the new Czar?

Chrzanowski.—He seems to be less of an impostor than his father was. Nicholas was an actor. I have been present when, in the most theatrical attitude, he has declared his immutable will as to certain measures. Objections have been raised; half an hour later he has declared an immutable will to the contrary effect. 'Il posait toujours.' He was not natural for one instant during his whole life. Perhaps he was right, for his nature was not fit to show.

He had neither courage nor intelligence. What was called his force of character was merely his belief in the flatteries of all around him. As for Alexander, he has possessed absolute power for nearly three years, and we hear of no improvement. Nicholas' management of the war was lamentable, and Alexander continued it. The maximum force of the allies was 125,000 men; the maximum force of the Russians was 180,000 men. With such a superiority, and with such an arsenal as Sebastopol, he ought to have driven you into the sea. The defence of Sebastopol is praised. What merit is there in the defence of a town strongly placed and amply provided, by a superior army, on its own ground, and constantly reinforced?

Senior.—What do you suppose to have been the Russian loss?

Chrzanowski.—About 500,000 men; 200,000 in and about Sebastopol, 300,000 more on their way thither. The Russian levies were absurd. They had more men at the beginning than they could employ. They started with 500,000 men; they raised 720,000 more. No additional hospitals were provided. The existing ones were overcrowded; hospital fever and mortification broke out, and at least half of the new levies died in them. In general, indeed, a man who enters a Russian military hospital is sentenced. It has been said that the Russians were careless in burying their dead, that many only wounded were thrown into the same pit with the really dead. It did not much signify, except that, perhaps, it was an easier death than they would have suffered in a hospital.

Dussard.—A mot is quoted of a French officer employed in that service, who, to the reproach of performing it à la Russe, answered, 'Mais si on voulait les écouter tous, il n'y aurait pas un seul de mort.'

Something was said about raw meat.

Chrzanowski.—I will not affirm that cooked meat is not better, but one can live on what is uncooked. I did so once for two months. My only sustenance was raw beef and water. I did not dislike it.

Senior.—What effect did it produce on your health and strength?

Chrzanowski.—No perceptible effect. I felt neither better nor worse than usual. But I found it difficult to return to cooked food. The first time that I attempted to feed on it I was repelled by an irresistible loathing. 'Du reste' raw meat is not a very uncommon military resource. In our retreat from Moscow, if a horse fell every soldier who passed cut a bit out of him till nothing eatable remained.

Dussard.—I have dined with the hippophages of Vienna. I was strongly reminded of the taste of the portions of beef in certain two-franc ordinaires in Paris.

Dussard outstaid Chrzanowski, and talked of the ruin of the fusion.

Dussard.—I believe that the three demands made by the Orleans princes were made in order to be rejected.* A continuance of this dynasty is, however, impossible. If

---

* This is the letter from the Duc de Nemours to the Duc de Broglie which put an end to the projected fusion.

Claremont, 25 Janvier, 1857.

CHER MONSIEUR,—Dans une lettre de Monsieur le Comte de Chambord, écrite à l'occasion de la mort de Monsieur de Salvandy et publiée par les journaux, se trouve une phrase qui représente la réconciliation accomplie en 1853, comme une des plus fermes garanties de la France.

Cette phrase, nous en avons acquis la preuve, a un sens sur lequel le doute n'est plus aujourd'hui possible, et elle a pour effet de faire croire à des engagements que mes frères et moi n'avons contractés. Nous sommes dès lors, quoique bien malgré nous, obligés de rompre

the Bonaparte family resembled the Orleans family, if they had such men as Joinville, Nemours, or Aumale, it might have a chance. It had a chance in 1833 and in 1834. Louis Philippe was tottering; a slight impulse would have overthrown him more easily then than in 1848. The Republicans were willing to adopt a Bonaparte, with Republican institutions. The first plan was to take the Duc

---

le silence que nous nous étions promis de garder sur les relations que nous avons eues avec Monsieur le Comte de Chambord.

Lorsqu'en effet, dans une pensée de concorde, je me suis rendu auprès de Monsieur le Comte de Chambord, je ne l'ai fait que sur l'assurance formelle que cette démarche n'impliquait aucun engagement. En lui exprimant ensuite notre désir sincère de voir la France l'appeler un jour au trône, et notre volonté de consacrer dans l'occasion tous nos efforts à obtenir ce résultat, j'ai été bien loin de lui offrir un concours aveugle et indéfini. Un accord préalable devait nécessairement en déterminer les conditions. Ces conditions, de notre côté, se seraient résumées en trois points principaux que nos convictions, comme le respect dû au passé de notre famille, nous commandent de ne jamais abandonner.

1°. Maintien du drapeau tricolore qui aujourd'hui aux yeux de la France est le symbole du nouvel état de la société et le résumé des principes consacrés depuis 1789.

2°. Rétablissement du gouvernement constitutionnel.

3°. Concours de la volonté nationale à ce rétablissement ainsi qu'au rappel de la dynastie. De ces trois points, le premier seul a été abordé avec Monsieur le Comte de Chambord lors de sa visite à Nervi, et le résultat de cet entretien a été tel, que nous avons cru devoir l'informer qu'aussi longtemps que ce point resterait indécis, toute communauté de vues entre lui et nous était impossible. Depuis lors cette situation, à notre très-grand regret, ne s'étant point modifiée, et toute idée d'une entente préalable étant même repoussée par Monsieur le Comte de Chambord, il est devenu obligatoire pour nous de mettre un terme à des tentatives d'accord aujourd'hui inutiles.

Nous regrettons vivement de n'avoir pas mieux réussi dans nos efforts pour réunir sous un même drapeau toutes les nuances du parti constitutionnel, car c'eût été encore là pour nous une manière de servir la France. Notre résolution est désormais d'attendre les événements, et de prendre en chaque occasion conseil de la raison et de nos devoirs envers le pays.

Recevez, &c. &c.

(Signé)   LOUIS D'ORLEANS.

de Reichstadt, whom Austria agreed to support. On his death I was sent to London to negotiate with Joseph. The treaty went so far that I was employed by Joseph more than once to draw up a manifesto in his name. I always omitted from it, and he always inserted, a claim of hereditary right, as the eldest of his House. In other respects he was liberal, much more so than any of the rest of the family. They were all opposed to any concert with the Republicans, none more so than Louis Napoleon and Lucien. And in fact it was the opposition of Lucien, who came to London for that purpose, that prevented the attempt.

Senior.—Do you *now* think that it would have had any chance of success?

Dussard.—Considerable. The Strasbourg and Boulogne attempts appealed merely to the Bonaparte feeling. We should have had with us also the Republicans, the most honest, the most devoted, and the most enterprising of all our parties. We should have tried rather to seize an occasion than to make one. If a Bonaparte could have shown himself when Lyons was in the hands of the workmen, the insurrection against Louis Philippe would have spread like wildfire. *Then* the name of Bonaparte was a spell; *now* eight years of familiarity with it have destroyed its force, at least in Paris, and, whatever the provinces may say, Paris still is France. In private life Louis Napoleon is good and kind. He is fond of those about him, and they are fond of him. He remembers all his old friends. I know that he has been trying to renew his friendship with Madame Cornu, who, much to her honour, broke with him on the coup d'état. In public life, considering his position, he cannot be called violent. But he has lately committed one or two capital errors. The greatest probably is the creation of an Imperial Guard, with extra pay and privileges as to promotion.

This has enraged the line, and the army is dividing itself into two camps. A friend of mine, a colonel of the line, told me the other day that some of his men, having had a quarrel with some men in the 'Garde,' offers of support had been made to his regiment from the other regiments quartered near him. As for the bourgeoisie of Paris, they of course hate him—as Orleanists, as sufferers in the massacre of the 5th of December, 1851, and as stripped by him of political power.

Senior.—Has he not given great impulse to the trade of Paris?

Dussard.—He has stimulated the building trade by pulling down and reconstructing a whole city, and the extravagance of the Court has enriched the modistes; but as all this is unproductive expenditure, it cannot have increased the general wealth and employment of Paris; it has only altered their distribution.

Senior.—But has he not, by restoring confidence, increased also the productive expenditure?

Dussard.—Not much. You see scarcely any considerable undertakings except in building or by joint-stock companies. Confidence is *not* restored. There is less terror of the Rouges, but there can be no confidence in a political system which depends on the life of one man. A life which, on that very account, because it is seen and felt that on its termination the whole imperial bubble will burst, is exposed to a thousand times as much risk as yours or mine. Then, economist as I am, I must reckon among his errors his attempt to improve our tariff. He wished very wisely to abolish its prohibitions. Relying on the discipline of the Corps Législatif he proposed to do it by a law. If he had done it by a decree there would have been complaints for six months, and after that time the utility of the measure would have become obvious, and every one would have approved it. But its proposal as a law gave time and means of opposition. Billault, the Minister of the Interior, a violent protectionist, under pretence of making inquiries in the manufacturing districts, went himself to Lille, and sent emissaries to Rouen, Mülhausen, and other towns of the same kind, who stirred up resistance, and reported even more than they actually found or created. Rouen solicited Thiers, as a protectionist, to be their candidate at the next election. The Corps Législatif referred the matter to a committee, and by our parliamentary law a bill so referred cannot be considered by the House until the committee has reported. The committee has not reported. And now, after the loss of two sessions, the Government announces that the measure is withdrawn for four years. All this has been mischievous to the Government as a defeat, but still more so as a threat. The manufacturers, all blind protectionists and prohibitionists, are frightened and angry, and communicate their fears and resentment to their workpeople.

Senior.—I should have thought that prohibitory duties would have served their purpose as effectually as prohibitions.

Dussard.—No; there is always a fear that duties may be reduced. Then a commodity which is excluded only by duties may be smuggled, and as soon as it has got through the Custom House lines it is safe. A prohibited commodity may be seized wherever it is found, in the shop, or even in the house. The enormous loans, too, have alarmed all the holders of 'rentes.' He borrowed sixty millions during the war, he is borrowing indirectly ten millions more now, and there is a suspicion ' qu'on allonge le grand livre,' that is, that fresh 'rentes' are secretly created and sold for the benefit of the Treasury at the Bourse. So much for his unpopularity with the army and with the bourgeoisie. As to the workpeople of Paris, he has professed to be a Providence—to be able to diffuse prosperity. He is made responsible therefore for the want of it. There is deficiency of employment in many trades; lodging is become very dear, in a great measure in consequence of his own conduct. Bread and wine have been made scarce by bad seasons, meat by an undue consumption during the war. There is considerable distress. The common people are beginning to despise him; they call him a ' drôle' and a ' farceur,' in English a humbug. And now I think that I have explained to you how it is that the name of Bonaparte is no longer a spell.

Monday, April 20th.—I dined with the Circourts, and met Tocqueville, Sumner, Viel Castel, Mérimée, and M. Le Play,* the author of a great work on the condition of the labouring classes. We talked on a subject now frequently discussed in Paris, its increased expensiveness.

Senior.—For what could a lady in Mrs. Senior's position dress in Paris?

Madame de Circourt.—If she went out much, for 10,000 francs.

Senior.—And my daughter?

Madame de Circourt.—Oh, with her youth and advantages, for about 3000 or 4000 francs a season. As unmarried women do not dine out or pay morning visits, less is required from them. Their gowns are not so soon got by heart. The Empress is said to have a wonderful memory, and to display it by reminding people that she has already expressed her admiration of a particular dress, which is supposed to be a hint that she ought not to see it again. They say that she seldom wears a gown twice.

---

* Le Play, conseiller d'état, an engineer, and author of several scientific works. The book referred to in the text is called 'Les Ouvriers Européens.' It made a sensation in France.—Ed.

Mérimée.—A friend of mine, by no means rich, was invited to Fontainbleau for a week. She took with her fifteen gowns; two a day, and one for accidents.

Senior.—How do you account for the neglect of Sunday by the workmen of Paris? It does not arise from indifference to holidays, for they generally take one on Monday instead.

Le Play.—It is difficult to account for it. It may have arisen from the ostentatious irreligion of the earlier revolution. It is helped by the frequent practice of paying wages at two on Sunday afternoon. The man works all Sunday morning because he has no money to drink with until the afternoon.

Senior.—Does the French workman save?

Le Play.—Seldom. His companions will not allow it. A man who has money is forced to drink it out.

Senior.—But how does he maintain his wife and children?

Le Play.—He frequently has *no* children; scarcely ever more than one, or at most two. In the great majority of cases he is not married. In the Faubourg St. Antoine the number of men much exceeds that of women. The woman, wife or not with whom he lives, generally earns her own maintenance.

Senior (to Circourt).—What is this dispute between the Emperor and the Bishop of Moulins?

Circourt.—The Emperor is in the right. The Bishop has created canons whom he cannot legally create. He has deprived of their benefices men who were legally irremovable. He has excommunicated all who have had recourse to the protection of the law, and he has refused to celebrate mixed marriages. The Emperor has complained to the Pope, and, if the Bishop had not been a man of high family and connections, the Pope would have deprived him. As it is, he has been merely admonished by the Conseil d'Etat. The clergy, however, sympathise with him. The Archbishop of Rheims informed the Emperor that all the Bishops in his province had agreed to act in a similar manner. 'If they do so,' answered Louis Napoleon, 'they shall all be prosecuted.' The Church, at least the Bishops, are further offended by his scheme of creating a grand aumônier. The grand aumônier is independent of all episcopal authority; he is subject only to the Pope. The royal palaces, the army and the navy, are under his jurisdiction. The person selected for this high office is a youth of three and twenty, a son of the Prince of Canino. He is to receive it as soon as he attains the canonical age of twenty-four.

Thursday, April 23*rd.*—Chrzanowski, Wolowski, Lord Ashburton, and the Mohls breakfasted with us. Chrzanowski came early, and gave to Lord Ashburton and me a sort of lecture, controverting the opinion expressed by Thiers, in his fifteenth volume, that Napoleon's invasion of Russia was necessarily unsuccessful.

Chrzanowski.—The object of that invasion[*] was not to conquer but to intimidate; it was intended rather to be a demonstration than a serious war. The day that he crossed the Niemen the Russian army was divided into two corps— one under Bagration, with its head-quarters at Wolkowitz; the other under Barclay, at Wilna, separated by one hundred miles. *Their* object, of course, was to unite; *his* to keep them apart, and to beat them separately. What did he do? He sent Jérôme and only two divisions, under Davoust, to stop Bagration's way, marched himself to Wilna abandoned by Barclay, reached it in four days from the opening of the campaign, and stayed there for eighteen

---

[*] General Chrzanowski read and corrected this conversation. The additions in French are his.—N. W. SENIOR.

days, waiting for an answer to proposals which he had sent to Alexander by M. Balaschof. It has been supposed that this delay was for the purpose of getting fresh horses and supplies. But his numerical superiority in cavalry, as well as in infantry, was such that his losses during four days had not sensibly affected it. Nor could he recruit his cavalry in eighteen days. The country was cleared of horses, and the absence of all the local authorities would have made it impossible to collect them if there had been any. If an army wants supplies it can get them much more easily when it moves and is every day in a new unwasted country than when it is stationary. These proposals were rejected, and Napoleon had then to turn a demonstration into a serious war; but, as is always the case, the false plan on which the campaign had been begun influenced it up to its latest results. Barclay and Bagration, the former scarcely pursued at all, the latter inadequately pursued, effected their junction. Napoleon would not venture at Smolensko to establish himself in winter-quarters with such an army before him. He kept following them in the hope of breaking them by a victory. At Borodino he gained his victory, but it was incomplete; nor is it clear that he could have made it more decisive by employing his guard, and perhaps depriving himself of an indispensable reserve. And though victorious he was too much crippled by that most sanguinary contest to continue to act offensively with vigour.

The burning of Moscow did not really influence the fate of the war, except so far as it excited the Russians. When the French army established itself at Moscow it changed its character. From an active army it became a garrison, and, like every other garrison, had only three alternatives: to evacuate, to be relieved, or to perish by starvation. Even if it had not been attacked, it must have lost all its horses during the winter, for there was nothing for them to feed on, and the next spring it would have been helpless. Napoleon's proposals of wintering there or at Kalouga, a town of only thirty thousand inhabitants, whose provisions would have been consumed in a few weeks, and whose climate resembles that of Moscow, or of marching on St. Petersburg in the beginning of winter with exhausted troops and with Kutusoff in his rear, were not serious. He knew perfectly well that they were all impracticable. They were intended merely to frighten the Russians. If the Russians held out he saw that he must retreat behind the Dnieper, and, indeed, behind the Niemen, and whether he carried back across the Niemen fifty thousand men or none did not much signify. He had long been accustomed to rely on the favours of fortune, and among them he reckoned on a reconciliation with Alexander. He believed here that an appearance of obstinacy would at last intimidate the Russians. When Kutusoff's attack on Murat showed that this hope had failed, and that he could no longer remain inactive, his first scheme was to fight a decisive battle with Kutusoff. The discouragement of his troops and the immense baggage that encumbered them made him despair of such a result, and he resolved to retreat by Malo Jaroslavitz to Smolensko through an unwasted country. He failed to effect this by a surprise. Kutusoff met him there, fought a furious battle, was beaten and forced to take a defensive position in the rear.

I am inclined to think that this intended line of retreat was still possible, and so thought Davoust, who was to have commanded the rear. But the spirit even of Napoleon was broken. Every hope which had successively gleamed on this unhappy campaign had proved delusive. Every effort had made his position worse. The frightful slaughter at Malo Jaroslavitz showed the resistance that we had to conquer; he hardly escaped being carried off by the Cossacks; he lost his force of will; took advice instead of giving orders, and allowed the opinion of the majority to precipitate his army into the gulf of the wasted road by which it had advanced.

Now if Napoleon, instead of a demonstration, had intended a war, would he not have used the immense superiority of force with which he crossed the Niemen on one side to crush Bagration, for which purpose he had the fourth, fifth, sixth, seventh, and eighth corps d'armée, about 150,000 men, and on the other to destroy Barclay, who must have been beaten if he had moved from his entrenched camp at Drissa, and would have been taken, like Mack at Ulm, if he had remained there? I have no doubt that such would have been the conduct of Napoleon if he had been governed by merely military motives, and—in opposition to M. Thiers—I believe that it would have succeeded. The main armies of Russia having been destroyed, even supposing his own force reduced from 400,000 to 300,000, he might with 100,000 of them have driven away Tormansow and Tchitchakoff into the south, and with 80,000 have driven Wittgenstein to the north, and with the remaining 120,000, if he thought it worth while, he might have made a 'pointe' on Moscow, dictated a peace from thence, or retired behind the Dnieper before the winter. If superiority of numbers, superiority of discipline and skill, and superiority of generalship cannot secure success, war must be considered as a matter of chance, not of calculation. The next spring he might have marched on St. Petersburg, or, what would have been better, might have re-established Poland. With 50,000 French troops and 50,000,000 of subsidy, Poland would have been able to resist Russia. Poland would not have been a Spain to him; the whole nation would have supported him. Though his indecision and his fear of alarming Austria and of exasperating Russia prevented his taking any serious measures in our favour, the Polish army fought for him to the last man. The Poles are the only allies of whom he never complained.

Senior.—How came Bagration and Barclay to be one hundred miles apart? Why did they separate in order, by vast efforts and through great dangers, to reunite?

Chrzanowski.—You may well ask the question; because they were fools. An army in cantonments must always spread in order to live, but its different corps should never be more than a day's march from a common centre, selected as a point of rendezvous. The early plan of the Russians was absurd; they ought not to have approached their frontier; they ought not to have thought of making a stand at Drissa. The further from their frontier they fought the fewer and more exhausted were their enemies. As I said before, by dividing their forces and by advancing to their frontier, they gave to Napoleon the means of certain victory.

'Et certainement il les aurait employés si dès le début de la campagne il s'était décidé à faire une guerre sérieuse; mais, comme il a eu l'idée qu'une simple démonstration suffirait pour forcer la Russie à une coopération contre l'Angleterre, unique but qu'il se proposait d'obtenir, en s'arrêtant à Wilna il a laissé échapper l'occasion de détruire l'armée russe. S'étant aperçu de sa faute, il a fait tout ce qu'il a pu pour la réparer, mais ce n'était plus possible sans une grande faveur de la fortune, et elle s'est montrée rebelle. Les dix-huit jours perdus à Wilna ont perdu tout. Il y a des circonstances qu'on ne rencontre nulle part ailleurs qu'en Russie qui donnent à une guerre contre cette puissance un caractère spécial. Les grandes forces dont dispose la Russie exigent des forces très-considérables chez l'aggresseur. Son climat rigoureux rend les interruptions des opérations inévitables, et double ainsi la durée de la guerre tandis que l'immense étendue peu peuplée de ce pays et le peu de bonnes routes rendent à l'assaillant l'entretien de ses troupes bien difficile. Une attaque avec un but restreint peut réussir, mais seulement dans le cas où le Gouvernement russe se trouverait disposé à faire des concessions. Une attaque de fond n'a de chances de réussite que si elle parvient à se créer une force auxiliaire sur le sol même de la Russie. Napoléon, dans la première inspiration de son génie, se proposa de réconstruire la Pologne, et de la charger, tout en lui prêtant l'assistance, d'achever l'œuvre qu'il ne pouvait terminer avec ses forces seules; mais, par des considérations politiques postérieures, il tomba dans le faux, et s'attira tous les désastres connus.'

There was no enemy against whom Kutusoff's plan of retreat could be more effectually employed than Napoleon, for, on his system of war, his men melted away like snow. He used constantly to repeat that war must support war; he clothed and fed his men by requisitions or by plunder; he never spent a farthing in buying supplies for them. No army but a French one could, under such a system, have been kept together for two months. An English, or a German, or a Russian army so treated would disband. The French did not disband, but they died of want and fatigue.

Senior.—Was that the case with the armies that fought at Austerlitz and Jena?

Chrzanowski.—Certainly it was. Ten died in the hospitals for one in the field. Theoretically he knew the value of old soldiers; he knew that for marching, for manœuvring, and for fighting, except a mere sudden rush, one thousand old soldiers are worth two thousand raw ones; but he did not act on it in practice; he used up his men so rapidly that he had no old ones, scarcely any adult ones. When, by an expense of perhaps ten millions of francs he might have saved ten thousand lives, he seems to have thought it best to save the money and to replace the men. But an old soldier cannot be replaced. Even one of three or four years' experience is almost invaluable. Napoleon's soldiers often had not four months' experience; in his later campaigns they used to learn their drill on their march, and accordingly the vast armies with which he opened his campaign in the spring of 1812, and again in 1813, had, in both cases, almost perished before the autumn. Their numbers, indeed, were kept up, but it was by conscripts, often taken before the legal age. This part of Napoleon's military character you will not find in Thiers; he did not know it, or he would have told it. I, who served under him for years, knew it and suffered from it.

Jobez,[*] Deputy to the Constituent Assembly from the Jura, came in before we separated. He praised the honesty and the good sense of the Assembly.

Senior.—And yet it made your impracticable constitution.

Jobez.—It did that from want, not of sense, but of courage. Cavaignac was a brave soldier, but a timid politician. He and his party feared and obeyed the ultra-Republicans in the Chamber, though they braved them at the barricades. During the insurrection of June, I was with nine or ten of my colleagues in the Faubourg St. Antoine. Our business was not to fight or even to direct—we left that to the military men—but to encourage the National Guards by our presence under fire. Two of us were killed. I said to one of them just before he was hit, 'I only wish that there

---

[*] Author of 'La France sous Louis XV.,' now in course of publication.—Ed.

was as much moral courage in the Assembly as there is physical courage.'

Chrzanowski.—Neither is common, but moral courage is the rarer; the rarest quality of all is calmness. When a man is in imminent danger his own mind is a sort of field of battle between the passions which urge him to advance, and those which tempt him to run away. Most men have no room in it for any other thoughts.

Senior.—Of the passions which combat fear, which is the strongest—anger, ambition, or honour?

Chrzanowski.—Anger, hatred of the enemy, and a fierce desire to kill him. Then comes, in the higher ranks, ambition. As for honour, meaning by honour the fear of disgrace, that is not a feeling which can inspirit a man or urge him on. The most that it can do is to keep him stationary. For 'élan' you must be excited by more active principles—by rage or by glory.

I dined with Kergorlay, and met there the Procureur-Imperial and Circourt. The procureur assured me that all the reports of attempts on the Emperor's life were unfounded.

Procureur.—At least they are founded only on the facts that secret societies exist in Paris, and that there are men who would make such attempts if they dared. We are forced to watch them narrowly. But as yet they have been guilty of no overt act.

We talked of Lamartine.

Circourt.—I am sorry for his difficulties, but they are self-created. He is a great poet, and a great speaker, and has some great merits as a historian. But his favourite employment is commercial speculation, and there he is great only in the extent of his dealings. A few years ago, expecting a bad vintage, he borrowed money and bought up all the wine round him. The vintage was good, the price fell; he got frightened, sold immediately, of course drove down the price much lower, and lost thirty or forty per cent. on the operation. He sells his books to booksellers who are speculators like himself, at nominally high prices, and is paid by bills which are dishonoured. He accused Thiers of giving away his property by selling an edition at 8000 francs a volume. 'I,' he said, 'ask 40,000.' 'Yes,' answered Thiers, 'but *I* am paid.' Then he buys all the land that is on sale near him, indeed much that is not on sale. His sister-in-law, whom he has established in a country-house near him, because he wishes to have her daughter always about him, complained of the noise from a neighbouring cottage. Lamartine proposed to purchase it of the proprietor, a small vigneron. 'I cannot,' said the owner, 'sell it to you for any price which you could prudently pay, for it is worth ten times as much to me as it would be to you. I work and live on my little vineyard; you would merely throw it into your estate.' 'Name your price,' said Lamartine. After two days' consideration the man asked 40,000 francs. Lamartine had not the money, but he had a volume of his early autobiography, unfit for publication during his life, and for which probably, on that account, a bookseller had offered him 40,000 francs. He went to Paris, sold the manuscript, which appeared under the name of his 'Confessions,' bought the little property, pulled down the house, and at an expense of 40,000 francs added perhaps 5000 francs to the value of his estate. He has now 14,000 subscribers at twenty francs a year to his 'Entretiens Littéraires.' This must give him a large revenue; but though he lives apparently inexpensively, he is as distressed as ever. It all goes in unsuccessful speculations.

Friday, April 24th.—St. Hilaire, Mérimée, Kergorlay,

and Manin breakfasted with us. Manin is, as might be expected, in low spirits.

Manin.—I see no immediate hope. The courage, indeed, of the Italians, and their aversion to foreign and to priestly rule, are undiminished. If the French were to withdraw, the Pope would not retain his temporal power for a day. But this makes the problem almost insoluble. Will they venture to withdraw? Will Europe allow them to remain? Is not the Pope even more effectually a subject than if Bonaparte's scheme of placing him at Avignon had been acted on? *Then* he would have been held in subjection only by fear, and indeed would not have had much to fear, for what harm could the French have done him? *Now* they have over him every sort of empire: they protect him against his subjects, they enable him to collect his revenue; he depends on them for his sovereignty, he is their puppet. It would be far better for Catholic Europe if Elba were given to him, or any small district, to be erected into a little principality and neutralised, in which he could have only spiritual affairs to attend to. The profit and employment arising from the presence of the Pope and of his Cardinals, and of his foreign ministers, does not reconcile the people of Rome, and still less the people of the Roman States, to the evils of priestly government. They are too proud of their history, too numerous—too anxious to be again a great nation. But the inhabitants of a country town like Albano or Frascati would be delighted to be the seat of a Court.

Rome, too, is the only town in Italy which the other great towns would acknowledge as a capital. The amalgamation of France is owing, in a great measure, to the pre-eminence of Paris. If France had had such towns as Venice, Milan, Turin, Genoa, Florence, Pisa, Bologna, and Naples, each with its past independence, its glorious recollections, its local patriotism, ambition, and jealousy, it would have been difficult, perhaps impossible, to consolidate it into one State. In 1848 the people of Turin scarcely regretted the defeat of Charles Albert, since it removed their fear that their Sovereign would remove to Milan. The most important modern event in Italy is the formation of Roman railways. No extension of railways in the north or in the south would have much contributed to unity, while the Roman States, intersected by mountain chains, and traversed only by a few bad, unsafe roads, were interposed. Gregory XVI., who was a cunning and consistent tyrant, said that railways transported ideas as well as commodities, and forbade them. Pio Nono, kind, short-sighted, solicitous—first, indeed, for his soul, but after that for his honour and glory—is not only promoting them, but is persuading the ecclesiastical corporations to invest their accumulations in them. Gregory was right. Ideas *will* travel by them; and instead of tribes, each with its dialect, its city, its laws, and its insociability, we shall become a nation.

Senior.—Will you breakfast with me to-morrow and meet Montanelli?*

Manin.—No; I value Montanelli: I think him perhaps the first man among us, but I cannot meet him. .He has accused me of inconsistency, indeed of worse than inconsis-

---

* Giuseppe Montanelli, a Tuscan, began life as a musician, then became a poet, and afterwards, by the desire of his family, he entered the profession of the law, in which, thanks to his gifts as an orator, he obtained great success. In 1840 he became Professor of Law in the University of Pisa, and propagated liberal opinions by means of secret societies and newspapers. In 1848 he entered the army, fought for the liberty of Italy, and was severely wounded and taken prisoner by the Austrians. He was soon set free, and was received in triumph on his return to his native country. For a short time he was Minister to the Grand Duke, and afterwards one of the Triumvirs with Guerazzi and Mazzini. The counter-revolution made him an exile. He lived in Paris, and once more took part in politics in 1859.—ED.

tency, because I, a Republican, wish to see Victor Emmanuel King of Italy; the fact being that he, also a Republican, wishes to see Murat King of Naples. The differences between us are these—first, that my wishes for Victor Emmanuel are openly expressed, while his intrigues in favour of Murat are concealed; and secondly, that I consent to royalty provided it give me, what I prefer to everything else—unity. I would take Murat, the Pope, Napoleon Bonaparte, the devil himself for King, if I could thereby drive out the foreigners and unite Italy under a single sceptre. Give us unity and we shall get all the rest. No one will govern Italy despotically, except through a foreign intervention. Let us only drive out the foreigners and we shall get liberty under one form or another, that of a constitutional Monarchy, a Confederation, or a Republic—I little care which. But if we are to have two Kings, one in Naples, the other in Piedmont, they will always be at variance and always leaning on foreign support—Piedmont on France, Naples on Austria. A Murat in Naples would be more Austrian than Ferdinand. If these views be correct, no calamity would be greater than a Muratist dynasty. And for such a dynasty Montanelli is willing to pay the great, the frightful, price of a revolution. I would pay that price for freedom. I have paid it already, but not for a change of masters.

Senior.—How goes on the subscription for the arming of Alexandria?*

Manin.—Fairly. I have tried to alter its signification. It began as an expression of the national feeling of the Piedmontese; that was well, but I wished it to be something more; to be also an expression of the national feeling of the Italians; to be more still, to be an expression of

---

* The Alexandria between Turin and Genoa is here meant.—ED.

the anti-Austrian feelings of all Europeans. I have endeavoured therefore to open a subscription in the principal towns on this side of the Alps. I have succeeded partially in London, through the *Daily News*, and to a considerable extent here. Early in last September, three days after I had opened the subscription here, I received a summons to attend the Minister of Police. M. Pietri informed me that I was disobeying the law. 'It was done in ignorance,' I answered; 'my knowledge of French law is very slight.' 'The law,' he replied, 'which you have broken belongs to a portion of our law which every one ought to know, the 'Code Pénal.' It forbids all acts of hostility against a foreign power, and your subscription is declared by the very letter in which you propose it to be an act of hostility against Austria.' Of course I submitted. A few days after I received a second summons. 'I communicated,' said M. Pietri, ' the substance of our conversation to the Emperor, who is at Biarritz, and I have just received a telegraphic message ordering me to inform you that you are at full liberty to reopen your subscription.' I afterwards ascertained that the Austrian minister had complained of my subscription to Walewski, and that Walewski, without consulting the Emperor, had instructed Pietri to order me to close it. The revocation of that order was a slap in the face administered by the Emperor to Austria and to Walewski.

Saturday, April 25th.—Montanelli, Arrivabene, Circourt, and Duvergier breakfasted with us. We talked of the prospects of Italy.

Montanelli.—Union is at present impossible. We cannot effect it without foreign assistance, and foreign assistance for such a purpose will not be granted. But the destruction of the Papal tyranny, which interposes a moral desert between the north and the south, and of the smaller despotisms, such as Tuscany, and Parma, and Modena, which extend that desert, I believe to be not only possible, but probable. The King of Naples is thoroughly frightened. He is imprisoned in his palace, and sees no one but his Minister of Police. A slight impulse would, I believe, drive him to abdication in favour of his son, and his son would be ready to purchase the crown at the price of a constitution. We could hold up to the father and to the son the fears of a Republic or of Murat. Such an arrangement would be favoured by England, and, I think, not opposed by Austria or France. Austria fears a Republic, fears Murat, and fears a constitutional Monarchy, but, I think, fears most the two first. France likes Murat, and fears a Republic and a constitutional Monarchy, but most the former. England fears Murat, and does not love, but perhaps does not hate, a Republic, and earnestly desires a constitutional Monarch. So that all three votes would be against a Republic, and two against Murat, and all the three Powers prefer a constitutional Monarchy to at least one of the other alternatives.

Senior.—What are the chances in favour of an attempt by Murat?

Montanelli.—He has a considerable party, but I do not think that he could occasion a revolution. It is possible that he might take advantage of one. If there were a cry of 'à bas les Bourbons!' and he were to come forward offering a constitution and French support, he might be accepted; at least he might prevent a better solution. I consider him therefore as one of our dangers.

The conversation turned on Mazzini.

Montanelli.—I have long known him. I admire his courage and his enthusiasm, but experience is wasted on him. He is still a child; he will die a child.

Senior.—Is he sincere?

Montanelli.—He is sincere so far—that he believes that all that he proposes will be beneficial to Italy. He would not knowingly do anything which he thought injurious to her; but he is not self-devoted. He is vain and ambitious, and the conduct of a man who has either of those qualities is always somewhat warped by selfishness, whether he knows it or not.

We passed the evening at Lady Cowley's, and M. and J. said that they had never spent two hours so instructively. They never saw such good models for the head or for the body.

I asked Kergorlay, 'What is the average expense of one of these gowns?'

Kergorlay.—From one thousand to one thousand two hundred francs.

Senior.—But that must be ruinous to moderate fortunes.

Kergorlay.—You must recollect that we economise in children, in apartments, in servants. In Paris most men have only a lodging, with two sitting-rooms and a bedroom apiece. In the country, where we are more at our ease, we do not, like you, keep open house. Then most of the French in these rooms belong to the Court; the Court distributes about 40,000,000 francs a year in places and pensions, and a man who gets an additional 50,000 francs may well give to his wife half of it, and in fact generally does so.

Senior.—How is it in the Faubourg St. Germain? No places or pensions are distributed there. Are the ladies there as gorgeous?

Kergorlay.—They are as gorgeous in their great reunions,

but in general life in the Faubourg St. Germain is quiet. A few persons, almost always the same, form a little circle, and visit without show.

Sunday, April 26th.—Dumon breakfasted with us. We talked of Louis Napoleon's position.

Dumon.—It is certainly stronger than it was last year; every day of continued prosperity strengthens it, and whatever be the partial complaints, the constant improvement in the revenue, in defiance of bad harvests and bad vintages, shows that the general prosperity is great. The expenses of the Court and of the public buildings in Paris alarm a stranger; but they do not seriously affect our finances, and they flatter our imagination and our vanity. So as to the colossal and sudden fortunes which are springing up, they are obtained perhaps scandalously; they represent perhaps almost as much loss as gain; but those who are ruined by the game disappear. Those who succeed in it stimulate the cupidity and raise the courage, and perhaps blunt the consciences and the moral sense, of the standers-by. They are like the gainers of the great prizes in the lottery. The forty per cent. profit of the Crédit Mobilier last year, its twenty-three per cent. this, the doubling and tripling of the value of its shares, have drawn to the Bourse millions and millions which, in quieter times, would have been spent in buying bits of land at forty years' purchase, or lent to a notaire, or perhaps buried in a garden. I believe that they have contributed more to the sudden development of avarice and vanity in France, than what is called the return of confidence or Californian gold, or what is not without its effect, the closing of all the paths of ambition, except through wealth. A serious check to our prosperity, an unsuccessful war, more inundations, more bad harvests, more bad vintages, might produce a crisis which would sweep away the

Empire; but in the absence of such contingencies, I think that he has it for his life.

Senior.—And no longer?

Dumon.—No longer, unless his life be prolonged for eighteen or twenty years.

We talked of the state of society in Paris.

Dumon.—We are trying to resume the habits of the eighteenth century. Yesterday Villemain read to us at the Duc de Broglie's some comments on Chateaubriand's autobiography. It was very flat. He began by saying that, as some young ladies were present, he must pass over a few details. This damped our curiosity. No one likes an expurgated edition. Some went to sleep; but Villemain is too energetic and self-engrossed a reader to exercise much surveillance over his auditors.

Tuesday, April 28th.—We breakfasted with the Mohls. I sat next to M. Tourguénieff,* a Russian author of a picture of Russian life, which the French translator has called, much to Tourguénieff's disgust, 'Mémoires d'un Seigneur Russe.' He confirmed Chrzanowski's description of the weakness of Nicholas.

Tourguénieff.—He showed vigour and determination only when he was unresisted. He was not accustomed to opposition, and was discouraged by it. From the beginning of the war he lost heart, and in fact died of anxiety and regret. Had he been a man of courage and decision he would have roused against Turkey the Sclavonic populations.

Senior.—This would have produced a war with Austria.

Tourguénieff.—I think not. Austria is too prudent, too conscious of the disaffection of her Magyar, Croatian, and

---

* Ivan Tourguénieff's name is too well-known now to need explanation.—ED.

Transylvanic populations to declare war against Russia. She will not fight until she is invaded; and when she is invaded she will find that her nine millions of Germans are all that she can really depend on.

Friday, May 1st.—We went last night to see Ristori in 'Camma,' a new tragedy by Montanelli. There are some fine theatrical situations, in which Ristori displayed her passion and dignity; and some regrets for Sinato, and anticipations of happiness with him in the Celtic paradise, which she gave with great tenderness. The rest of the actors were detestable.

Manin, Tocqueville, Arrivabene, Rémusat and his son, and General Fox breakfasted with us. As we rose from the table Chrzanowski joined us. He and Manin talked of the Principalities.

Senior (to Chrzanowski).—What say *you*, ought they to be united or separate?

Chrzanowski.—It is utterly unimportant. I would not cross the room to produce either event. To talk of their being a bulwark against Russia is nonsense; a bulwark of four millions of servile peasants or shopkeepers, debased by centuries of oppression and intrigues, without an aristocracy, or a reigning family, or a history, or a nationality. United or separate, they will be under the influence of Russia.

Manin.—I wish them to be united, not because I think that when united they will be a barrier against Russia, but because they will be mischievous to Austria. A tolerably governed, quasi-independent, semi-Sclavonic population will be another Piedmont to her. It will set a bad example to Croatia and Transylvania. Austria shows her good sense when she wishes all her neighbours to be enslaved and impoverished. The sight of freedom and prosperity on the other side of her frontier puts bad ideas into the minds of her subjects. I believe that Piedmont alone, if the rest of Europe will only stand by, can beat Austria. I know a part of her empire in which Austria is vulnerable, in which a fire could be lighted which would spread over all her non-German provinces.

Rémusat.—I should not be surprised at such an event, and I believe that our great man is of the same opinion. So far as he has any sympathies they are Italian. Austria has no real friend, except England.

Montanelli came in. We talked, of course, of the re-presentation of yesterday.

Montanelli.—I am half-mad with the subordinate actors. The principal scene of the second act was ruined by one Gleck who misrepresents Sinoro. Ristori herself, in her vexation, lost her presence of mind.

Senior.—Where did she pick up such a set?

Montanelli.—It is very difficult to find better in Italy. We have sometimes one or two who are first-rate; but all the rest are execrable. France is the only country in which the general average of acting is high. If Ristori could have one good supporter, such as Modena, she could do; but he asked a price which she and her husband, Marquis Capranica, who are the managers of this itinerant theatre, did not think it prudent to give. I am a sufferer as well as Ristori. I was forced to cut three scenes out of the second act, without which it is meagre, because I was sure that the actors would spoil them.

Senior.—As your tragedy is on the Greek model, might it not have been improved by adding a Greek chorus?

Montanelli.—I thought when writing it that it might be so improved, and the effect of the harp in the last act confirms me. But there again I wanted the ' personnel.'

Senior.—Perhaps when you write, not for a given actress or theatre, but to be read over the whole world, you will introduce a chorus.

Montanelli.—I do not think that I shall write another tragedy for fame, though I may write some for the use of Madame Ristori. History and philosophy, especially political philosophy, are my studies. My friendship for Ristori induced me to write for her, but I wish to return from the world of imagination to that of reality, painful as that reality now is. Then this grey sky, and harsh climate, and monotonous plains and poplars, are unpoetical. If I were at home, looking over the valley of the Arno, in an amphitheatre of mountains, and with a bright sun and soft air, I could write verses. In Paris I am fit for nothing but prose.

Senior.—Ristori's action is fine, but it sometimes seemed to me excessive. When people are merely telling their dreams they do not make faces. But in the first act, when she tells her dream, she gesticulates as violently as if she were actually suffering all that she describes.

Montanelli.—She feels painfully that her words are not understood, or, at best, are imperfectly understood, so she tries to aid them by pantomime. Her action is more vehement here than it is in Italy. But to see her in perfection you should see her in comedy. In 'Goldoni,' for instance, her grace, vivacity, and fun are incomparable.

I spent the evening at Montalembert's. He gave me a paper which he has published in the *Correspondant* on the censure by the Conseil d'Etat of the Bishop of Moulins.

Montalembert.—Notice was given to all the periodicals to avoid the subject. *We* resolved to disobey. The notice had no legal force, even according to our present ideas of what is legal, and if they suspend us, well and good, we can reappear under another name. A daily paper is ruined by suspension. A man cannot go without his newspaper, and takes another; but he waits patiently for the reappearance of a monthly journal. I have not undertaken a formal defence of Monseigneur de Brézé. He does not want my support; but I have protested against the right of the Conseil d'Etat to take cognizance of the spiritual conduct of a Bishop. The right is supposed to be founded on the 'Articles Organiques' of 1802, a codicil to the concordat of 1801, an addition against which the Pope always protested. Such arrangements are treaties; and what should we think of articles appended to a treaty by one of the contracting parties, without the assent, or even the knowledge, of the other? Those articles treat the Pope as a French subject. One of them enacts that 'Every Pope, on his accession, shall swear to respect the four Gallican propositions of 1682,' propositions, not only indignantly rejected by the Pope, but now abandoned even by the clergy of France. We are all now Ultramontane. Napoleon was Ultramontane when, in 1801, he signed a concordat which surrendered all the Gallican liberties. Louis XVIII. was Ultramontane when he requested the Pope to deprive Cardinal Fesch of his archbishopric. Celui-ci was Ultramontane when he employed the Pope to get rid of the Bishops of Pamiers and Luçon. Whenever the Government wants the aid of the Papal authority it becomes more Ultramontane than the Pope; when it wishes to trample on the Church it becomes more Gallican than Bossuet.

Senior.—The jurisdiction assumed by the Conseil d'Etat may be objectionable, but its exercise in this particular case seems to be approved by the public, as far as my means of judging, which are of course very imperfect, extend.

Montalembert.—It is popular with all the Liberal party,

for it is popular with the enemies of the Government, and it is popular with the enemies of the Church; and what Liberal is there who does not belong to one, or rather to both, of these parties?

Senior.—Is the Church unpopular with the Liberal party?

Montalembert.—Not only the Church, but religion itself, and not only among the educated classes, but even among the workmen. This deplorable fact is the result of the conduct of the Church ever since the coup d'état. It is not merely that it submitted to the Empire. All France did so. It is not merely that it voted and preached in favour of the despot. That might have been forgiven. But it has gone much further than he has ventured to do. *He* talks of the time, distant perhaps, when he may be able to crown his labours by restoring liberty. The Church, or at least the clergy, protest against liberty. They have been maintaining ever since 1852 that liberty in a Christian country is a contradiction in terms; that the rights of the people are things not to be discussed, but to be denied; that constitutional government is the squaring of the circle. What makes this self-abasement more revolting is its apostacy. The principles, the institutions, the safeguards which they are now offering as a holocaust to their idol, were those which under Louis Philippe, and during the Republic, they invoked for themselves, and for all around them. They then asked for the Church, ' La seule liberté, la liberté de tout le monde.' Those who were then Republicans, and something more, are now pouring themselves out in flatteries and self-abasement which must disgust the object of them, as much as they do those who have the misfortune to hear them and to read them.

Senior.—You have shown that the censuring the Bishop must please the enemies of the clergy. But how can it please the enemies of the Government? If it be a popular act, the enemies of the Government must be grieved by it.

Montalembert.—The enemies of the Government think that they see in it a step towards the destruction of this unholy alliance between despotism and the Church. Many of them, like myself, while they deplore the conduct of the majority of the clergy are devotedly attached to the Church herself, considered abstractedly from the clergy for the time being representing her. The real friends of the Church believe that she can be free only while the people is free; they are the friends of liberty therefore, not only as citizens but as Christians. I no more believe in the co-existence of a free Church and a servile laity than I do in that of a free laity and an oppressed Church. The freest portions of the world—England, Holland, Belgium, and the United States—are those in which the liberties of the Church are the greatest. I earnestly hope that the Government will go on in its present course, and make these votaries of absolutism feel that they are slaves like the rest of us. Nothing is to be hoped from their patriotism or from their wisdom, but we may gain by their selfishness or by their fears.

Monday, May 4th.—I breakfasted with Buffet, Minister of Commerce before the coup d'état. We talked of the smallness of the Parisian rooms.

Buffet.—They are diminishing every day. As our parties are small we do not want large rooms, and our habits require many. The husband has his bedroom, salon, and cabinet de travail. The wife wants her bedroom, salon, and boudoir. Then there must be a dining-room, a drawing-room, and an ante-room. If these were to be as large as the London rooms, our house-rent, already oppressive, would be intolerable. All the new hotels therefore are cut up, as this is, into a number of pigeon-holes.

In fact, though we were only six, the table almost filled the room.*

Wednesday, May 6th.—Tocqueville, Corcelle, Arrivabene, Sumner, and the Clives breakfasted with us. We talked of Algiers, which Tocqueville and Corcelle visited in 1842. The French outposts were then only a few miles from the town.

Corcelle.—We are going to try to introduce a new element into Algiers, 'les honnêtes gens.' Up to the present time it has been the theory, and still more the practice, to colonise with rogues. The mother country gets rid of them, and it was supposed that in the colony, removed from their old habits, they would reform. This may account for the strict, perhaps arbitrary, way in which we governed them. I was with Bugeaud when he visited Deli Ibrahim, now almost part of Algiers, then one of our frontier villages. St. Arnaud, his aide-de-camp, was with us. 'J'espère,' said the Marshal, 'que nos colons sont contents.' 'Parbleu,' said St. Arnaud, 'je crois bien qu'ils sont contents. S'ils n'étaient pas contents par Dieu on les flanquerait bien.' Louis Philippe used often to talk to me about Algiers. Its conquest was not *his* doing, and he always doubted the wisdom of its retention. 'It is our opera-box,' he said to me, 'but a terribly expensive one.' I do not believe that we should have kept it if you had not required us to give it up.

He spoke highly of M. and Madame Cornu.

---

* The conversation which followed is omitted.—Ed.

Corcelle.—She wrote for Louis Napoleon a great part of his book on artillery practice. She used to read and make notes for him in the Bibliothèque when he was at Ham. Two days after the coup d'état she was to have breakfasted with the Princesse Mathilde: she sent word that she would not go. The Grande Duchesse Stéphanie called on her in her cottage in the Rue Rousselet to persuade her to change her mind; she spoke out against Louis Napoleon and the coup d'état with a violence which frightened the Duchesse. 'Tell him,' she said, 'that the gipsy's prophecy will be fulfilled. He has accomplished one-half of it; the people will do the rest.'

Senior.—What prophecy?

Corcelle.—It is a story well known in the family. Queen Hortense, when he was a child, had his fortune told by a gipsy. She prophesied that he would rise to the highest eminence of power and of fame, and would be killed by a bullet entering his forehead. The Grande Duchesse delivered the message. 'Nothing is more probable,' he answered.

Thursday, May 7th.—I went with Dussard and Circourt to see Delaroche's pictures. Dussard's daughter, about twelve years old, is to make her first communion in about two months, and he complains that she and her mother are worked to death in preparing for the previous examination.

Dussard.—She has to learn how many persecutions there were; how many 'péchés' there are; the difference between 'péchés' original, venial, semi-venial, and mortal; what is the meaning of the immaculateness of the Virgin; what is the difference between the authority of the Pope and the authority of a General Council; with no end of stuff of the same kind, all of which I trust that she will forget as soon as the examination is over.

Circourt.—The education of our boys is bad enough, but that of the girls is absolutely detestable. It is an exercise of memory and cunning. They have to prepare themselves for strings of questions, the answers to which not the whole Academy could carry in their heads. The business of the crammer is to teach them how to elude them, how to conceal their errors in generalities. If it were not for the admirable natural disposition of the French they would be turned into idiots or worse. As it is they become only *bête,* superficial and médiocres.

Friday, May 8th.—I breakfasted with Mérimée.

Mérimée.—I am somewhat fatigued with my exertions of yesterday. I breakfasted with the Court at Villeneuve l'Etang, and we amused ourselves with what you call romping, and we des jeux innocents. The Empress and her ladies occupied a hill with a steep slippery slope, the gentlemen tried to mount it, and were repulsed by nosegays and parasols, till at last the Emperor threw himself, when half-way up, on all fours, scrambled to the top, made way for himself and his followers, and established himself 'maître de la position.' The display of pretty feet was charming, all the more so to us who have not seen a lady's foot for the last four years. The Rouges give him a spine complaint; I never saw a man stronger or more active.

Senior.—Do you believe in the stories of recent attempts on his life?

Mérimée.—I know of two, for the Empress related them both to me. The first was by means of a hat left on a sofa in a passage which he was to pass through in returning from the opera. In it was a handkerchief, and under that a small box; it contained a piece of fulminating silver, with a clock-work wheel like an alarum, which would cause it to explode at the time for which it was set. As fulminating silver produces perhaps forty times the effect of gunpowder, if the explosion had taken place, as seems to have been intended, while he was passing, it would probably have destroyed him; but it was not wound up, probably the heart of the person intrusted with it failed. The other was at the Théâtre Français, where bags of gunpowder were found in a mine which had been driven under the wall. What gives importance to these attempts is the expenditure of time and money which they required. The fulminating box could not have cost less than 20*l*.; it is supposed to have been made in Switzerland. The hiring a shop and driving a mine under the theatre cost less money, but required the concurrence of several persons for some weeks. Yet no traces of any of the conspirators have been discovered.

Senior.—Do you believe in the attempt to seize him near Madame de Castiglione's house?

Mérimée.—No, I do not believe a word of it.

Senior.—Does the fear of assassination much disturb him?

Mérimée.—Not at all. He is brave, and he is a fatalist. The Empress is also a woman of courage; under certain circumstances she may render great services; she systematically tries to avoid dwelling on the danger.

I was at Nice when the Archbishop of Paris was killed. I saw there a coat of mail, very light, yet capable of resisting a dagger. I sent a description of it to the Empress's secretary, and made my letter amusing that it might be read to her, which it was. On my return she alluded to it. 'I might,' she said, 'have persuaded him to wear it one day, but he would have been tired and would have thrown it off the next. If we were to take precautions we should have nothing else to think of.' It was then that she related to me the two attempts that I have mentioned.

Both he and she seem to enjoy life very much, and not the less so because it may be short.

Senior.—Evans describes him as laborious.

Mérimée.—Nobody knows so much of his habits as Evans, for he sees him at all hours; but, considering how much he has to do, I scarcely call him laborious; he has not his uncle's greediness for business; he works from about half-past seven to eleven, but he does not do much that requires thought after eleven. Sometimes, indeed, he has fits of irregular exertion, and at all times he gets through his business very rapidly; he has read much and thought more, and has great knowledge of human nature; his conversation is attractive, not only from the charm of his manners but from its originality.

What are Dumon's expectations as to the dynasty? I have great respect for his sagacity.

Senior.—He thinks that the Emperor will reign during his life, and that if that is prolonged to the usual age of man his son may succeed him; but he will not prophecy as to what may happen if he should die within a few years.

Mérimée.—Did you read the allusion to Thiers in the Emperor's speech?

Senior.—Yes; it seemed to me to be a little grenade thrown into the enemy's camp.

Mérimée.—So it was; and it exploded. Guizot and Montalembert and Duvergier are furious. The Emperor begged me to talk to Thiers about it. 'You may tell him,' he said, 'that I think his work the greatest monument that has been erected to the glory of my uncle.' 'Vous pouvez répondre à l'Empereur,' said Thiers, 'que je m'occupe peu de la politique; que j'ai toujours mes chimères constitutionnelles, mais que je suis très-sensible à une éloge qui vient de si haut. My friends see nothing in it but a trick to ensnare me. I take it as a compliment to one who merely writes history from one of those who make history.'

I spent the evening at Lamartine's. His conversation was unusually agreeable. In general he addresses commonplaces to half a dozen bearded persons, apparently political refugees, who merely re-echo them. To-night he sat on the sofa and talked only to me.

Lamartine.—The founders of modern French literature were Voltaire and Rousseau. Our wit, our freedom, our badinage, our brilliancy, we owe to Voltaire; our vigour, our passion—a passion not inconsistent with the gravest dignity —in short, our eloquence, we owe to Rousseau. Our journalists are the offspring of the former, our orators of the latter. We have been called a military nation; we are far more a literary one. Richelieu, when he created the Academy, did more for us than Louis XIV. when he created the army; not that Richelieu knew what he was doing. He thought that he was founding a school of great writers and servile courtiers; what he actually did was just the reverse. Academies do not produce great writers; they spoil them. If a man of genius is betrayed into one, he breaks out of it or is pulled down to the general level, and the level of every Assembly is the dull plane—somewhat above that of its humblest members and far below that of its best members—which is called mediocrity. But by collecting into one body the most eminent men of France, by enabling them to recruit themselves by re-elections, he gave to literature social and political power. He made the 'hommes de lettres' the real aristocracy of France, the only aristocracy which could resist the Crown before 1789, or the people afterwards; the only aristocracy which has withstood or could have withstood the storms which have levelled every other eminence. Have you read Tocqueville's new book ?*

Senior.—Of course I have; who has not?

Lamartine.—It is a book of wonderful sagacity and good sense; but Tocqueville has examined the ancien régime so closely, and has so familiarised himself with its anomalies and abuses, that he believes that those anomalies and abuses account for the Revolution. He treats the Revolution as a reform, wide-spreading and logical, but while planned by theorists, violent and sanguinary, it was executed by savages. The Revolution was much more than a reform; or if a reform, it was a reform of much more than the government of France. It was an insurrection against the slavery, not of the body, but of the mind. It was an attempt by France, which personifies modern civilization, to break out of the feudal and religious prison in which she had lived for ten centuries, and to begin a new life, with new ideas, new objects, new habits, new means, new hopes, and, as was inevitable, new dangers and new calamities. Some humbler motives were necessary to render the overthrow of the ancient institutions of France so rapid and so complete. Envy and vanity supplied them. The working clergy envied and hated the dignitaries and sinecurists; the provincial nobles hated the courtiers; the courtiers hated the favourites; the Parliaments kicked against the overruling power of the Crown; the bourgeoisie were indignant at the usurpations of the Parliament; the people complained of the arrogance of the 'bourgeoisie;' the 'roturiers' hated the 'anoblis,' the 'anoblis' hated the 'gentilshommes,' and the result was a conspiracy of everybody against everything. These local passions, however, would have excited no

---

* The 'Ancien Régime.'—ED.

sympathy in Europe. Europe cared no more about the French Parliaments than it did about the English Reform Bill. But it saw that France was fighting the battle of moral freedom and of intellectual freedom, as well as of political freedom. It knew that though the last might be gained and lost again, the others, if once acquired, would be immortal; that the chains of custom, and prejudice, and authority, and routine, if once broken, could never be repaired; and it felt that those who seemed to be merely remedying the municipal abuses of France were really destroying the obstacles to the progress of mankind.

Senior.—One of the misfortunes of your revolutions is that those who begin them seldom carry them on. In 1789, and again in 1848, your Constituent Assembly was admirable. But the Legislative Assemblies of 1791 and of 1849 had neither courage nor wisdom, nor even patriotism.

Lamartine.—That is true, and it was to be expected, for the Legislative Assemblies were the produce of a reaction; the Constituent Assemblies were the creatures of enthusiasm. In 1789 and in 1848 all was hope and trust. They were times of patriotism, of confidence, and generous illusions; the foremost, the most active, the least selfish spirits rose to the top. The nation was superior to itself, the Assemblies were superior to the nation. In 1791 and in 1849 these illusions had been dissipated, or rather other illusions of an opposite kind had been substituted for them. Disappointment, mistrust, and despondency had taken the place of confidence and hope. The great men of the Constituent of 1789 voluntarily abdicated; many of the best members of the Constituent of 1848 were not re-elected. The metropolitan constituency rejected its most illustrious candidates— Bugeaud and Thiers, and its most respectable ones—Faucher, Falloux, and Marie, and brought in at the head of the poll Lucien Murat, Ledru-Rollin, Lagrange, and Boschot.

Abroad and at home all was disappointment and alarm. The priests were allowed to send French soldiers to destroy freedom in Rome. France looked on while Italy lost her best chance of independence, and while Hungary was conquered by Russia for the benefit of Austria. A pseudo-Montagne imitated the language and the violence of the giants of the Convention without their strength, or even their passions. Pseudo-Socialists attacked property, industry, and marriage. A drowning man will catch at a red-hot iron, and society, threatened by anarchy and plunder, will clutch the blade of a sword or of a bayonet. The country was terrified by the Rouges; trusted neither the wisdom, nor the honesty, nor the courage of the Assembly, and ran for refuge to a despot.

Saturday, May 9th.—The Rivets called on us.

Rivet.—What astonishes me most in the present state of public feeling is the indifference to parliamentary government. One would have thought France proud of her speakers and interested in their speeches, and that such a gratification to her vanity and to her amusement would have been what she would have most regretted in the loss of her liberties. Nothing of the kind. No one except those who were, or hoped to be, Deputies mourns over the Chamber. All that we want is a Government which will enable us to make our fortunes and will allow us to spend them. Whether that be effected under a despotic, or a parliamentary, or a republican form, no one cares. Tocqueville and I are among the proprietors of the *Siècle*. When we bought our shares we were told that they would enable us to control its politics. That was not true. The director is the tool of Fould; but Fould allows him, from time to time, to make a little opposition. We have sixty thousand 'abonnés,' who fancy that they are taking in an opposition paper. The political tact of the public has become so callous that it can read a journal every day for years without finding out what are its real politics.

Senior.—Sixty thousand ' abonnés' is enormous.

Rivet.—It is. The suppression of many other journals has made those which remain productive. We bought our shares at one hundred and twenty per cent. Even on that price they give us twenty-five per cent. If we had succeeded in getting the direction we should probably by this time have been ' avertis,' ' suspendus,' and ruined.

We talked of the elections of Paris.

Senior.—How will Cavaignac, if he should come in, deal with the oath of fidelity to the Emperor?

Rivet.—I do not think that if he takes it it will influence his conduct. No promise to do what appears to you to be mischievous, or to abstain from doing what appears to you to be useful, is binding. It cannot be your duty to God to keep a promise which it is your duty to your country to break. Once in the Corps Législatif, Cavaignac will do and say whatever he thinks that the welfare of France requires, and will hold all promises to the contrary void. The question is not whether he will obey the oath, but whether he will take it. If he refuses, he enables the usurper to pack the Corps Législatif, and to exclude from it all who hold that his tyranny is a nuisance which ought to be abated. Among the few gains which liberty has made during this century is the necessity imposed on even the least scrupulous despot to summon an Assembly elected by the people, and having power to enforce its opinions by refusing the budget.

Ought *we*, the friends of liberty, to abandon this advantage by allowing the door of the Assembly to be shut against us by an oath? Is not Cavaignac justified in attacking the usurper with the only weapon that is left to him? May we not say to him, 'You attempt to fetter or to exclude the friends of liberty by an oath. We think the oath void; we take it as a mere form, imposed on us by force, as we should obey a robber who threatened us with death unless we swore not to give evidence against him; and we shall break it just as we should break our oath to the robber.' It appears to me difficult to answer this reasoning, though I own I should be sorry to act on it. My scruples would be not so much scruples of conscience as scruples of honour. As between God and me, I should think myself justified in doing what I thought best for the country; but I should not like to appear to men to have voluntarily taken and broken a solemn promise. My motives might be misinterpreted; they might be supposed to be avarice, or ambition, or vanity. But as I am not a candidate, I shall not be put to the test.

Senior.—Could you not be elected without coming forward as a candidate?

Rivet.—No. The Court of Cassation, under the influence of M. Troplong, has decided that a 'billet d'élection'—that is, a bit of paper containing nothing but a name—is a book, and therefore is subject to the law of 'colportage.' Under that law no book can be 'colporté,'—that is, distributed by hand—until a copy of it has been signed by the author and deposited with the prefect. As few of our electors can write, no one can be elected unless he or his agents distribute among the voters papers containing his name. To do this is 'colportage,' and, as I said before, is unlawful, unless such a paper signed by the candidate be previously deposited with the prefect. No one therefore can now be returned for two places, or can be returned unless he has formally presented himself as a candidate. This increases the probability that Cavaignac has made up his mind to take the oath. He would not require his supporters to run risks in order to give him a seat if he did not intend to fill it.

Senior.—Has the prefect a right to refuse a candidature?

Rivet.—Not wantonly; only on the ground that the candidate is a 'perturbateur,' and *that* right has not been exercised. In the provinces, however, the Government has little to fear. The ballot is no real protection. The billet distributed by the Government has always a peculiar colour or fold. The voter, as he comes to the polling-booth, shows a card containing his name and his number in the register. They are taken down. He then throws his billet into the ballot-box, and of course it is easy to see whether he throws in the Government billet or another. I have watched, during the Republic, the voters, and made a list of their names and their supposed votes, and scarcely ever was materially wrong. The Government has a further power of controlling the elections. The poll is open for two days. On the evening of the first day the ballot-box is taken possession of by the maire, and sealed with his seal, and remains in his custody until the evening of the second day, when, immediately on the closing of the poll, the boxes are opened and the votes are counted. This is done by the bureau, consisting of two or three officers appointed by the maire.

Now there is nothing to prevent the maire, during the night in which the box containing the first day's votes is in his possession, from opening it, taking away all the opposition votes, putting in their place Government votes, and resealing it. Nothing connects the vote with the voter. It is a mere slip of paper, with a name written or printed on it. There is nothing to prevent the bureau from miscounting or misreporting the number of votes; and as the bureau is appointed by the maire, the maire by the prefect, and the prefect by the Government, you may be sure that every sort of abuse is suspected. All this will give great importance to any opposition returns. There are so many difficulties in the way of them that two or three will be hailed as great victories. Then the Government is increasing that importance by the anxiety that it betrays. Fortunately for it, Cavaignac, the most formidable opposition candidate, is odious to the Republican party, whom he crushed in June, 1848. On the other hand, if he should be returned, the defeat of the Bonapartists will be still more marked. He can come in only as the product of deep and widely-spread anti-imperial feeling. Half a dozen opposition members will be a nucleus of disaffection. Louis Napoleon will scarcely venture to dissolve. The next Corps Législatif, whether the product of a dissolution or of the expiration of the five years' service of this Assembly, may contain a majority in opposition. He may be forced either to liberalise his Government or to attempt another coup d'état.

Before Rivet left us Dumon came in. He asked me about the English elections, which led the conversation to Palmerston.

Senior.—Are you among those who believe that he contributed mainly to 1848?

Dumon.—I am. If the Spanish marriages contributed to that revolution, Lord Palmerston is remotely answerable for them. It was agreed between Guizot and Aberdeen that the Queen should not marry either a French Bourbon or a Coburg. Yet in Palmerston's celebrated despatch he mentioned Coburg as still a suitor, and as the first on the list. Guizot thereupon decided to effect the marriages in the manner in which, in fact, they took place. I was with the King at Eu, in September, 1846. He wished to have always one of his ministers with him. When I visited him one morning he said, ' Glücksberg has come to me from

Guizot. I wish that he would come himself, or that there was a telegraph between Eu and Val Richer. Guizot wants Montpensier to marry Marie Louise. Je m'en garderai bien. Je ne mettrai pas le bout du doigt dans les affaires d'Espagne. Si Montpensier veut absolument une femme, il faut qu'il aille la pêcher ailleurs.' Yet, in two months after, the marriages were made. The King saw more deeply into the matter than Guizot did.

I spent the evening with Cousin. He is sentenced to a warm climate. I recommended Algiers or Egypt.

Cousin.—Without doubt they would be the best, but I fear the voyage; and, as to Egypt, I fear what would be a recommendation to most persons, the new ideas and emotions. I have far more to do than can be done in the little time that is left to me. I have mapped it all out. When I was young I felt immortal. I cared nothing for the loss of a month or a half-year. Now I cannot spare a day. My imagination has so long dwelt on Egypt, that while there, and perhaps for months afterwards, my thoughts would be wholly Egyptian. I have not room in my short life for a new subject. I shall try the south of France—Cannes, or perhaps Hyères.

Senior.—What think you of Montpelier?

Cousin.—It is a charming country, and there is an excellent society there, ' mais l'air est trop vif.' Hyères is warm and unexciting, and is free from mistral.

Sunday, May 10th.—I called on Thiers, and assisted as usual at his breakfast and his subsequent toilette. He is the most conscientious shaver that I ever saw. Long after the chin and cheeks appeared to me to be smooth even to polishing, he went over them again and again.

Thiers, who is just returned from the coal mines at Anzin, of which he is a director, poured out his protectionist prejudices.

Thiers.—If I were in the position of Louis Napoleon, that is, if I had absolute power, I would to-morrow double or quadruple the duties on foreign coal.

Senior.—What are they now?

Thiers.—They differ according to the place of origin and the place of consumption. The country is divided into zones. As you go south, and the place of consumption is further from the place of production, and the advantage of the foreign producer therefore is smaller, the duty diminishes. It is lower at Bordeaux than at Boulogne, and at Marseilles than at Bordeaux. The duty on Belgian coal in the north of France is fifteen centimes the hectolitre, about an English sack. That on English coal is thirty centimes a hectolitre, about two shillings and sixpence a ton.

Senior.—What does English coal cost in Paris?

Thiers.—Sixty francs a ton.

Senior.—I pay in London about twenty-four francs.

Thiers.—The proof that the duty is not too great is, that it is with difficulty we beat the Belgian coal. If all foreign coal were prohibited it would give such an impulse to the French collieries that in ten years coal would be as cheap in France as it is in England. If we were to reduce our duty you would raise your price, and if we were to allow our mines to be abandoned, as would be the case if we let in English coal without a duty, you would soon make us pay a monopoly price. And what would be our state in time of war? Maritime wars in future will be coal wars. If a war were to break out now we should soon be in want of coal. Our mines however are advancing, and in a few years we shall be independent of you. It seems that at St. Etienne there are great coal-fields below those that are now worked.

I did not answer him. It is seldom worth while to argue

with anybody, never with Thiers. Madame Thiers put in her head, and seeing that we were alone, sat down. They both spoke with the greatest affection of Lady Ashburton.

Thiers.—I never knew so clear a head, so bright a wit, and so kind a heart combined.

Madame Thiers.—She was the most distinguished Englishwoman that I have met with. Little as she has lately been in Paris, her loss will be felt widely and deeply. It has shed a gloom over our society.

Monday, May 11th.—I called on Mérimée and enjoyed one of his long Turkish pipes. I asked him what he supposed to be the real purpose of the new military system.

Mérimée.—The object of the Emperor is to have a very large *land-wehr*, or military population, and a comparatively small and thoroughly effective army. He thinks that war is now so complicated an art that those who practise it should devote their whole lives to it. When it was first proposed, every military man in the Senate opposed it. They did not believe that the remplaçant—the volunteer—would have the *élan* of the young peasant taken from the plough. Experience, however, has decided against them. The older regiments, and those which had the most 'remplaçants,' behaved best in the Crimea.

The conversation passed on to marriage.

Mérimée.—If I had a daughter, my great object would be to teach her to look without fear on an unmarried life. The horror with which it is contemplated by French girls, and by their mothers, leads to most unhappy marriages.

Senior.—There is much to be urged in favour of your marriages arranged by the parents. They are likely to make as good choices as the young people themselves, when you recollect how little the young people generally know of one another.

Mérimée.—I have known as great a proportion of the 'mariages d'inclination' turn out well, as of 'mariages de convenance.' The latter are generally made by the mothers, and often for selfish purposes. We remark that a husband generally agrees better with a mother-in-law than a wife does. A ménage in which the married couple live with the wife's mother goes on better than one in which they live with the husband's mother. But of all marriages the worst are the 'mariages de terreur.' When a girl gets to be six or seven and twenty, her mother tells her that she absolutely must marry, or go into a convent. That for an unmarried woman to be living in the world, 'n'est pas reçu, n'est pas dans nos mœurs.' As a middle course, I have known ladies call themselves chanoinesses. If our families were as numerous as the English families none would remain gentry for more than two, or at most three, generations; but as in many cases they have no children, and in scarcely any more than two, or at most three, children, they do not sink into poverty, they become extinct. Half the really noble families that existed, even at the beginning of this century, have disappeared. Many are represented by only one child. The fear of poverty has been far more destructive to our aristocracy than our sixty years of revolutions.

Senior.—What do you mean by really noble families? What is the meaning of the proverb that the King can make a nobleman, but not a gentilhomme? What precisely is a gentilhomme?

Mérimée.—There are three theories. One is, that no family is gentilhomme that is known ever to have been 'vilain.' This would exclude nine-tenths of the greatest names in the Faubourg St. Germain. Another is, that all the families reputed to be noble before the 1st of January, 1400, are 'gentilshommes.' This was the theory of the times of Louis XIV. The third doctrine, and I think that now received, is, that the grandson of an anobli is gentil-homme.

Thursday, May 14th.—We dined with Mérimée at St. Germains, in the house in which Louis XIV. was born, now turned into an inn. The situation is exceedingly fine, overlooking the valley of the Seine, with Paris in the distance. The palace is ugly, but imposing from its size and its site. The forest, like all French forests, is a thick grove of closely-planted, drawn-up, middle-aged trees, without any lateral branches, growing out of thick underwood, profitable, but intensely ugly. I never saw a really fine tree in France. After dinner I walked for a couple of hours with Mérimée along the terrace overlooking the valley of the Seine. We talked of the elections and of the attempts at opposition.

Mérimée.—The Emperor is far more liberal than his 'entourage.' They care only for themselves and for the fortunes which they have amassed or are amassing. He cares for France and for his dynasty, and he has too much sense to believe that the country will permanently submit to such a mockery of a Constitution as this. We must have a real Constitution, or we shall take for the third time the desperate plunge into a Republic. But I think him quite right in excluding from the Corps Législatif the Republican party, the party that is resolved that no form of Monarchy shall work well, and which enters the Government for the express, or rather for the concealed, purpose of discrediting it.

Senior.—No one is better fitted to see through and to appreciate such a game, for he played it himself during the whole of his Presidency.

Mérimée.—It has been played from 1789 up to 1852. The five years of comparative tranquillity which we have enjoyed since the coup d'état are mainly owing to the absence of such intriguers from our governing bodies. I trust that we shall continue to exclude them. This is the only use of the oath. The misfortune is, that those whom it repels are the best of their kind. 'Du reste,' considering my age, and that I probably have not above twenty years before me, I ought not perhaps to amuse myself with the vision that *I* shall live to see anything permanent in France. I believe that we are too enlightened to submit permanently to a despotism, and every other form of government seems to require what we have lost, an aristocracy.

Senior.—What are your expectations as to Spain ?

Mérimée.—Not much more sanguine than as to France. The Queen is utterly without influence, worse than without influence; she is hated, worse than hated—she is despised. She will not be allowed to reign much longer, or to be succeeded by her son. Montemolin is feared as an enemy by three-fourths of the people, and Montpensier is hated as a Frenchman. His conduct too, as a Spaniard, is exceedingly offensive. He visits his estates, throws farms together, raises his rents, turns out bad tenants, in short, he is an improving landlord. Such a man is as obnoxious in Spain as he would have been in Ireland before the famine. A Spanish grandee never raises his rents, never interferes with his tenants, in fact, never goes near his estates. The Duke of Ossuna has a whole territory in Andalusia; he has never crossed the Sierra Morena. His father never did so, nor his grandfather, nor his great-grandfather. The Duke of Medina Sidonia's rental is called 13,000,000 of francs, about 500,000*l.* a year. He would be distressed by an unexpected demand for 100*l.* There never was so unaristocratic an aristocracy at that of Spain. They live and talk and jest with their inferiors, without apparently any consciousness that they *are* inferiors. The chief advantage of the grandee over his household is, that he has a little more trouble. His servants treat his house, and his tenants treat his lands as if they were their own. They live there, marry there, breed there, and are much more difficult of extirpation than rabbits from a warren. The Countess ——— has a nominal income of about 100,000 francs a year. With that, one would suppose, that in so cheap a country as Spain, she would be rich. But, in the first place, she has two houses in Madrid, one for herself, the other for her business, her 'chancellerie.' Her own house is a large one, and it swarms with old servants, and the children and grandchildren of old servants. Then she has her *contador*, who receives all her income; he has 6000 francs a year. Her house-steward has as much; the land-stewards of her different estates have each their salary, and, what is worse, their percentage. At least 50,000 francs a year goes in paying for services which in France might be obtained for 4000 or 5000. Out of the other half of her income she has to keep up her establishments in Madrid and in the country. You may easily believe that she is really poorer than any of her servants. All this carelessness and waste, though they may be unfavourable to the power of the Spanish aristocracy, give it popularity. Their persons, their properties, and their titles have been safe during these fifty years of revolutions.

Senior.—Would France tolerate a Republic in Spain? Would not the events of 1821 be repeated?

Mérimée.—No; at least if the crisis occur, as it probably will, during the reign of Celui-ci. I had a long conversation with him on my last return from Spain. When I talked of the fall of Isabella and the succession of the Duchess of Montpensier his eye glistened, but it resumed its usual calm fixedness when I described the unpopularity of the Bourbons and the probability of a Republic. The example of a Republic, as the Spaniards would manage it, will be rather a warning than a temptation to France.

Senior.—Will they be able to manage one at all?

Mérimée.—Yes, by means of their municipal and provincial institutions. Our Republics fail because our centralization has deprived us of the habit, and therefore the power, of self-government. What we call a Republic is merely exchanging the despotism of the Tuileries for the despotism of the Hôtel de Ville. Spain is less centralized than even England; every province, every town, every village has its aristocracy, its democracy, its representative assembly, its local pride and patriotism, and provides roughly enough for its own administration. If her neighbours will let her alone she will naturally crystallize into an aggregate of municipalities like Switzerland, under the nominal sovereignty of a Cortes at Madrid; she will have no army, no fleet, no railroads, except those which are made for her during the Monarchy, no trade, no colonies, no influence in Europe; she will be weak, obscure, quiet, and prosperous.

Senior.—And in such a state of prosperity you think that she will be a warning to France?

Mérimée.—Certainly. France would not pay that price for the utmost prosperity which the most sanguine Utopian could imagine; she would no more consent to it than you would consent to change places with an old woman at an apple-stall, though you might be convinced that it would increase your happiness.

We left Paris on the following day.

1858.

[MR. SENIOR spent the winter of 1857-58 in Turkey and Greece,* and reached Paris, on his return, on the 3rd of March. A most important event had taken place six weeks before—the 'Attentat.'

Louis Napoleon had passed many years of his early life in Italy; he belonged to the *Carbonari*, and was bound by their laws to help them. As years went on, and nothing was done, they became impatient, and Orsini and four others attempted to assassinate the Emperor by throwing bombs under his carriage as he passed with the Empress on his way to the opera on the 14th of January. This was called the *attentat*, and it produced a great change in the feelings of France towards this country. As some of the conspirators had resided here we were accused of encouraging conspiracy and harbouring assassins, and the colonels of the French army addressed congratulatory letters to the Emperor which bristled with offensive remarks concerning England and awoke a corresponding indignation in our country. Although the Emperor had shown much courage at the time, his nerves were severely shaken by the attentat, and the result was a stringent law of public safety, or 'loi des suspects,' as it was sometimes called, of which the principal clauses were:

1. Punishing with five years' imprisonment every one publicly exciting (but without success) the breach of the

---

* He afterwards published an account of his travels ('A Journal kept in Turkey and Greece,' Longmans, 1859), translated under the name of 'Questions Orientales,' A new edition appeared last year. —ED.

eighty-seventh and eighty-eighth articles of the present code.

2. Punishing with two years' imprisonment any one 'qui, dans le but de troubler la paix publique, ou d'exciter à la haine ou au mépris du Gouvernement de l'Empereur, a pratiqué des manœuvres ou entretenu des intelligences, soit à l'intérieur soit à l'extérieur.'

5. Every person convicted of *any* crime punished by this law may be expulsé, interné, or transported to Algeria.

7. Any person who has been convicted, or interné, or expulsé, or transported, with reference to the events of May or June 1848, June 1849, or December 1851, 'et que des faits graves signalent de nouveau comme dangereux,' may be interné, expulsé, or transported to Algeria.

10. The Minister of the Interior is to put this law into execution, on the advice of the prefect, the general in command of the district, and the Procureur-Général.

To be interné is to be required to reside in a place fixed by Government, under the surveillance of the police; it is a sort of imprisonment, mild when inflicted on the rich but ruinous to those depending on a trade. An interné is not lodged or fed; if he cannot support himself in a strange place he must beg or starve.—ED.]

Paris, Wednesday, March 3rd.—The first person that I saw was Cousin.

Cousin.—I wish to devote what remains of my life, as I have all of it that has passed, to two subjects, philosophy and the political and literary history and biography of the seventeenth century. The first is my business, the second my amusement; but the dreadful state of public affairs is always, against my will, occupying my thoughts. You find the horizon far darker than when you left us last year.

Senior.—When I first heard of the 'attentat' I thought

that sympathy for the frightful dangers which he and the Empress had escaped as yet, but were still exposed to, and admiration of their calmness and courage would have given them some popularity.

Cousin.—So I expected, and so it was for the first three days; but what we took for calmness was stupefaction. He thinks slowly; his first feeling seems to have been delight at his escape; his answer to Morny and his address to the Corps Législatif were admirable. Gradually, however, anger and terror got possession of his mind; the people about him—Troplong, Baroche, and Morny—whose whole fortunes are bound up with his, and who think about nothing but their fortunes, were still more frightened and still more enraged; they were in the terrible state of people who think that they must do something and do not know what to do; they proposed to him to please the army by letting it insult England; at the same time to erect revolutionary tribunals, and place all whom they knew or suspected to be *his* enemies or *their* enemies at their mercy.

Senior.—We suppose in England that he still adheres to our alliance; that the military addresses were inserted in the *Moniteur* by mistake or negligence, and that Walewski was ordered to be conciliatory.

Cousin.—I have not the least doubt that he adheres to your alliance, and I think it probable that Walewski was ordered to be conciliatory, and indeed intended to be so, but is too stupid and too bad a writer to see the construction to which his despatch was open; and, in fact, the mischief produced by the despatch was your doing. Lord Clarendon suggested to Persigny that it might do harm. Persigny answered that in that case it might be well to withdraw it. While this was under consideration Lord Palmerston threw it on the table of the House of Commons. But as to the military addresses, they were inserted in the *Moniteur* for four successive days. From the very first day they disgusted and alarmed us. It was not through mistake or negligence that their insertion was continued day after day. Perhaps he thought that you would not notice them, perhaps that you would swallow them. He and those around him mutually excited one another, until they lost their heads, and did not see all, or indeed any, of the consequences of their acts. The law as first proposed shows this. Ten years' imprisonment in irons was its slightest punishment. Its penalties affected all who by writings, or even by words, should express disapprobation of the present Government, or who should maintain any correspondence with the Bourbons. The Council of State rejected the first draught. The Emperor himself saw the iniquity of subjecting to transportation all who had, for any reason, right or wrong, been required to leave France in 1851. 'What,' he said, 'I called Thiers, a year ago, 'illustre et national;' and am I now to put him 'hors la loi?'' So the law was modified, and assumed its present form. Even in that form it had great difficulty in passing through the Conscil d'Etat. All the Conseillers Extraordinaires, who have never been accustomed to vote, were summoned. Six ministers attended, and after all it was carried by a majority of only four—thirty-one to twenty-seven. In the real Conseil d'Etat there was a majority against it. Michel Chevalier behaved exceedingly well. It is said that his exertions in opposition to the law, and his grief at its passing, aggravated a disease of the heart, under which he has been suffering for some time, and which has forced him to leave Paris. General MacMahon opposed it in the Senate. Public opinion has for some time pointed him out as the next Marshal. Vaillant heard of his intention, and remonstrated. 'You are going,' he said, 'to deprive yourself of the bâton. Stay away.' But MacMahon not only voted but spoke against it at great length: the speech is unreported. The law has created innumerable enemies. Two thousand persons have been already arrested. No one feels safe when an *ex post facto* law may send him without trial to Algeria.

I spent the evening at Duvergier's. Montalembert came up to me in great spirits.

Montalembert.—At length one can read an English newspaper; at length you have found out the composition of the idol that you have been adoring. You invented for yourself a god, with courage, and calmness, and moderation, and wisdom; the friend of England; the saviour of France, who was gradually to restore to us as much liberty as you think that we deserve. See what your god has turned out in the presence of a new form of danger. What has become of his sang froid, or of his moderation, or of his intelligence? More corruption, more violence, more injustice, more threats, are his only resources. He has only one weapon, intimidation. He has tried it at home; he has tried it abroad. He has threatened the Pope, and Naples, and Belgium, and Austria, and Piedmont, and at last he ventures to threaten England. Not one of his menaces has been effectual; not one has been followed by any act on his part or, except in your case, on the part of those whom he has threatened. You have given him a rude lesson; but he will not profit by it. He will go on compressing the gas until it explodes.

Saturday, March 6th.—I breakfasted with Mérimée. He confirms what I hear from everybody, that the Emperor's conduct for the first two or three days after the attack was calm and courageous. He drove the Empress along the Boulevards on the 15th with only one attendant.

Mérimée.—The people about him excited and frightened him, and impelled him to the unfortunate steps which he has taken. I had a long conversation with the Empress on Monday last. I found her calm and resigned, but convinced that she and the Emperor will perish by violence. You know that in a certain class of Parisian society there is great sympathy for Orsini. He is a gentleman, and brave, and young, and handsome, and an enthusiast. The Empress is an enthusiast too; she has a vivid imagination, which she rather encourages than checks. She is bent now on obtaining Orsini's pardon, not from fear, for she sees too clearly that neither his pardon nor his execution will influence the Italian conspirators. She knows that they wish to destroy the Emperor, because they think his life an obstacle. But she admires Orsini. She sympathises with his devotion, and, as one of the persons whose life was aimed at, she thinks that she has a right to forgive. The Emperor himself is said to lean towards a pardon; the ministers are opposed to it. After the execution of Pianori, who attempted the life of only the Emperor, to pardon those who have killed and wounded one hundred and fifty people would irritate the Parisians, and perhaps would be attributed to fear. It is one of the faults of Sovereigns who have risen from the ranks that they think too much about public opinion. Born Kings and Queens have been accustomed all their lives to be talked about, and are indifferent to it. They are not driven out of their course by their fears or their hopes of what will be said about them. A man who, after having passed forty years in obscurity, suddenly becomes the centre of observation, who finds all the newspapers of all Europe commenting on what has been done, and speculating on what he will do, is stunned and bewildered by the hubbub of praise and blame, of encouragement and threats, which rises all round him. He is like the princes in the 'Mille et une Nuits,' who attempted to scale the mountain of the talking bird, and were driven out of their path by no tangible object, but merely by the voices which assailed them on every side. No one suffers under this misdirecting influence more than the Emperor. He is morbidly sensitive to the gossip of the salons of Paris and of London. He glances over as many newspapers as he can find time for—Italian, English, Belgian, as well as French—and there is no doubt that much of what he reads worries or enrages him, or alarms him. His wish to pardon Orsini may arise from a desire to conciliate the Italians or the Republicans, or from his old relations with Orsini's father, or from his natural kindness of disposition. I do not believe that even yet his mind has recovered its perfect composure. But you need not fear a breach of the alliance; he knows too well its value. He was very angry with Morny's speech.

Senior.—How do you account for Morny's dislike of England?

Mérimée.—It began by his resentment against the English papers, which accused him of having made a fortune by abusing his influence and his information. It was encouraged by his embassy to St. Petersburg, where he fell in with an anti-English party; and it was completed by his marriage with a Russian.

Senior.—What is the history of Billault's disgrace?

Mérimée.—A Minister of the Interior, whose master is assailed by conspirators, has a difficult part to play. If he reports all that he hears he must often tease his chief by stories which turn out to be false. If he tells only what he has ascertained to be true he may conceal what ought to have been told, or delay his communication until the risk has been run. Billault belongs to the sanguine and sceptical class. He tells only a portion of what he hears. While the Emperor was calm and confident this suited him; but in his present state of mind he is fidgety and anxious. He wishes to know everything. One morning, without any warning, he told Billault that he wished him to replace Turgot, who is dying at Madrid. Billault ventured to represent that he knew nothing of diplomacy. The Emperor has taken up his uncle's fancy that he has la main heureuse, that any one whom he selects soon becomes fit for his office, and he insisted. Billault still refused, and has consequently been turned out altogether. But he has made his fortune.

Senior.—Do you agree with those who think that the conspiracy was purely Italian?

Mérimée.—No; I think that it was European. I believe that there were more French than Italians among its organisers, though Italians, who are more secret and more resolute, were chosen for the execution. The Rouge party in France was warned in the beginning of February that something would happen on the 14th or the 15th.

I dined with L——, and met Commandant Blanchard. He belongs to the Ministry of the Interior, and corresponds with the gendarmerie.

Blanchard.—Their reports are interesting and amusing; they are intended to reflect public opinion on every subject. At first they used to alarm me, but one gets callous to the repeated denunciations of hostilities and plots. I was employed on them to-day from seven in the morning till five in the evening.

Senior.—Do you believe that the last plot was chiefly French or Italian?

Blanchard.—French. In more than thirty departments notice was given to the Rouges that some great event would happen on the 14th or 15th of February. In the Nièvre bands of peasants and of workmen from the ironworks collected, and were evidently intending to plunder Nevers and Cosnes.

Senior.—What was the number of the arrests made under the new law of public safety?

Blanchard.—I cannot at present tell you the precise number; but the principle on which they were made will enable you to guess it. That principle was numerical. Orders were sent to each prefect to arrest a specified number of persons. The choice was left to himself; the number alone was prescribed; it varied from twenty, the maximum, which was that of the Nièvre, to four, which was the minimum. The average perhaps was six, which gives about five hundred for the departments. The number in Paris was about one hundred. I shall not have the complete returns until next week.

Senior.—I thought that the object was to seize the most dangerous persons?

Blanchard.—No; the principal object was to intimidate. The number therefore of arrests prescribed was proportioned to the general spirit of the department. The selection alone was left to the prefect. Different prefects interpreted the order differently. Some understood it to be confined to the persons defined by the seventh clause, and arrested only those who had been condemned or expulsés with relation to the events of 1848, 1849, and 1851. Others took the persons, whoever they might be, whom they thought the most dangerous. These persons, about one hundred and fifty in number, will be sent to the tribunals and tried.

Senior.—For what?

Blanchard.—The prefect who arrested them of course will easily find matter of accusation against them.

Senior.—The others will be sent across the frontier with passports?

Blanchard.—Certainly.

Senior.—And how will they be described in the passports? As good men, for whom you ask the kindness and protection of foreign Governments?

Blanchard.—I have not read the passports, but I suppose that they will be in the usual form.

Senior.—And do you expect us to look after them?

Blanchard.—We hope that you will exercise over them a proper surveillance.

Senior.—It is a vain hope. We surveille nobody except ticket-of-leave men. To what classes do the persons arrested principally belong?

Blanchard.—In Paris they are chiefly the higher workmen. In the provinces they are the avoués, the notaires, the avocats, the doctors—I am not sure that *they* are not the most disaffected classes, certainly they are the classes who have most influence, and who can most easily conspire. If the police of a country town were to observe that the house of a rentier or of a shopkeeper was frequented by suspected or suspicious-looking men, they would make inquiries, and might obtain a clue to what was going on; but the doors of a notaire or of a doctor must always be open. His visitors pass for clients or patients. As I mentioned before, the great object of these arrests is to intimidate. The expulsion of one avocat or notaire is more notorious, and spreads greater alarm than that of twenty shopkeepers or propriétaires.

Senior.—But the expulsion of such men must be their ruin. A workman can get his living anywhere; everybody wants shoes or coats. There is no demand for French law out of France; the avocat or the avoué must starve.

Blanchard.—Such measures are a painful necessity.

We talked of the conspirators.

Blanchard.—We are much afraid of the 16th of March; it is the anniversary of the birth of the Prince Impérial. If the execution does not take place before that day, the Emperor may take advantage of it to overrule his ministers and pardon Orsini. We know that he is bent on doing so.

Senior.—How is the publication of Orsini's letter accounted for?

L.—I account for nothing that has happened since the attentat. Of course the Italians will distribute it by millions. A letter published by the Emperor's consent, urging him to drive the Austrians out of Italy, is no slight matter. Hübner, I know, has already asked for an explanation of it. It is said also that Bourqueney has gone too far at Vienna. Austria, too, complains that with respect to the Principalities, we who have no interest in the matter are violently opposing her, who has a deep interest in it. Altogether our relations with her are in a disagreeable state, and will become still more so if Orsini be pardoned.

We talked of the exiled generals, and of Bedeau's and Changarnier's refusal to return.

L.—Bedeau put himself into the hands of Changarnier. Drouyn de Lhuys was anxious to recall them all at the beginning of the war. He drew up the decree. 'Considering,' it said, 'that when the country is engaged in war, all party spirit ought to cease, considering that absence from France during war is a punishment which the generals have not deserved, Generals Changarnier, Bedeau, and Lamoricière are recalled to France.' But he was overruled.

Senior.—Did Vaillant agree with Drouyn de Lhuys?

L.—Certainly. He was at that time, as he is now, 'censé' to be too busy to be spoken with. I heard that Drouyn de Lhuys broke the 'consigne,' penetrated into his penetralia, and found him in his garden, watering his camellias. He entered warmly into the scheme, not only because he thought it right as respects the generals, but also because he thought it useful to the Emperor. Whether they accepted or refused, the generals would have ceased to be dangerous.

Sunday, March 7th.—Rémusat called on me.

Rémusat.—Louis Napoleon's conduct on this occasion has disappointed his friends and his enemies. We all gave him credit for coolness, courage, prudence, and temper. He showed them during the first three days, and then they deserted him. It was lucky for Pietri that he saw the Emperor before he lost his calmness. Pietri had received information that something was brewing. The warning was so serious that he advised the Emperor not to go to the opera that evening. The Empress was consulted. She wished to go; so they disregarded that warning, as they had disregarded similar ones a hundred times before. Pietri himself seems afterwards to have disbelieved the danger, for he dined out. The summons sent to him immediately on the attentat did not find him for some time. The Emperor at first received him roughly. 'Retournez,' he said, 'à vos plaisirs. Votre police m'obsède et ne me protège pas.' This, however, was a good sign. He is most formidable when he is kind. Since that time he has never reproached Pietri. Billault, whom he treated at first affectionately and allowed to bring forward his measures, has been the sacrifice. I hear from good authority that even now 'son esprit n'est pas dans son assiette naturelle.' He who was so silent and so self-confident now talks to everybody, asks everybody's advice, and is governed by the last speaker. The whole people of Paris and the educated classes throughout France have lost their confidence in him. The army is indifferent to him. It would like war, and the officers look to him for promotion, and will sign any addresses to get it, but it has no sympathy with him. It despises his affectation of military skill. His only friends are the peasants and the priests. His connexion with the Church is perhaps his greatest difficulty. It renders it impossible for him to alter his Italian policy. He cannot desert the Pope, and he cannot support him and break with Austria. He would give anything to pardon Orsini, but I do not think that he can venture it. It would offend too much the Parisians.

Senior.—I am told that Orsini is popular in Paris?

Rémusat.—Not popular, but he excites interest, as everybody does that is notorious. The young ladies cannot bear that so handsome a head should fall. The Empress has pleased us by her exertions for him. She alone has gained by all that has passed. Her courage, her kindness, her endeavours to save those who tried such frightful means to destroy her; and pity for the dangers to which so delicate, so charming, so fragile a being is exposed, have raised a sort of halo round her. But conduct which is admired in a woman deeply offends us in the Emperor. We think that it shows weakness, perhaps cowardice and indifference, to the sufferings of the one hundred and fifty people whom Orsini sacrificed.

Rémusat was followed by C——.

Senior.—What is the history of the appointment of Espinasse as Minister of the Interior?

C.—It is one of the odd freaks which show the disorder of our master's mind. Espinasse in 1851 was colonel of one of the regiments forming the garrison of Paris. They took their turns in mounting guard over the Assembly. Espinasse came to an understanding with Louis Napoleon in or about October, some weeks before the day on which it was the turn of his regiment to protect the Assembly. Louis Napoleon delayed the coup d'état until that day. He was anxious that Generals Le Flô and Baze, the questors, who resided and slept in the palace of the Assembly, should be arrested. To insure this, Espinasse, who was an old friend and comrade of Le Flô's, asked him whether he had secured the means of escape in the event of a revolutionary force seizing the palace. Le Flô showed him a private staircase leading from his bedroom to the garden and the quai, by which in such circumstances he and Baze intended to retreat. About five in the morning of the 2nd of December Espinasse proceeded to the palace, took the command of the regiment from the lieutenant-colonel, and told the officers and men that he had been ordered by the President to perform a special service. There was no opposition. He stationed men in the garden, at the exit of the private staircase, and proceeded to the bedrooms of Le Flô and Baze. They fled by the staircase, and of course were taken. Le Flô was brought before Espinasse in a state of frenzy. He reviled him, would have struck him if he had not been restrained, and actually spat in his face. Espinasse bore it with perfect tranquillity, and sent the two questors off to Mazas. He then proceeded to make the other arrests which were prescribed to him as the most urgent, such as those of Bedeau, Lamoricière, Changarnier, Cavaignac, and Charras, and to close the avenues to the palace. The representatives, excluded from their own hall, met at the Mairie of the tenth arrondissement, where they decreed the déchéance of Louis Napoleon. Espinasse and his soldiers appeared at the door. The President of the Assembly, Bénoit d'Azy, read to them the decree. Espinasse hesitated; sent to the Elysée for orders; received them; ordered the President and the Vice-President to be collared, and dragged them, followed by the rest of the Assembly, to the courtyard of the barracks on the Quai d'Orsay. Of course he was made general and promoted in the Legion of Honour, and has been a favourite ever since; but no one expected anything so grotesque as to see him Minister of the Interior.

Ferdinand Barrot is at the head of a hospital which the Emperor has founded at Vincennes. It is not yet endowed, so that the Minister of the Interior has to provide the funds. Barrot called on Espinasse. Espinasse asked him if he was related to Odillon Barrot. 'Yes,' said Ferdinand, 'I am his brother.' 'And what else do you do?' said Espinasse. 'Not much,' answered Barrot, 'since I was Minister of the Interior.' 'Oh,' said Espinasse, 'you were Minister of the Interior! I am delighted to see you. Sit down and let us have a talk, for you can tell me something about my office. I know nothing. I attend to the conspirators and the arrests, my secretary-general does everything else. He is very clever; but I am forced to trust him so blindly that I am sometimes afraid that he may get me into a scrape. Tell me what you want, and how to do it; or rather do it for me, for I am totally unacquainted with civil matters.'

Experiments have been made as to the inflammability of the bombs. They were thrown on a wooden floor, and against plate-glass, and exploded; but flung on a carpet, on cushions, and against wire-gauze, they did not kindle. All the passages and rooms will now be thickly matted and carpeted. The houses in the Rue de Rivoli, opposite to the Carrousel, have been bought, lest anything should be flung from the windows on the Emperor's carriage. That which he used on the night of the attentat was one of Louis Philippe's, made of wrought-iron. It is supposed to have contributed to his escape.

Among the effects which the attentat seems to have produced in our master's character is a readiness to submit to take precautions. Formerly he relied on his star. When his ministers talked to him of danger, he used to answer that he had a mission, and that until he had executed it his life was safe. Now the events of the 14th of January unquestionably favour this theory. If Pieri had thrown his bomb, and Orsini his second, they could scarcely have failed. Perhaps there was only one police-officer in Paris to whom Pieri was known, and he met that man face to face under a gas-light. At the same instant Orsini was blinded by a splinter from his own weapon, and thus the two last bombs were unexploded. This does look like the work of a special protecting Providence, but his faith in such a Providence seems to be weakened. When he was going to Lady Cowley's ball he had the road through the Champs Elysée, from the Tuileries to the garden door of the embassy, kept clear. There was a line of troops on each side, who allowed no one to pass. Instead of taking that road, he drove at a gallop down the Rue de Rivoli, and entered by the Rue Faubourg St. Honoré. He told Lady Cowley that it had been thought necessary that about twenty officers of police should attend her ball. 'They are very well dressed,' he said; 'many wear ribbons and crosses, but you will distinguish them by their silence. They know nobody, and they will speak to no one.'

Monday, March 8th.—I breakfasted with the Duc de Broglie. Only the family were there, including M. Doudan, the Prince's former tutor, who, indeed, makes a part of it. They affected to wonder at my thinking of returning to Paris, but promised that if Mrs. Senior and I were sent to Verdun they would give us good letters of introduction.

They talked about our late change of Ministry, and expressed a fear that on the return of a Liberal Government Lord Lansdowne might claim the privilege of age, and prefer the rôle of an independent observer to that of a member of the Cabinet. This led us to talk of Bowood, and from Bowood we went to Bentham. The Duke had never seen his Bowood correspondence; indeed, he seemed to be little acquainted with his works. The Prince knew more of them, but admitted that he had not studied them accurately.

Prince de Broglie.—There are valuable hints in them, as there must be in the works of a man of diligence and originality, but they scarcely repay the labour of mastering a system based on an error.

Senior.—Do you reject then utility as the foundation of morals?

Prince de Broglie.—Certainly I do. It is generally rejected in France.

Senior.—And what do you substitute?

Prince de Broglie.—Our innate feelings of right and wrong.

Duc de Broglie.—I remember a conversation at Coppet, which lasted for one or two days, between Ricardo and Dumont, as to Bentham's Political Economy. Dumont produced many manuscripts of Bentham's on that subject. There were few of his doctrines to which Ricardo did not object, and, as it seemed to me, victoriously.

Senior.—When I was drawing up the report on the Amendment of the Poor Laws I consulted Bentham's manuscripts on pauperism. I derived from them very valuable suggestions. On that portion of political economy his views were sound at a time when some of our ablest men—Pitt, for instance, and Whitbread—were thoroughly wrong.

I spent the evening at Madame Mohl's. I spoke of the unpopularity, or worse than unpopularity, into which Louis Napoleon seemed to have fallen as far as I could judge from the conversation of the few people whom I had seen.

Mohl.—It is much greater in the class of society which you do *not* see. The ouvriers have been principally struck at. They were already angry at the high price of apartments and of food. Like all uneducated persons, they exaggerate the power of a Government, and think that the Emperor could give them cheap lodgings and bread and wine if he liked. Instead of doing so, he inflicts imprisonment and banishment on persons who, perhaps, were 'émeutiers' in 1848, but have been for years well-conducted 'pères de famille.' The number so treated is, of course, enormously exaggerated. These arrests, and the law which has sanctioned them, have produced, as it was intended that they should do, much fear; but they have excited more irritation. I do not think that he was ever before so unpopular among the working classes in Paris. The natural effects of that unpopularity will not be prevented by compression. He is compressing an elastic gas. Some day the resisting force will be greater than the compressing force, and then woe to those who are near to the explosion.

Tuesday, March 9th.—I breakfasted with Guizot.

Guizot.—What has just taken place with you and with us shows the disadvantages of each form of monarchical Government. No despotic Sovereign would have dismissed Lord Palmerston.* No constitutional Sovereign could retain Walewski or Morny. The balance is in favour of Constitutionalism. The retention of a bad minister is yet more dangerous than the dismissal of a good one. Palmerston, even assuming him to have been a good minister, may

---

* Lord Palmerston resigned in February, in consequence of a defeat in Parliament on the Conspiracy to Murder Bill. Lord Derby became Prime Minister in his stead.—ED.

have a good successor; but it is certain that Walewski will be mischievous as long as he is retained. As for Palmerston his fate is not an uncommon one. After having committed absurdities for twenty years with impunity, he is upset for having behaved once in his life with prudence and temper. A man ought to be consistent. If bullying and chicane are his natural rôle, he should keep to them. If he deviates into moderation and good sense, he is lost.

I called on Madame ——.

Madame ——.*—You can have no conception, unless you stay here for a couple of months, and mix in every sort of society, of the exasperation of the French against England. The colonels expressed very mildly the national feeling.

Senior.—It is hard that we should be unpopular both with the oppressor and the oppressed. Formerly I was told that they hated us for supporting him; now you tell me that they hate us for not sufficiently protecting him.

Madame ——.—That is only the pretext. The real cause of their hatred is that we have roused their strongest passions —envy and jealousy. As long as we yielded to them the laurels of the Crimea they were our best friends; 'Les bons Anglais,' they said, are not a military nation, and they have the good sense to confess it, but they are 'de braves gens,' and pay well. Our success in India has shown them that we are a nation, not merely of soldiers, but of heroes. They feel that we have done what they could not have done. And until we have some great reverse they will not forgive us. You have read the wonderful speech of Jules Favre?

Senior.—It is a good speech; but I scarcely call it wonderful.

Madame ——.—You must recollect in the first place the

---

* An English lady.—ED.

difficulties under which it was made. Favre had to defend a man whose guilt was not only notorious, but confessed. The advocates for the other prisoners tried to explain away the evidence, or to excite commiseration. Of course they failed lamentably. Favre, like a man of genius and of courage, threw away the personal interests of his client. He gave up to the Court Orsini's head, and then pleaded the cause of Italy. The under-current which runs through the whole of it is the identification of Orsini with Louis Napoleon, as conspirators for the same object, as using the same instruments, as equally tenacious of their purposes, and equally unscrupulous as to their means. I was present during the whole trial. It was conducted with a fairness and moderation unusual in France. I tried to compute the number of spectators, and reckoned them at about six hundred, perhaps the élite of the Parisian world. During the first days they listened in silence, but the speeches of Chaix d'Est-Ange (the Procureur-Général) and of Favre produced, on four different occasions, bursts of applause, which Langlet, the President of the Court, was unable to repress.

Senior.—What could there have been in the speech of Chaix d'Est-Ange to provoke applause?

Madame ———.—A passage of which he little perceived the tendency. He had been reproaching Orsini for having broken the oath, never to conspire again, which he took on his release in 1846.

'Je sais,' said Chaix d'Est-Ange, 'qu'il y a des hommes, une secte politique, qui pactise avec la conscience, qui apporte au serment, à la foi jurée, des restrictions mentales, mais je sais que tout homme loyal, tout homme de cœur repousse ces misérables transactions, et qu'il tient le parjure pour un acte immoral et honteux.' These words were followed by thunders of applause. Poor Chaix d'Est-Ange looked bewildered as if he did not know that he had been so eloquent.

Jules Favre's blows were intentional. 'S'il était,' he said, 'une nation assez malheureuse pour tomber entre les mains d'un despote, ce ne serait pas le poignard qui briserait ses chaînes. Dieu, qui les compte, sait les heures des despotes ; Il leur réserve des catastrophes plus inévitables que les machines des conspirateurs.' This procured a general murmur and cries of ' Bien, très-bien !'

Another general whisper followed Favre's allusion to the Roman insurrection of 1831 in which 'un des principaux conjurés tomba sous les balles des sbires de l'autorité' —this having been the insurrection in which Orsini the father, Louis Napoleon, and his brother took part, and the brother was killed. The last words, too, were much applauded. 'Aujourd'hui Orsini va mourir. Dieu qui est au-dessus de nous ; Dieu, devant qui comparaissent les accusés et leurs juges ; Dieu qui nous jugera tous ; Dieu qui mesurera l'étendue de nos fautes ; Dieu prononcera sur cet homme, et lui accordera peut-être un pardon que les juges de la terre auront cru impossible.' But the greatest sensation perhaps was produced by the reading of Orsini's letter.

Favre handed it up to the President. Langlet looked at it, as far as we could judge from his countenance, with dismay, which was increased when Favre added, ' I propose to read it, having the permission of him to whom it was addressed.'

The Emperor, as perhaps you know, has always preserved some relations with Favre. It is a part of his policy to coquet with the Republicans. Favre with great difficulty persuaded Orsini to write the letter. He took it immediately to the Emperor. The Emperor altered very slightly one or two passages, and gave it back to Favre with permission to read it. The magistracy are exceedingly angry. They say that such an interference of the Sovereign in the course of a trial, without the consent, or even the knowledge, of the President of the Court is unheard of. Many of them blame Langlet for letting it be read, whatever were the permission.

In the Cour d'Assises the prisoner stands immediately above his advocate. As soon as the sentence had been pronounced, Orsini bent down and repeated to Jules Favre the two last lines of the 9th canto of la Gerusalemme Liberata—

> 'Risorgerò nemico ognor più crudo
> Cenere anco sepolto e spirto ignudo.'

Senior.—What are supposed to have been the motives which induced Louis Napoleon to allow the publication of the letter?

Madame ———.—Many motives are ascribed to him; a wish to conciliate the Italian Republicans, a wish to show magnanimity, perhaps real magnanimity, and a desire to soothe the last days of a man with whose Italian feelings he himself sympathizes, and whose father was his early friend. Then the trial, damaging as it was to him, might have been made still more so. Several early letters of Louis Napoleon were found among the papers seized at Orsini's. It was not certain that others might not exist. Every means that public opinion would allow were used to conciliate the prisoners and their counsel. The impartiality of the trial was ostentatious. But it is difficult to explain any part of Louis Napoleon's conduct since the attentat, or rather after the first three days subsequent to the attentat. Many persons affect to think that he was mad. Others throw the blame of his violence on Troplong and Baroche. The ferocity of the Imperialists is indescribable. I have heard young women exclaim that if a bourreau were wanted they would tender their services. Others lament that Orsini can only be beheaded. If he could be tortured a little, they say, or flogged at the bottom of the scaffold, or broken on the wheel, it might intimidate; Italians do not fear the guillotine.

They think their own lives and fortunes wrapped up in Louis Napoleon's; they would joyfully rush into a war with us, if they thought it a safety-valve; hence their fury when his wish to pardon Orsini is alluded to. It is certain that he is anxious to do so, and the Empress still more so.

[On the next day Mr. Senior ran over to London for a few weeks. He returned to Paris on the 14th April.—ED.]

Friday, April 16th.—I dined and slept at Vaux, Baron Marochetti's château, near Meulan, about fifteen miles from Paris. It was an ancient rendezvous de chasse, given by Louis XI. to Olivier le Daim, and purchased in the early part of the Revolution by Marochetti's father; it stands in a park of forty or fifty acres, sloping down from a wooded hill to the Seine; the architecture of many centuries is recorded in it; the principal gate, with the traces of its drawbridge and portcullis between two large central towers, was probably the work of Olivier le Daim; a wing containing the principal living room is in the taste of Louis XIV.; the kitchens and out-offices, among which are several small circular towers, with loopholes instead of windows, may well belong to the tenth or eleventh century. The temperature was that of early summer. We sat in the park, drinking coffee by moonlight till half-past ten at night.

Marochetti.—The château requires much greater expenditure than I shall venture to bestow on it. We are popular here, though what we do for the people is not half what is done by almost every English squire; still it is so much more than is usually done by a French country gentleman that we have won their hearts; they protected us in 1848 when many neighbouring châteaux were burnt. But I fear that the next revolution will be much fiercer than the last. In 1848 the people had been civilized and instructed by thirty-four years of constitutional rule; there was no hatred, no vengeance, the bulk of the nation was indifferent, and even the revolutionary minority, which surprised the Government, was impelled by selfish passions —vanity, ambition, the desire of money or power—not by malignant ones. Now a fierce indignation is rising among the people; they hate the Government which has oppressed them and deceived them, and has sent thousands to perish under the sun of Africa, and thousands to die in the marshes of Cayenne; they consider all the higher classes as parts, or at least instruments, of the Government. I believe that this château will be among the last that will be burnt, but I scarcely hope that it will escape.

Senior.—You fear, then, a Rouge revolution?

Marochetti.—I not only fear it but I expect it. This régime cannot continue; it has all the oppression of the Empire, without its glory. How the revolution will burst forth, who will be its leaders, what will be their instruments, I will not venture to guess; I only know that it must come, and that it will be destructive, far more destructive than any we have had to suffer.

The park is pretty, but I remarked the absence of fine trees.

Marochetti.—It is impossible to persuade a Frenchman that trees are anything except a source of profit. My intendant values them according to their cubic contents. As soon as my back is turned he finds an excuse to cut down every one which he thinks has reached its maturity for sale; so does every one else. There are more fine trees in Hyde Park and Kensington Gardens than in all France.

Saturday, April 17*th.*—I called in the afternoon on Cousin. I found him grieved and desponding.

Cousin.—My mind is turning over and over the chances of the greatest of calamities, a war with England. I give up all Louis Napoleon's conduct since the attentat; it is senseless; it shows into what follies a new danger and frightened advisers can drive a man of courage, calmness, and good sense, for he has all these qualities. But *you* are not free from blame; Bernard* was as much an assassin as Orsini, though he had not courage enough to throw the bomb; to acquit him against all evidence and to applaud the acquittal is taking a bitter revenge for some silly addresses, an intemperate speech, and an impertinent letter; it shows what value you put on the alliance; it shows the strength of English gratitude, if such comparatively slight offences wipe out the remembrance of his fidelity to you during six anxious years. You require all the concessions, and make none. The cup may overflow at last, and *that* I repeat is the fear which torments me. I believe Louis Napoléon to be sincerely anxious for peace, but he may be carried away by the public indignation; he may die; he may be overthrown.

Senior.—Do you think the chances of his overthrow increased?

Cousin.—Certainly. He has lost his prestige, the public reliance on his courage, calmness, and prudence; he has set us a bad example, for he has obviously lost confidence in himself. The institution which France wants more than any other

---

* Bernard had resided in London, where he was tried and acquitted.—ED.

is that of a dictator—a temporary despot, legally appointed
—who can remedy evils which the ordinary authorities cannot
reach. From time to time we have a self-created one;
he cannot depend on our obedience unless he performs the
duties which we expect from him; Celui-ci was submitted
to because we expected him to put down the Rouges; it is
the belief that he stands between us and the Rouge spectre
that has maintained him during the last six years. But it
does not seem that he is delivering us from that spectre;
during the last three months it has been growing and
growing. The greatest proof of our alarm is the general
stagnation of industry and trade; the monetary crisis has
passed, it never was severe; the harvests are promising;
bread is cheap; yet all business is at a stand. A general
distrust of the future disturbs us; the security which was
to have been the price of our liberty is wanting. I believe
that we shall rise and put down our dictator as incompetent, though how or when, or with what ulterior purpose,
I will not venture to guess.

Sunday, April 18*th*.—I passed a couple of hours with
Thiers.

Thiers.—I am grieved and anxious at the state of our
affairs, internally and externally. Internally, the sickness
which did us so much mischief in 1850 and 1851—the
want of confidence—is returning. Every one is trying to
save; but the savings, instead of being employed productively, are hoarded or invested in foreign securities. We
shall not have a commercial crisis like yours, because, there
being no credit, there can be no failures; but there will be
great distress, great indigence, and, among the working
classes, great want of employment. Externally, our relations with Austria are becoming every day worse and worse.
We opposed her, and we were right, on the Danubian

question. We opposed her again, and we were wrong, on that of the Principalities. In a matter in which she has a vital interest and we have none, we have thought fit to join our old enemies against our allies—to take part with Russia against Turkey, England, and Austria.

When poor Lady Ashburton was dying last spring at Passy I used to go to her every day. I met Walewski there, and I wasted once two hours in trying to show to him that he was taking a position which he could not maintain, which he would be forced to abandon disgracefully in the face of Europe. Then Orsini's letters, the first published avowedly by Celui-ci, the second evidently so, in which he is called on to free Italy from the German, are affronts to Austria, almost menaces. With England the differences, though slighter in appearance, are still more serious. The relations between the two countries resemble those between husband and wife; they are so intimate that the least coldness is likely to degenerate into enmity. I believe him to be sincerely anxious to preserve the alliance, and I believe you to be so too. Yet two or three 'maladdresses' might produce a rupture. Now, during the last two years there have been several, and on each side. We were in the wrong about Belgrade, and, as I said before, about the Principalities. You committed, or rather are committing, a fatal mistake about the Suez Canal. I know nothing about the engineering questions; politicians have nothing to do with them; they interest only shareholders. But in declaring that the attempt shall not be made, that Europe and Asia shall be deprived of a great highway in deference to the interests—as we hold, the ill-understood interests—of a single country, we think that you exhibit the faults which most irritate and disgust us, insolence and selfishness. Unless you mix as much as I do with people of every part of Europe you cannot estimate the mischief which your narrow-mindedness is doing to your national reputation. It confirms all that your enemies have long been saying of your selfishness, and makes us treat your affectation of liberality and cosmopolitan sympathies as mere hypocrisy. Then comes Perim. It is the key of the Red Sea. We do not admit the right of any one nation to seize it. If you had done so merely as a precaution against the dangers which you profess to fear from the canal, and had then allowed the canal to be made, we might have acquiesced; but you stop the passage at each end.

Senior.—But you have no real interest in either of these questions. Not three French vessels a year will go through the canal or pass within sight of Perim. You are treating us just as you are treating Austria, opposing us in a matter in which we are deeply concerned and you not at all. We do not interfere with you in Algeria; you ought not to trouble us in India.

Thiers.—It is true that we have little interest in Perim; but the canal is a French enterprise. A Frenchman, a near relation of the Empress, is at its head; the majority of the shareholders will probably be French, and you have seen enough of us to know, strange as the feeling may appear in England, that we are 'passionnés,' and sometimes 'passionnés' for objects not purely selfish, for objects which concern the whole civilized world, and *us* merely as a part of it. Such appears to us to be the Suez Canal. We probably exaggerate its utility. I will not admit that it cannot be made. Everything can be done with money, and money will not be wanting; but when made the tolls may not be sufficient to keep it in repair. It may be a gigantic failure, a magnified Thames tunnel; but we have set our hearts on making the experiment, and it requires all Louis Napoleon's devotion to the alliance, a devotion never more prominently manifested, to restrain us from breaking out and exclaiming that 'coûte que coûte' it shall be tried. And now comes a new series of mutual blunders. There is no doubt that both the mind and body of Louis Napoleon gave way under a new and frightful form of danger; his self-reliance failed; he asked advice, and those about him were still more frightened than he. Frightened people are evil councillors; the only remedies that occurred to them were violence and threats—violence at home; abroad, where violence cannot be used, threats. Billault produced a Bill which outlawed all who had ever been the subjects of any measure of 'sûreté-générale,' that is, all the most eminent political men in France.

Senior.—Is it true that he exclaimed, ' Quoi ! j'ai appellé Thiers illustre et national, et on veut que je le mette hors la loi !'

Thiers.—It is true. When Billault's Bill was proposed to the Conseil d'Etat my name was in everybody's mouth. All this was wretched folly; the threats against you were still worse; but I do not believe that he looked at the addresses or at Walewski's letter, and we know that he disapproved Morny's speech. Putting aside the rashness of menacing England, even if there were good cause of complaint, there was in fact no cause; the presence of the conspirators in England was a geographical, not a political, cause. If they did not conspire in England they would in Belgium, in Holland, in Spain. As for your laws, they are already much more repressive of attacks on foreign Sovereigns than ours are. If an Englishman had thrown Orsini's bomb you could have punished him. If a Frenchman were to go to London and kill Queen Victoria, and return to Paris, we could not even try him. Our laws take no cognisance of what is done out of French territory, except as to a few offences, such as treason or coining, which, though committed abroad, affect us at home.

Senior.—The change which you wished us to make in our laws was not the one which we attempted to make. What you required, and what I am told Persigny enforced almost intemperately, was an Alien Act. We once had such an Act, but it was passed for our own protection, to enable us to send away foreign agitators. It has long expired, and no one proposes to renew it. You wanted us to pass an Alien Act for the protection of foreign Sovereigns, to enable the Government to send away any foreigner to whose presence in our territories a foreign Sovereign objected.

Thiers.—We were fools, or, what is more probable, Persigny was a fool, for making such a proposition. All these were our blunders; your blunders were the not allowing for errors committed under the pressure of terror and anger, the not accepting frankly a frank excuse, the harping month after month on an old provocation. We learn now that Bernard has been acquitted in the teeth of the fullest evidence. Your resentment has so little cooled during the three long months that have passed since Walewski's letter, that twelve men are ready to perjure themselves in order to acquit an assassin; that the crowd applauds their crime, and that the judge by his silence approves it. It is now our turn to be angry. That applause indicated hostility to Louis Napoleon and hostility to France; there was not a man in that crowd who did not know that Bernard was an accomplice in one of the most mischievous, one of the blackest, crimes that has ever disgraced humanity; they applauded his acquittal because they thought it an insult to us. I will not say which is the most to blame in this wretched series of mutual provocations, but you must agree with me that the situation is very formidable. I know that a war with England would be his ruin, and I believe he knows it too. But I no longer rely on his prudence or self-command, still less on that of his entourage. A sudden fit of irritation, perhaps of well-founded irritation, may drive him to take a step from which he may be unable to retreat—to make, for instance, some demand which *you* cannot grant and *he* cannot retract.

Senior.—And what would you advise us to do?

Thiers.—I advise you, as a sincere friend of the alliance, to give up frankly and immediately your senseless irritating opposition to the Suez Canal, keeping Perim as a set-off if you want it. I advise you, as I advise France, to improve your legislation as to crimes committed abroad or against foreign countries. Our mediæval legislation is inconsistent with the present international intercourse. I advise your newspapers to avoid ripping up old sores; but above all I advise you to take care of your army and of your navy, and not to leave the Channel unguarded in order to blockade the ports of Guinea.

Duchâtel called on us in the evening. We talked of Louis Napoleon.

Duchâtel.—Never was so fine a game so utterly ruined. The first effect of the attentat was to give to him the sympathy of every one. For a couple of days he was almost popular in France, and, as I am told, almost idolised in England. He had merely to keep quiet, and these feelings would have continued. But he rewarded the sympathy of England by threats, insults, and abuse; that of France by a law formally, distinctly—in so many words—placing our fortunes and even our lives at the mercy of a secret tribunal consisting of the préfet, the general, and the Crown lawyer of the department. I say our fortunes and our lives, for those sent to Cayenne and to Lambressa are sent to die; those merely internés or expulsés are ruined. What shows more strongly the folly, the madness of his law, is, that it was not necessary even for his purposes. He was already absolute. He could already send to Cayenne or to England any one whom he or any of his creatures disliked or feared. He cannot guillotine—that requires a court and a sentence; he cannot shoot, except on the pretence of an émeute. But par mesure de police, he can imprison, exile, transport—inflict every punishment that is known to our laws short of death. The proof that the new law was unnecessary is that a large proportion, perhaps more than half, of those who have been deportés and expulsés, are not within it. They are men who either were *not* punished in 1848, 1849, or 1851, or who have given *no* subsequent cause of complaint. But they cannot resist; they cannot even protest. We have no *habeas corpus*, no power to oppose any officer of the Government, no appeal, no newspaper even that will tell the story. We are told that the secret societies are spreading, and it is no wonder. Instead of terrifying he has exasperated. As for *you*, we acquit the nation of sympathy with assassination. We do not believe that the jury which perjured itself to save Bernard, or the mob which applauded them, represent the feelings of the nation. But we think your public conduct unfriendly and haughty. The French nation does not require you to pass Alien Bills, or Conspiracy Bills, for the benefit of its tyrant; but it wishes you to exercise your great power and your wide influence with less selfishness and with more moderation.

I hear of fresh plots. A week or two ago twenty-five men were found in possession of a house in the new Boulevard de Sebastopol, under which Louis Napoleon was to pass at the head of the procession on the day that the boulevard was opened. They could not account for their presence there, and have been sent to Cayenne.

Tuesday, April 20th.—The two Guizots, Corcelle, and Lanjuinais breakfasted with us. We talked of the alterations in Paris.

Guizot.—If Celui-ci reigns for ten years longer, old Paris, its buildings as well as its institutions, will have disappeared. The two towns most full of historical recollections were Rome and Paris; and for the same reasons—namely, that more than any other capitals they have been political centres. The history of Rome is the history of Italy. The history of Paris is the history of France. There was not a street that had not been the scene of some important event. The new Rue de Rivoli and Boulevard de Sebastopol, with the vast open spaces which adjoin them, are fine communications, especially for military purposes, but they are hateful to the historian and to the artist. The Boulevard de Sebastopol is my special aversion. It cuts in two the most picturesque and the most beautiful of our districts, the Isle St. Louis.

Senior.—You put me in mind of Cousin, who says Paris 'était une belle ville;' but modern Paris, though less interesting, is a pleasanter residence.

Guizot.—I do not admit even that. The streets of old Paris to be sure were narrow, ill-lighted, and ill-paved, but they were less thronged. Forty years ago the population was not 700,000, now it is 1,400,000. There are twenty carriages and carts now for one that there was then. The Champs Elysées were a grove, now they are streets. We were then all so near one another that everybody walked; now the distances are so great that everybody drives. We then formed one large society, subdivided of course by intimacies, but still with such mutual relations, that every one was known, it resembled in that respect the society of London. No one in London could usurp a title or even a name. The society of Paris now consists of coteries which know nothing of one another; the Faubourg St. Germain is full of false names and false titles; I do not believe that there are forty families in it who really are what they claim to be. Wealth *now* gives distinction. Anybody with a fine apartment and fine dinners and parties can become fashionable; *then* people were valued for their personal merits.

Talleyrand used to say that no one who had not seen the first fifteen years of Louis XVI. knew how happy human life can be. This, indeed, was a period of hope; men lived in the only real utopia, the utopia of the imagination: they enjoyed reforms without sacrifices, because their reforms were all future. Like the Catholic ascetics, they looked forward to an indefinite amount of happiness, but it was to be in this world, and it was to be purchased by no austerities. Their state was that of a religious order, whose rule should be not mortification, but pleasure. All this of course had passed away when I entered the Parisian world in the latter years of the Empire; but a few of those who had adorned the eighteenth century remained. Chateaubriand, Madame de Houdetôt, and Madame de Rumford.

Senior.—Were *you* among the worshippers of Madame de Houdetôt?

Guizot.—Of course I was; I should have been a heretic if I had not been. She turned every head that approached her. Not by her beauty, for though she had a fine figure, and fine hair and hands, her face was positively plain: her complexion was one of those which never could look clean. Madame Geoffrin used to say that she longed to take a wet towel and wash off a little of the worst dirt. Nor was she fluent in conversation: she said little, but the little was admirable, and set in motion more voluble talkers. At the beginning of the winter she invited twenty-five persons to dine with her every Tuesday. No one sent an excuse or announced that he was coming. Sometimes the party consisted of nine or ten, sometimes there were fourteen or fifteen. She knew from experience the average number. If fewer came we collected at the top of the table; if more, a leaf was added. There was a want of earnestness perhaps in that society. No one had any plans of action. Every one hated the despot, but no one proposed to overthrow him. They scrutinised his conduct, they criticised his errors, and at last they came to predict his fall; but they thought much more of the pleasures of society, of taste, of knowledge, and of literature, than they did of politics. They were intelligent, refined epicureans, without passions, or prejudices, or objects, except to amuse and to please, and to be pleased and amused.

I am going to give the English some praise and a little blame. No people have more of the elements of good company, more knowledge, or imagination, or taste, or humour, or wit. But they are too reserved, or too indolent to make the best use of them; they want free trade in ideas, and often substitute words for them. From time to time I have lived in an English country neighbourhood; in every house I ate the same dinner and heard the same conversation.

We talked of Val Richer.

Guizot.—The house was a monastery. When I took possession of it I was taken to an open space in one of the woods, which they told me had always been kept clear, because it was venerated as the place in which many hundred years ago an English saint used to pray. This saint was Thomas à Becket. He passed at Val Richer a few months before he returned to die at Canterbury.

This led the conversation to the Trappists, whose original house is in Normandy.

Corcelle.—I have talked much with the few members of the Order who are allowed to speak. I have often inquired into the cause of their retirement, and very seldom found that it was repentance or grief, or any sudden, or indeed any single event. The motives seemed in general to have been ennui, fatigue, disappointed expectations, and a wish for repose.

Guizot.—Such are among the most frequent causes of suicide, and monastic vows have been called a Christian suicide.

Senior.—A Carthusian, the Fra Dispensatore, with whom I talked for a couple of hours in the Certosa of Pavia, much to the scandal of the lay brother who accompanied me, appeared to regret his suicide, and cast many longing looks at the cheerful external world.

Corcelle.—I never perceived any trace of such feelings; but my opportunities of observation have not been great, as the Trappists and Carthusians with whom I have had an opportunity of conversing have been few, and were a selected portion of their communities.

Senior.—You know the Pope well. Is it true that disappointed love drove him into the Church?

Corcelle.—Perfectly false; from a child he wished to be an ecclesiastic, and delayed doing so only in consequence of his health, which was weak in early youth and gradually strengthened.

Thursday, April 22nd.—Dumon called on us. I asked him about the state of the finances.

Dumon.—I have not been able to see the budget, but I am told that there is a deficit. We are spending nearly twice as much as Napoleon did, though we have not much more than half his territory. The money goes in luxuries, the greatest, that is, the most expensive of those luxuries, being war, or preparations for war.

Senior.—Do you consider the Russian war a luxury?

Dumon.—Certainly I do. What has France got by it, and what has she lost? Two milliards and one hundred and fifty thousand men. I admit that it did Louis Napoleon good while it lasted. Its mischief is seen now that we have to pay for it. He is like a man who spends his capital on his marriage feast and is straightened for years afterwards.

Senior.—I hear that you had a long interview with him the other day to protest against the tax on the transfer of railway shares, and that you produced a strong impression.

Dumon.—He was very kind and said that if the thing had not been done, he would not do it. But he gave us no hope of its being removed. Chasseloup Lobat, one of the deputation, who was once his minister, outstaid us, and talked to him about the state of France. Lobat, as is often the case with persons who have *têtes-à-tête* with Sovereigns, describes himself as having spoken boldly, as having told him that what France wanted was a good foreign policy and a good home administration. 'Louis Napoleon,' he says, 'took it very well.' As to his foreign policy, I do not believe that he has any aggressive intentions. When the military addresses appeared I was frightened, but my Imperialist friends set me at ease. 'What he wishes,' they said, 'is to make each country believe that the other is eager to attack it, and that he stands between it and war.' If we were increasing our navy, I might feel alarmed.

Senior.—But you *are* increasing your navy; you are spending from fifteen millions to seventeen millions a year in building new war steamers, and more than thirty millions a year in altering your old ones.

Dumon.—If that can be proved, it is serious; my impression was that we had neglected our naval arsenals during the Russian war and were now bringing them merely to their normal state. The state of our finances would make a war mischievous, even beyond the average mischief of war. It must be carried on by loans. The utmost addition that we can make to our taxation is to provide for the new interest. Our statesmen are deceived by the constant increase of the indirect taxes. They believe it to be a symptom of increasing wealth. My fear is, that it arises from a diminution of accumulation. Everybody appears to me to be spending all his income, many to be spending more. I can recollect the style in which people of my rank lived thirty years ago, a petit bourgeois would be ashamed of it now. The other day the wife of Count ———, Conseiller d'Etat, informed her husband that she owed to milliners and others 500,000 francs. He sent her to a convent, but he must pay. The example is set from above. What the Emperor does he will not tell us, but the State has an annual deficit. Paris owes a milliard, and is going to borrow 120,000,000 more. All the departments and all the towns are in debt. There is a general feeling that this cannot go on, that it must end in the ruin of many, and in retrenchment by all, and I believe that this feeling occasions the stagnation which you must hear complained of. I do not expect the revenue to increase, or even to be maintained. A diminishing revenue and a war supported by loans would lead to bankruptcy.

Senior.—What is the destination of the one hundred and twenty millions which Paris is to borrow?

Dumon.—It is two-thirds of one hundred and eighty millions which are wanted to carry on the improvements of Paris. Our old, mediæval, picturesque town is to be turned into a St. Petersburg, with long broad streets of pseudo-classical and pseudo-Gothic architecture, full of wind and dust, taking the place of all that was historical in Paris. It was opposed in the Corps Législatif. Haussman, the prefect of the Seine, ventured to attribute the opposition to hostility to the Emperor, a reproach so unexpected, and I must say so undeserved, that the members thought fit to be angry. They invented a formula, and used it whenever he invited any of their body. 'M. A. B., étant membre du Corps Législatif, ne peut pas avoir l'honneur,' &c. &c.

Senior.—Will the loan and the expenditure go on?

Dumon.—Of course they will. In fact they began before the Corps Législatif was consulted. That is the present system, and saves much time. It being known that every law proposed by the Government to the Chamber will pass, it is acted on as soon as it has been introduced. Many hundreds were arrested by virtue of the 'loi des suspects' before it was passed.

Tuesday, April 27th.—Grimblot breakfasted with us. He has been appointed French consul at Monastier, a considerable town in Thessaly, and starts in a couple of days. Few men have relations with so many different parties. He has therefore great opportunities for acquiring information, and he is a calm, impartial judge of its value. He believes Louis Napoleon to be sincerely attached to the English alliance.

Grimblot.—It has been useful to him, and he expects it to be useful to him in future. He is grateful, too, for the hospitality of England when he was an exile, and for his reception in 1855. And though it may be true that he has little moral sense, little perception of what we call right and wrong, he has strong sympathies, strong and permanent friendships, and as quick and lasting a remembrance of benefits as he has of injuries. He is as grateful as he is vindictive. On his return from the opera he sent for all the papers relating to the attempt to destroy Napoleon by the infernal machine, and sat up all night reading them. At seven the next morning he went to the Rue Le Pelletier and looked at the destruction. The horror of the attack, the excitement produced by his sleepless night and by the scene which he saw in the morning, and the terror and rage of those about him, certainly turned his head for a time. He allowed Billault to bring in the ' loi des suspects,' which was an exaggeration of one which had been previously contemplated. I do not believe that he understood it, and it is certain that he was indignant when it was explained to him. I doubt whether he saw the military addresses the first day. Lord Cowley pointed out to Walewski their danger; but after their insertion had been begun it was thought too late to suppress the remainder. I have reason to believe that Walewski saw his own letter to Persigny first in the English papers.

Senior.—Who then wrote it?

Grimblot.—Somebody in his entourage. Louis Napoleon has long, as you know from his celebrated letter to Ney,[*] been in the habit of corresponding directly with his foreign ministers, and in this Government false signatures are common. I know that Walewski himself wrote the excuse. It is said, I believe with truth, that Louis Napoleon announced to Walewski Pelissier's mission, and that Pelissier asked for it, being anxious to re-establish the alliance, and thinking that his long intercourse with the English in the Crimea gave him peculiar means of doing so.

Senior.—Do you believe that Louis Napoleon is looking forward to another war?

Grimblot.—I do. A war is necessary to him in order to regain his prestige, to divert public attention from what is passing at home, and above all to employ and please the army. But it will not be with England; not, however, for want of naval means. ——'s[†] remark that he has no ships

---

* In 1849, approving of the Roman expedition.—ED.
† This refers to a conversation which is not published.—ED.

is a proof of the inattention of even political men to the state of the country. —— lost all interest in public affairs in 1852, and cannot have looked at a budget since, or he would have known that for five years we have been systematically and perseveringly increasing our steam navy; that we have already a formidable one, and that by the end of the year we shall have an enormous one, quite large enough to give us, if concentrated, the command of the Channel, at least for a time. But, as I said before, he likes England. The English alliance is his settled policy, and he does not change his plans. If he attempted an invasion and failed, his ruin would be immediate. If he did not venture to attempt one, the war would be disastrous to our commerce, and in a few months would rouse the Continent against us. He is not desperate enough to risk all on a single throw. His war will be in Italy; that is the country of his sympathies. Italians have at all times access to him by private channels. You know how anxious he was to pardon Orsini.

Senior.—Ought he to have done so?

Grimblot.—I think that he ought. It is clear that punishment does not do good. I will not say that clemency would, but its results could not have been worse than those of severity have been.

Senior.—I am told that the pardon of a man who had killed and wounded one hundred and sixty persons would have disgusted the Parisians.

Grimblot.—I do not believe that the Parisians would have cared much about it. They would have acknowledged that as the person most endangered he had a sort of right to be merciful. Then the deliberate execution of a single man revolts us more than the massacre in the streets of a hundred. On the other hand, the Italians might have accepted Orsini's pardon as an atonement for the past and a promise for the future. Orsini's popularity in Italy is enormous. A friend of mine who passed through Piedmont a few days ago saw his portrait on the walls in the cottages. Louis Napoleon's Italian war must be a revolutionary one. He ought therefore to put himself early at the head of the revolutionary party.

Senior.—If his war is to be in Italy, why is he building ships?

Grimblot.—They would be useful in an Italian war. Italy is almost an island. They may be intended, too, to menace you if you interfere against him.

Senior.—Will he make his war soon?

Grimblot.—There are grounds for believing that he will and for believing that he will not. His temper is procrastinating. He resolves, and what he has resolved he executes; but the interval between the resolution and the execution is often long. We know that he had decided on the coup d'état in January, 1849; he did not execute it until December, 1851. On the other hand, the motives to an early war are strong. Public opinion is turning against him; the attentats are likely to be repeated; even in the Corps Législatif an opposition is springing up. If there were in that assembly a single man of courage, knowledge, and eloquence, he might make the Corps Législatif a real power. And in that case a war of aggression would be impossible. No portion of the French nation, except the army, desires war, and even in the army I doubt whether a war would be popular, except among the officers.

Thursday, April 29th.—General Chrzanowski and Michel Chevalier breakfasted with us. I asked Chrzanowski whether, if Louis Napoleon should attack Austria, he could hope for the assistance of Russia.

Chrzanowski.—The conduct of these absolute Monarchs

can never be predicted. It may depend on an extra glass of champagne. A war between Austria and Russia would be very dangerous to both of them. Each is so strong in some respects and so weak in others, that either may destroy the other. Russia at this instant is weaker than she has been since the death of Peter III. No enemies have done her so much harm as her late Emperor.

Nicholas destroyed the higher education of Russia. He reduced the universities to five, and restricted the students in each to three hundred. To have a son at a university was a distinction. The rich and great families monopolised it; but their young men were not likely to make the best of their opportunities. The consequence is an absence in Russia of men of ability. Alexander is forced to take his foreign ministers and generals from Poles and Germans. But the interior administration must be in the hands of natives, and therefore of half-educated or uneducated men.

Senior.—Who are the notables?

Chrzanowski.—The notables are the nobles who possess one hundred males and upwards; females are not counted. At irregular times, originally once in twenty-five years, but now once in twelve or fifteen, a census is taken, and the taxes, the conscription, and in fact the relation of each property to the State remains unaltered until the next. There are always therefore on the register of an estate names of persons who have died since the last census. A profitable use has been made of this. A man buys twenty thousand or thirty thousand acres in one of the steppes where land is worth nothing. He then peoples it with dead men, that is, he buys from landowners names of men who have died since the last census, and has them regularly conveyed to him as if they were living. He goes to the Russian Land Bank, an institution resembling the Crédit Foncier, shows his title to land and to people, and borrows money on them. The bank generally advances sixty roubles, or 9*l*. per man. On an apparent property of one thousand men he can therefore borrow 9000*l*. He sends it to Paris or London, and leaves Russia never to return.

Senior.—What do you know of this Emperor?

Chrzanowski.—I knew him about twenty-eight years ago, when he was eleven or twelve years old. He was a fine, intelligent, spirited youth. I hear the most contradictory accounts of him. I cannot venture on an opinion. His father was ignorant and stupid; but he was presumptuous and rash, with intervals, in cases of failure or even of difficulty, of depression almost amounting to helplessness. I had opportunities of studying his character, for, as aide-de-camp to General Diebitsch, I lived under the same tent with him for six weeks. His management of the late war may be taken as a test of his powers. When he began he had, besides the armies in the Caucasus, in Finland, and in Siberia, a disposable army of 450,000 men. He immediately doubled it, that is, for every regiment consisting of four battalions of 1000 men each, he raised four more battalions of equal strength. The men of course were mere recruits; the officers were even worse, since it takes much more time to make an officer than a soldier. Besides these 900,000 men he raised about 200,000 more during the course of the war. At the peace not more than 200,000 out of the 1,100,000 men remained. They perished from forced marches, bad food, bad clothing, and hardships of every kind, a very large number, perhaps the greater part, before they had been actually embodied in any army. I know of regiments which marched from Odessa to the Baltic, and back from the Baltic to Perekop, starting 4000 strong and wasted at the end to 1500, without having seen an enemy. His only generalship was to overwhelm the allies by numbers; but as he made no adequate provision for their maintenance or for their hospitals, their numbers were formidable only to themselves. The 450,000 good troops with which he started were soon used up, and at last his army became a mere rabble.

Senior.—I am told that we never encountered the best Russian troops; the army of Poland, for instance, and the Imperial Guard.

Chrzanowski.—You did not encounter the Guard, but it was only 40,000 men. As for the army of Poland, it was reduced during the war from 200,000 men to 25,000; principally, I believe, by marches, but certainly a large portion of it died in the Crimea. The scenes that took place at Nicholas' death have been described to me. For the first day scarcely any one ventured to mention it; they seemed to be in awe of his spirit. At last the corpse was shown, and there was a burst of joy. A load was taken off every man's breast. They could breathe freely.

Senior.—You say that in a war between Russia and Austria each could ruin the other. How could Russia ruin Austria?

Chrzanowski.—By promising to restore the old constitutions which Francis Joseph abolished when he introduced centralisation and despotism in 1851. The Austrian empire is so heterogeneous, its component parts have so little sympathy, so few interests in common, and in many cases such mutual hatred, that there is scarcely a province that would not be delighted to regain the independence which it lost when conquest, or inheritance, or marriage, made the house of Hapsburg its Sovereign, though in almost every case its constitutional Sovereign. But to obtain this result the war must be a serious one. Those who desert the Austrian cause must not have to fear that they will be disavowed or abandoned when peace is made.

Senior.—You are speaking of wars in which each nation

would be a principal; but if Austria were attacked by France, could not Russia without much danger join France as an auxiliary?

Chrzanowski.—She could, and perhaps hatred and revenge might lead her to do so; but she will not if there is any prudence in her councils. What would she gain by strengthening France and bringing her almost in contact with herself? I believe that she will take little part in European politics during the next ten years. Her own internal affairs are quite enough to employ her. But if she does take part in any European war, I think that it will be against France. She fears France politically and militarily. France must soon become a constitutional Monarchy or a Republic, both of them forms of government distasteful to Russia. Her literature is the only literature of the Russian higher classes. Her habits of thought are imitated. If a revolution breaks out in Russia, the impulse will probably come from France. I believe that she would willingly join in crushing France, even though it might profit Austria.

Senior.—What is the present state of the Russian army?

Chrzanowski.—Bad, and getting worse. An army is never stationary; it is always improving or deteriorating. The Russian army has been deteriorating ever since Suwarrow. It has neither generals nor officers; it is ill-armed. I had a rifle made for me at Liége. The manufacturer showed me one which was the model after which he was to make fifty thousand for Russia. It was a barbarous weapon, weighing thirteen pounds, and in every respect ill-constructed. 'Are you not ashamed,' I said to the gunsmith, 'to turn out such a machine?' 'I am not consulted,' he answered, 'and I am well paid—fifty francs per gun; but I give a receipt for one hundred francs.' Thus in one transaction the State is robbed of a hundred thousand francs, and the infantry of a whole corps d'armée will be almost defenceless against really well-armed troops. This is a sample of Russian administration.

Senior.—What ought a rifle to weigh?

Chrzanowski—The Minié weighs ten pounds, but I believe that one weighing only eight would be as efficient. An attempt has lately been made to give men double-barrelled rifles. It will fail. The soldier is already loaded to the utmost. The weight of another barrel, and of the ammunition for another barrel, would be intolerable, or some of his other necessaries, now reduced to their lowest, must be left out.

Senior.—Do you believe that in future actions batteries will be rendered useless by the artillerymen being picked off by the rifle?

Chrzanowski.—It is certain that the improvement in small-arms has been greater than that in artillery, but the cannon has an advantage over the rifle which nothing can destroy. It rests on the earth; the rifle rests on the arm, and trembles with the excitement of the man. There will probably be greater destruction of artillerymen than there was formerly, but not such as to influence the fate of a battle.

I never recollect a time in which the great European Monarchies were so helpless. Russia has her hands full; so has Austria. France may to-morrow be in a state in which she can think of nothing but her own affairs, and England for years will be rendered powerless by India.

Senior.—We are inclined to hope that the worst of the mutiny is over.

Chrzanowski.—I fear that the worst is not begun. There is a proportion between the numerousness of an army and the extent of country which it can occupy which cannot be violated with impunity. You are attempting to hold that vast empire, almost as big and as populous as Europe, with merely English troops. I do not believe it to be possible, and if it be possible it will exhaust your whole strength. You cannot afford to send every year fifteen thousand fresh soldiers to India to replace those who will die, besides those whom you must send to replace those who return. Your army is scattered over the whole world, and therefore really in force and efficient nowhere. A seventh of it is always at sea.

Chevalier.—That portion will be diminished when the Suez Canal has been made. *You* will gain more than anybody else by it, as it will enable you to relieve and reinforce your Indian armies in half the time. When Turkey falls to pieces, as soon it must, you will take Crete or Cyprus, and establish there a depôt half way to India.

Chrzanowski.—What is the value of a depôt of ten thousand men on the scale on which the Anglo-Indian army must be placed? Recollect that it is not only your own subjects that you will have to contend with. Unless the Sikhs and Ghoorkas differ from all other Asiatics they will turn against you.

Chevalier.—What will they get by it?

Chrzanowski.—Plunder; perhaps India. And do not think that this is a distant danger. It will occur in two years, perhaps in one year; in fact as soon as they demand some extravagant, absurd payment for their services, and you refuse it.

Friday, April 30th.—I called on Lord Cowley. I asked if Louis Napoleon had recovered his tranquillity.

Lord Cowley.—I fear that he has not; the shock was severe, and all that has passed since has tended rather to aggravate his excitement. His situation is frightful: every day he receives letters threatening death to the Empress, to the Prince, or to himself. He can never leave his apartment and be sure of returning to it. He can never let his wife and child go out and be sure that he shall see them again. The strongest mind, and his is a strong one, may well be weakened by such constant shaking.

I wish that you would inquire further into the manner in which the 'loi des suspects' has been executed. My information differs from that which you have received. I am told, for instance, that the orders given to the prefects were limited by a maximum; that to temper the desire to show zeal, which is the bane of despotic administration, they were desired not to exceed in their arrests a given number, that number varying in each department. I am told, too, that scarcely any have been merely 'expulsés'—few neighbouring countries, except Spain, consenting to receive them—and that the 'déportés' amount to only three hundred and fifty. Certainly a list containing only three hundred and fifty names, with the cause of deportation appended to each of them, was shown to me as a copy of that which was furnished to the Emperor as the whole result of the law.

Senior.—Rogier, the Belgian minister, informed M. Simon's friend, whose name I think was L'Entade, that he had refused three weeks ago his vizé to three hundred and sixty passports of expulsés, and Commandant Blanchard, belonging to the bureaux of the Minister of the Interior, described expulsion as having been more employed than deportation.

Saturday, May 1st.—I dined with Wolowski. He belongs to the 'nuance' of the Liberal party which has approached most to the Imperialists, and was supported by the Government as candidate for the Institut. He and Louis Napoleon were colleagues as Deputies for Paris in the Constituent Assembly, and sat side by side for six months. I asked him if he could tell me anything as to the manner in which the 'loi des suspects' had been executed.

Wolowski.—Not much, except that it has been done ' à tort et à travers.' An ouvrier, of whom I knew something, an excellent man, quiet and inoffensive, was arrested in Paris. I interceded for him in the bureau of the minister, and got no answer. I wrote to the Emperor and got none. On Monday evenings he receives the 'Corps Constitués.' I attended as a member of the Institut, attracted his notice, and mentioned the subject of my letter. He had not received it, but he sent for his secretary, got it, read it, and promised that it should be attended to. But my protégé has not been released—he has not, indeed, as yet been déporté, but he may be. Espinasse's system is, never to admit that he has made a mistake; he has no sense of justice, and nothing but an express order from above will induce him to relax his grasp on any one whom he has seized.

Senior.—Do you believe Louis Napoleon to be as 'ébranlé' as is said?

Wolowski.—I do. One of his aides-de-camp who sees him every day said to me only yesterday, 'On dit qu'il a reçu un éclat dans le dos, mais moi, je crois que c'était dans la tête.'

Monday, May 3rd.—I breakfasted with Buffet, and met Duvergier, Target, Lanjuinais, Lavergne, and Freslon; they all agreed in believing that the orders given to the prefects were to arrest a minimum.

Duvergier.—In the Charente I know that the prefect was ordered, or at least considered himself ordered, to arrest six. He found five fit subjects, but was puzzled as to the sixth. At last he selected a man of some fortune, living at Angoulême. He was not a man of very good moral character, not very popular—the prefects of course try to avoid meddling with persons with whom the public sympathises. This man had been a priest, had thrown off his orders, and lived rather a disreputable life, but could not be called dangerous. The arrest, however, of a man who was rich, and therefore belonged in some measure to the higher classes, excited alarm, and a deputation from Angoulême called on the prefect to remonstrate. He admitted that the man was not dangerous. 'But,' he said, 'I *must* arrest six, whom will you put in his place? As he is rich he will suffer less inconvenience than a poorer man would do, and I do not think that he will be a loss to our society.' Many substitutes were proposed, objections were raised to each, and at last the deputation agreed with the prefect that his list had better remain unaltered.

Lanjuinais.—Admiral Barbier-Tinant has a brother or a cousin of the same name, an ' armateur' in one of the channel ports, I believe Rochelle. He has large docks, and employs a numerous body of workmen. One of his ' contre-maîtres' was arrested. Barbier-Tinant (the armateur) went in great alarm to the prefect. ' You have taken from me,' he said, ' my right hand man, a man absolutely necessary to me, and so far from being dangerous, that he does not even think about politics.' ' I did not act,' said the prefect, ' without grounds.' He sent for the man's ' dossier,' and showed to Barbier-Tinant a letter denouncing the ' contre-maître' as a Rouge. ' I know,' said Barbier-Tinant, ' the hand-writing. The writer is a man who was in my employment, was detected by my ' contre-maître' in robbing me, and is now in prison for the theft.' The prefect of course was horror struck. ' The affair,' he said, ' has passed out of my hands. The man is at Havre, on his way to Cayenne, but I will write to Espinasse and obtain his release.' Espinasse's answer was, ' Nous ne revenons pas sur nos pas. C'est une affaire finie. Il faut qu'il parte.' And the poor man is now at Cayenne.

Duvergier.—I know two brothers living at Auxerre, named Meron. One is a lawyer, the other a physician. The physician was arrested, handcuffed, and marched towards Marseilles on his way to Algiers, and thence to Lambressa. The lawyer was a strong Liberal politician, but the physician perfectly inoffensive. The people of Auxerre represented to the prefect that he must have mistaken one brother for the other. He inquired, found that it was so, and as the prisoner was still within his department released him; the other brother had fled to Geneva.

Senior.—Was the physician's place on the list of proscriptions supplied?

Duvergier.—I have no doubt that it was, but I have not inquired. All that is going on is so utterly abhorrent to my wishes, and feelings, and opinions, that I try to know as little as possible.

Senior.—Is Lambressa unhealthy? The desert is in general eminently healthy.

Lanjuinais.—Lambressa was described to me when I was in Algeria last year as very unhealthy. There are marshes near it. I was told that out of about fifteen thousand men who have been sent thither by Louis Napoleon, not one-half are living.

Senior.—If they are employed in opening the ground, I wonder that any of them are alive.

Lanjuinais.—I heard that their chief duty was stone-breaking, and that, as they were allowed no shelter when at work, the summer sun quickly destroyed them.

Freslon.—I was at Tours a month ago. A woman ventured to foretell the reappearance of the vine disease. She was arrested, kept for some days in prison, and discharged with a threat from the prefect, that if she spread any more bad news she would be shut up for life. This took place while I was there. I heard a more characteristic story of what took place a little before to a barber at Tours. On the day before the 14th of January, a customer said that great news would soon come from Paris. The barber laughed at him, in short, treated him as an imbécile. Another customer came in just as the first was going out. He asked what they were disputing about. The barber told the story, expressing great contempt for his informant. Soon after the news of the attentat arrived. The barber was arrested, accused of spreading false news, sentenced to six months' imprisonment, and is now undergoing it.

Duvergier.—How low have six years of servitude sunk us! Such stories as these, told of Russia in Louis Philippe's time, would have almost impelled us to make a crusade to put down such tyranny. Now we hear of them as occurring among ourselves with almost indifference.

Wednesday, May 5th.—I called on Madame Cornu, and found with her an Italian, a man about thirty-five. She afterwards told me that his name was Ceruschi.

Madame Cornu.—Unless Louis Napoleon's character is much changed since 1852, when I ceased to see him, it is little understood; he is supposed to be calm, unimpressionable, decided, and obstinate; he has none of these qualities except the last, and even his obstinacy sometimes deserts him. I have known him build castles in the air, dwell on them for years, and at last gradually forget them. When he was young he had two fixed ideas—that he was to be the Emperor of France and that he was to be the liberator of Italy; and I do not believe that even now he has abandoned the latter.

Ceruschi.—If he would frankly declare himself favourable to Italian liberty these plots, as respects the Italians, would cease. We care nothing for his treachery to France, or for his usurpation, or for his despotism; those are the affairs of the French, in which we do not presume to interfere. The Italians try to kill him as the supporter of the Pope, the supporter of Austria, and the enemy of Italian unity. I do not believe they would meddle with him if he were merely neutral.

Senior.—Has not his treatment of Orsini done him good with the Liberal Italians? Never was a man's head cut off more politely. Short of pardon, which was impossible, Orsini had everything that he could wish.

Ceruschi.—It has done him good for a time. He has shown sympathy with our cause, he has shown hostility against our enemy, he has raised our hopes, he has obtained perhaps a respite; but if he disappoints those hopes, if in order to court the French clergy he continues to support the Papal tyranny and to allow the Germans and the Bourbons to oppress four-fifths of Italy, I fear that it will not be more than a respite.

The Italian left us, and Madame Cornu told me his history.

Madame Cornu.—He is a Milanese. He took a prominent part in the Milanese revolution; on its failure he emigrated to Rome, was a member of the Roman Parliament, and was one of the leaders in the defence of Rome against the French. When we entered, Oudinot had him tried—I know not on what pretence—by a court-martial; he was acquitted unanimously. The Pope, or the people about the Pope, prevailed on Oudinot to appeal, a thing of most unusual occurrence when the acquittal has been unanimous. He was tried again, and was again unanimously acquitted. The Pope then, admitting that the French could not punish Ceruschi, required him to be delivered up for trial and punishment to the Roman tribunals, and I am sorry to say that he was supported by M. de Rayneval. My intimacy with Louis Napoleon then continued. I saw him and told Ceruschi's story; he behaved well, as he usually does in individual cases, especially when an Italian is concerned, and ordered Ceruschi to be released and sent to France. The Roman authorities however were so bent on seizing him, that they managed to detain him twenty days at Civita Vecchia while they were intriguing to get the order for his discharge reversed. They failed; he came to Paris, and is now employed in the Crédit Mobilier. He has so much influence among his countrymen that Orsini, though unacquainted with him, named him his executor. The tribunals refuse to acknowledge the validity of Orsini's will, but have allowed Ceruschi to act as in the case of intestacy.

Senior.—You say that Louis Napoleon is neither calm, unimpressionable, nor decided?

Madame Cornu.—I do. He has a calm crust, but furious Italian passions boil beneath it. As a child he was subject to fits of anger, such as I never saw in any one else; while they lasted he did not know what he said or did; he is procrastinating, undecided, and irresolute; courage he certainly has, and of every kind, physical and moral.

Senior.—Do you believe that his courage gave way under the horrors of the attentat, and that the conduct which followed it was the result of alarm and anger?

Madame Cornu.—I do not. As to the 'loi des suspects,' I know that it was decided on last summer after the Parisian elections; they astonished him as much as they irritated him; he believed himself to be adored in Paris, and could account for one hundred thousand persons voting against his candidates only by supposing that some Rouge element was fermenting among them, which must be extirpated. For that purpose the law was prepared; the attentat was merely its pretext. And as to the unhappy insults against England, I firmly believe that they were concocted by the anti-English party, and took him by surprise. A friend of mine, a Deputy, came to me on the 18th of January, immediately after the addresses of the Senate and of the Corps Législatif had been received by him. 'I fear,' he said, 'that we have made a great blunder. Morny assured us that the Emperor was furious against England, and induced us to agree to an anti-English address, and prefaced it by a speech still more extravagant in the same sense. I never saw surprise and anger so marked as in the Emperor's face; he could scarcely contain himself, and dismissed us with this sharp reproof—that he should not alter his foreign policy.' But that policy has received a serious blow; the alliance is not destroyed, but there is a terrible rent in it.

I have just returned from Germany; I was there last year. *Then* everybody believed your power and ours to be united in one mass, and to be irresistible; no one thought of opposing it. This time I found every one speculating on a quarrel, and on the means of provoking one. The prestige of the alliance has fallen as much as the prestige of the Emperor; his prestige was founded on the success of the war, on the general sympathy of the country, and on the English alliance. The success of the war remains; it has been greater than we believed it to be. Russia, deprived of her army, of her fleet, and of her courage, and entangled in an enormous social revolution, has ceased to be formidable. But the general prosperity, like the alliance, has received a shock, and has received it from him.

Senior.—How has the 'loi des suspects' been executed in Paris?

Madame Cornu.—Very harshly. I have many relations with the bourgeoisie and the ouvriers, and have witnessed scenes of wanton cruelty which have almost turned my blood.

I obtained the release of one man; he is a druggist, he incurred the anger of the Provisional Government in 1849, and was expulsé. In 1850 he asked permission to return, was informed by the then prefect that there was nothing against him, and has lived quietly in Paris ever since; as the only pretext for arresting him was that he had been thought dangerous by a revolutionary Government ten years ago, he was released. The wife of an ouvrier, one of the most respectable men in the quartier, came to me; her husband had been seized that night, and hurried to Mazas; as he had never been prosecuted before, it was clear that he had been dénoncé. I thought the matter beyond my competence, and begged Prince Napoleon to interfere; he hates oppression and hates Espinasse, and took up the poor man's cause warmly; he saw the Emperor three times. All that Espinasse could say was that the man had been dénoncé as one of the most dangerous men in Paris. The Prince asked for the grounds; the denunciation contained none; it merely stated him to be dangerous. This Espinasse maintained to be enough, and the Emperor seems to have thought so too, for the man has been sent to Cayenne. Another case was that of a physician at Senlis. He was accused of belonging to a secret society; he denied it, and asked for the name of the informant, or at all events of the society, and for some proofs of his belonging to it; no answer was given. Then he asked to see his wife in order to make some arrangements as to his two children. She was allowed to visit him, and came from the prison to me; she protested that she could not guess on what evidence the accusation rested, as her husband most carefully avoided all connection with secret societies. Again I obtained Prince Napoleon's interference, and again it was fruitless; the wife was allowed to visit him once a week, but the second time that she went she found that he had been sent three days before on his way to Lambressa. The whole family are ruined.

We spent the evening at Madame Meynieu's, and met there M. Passy and M. Parieu, Conseiller d'Etat. Parieu was at the Tuileries on Monday, and amused us by repeating some remarks addressed by the Emperor to M. St. Pol and M. Devine, members of the Corps Législatif, apparently with an intention that they should be overheard. To M. Devine he said, 'I hear that you maintain that the Corps Législatif ought to have the power of amending the budget. What right have you, a Government member, to attack the constitution? And I hear that you, M. St. Pol, affirm, in defiance of the figures presented by my ministers, that there is a deficit. When you were a candidate you asked for the support of the Government, and you received it. Are you acting constitutionally in now opposing it?'

Passy.—In fact he becomes every day less tolerant of resistance. I believe that he has really convinced himself that an Opposition is a revolutionary element, quite unsuited to the constitutional empire which he believes himself to have founded.

Tuesday, May 11th.—Duvergier, St. Hilaire, and Chrzanowski breakfasted with us. Duvergier talked with much delight of the election of Picard, a young Liberal advocate, for the fifth arrondissement of Paris.

Duvergier.—Nothing could be more unscrupulous than the opposition of the Government. At the Belle Isle pollingplace the votes of four hundred workmen, who came in a body to vote for Picard, were absolutely rejected. The clerks would not receive their voting papers. A Dr. L——, a physician, has great influence in the Faubourg St. Antoine. He was a minister under the Republic, and from seven to nine every morning the door of his ministerial hotel was besieged by persons who came to consult him, and to whom he gave those two hours every day. As it was known that he would help Picard, he was ordered to quit Paris a week before the election began, and to be absent until it was over. You may conceive the indignation of the ouvriers, who have thus been deprived of their favourite physician, lest he should assist their favourite candidate.

Chrzanowski has been reading my Turkish Journal.

Chrzanowski.—I recognise the country as I left it twenty years ago, except that it seems to have become poorer, that corruption seems to be increasing, and that a new element of disorder, debts of the State and debts of the Sultan, has crept in. In my time the State and the Sultan were rapacious and extravagant, but they were not in debt. The great ship was even then waterlogged, and slowly sinking. This is a fresh leak.

Senior.—Do you agree with those who attribute its ruin mainly to the diplomatists?

Chrzanowski.—Certainly I do. I believe diplomacy to be the specific poison that kills weak, decaying Governments. It killed Poland; and if ever Poland should be reanimated the fundamental law of the Government, whether Monarchical or Republican, ought to be to send out and to receive no diplomatists. The history of Russia appears to me to run parallel with that of Turkey, but at an interval of almost three hundred years. Three hundred years ago the Turks, having risen, under the guidance of ten such Sovereigns as never succeeded one another since the beginning of the world, in a couple of centuries from a tribe to an empire, were at the height of their power. From the death of Soliman the Great they began to decline, though the ignorance of Europe as to their internal state enabled them still to hold a high rank among the great powers. The Russians were then a barbarous horde almost unknown to us. A succession of great Sovereigns raised them in about two hundred and fifty years to a preponderance in Europe almost equal to that of Turkey under Soliman the Great. The same causes which have destroyed the power of Turkey, barbarism in the people, despotism in the Government, and corruption among all classes, are destroying Russia. I believe that after having been dangerous for a hundred and fifty years, and a scarecrow for thirty more, she will soon cease to be feared or even respected. Her empire may cohere longer than that of Turkey, but as it is suffering under the same diseases, I believe that it will perish by the same decomposition, slow or lingering, according to circumstances.

Senior.—What would you do with the Principalities?

Chrzanowski.—The question is one as to which Europe may conscientiously adopt the course which is most for its own interest, for nothing can do much good to the Principalities. The peasants are mere brutes. The *boyars* are more corrupt than any society that ever existed in Europe. There is no virtue or honour in any man or in any woman. If they are united under a foreign prince they are torn from Turkey. If they are united under a native Prince he will plunder and oppress them in order to provide his bribes for the Porte. If they are governed separately they will be under two robbers instead of under one. I really believe that the best course would be to give them over to Austria.

Wednesday, May 12*th.*—We left Paris.

1859.

[THE warlike spirit awakened in England by the threats of France, and, it is to be hoped, some regard for his old ally, induced the Emperor, after the first irritation had subsided, to endeavour to calm the French nation. Soon afterwards he provided occupation for them, and at the same time tried to satisfy the *Carbonari* by inclining a favourable ear to the proposals of Cavour, who was increasing the Sardinian army in spite of the representations of Austria.

Louis Napoleon entered warmly into the Sardinian alliance, and announced that he intended to free Italy from the Alps to the Adriatic. The Austrian army crossed the Ticino on the 1st of May, and on the 13th the French army joined the Sardinians, Louis Napoleon and Victor Emmanuel commanding in person.—ED.]

Sunday, April 24th.—We reached Paris late last night. The first person that I saw was Cousin. I was anxious to hear about his health, but he said that he could think and talk of nothing but politics.

Cousin.—Peace or war depended on England and Prussia, or rather on England. Louis Napoleon thinks, probably with truth, that he can beat Austria alone, but not if she is supported by a coalition. If you had peremptorily demanded, in the tone not unfamiliar to your Foreign Office, a disarmament by all parties in three weeks, had offered an armed mediation, and had threatened to attack the party that refused fair terms, there would have been no war.

Senior.—What would you have called fair terms?

Cousin.—Giving the Milanese to Piedmont, Wallachia and Moldavia to Austria, and Savoy to France.

Senior.—What would Savoy have said?

Cousin.—She would have been delighted. I am forced to pass some months every year at the baths of Ivade in Savoy. All whom I talk to are anxious to be French. They wish for the French market for their produce. The nobles, highly descended, brave, and popular, but very poor, look to France for a ' carrière.' Piedmont affords one only to the army. The priests, devout and Ultramontane, are disgusted by the way in which the Sardinian Government, and still more the Sardinian press, treat the Pope. The people are accustomed to the French language and laws. They complain that they are oppressed by a grinding taxation to enable Piedmont to get the Milanese. They wish to be part of a great country; their only connexion with Piedmont is the Savoyard descent of the King, which is a weak bond even now, and would become weaker if Sardinia were aggrandized, and Savoy sunk into a neglected province.

Nothing can be more unpopular than the war is here. The priests hate it as anti-Papal; the people as forcing into the army, as he enters his twenty-first year, every young man not protected by want of health, or of size, or by a legal exemption; the men of business as spreading ruin and threatening more, and the politicians as anti-French. 'What reason,' they say, ' have we to fight in order to raise Piedmont into a smaller Prussia, now friendly, but perhaps five years hence hostile? Why is France to waste her blood, perhaps to risk the integrity of her territory, because one man thinks himself a great general, or wishes ' se distraire,' or is afraid of Italian bombs? Other Sovereigns of France have been threatened with assassination, but no one was coward enough or selfish enough to let his policy be governed by such base fears.' There is no sympathy here for Italy, except the sympathy of the priests with the Pope, against whom this war is directed. Thiers has covered himself with honour; he and I exerted to the very utmost all our social influence in favour of peace. The power of the salons of Paris is very great, greater perhaps than it ever was, for theirs is the only voice that cannot be stopped. But this false move of Austria has produced a marked change in public opinion. *She* is now the aggressor.

Senior.—She is the aggressor, as a man is the aggressor who sees a tiger preparing to spring on him, and fires before it makes its bound.

Cousin.—If Austria could not rely on your active armed interference she was perhaps really in the right; but, either through your fault or her fault, she has given herself the appearance of being in the wrong. If the war is kept within the bounds of a duel between Austria and us it may not involve the rest of Europe. It will revolutionize Italy; that, in fact, is its object. Its real authors are not Louis Napoleon and Victor Emmanuel. They are the instruments of the *Carbonari* conspiracy, which has made use of their vanity, their ambition, and, above all, of their fears. Celui-ci is told that he is to be murdered. In February, 1858, two years were given to him; in the beginning of December last he was reminded that one of them had almost expired. Victor Emmanuel and Cavour know that if they were to follow the policy which the quiet Liberals of England recommend, diminish their army, restore their finances, and devote themselves to peaceful liberty and prosperity, their native revolutionists and their thirty thousand refugees, excited, perhaps assisted, by our imperial conspirator, would turn the kingdom of Sardinia into a Republic or a Republican Confederacy before the end of the year.

Senior.—I agree with you that if your war succeeds it will revolutionize Italy. How will it affect France?

Cousin.—Add two milliards to our debt and rivet our chains.

Senior.—And if it fails?

Cousin.—' Dieu sait; ou plutôt le diable sait'—it may produce partition; it may produce a Socialist Republic. The only desirable result, the return of the Orleans family, is only one contingency among many.

Monday, April 25th.—I called on Guizot at twelve, his hour of reception, and found a circle round him. He read to us a letter from a prefect in Brittany. 'The fear of war,' said the letter, 'seems to have reconciled all parties, the priest and the Jew, the seigneur and the peasant, the Republican and the Constitutionalist; even the Bonapartists forget their peculiar differences to join in execrating the war and the authors of it.'

Guizot.—But they will *do* nothing either in the provinces or in Paris. Some members of the Corps Législatif proposed an address in favour of peace. They were informed that they would be dissolved.

One of the company told us that he had accompanied a body of troops marching along the Boulevards to the embarcadère. What feeling there was was Democratic. The old émeutier cry, 'Vive la Ligne!' was raised; others shouted 'à bas l'Empereur d'Autriche!' It was only at the station that 'Vive l'Empereur!' or 'Vive Napoléon!' were heard, and obviously from a paid mob.

Guizot.—' La bonne canaille' is anti-Imperialist, and becomes more so every day.

Senior.—Is what I hear of your want of preparation true?

Guizot.—Quite true. General Niel, who took leave of me yesterday, tells me that it will take three months to cast balls for the new artillery; the army is neither well-armed nor well-clothed. It seems that we are to increase our garrison in Rome. Baraguay d'Hilliers expects to be sent thither.

Senior.—It is not a strategic point.

Guizot.—No; but it is an important political one. The Pope is Austrian; the people are revolutionary. This war comes from Rome; Garibaldi and Mazzini and their co-conspirators are its inventors. We are only accomplices.

Senior.—Have you formed any expectations as to the result?

Guizot.—None worth expressing. I am not a militaire, and do not talk on matters that I do not understand. Thiers, perhaps, will prophesy to you. He is our great military statesman.

I went from Guizot to Thiers. He began by bitter complaints of the British Cabinet.

Thiers.—You were masters of the situation. If you, and Prussia, which would have followed in your wake, had said there shall be no war, there would have been none. But to hold such language, and to be believed, presence of mind, and courage, and a determination to act on your threats were required, qualities which your Cabinet does not seem to possess; Celui-ci at least does not believe that it possesses them. He tried your Foreign Office in the 'Charles et Georges' question, found of what materials it was composed, and despised its timid interference.

Senior.—Our Cabinet *was* timid; a Cabinet always is so, like a council of war; but it had to fear the results of its conduct, not only as respects the Continental despots and revolutionists, but the English people. If Louis Napoleon had refused our mediation would Parliament or would the constituencies have sanctioned our thereupon declaring war against France?

Thiers.—What is the opinion in London as to the conduct of Austria?

Senior.—We think that her fault is that she has delayed the invasion of Piedmont too long.

Thiers.—Your statesmen do not hold that language.

Senior.—I think that I can account for the attacks on Austria by the ministers. They were warned against dissolving in the face of a probable war; they disregarded the warning; they hoped to get through the elections before it came. They have been disappointed, and they vent their ill-humour on Austria for having struck the first blow.

Thiers.—I cannot understand the state of public feeling, or rather of public speaking, in England. Everybody seems to speak with a false voice; every one wears a mask. I am told that all your statesmen, at least all that deserve the name, detest reform; that they see that the uneducated electors are already too numerous, and that to add to them would be only to push you faster down the inclined plane that ends in Democracy. Yet Government after Government is founded on the principle of a reform. Everybody with his public voice declares its necessity, and with his private voice its mischief. Then all of you talk in public of Celui-ci as your faithful ally, and in private call him a villain, a robber, and a traitor. What is one to believe?

Senior.—Nothing, except the evil that is spoken of public men; that is almost always true.

We went on to French affairs.

Senior.—I hear that you have been a bold and vigorous opponent of the war.

Thiers.—I have done the little that a man who is nothing in his own country can do. There was no boldness in it, for there was no danger; but it required perseverance in fighting a hopeless game.

What our master is doing is very dangerous. He is putting himself in the situation in which his uncle always tried to put the enemy. He has divided his army into three corps, which are to meet from different bases in one centre. If the Austrians can pre-occupy that central point they may beat us separately.

Wednesday, April 27th.—I called on the Corcelles. At first they could talk of nothing but the loss of Tocqueville,* ' l'âme la plus pure et l'intelligence la plus pénétrante' of modern France. Then came politics.

Corcelle.—There is no sincerity in Louis Napoleon's desire to give good Government to Italy. Rayneval assures me that since the coup d'état made it unnecessary for him to court the Liberals, he has never shown the slightest desire to improve the Government of the Roman States. While he was trying to get the Pope to crown him, he licked the dust of the Vatican and encouraged all its misgovernment. When that attempt failed, he ceased to care for Rome or for the Romans. All his thoughts, in fact, ever since 1852 have turned on war. He got his war with Russia, and it succeeded. But it had scarcely ended before he wished to turn her into an ally for some other war. He supported her in all the negotiations, where she was in the right and where she was in the wrong. You opposed, and he was always in a minority. Then came the attentat. He was frightened and irritated; first turned on you and got up the addresses of the colonels and the speech of Morny. But the Italians warned him that if he wished to live he must make his war for *them*. I believe that even in the summer of last year he had promised to do so.

He will support the Pope, but he will make him his

---

* M. de Tocqueville died on the 16th April, 1859.—ED.

slave. Two or three days ago the Pope had decided to take refuge in Gaeta. General Guyon said that the French would be happy to receive him in Civita Vecchia, and still more so in Avignon, but that he could not be permitted to be a guest anywhere but in France. This is a matter of great interest to all Catholic Powers. They cannot allow the Pope to be a dependent. It is important even to us. All the independence of the French clergy rests on that of the Pope. But for him they would be crawling on their bellies before the Government, which pays and promotes them; they are not like yours. They are not men of birth or of fortune; they have no wives, no children, no property. They have little knowledge, except their professional knowledge, little interest in politics or care for liberty. Their ruling motive now is obedience to the Pope. He is removed far above our local passions and interests, his advice is wise and benevolent, and while they follow it they contribute more than any other class to moderate our despotism and to keep together our distracted society. But if our master can make a tool of the Pope, he may make tools of the clergy.

I called on Duvergier. I asked him if he believed in the alliance between France and Russia.

Duvergier.—I believe in it. I believe that the plan of the present war was sketched long ago, and was matured, marriage and all, last summer, between Louis Napoleon and Cavour at Plombières. Cavour on his return told De la Rive, of Geneva, that there would be war in spring.

Thursday, April 28th.—I called on Madame Cornu.

Madame Cornu.—Louis Napoleon is delighted with the war. A war to drive Austria out of Italy, in which he should command, has been his dream from boyhood. He said to me once at Ham, 'I trust that some day I shall command a great army. I know that I should distinguish myself. I feel that I have every military quality.' 'Is not experience,' I answered, 'necessary?' 'Great things,' he replied, 'have been done by men who had very little of it. By Condé, for instance. Perhaps it would be better for me to die in the belief that I am fitted to be a great general than to risk the experiment. But I will try it if I can, and I believe that I *shall* try it.' Then the war relieves him from an anxiety which pressed on him from the 14th of January, 1858, until the 1st of January, 1859—the fear of the *Carbonari*. He has breathed freely only since he could give notice to them that he had accepted their terms.

Senior.—You do not believe then in the sincerity of his negotiations?

Madame Cornu.—They were sincere so far, that if Austria would have submitted without war to a sacrifice which would have satisfied the *Carbonari* he would have accepted it. The least favourable condition on which he would have remained at peace with her would have been the erection of Lombardy and Venetia into a separate kingdom, under a prince of the house of Hapsburg, probably the Archduke Maximilian, with an Italian army and Ministry, perfectly independent of Austria. What he would have liked better would have been to put those provinces under the Duke of Leuchtenberg, Eugène's grandson. This would have suited Russia, and perhaps may be the ultimate solution. But I *know*, I can affirm with perfect certainty, that he is resolved —first, that they shall *not* remain Austrian; and secondly, that they shall *not* be united to Piedmont. He hates Piedmont as constitutional, as a neighbour too strong to be a slave, and because the King has treated him from time to time somewhat roughly. As to the freedom or the prosperity of these provinces, when once they cease to be Aus-

trian, or indeed as to the welfare of any part of Italy, he is
nearly indifferent.

Senior.—Do you believe in the Russian alliance?

Madame Cornu.—I do, and I believe that it has existed,
in the shape at least of an understanding, for many months;
perhaps for years. I have no doubt that it was by his orders
that Russia proposed the Congress. Whether through his
skill, or his luck, everybody has played into his hands, no
one more so than England. The strange delays of Austria,
her notice that she should give Piedmont a further notice of
three days, and the wonderful slowness of her advance now,
are all attributed to your interference or to a wish to stand
well with you. They may cost her the campaign, for she
is far better prepared than we are, and ought to have begun
it a month ago. What strengthens my belief that the
Russian alliance exists is, that I know that the day that
the violent article of the *Times* on the subject reached us
the editor of the *Constitutionnel* went to the Tuileries to
ask how he should treat it, and that the answer was, ' Be
silent.'

Senior.—Is it true that the war is unpopular?

Madame Cornu.—Among the higher classes, yes; but not
among the lower. I talk much with the ouvriers and
ouvrières of my neighbourhood. They are all Republicans,
or rather Socialists; they delight in it, partly from the
vulgar love of excitement, and partly because they think
that in the fight something favourable to the Republicans
may turn up; that Celui-ci may be killed for instance, or
that he may be forced to throw himself on the Socialist
party. How many volunteers do you think have enrolled
themselves during the last fortnight? Fifty thousand. The
Rue Cherche Midi, in which is the bureau, was so filled with
them for some days, that the passage through it was
stopped.

Senior.—Will these 50,000 men be substituted for a part of the 140,000 conscripts now demanded?

Madame Cornu.—No, they will be added. We shall raise 190,000 men this year. The popular opinion as to the war is amusing. As the army begins the campaign by entering Piedmont, the soldiers all think that Piedmont is the enemy. 'Nous allons,' they say, 'étriller bien ces gredins de Piémontais.' And I daresay that it is true. Piedmont will be 'bien étrillé.' Our Zouaves and Turcos will respect nothing.

We spent the evening at Madame Mohl's. Some Russians were there, whom I asked if they believed in the Franco-Russian alliance.

'Our hands,' they answered, 'are full with the serf question. A Government indeed sometimes tries to escape domestic difficulties by a foreign war; but this is too great a question to be so solved or ' tranchée.' The expectations of the serfs have been raised. The Emperor has promised to them emancipation. The loss to the seigneurs will be ten milliards (400,000,000*l.*). If that falls on the seigneurs, the whole Russian aristocracy is ruined; if it falls on the serfs, the effect is nearly the same, for they can not or will not pay it; if it falls on the State, our finances are ruined. This is not the time for us to rush wantonly into war.'

Madame Mohl showed me a letter from the Marchioness Arconati.* She is a Milanese by birth, a Trotti. Her husband, who has large estates in Lombardy, Piedmont, and Belgium, settled in Turin when Piedmont became constitutional, and is a member of the Chamber of Deputies. It paints so well the state of feeling of the highest Italians that I copy it.

---

* See conversations at Brussels, vol. i. p. 107 of this work for account of the Arconatis.—Ed.

Turin, ce 1 Avril, 1859.

'L'Angleterre nous a fait défaut, les sympathies de la France également, nous n'avons jamais compté sur celles de l'Allemagne. Et pourtant je ne désespère pas. Une cause qui à chaque fois qu'elle rentre en scène a grandi, n'est pas en train de périr. Je me ferais scrupule de dire que la guerre est inévitable si personnellement elle ne m'exposait pas à des sacrifices.

'J'ai beaucoup de parents parmi les jeunes gens qui sont venus s'enrôler. Notre fortune, soit en Lombardie, soit en Piémont (nos terres se trouvent sur la frontière) est bien exposée. Il y a au monde de plus grands malheurs que des pertes de ce genre. Quand même notre chère armée piémontaise devrait succomber, je remercierais le ciel d'avoir vu ce que je vois depuis un mois—l'élan généreux de la jeunesse lombarde qui vient ici pour supplier qu'on la laisse entrer dans l'armée, n'aspirant à servir que comme soldats. Le Duc Visconti et ses deux frères—le Comte Cicogna, le Comte Taverna (ces deux-ci sont fils uniques)—sont du nombre. Mon neveu Trotti, veuf depuis deux ans, a quitté ses enfans pour venir s'enrôler.

'L'autre soir il est arrivé par le chemin de fer plus de deux cents Toscans. A Florence le Marquis Cappone s'est mis à la tête d'une souscription pour fournir aux jeunes gens qui veulent aller en Piémont les moyens de faire le voyage. La petite armée toscane a déclaré qu'en cas de guerre elle se joindrait à l'armée piémontaise. Nous vivons au milieu d'un mouvement irrésistible mais non point désordonné.'

Chrzanowski breakfasted with us.

Senior.—How do you explain this delay in the march of the Austrians—that they crossed the Ticino only yesterday?

Chrzanowski.—Its principal cause is without doubt diplomatic. Your Government wished to please the peace party in England by being peacemakers 'à l'outrance.' To this selfish party interest it sacrificed Austria, and almost forced her to await the issue of its absurd negotiations. But there were some real considerations which may have made the Austrian Government less unwilling to submit to the delay. If they had crossed the Ticino—as for military purposes they ought to have done—by the beginning of the month, they must have moved a large portion of their troops from their cantonments and exposed them to the discomforts of a bivouac for a fortnight. Now 100,000 men in that fortnight at this season would have lost 15,000 of their force, or at least have sent them to the hospital. I will not say that this was a sufficient reason for losing a fortnight, but it *was* a motive. They are too late therefore to establish themselves firmly at the foot of all the passes and beat the French as they come up, but they are not too late to lay a contribution on Turin, to live for a month on the country, and to destroy the Piedmontese army.

Senior.—But the Piedmontese army will not stand to be destroyed. It will retire into its fortresses.

Chrzanowski.—What fortresses? There is only one real fortress, Genoa, and by this time the Austrians must have possession of the railway and have intercepted the road.

Senior.—Is not Alessandria strong?

Chrzanowski.—It is just strong enough to be a trap to catch the Piedmontese and keep them till they capitulate. It *was* strong, but the Austrians with laudable providence dismantled it. The King begged that at least they would leave him the citadel that he might have a place for State prisoners. This motive was appreciated by the Austrians, and the citadel, not very strong, remains surrounded by earthworks. Now earthworks can never be defended except by really good troops, as they can always be escaladed.

Senior.—Were not the works of Sebastopol earthworks?

Chrzanowski.—Certainly; but Sebastopol was only a 'tête de pont,' behind which was an army of 160,000 men, attacked by only 130,000, who could not even invest it. Sebastopol could not have resisted if it had been merely garrisoned and had been invested.

Senior.—What was Silistria?

Chrzanowski.—A mere earthwork, not high enough to cover a man; but the Turks were far superior to the Piedmontese. The Turks could be fanaticised, and were so. The Piedmontese soldier is merely a tolerable machine.

Senior.—Did not they fight well at the Crimea?

Chrzanowski.—They fought neither well nor ill, for with one exception they did not fight at all. That exception was at the Tchernaya. The extreme right was confided to a Piedmontese battalion. Just at the time when they were being relieved, so that there were two battalions there, the Russians came up. The two battalions ran. The Russians followed them at full speed till they reached the French, who stopped them. A Piedmontese regiment next to the French joined them; the Russians were driven back, and the Piedmontese lost three or four men. Besides this a Piedmontese battery actually ventured to fire on the Russians; and this was all that they did in the war.

Senior.—What are your expectations as to the campaign?

Chrzanowski.—I think it probable that the Austrians, having destroyed the Piedmontese army and wasted the country, will gradually retire before the French. Their officers are good and so are their generals, but their men are probably much inferior to the French. They were so ten years ago, when I knew something of them. Twenty thousand French could then have beaten fifty thousand Austrians. The French, however, run one great danger. Their men are ill-provided; in general they are overloaded. A French infantry soldier carries on his back sixty pounds

French, about sixty-eight pounds English. This is far too much even in dry weather, and in wet weather, when their bits of tents and their clothes are made heavy by rain, it is intolerable. In the rapid marches which they have to make they must abandon a part, and they may have to pillage. Some of their men, the Arabs (Turcos as they call them), are pillagers by nature and by education. They sacked a part of Algiers on their way to embark. Now, besides the mischief done by exciting the terror and anger of the people and stopping supplies, a pillaging soldier is worth nothing. If he is intemperate he drinks; if he is sober he accumulates and deserts. I should not be surprised if the French army met with a great disaster. Another danger is the Emperor's presence. One of the reasons why the Crimean war was so ill-managed by both parties was the interference of the two Emperors. If he could do so much mischief at two thousand miles distance, what will he do on the spot? And yet his presence may be necessary. French marshals are always quarrelling and spiting one another. At Auerstadt, Davoust and Bernadotte were posted within two miles of one another with about thirty thousand men each. Davoust saw that he should be attacked, and asked Bernadotte to send him a division. Bernadotte said that he would come with it and take the command. Davoust would not accept the assistance on such terms, and Bernadotte with his thirty thousand men stood quiet all the day within two miles of the action. So it would be now if there were not some one to control them.

Senior.—What do you suppose to be the intentions of Celui-ci if he succeeds? Will he be content with driving the Austrians out of Italy?

Chrzanowski.—How do *I* know? How does *he* know? One thing only I do know—he will not give Lombardy to Piedmont. When I commanded the Piedmontese army in

1849 I was in communication with the head of the secret police. He told me that a French agent was travelling over the country. I desired him to get hold of the agent's papers. This was done; they were copied, and then replaced in his luggage. Among them I found his instructions from Louis Napoleon, then President. They were to use every means to prevent the annexation of Lombardy to Piedmont, and to procure the separation of Savoy. 'Piedmont,' said the instructions, 'is already too strong. We wish all our neighbours to be weak.'

Senior.—Do you believe in this Russian alliance?

Chrzanowski.—It is very probable. Russia, however, cannot exercise any immediate influence over the war. She can send across her frontier 200,000 men; but that would take five months; she can send 100,000 men in three months. Then this is a revolutionary war. To injure Austria seriously she must rouse against her her Magyar and Slav populations. Can she do this without exciting her own Germans and Poles? Her 21,000,000 serfs threaten to revolt if they are not emancipated. The nobles threaten to do so if their serfs are taken from them. They say that if they are no longer to be masters they will no longer be slaves.

Senior.—How many days' march is Turin from Lyons?

Chrzanowski.—Five; about the same distance as from Pavia. But the Austrians can march in a body over a flat country with their guns. Only two divisions can cross the Alps at a time—one by Mont Cenis, the other by Mont Genevre—and it will be very difficult to drag cannon with them. Louis Napoleon ought to have sent his cannon and heavy stores three or four weeks ago by sea to Genoa, and thence by the railway to meet him at Turin. But he has shown childish improvidence. He has rifled his guns and has no balls for them; it will take three months to cast them; so he must use the old pieces. Some months ago

he ordered the bore of a million of muskets to be enlarged.
After that had been done he had them rifled; they are so
thin that they cannot be depended on, and he must use the
old muskets. In the spring of last year, to frighten you,
he increased or transformed his fleet. This was an expensive operation. To get money for it he diminished his army,
sold half the cavalry and artillery horses, let many of the
men go home, and took the money of 'remplaçants' and applied it to other purposes. The army has no shoes, no
'ceintures de laine,' in short, it is unprovided. He has ruined
himself by finesse, by over-cunning, which does no better in
politics than it does in private life. He wished to appear
the attacked, not the attacker, so he would not arm ostensibly, and it is difficult to arm privately. He fancied that
Austria would give him time, especially as you played into
his hands. He is not an administrator; he is idle and
careless, and probably thought himself much better prepared
than he now finds himself. In war almost everything
depends on time. The man who runs straightest and fastest,
and stops least, wins. Louis Napoleon is idle and procrastinating; his wonderful luck may save him, as it has
saved him before, but it will be by the blunders of his
enemies, not by his own wisdom or activity.

Senior.—Do you attach much importance to this Tuscan
insurrection?

Chrzanowski.—No military importance. An army that
revolts ceases to be an army; neither officers nor men feel
bound. Some go home, some seek service elsewhere. Out
of ten thousand men not five thousand will join Victor
Emmanuel, and they will be an undisciplined rabble not
worth clothing and feeding.

Sunday, May 1st.—Dumon breakfasted with us. As an
ex-Minister of Finance he talked of the finances.

Dumon.—Our expenditure this year will be at least one hundred millions sterling, probably more. We have added five millions to the interest of our debt since 1848. For temporary purposes the new loan will be a good investment. Every Government will recognise the debts of its predecessors and pay in gold, while it can, and then in paper. It will come out at about 57 in a Three per Cent. Stock, and interest will run on the whole from the time that the first instalment is paid, so that it will pay more than five per cent.

Senior.—Does the unpopularity of the war continue?

Dumon.—Certainly, among all the educated classes, and among eighty per cent. of the uneducated. No one can pretend that it is made in the interest of France, and we have no sympathy for the Italians. We fear, too, that he must have made great concessions in order to get this Russian co-operation; and though our Crimean success produced no enthusiasm, we do not like to see the very man who forced us to purchase it so dearly, himself destroy its results. The only friends of the war are the Republicans. They see that it is essentially revolutionary.

Senior.—What do the Republicans want? A Democratic despotism like this seems to be the Government that suits them; they hate liberty.

Dumon.—They hate liberty and they love despotism, but not the despotism of an individual. They wish for a despotic Assembly, a Committee of Public Safety, and perhaps a Directory, constantly renewed. They like a rotation of office, under which every one may hope to hold it. Then the splendour and extravagance of the Court annoy them. They do not like to be forced to spend their money on dress and ostentation. They had much rather hoard what they steal. Louis Napoleon's death would open an enormous field, and what is going on multiplies much its chances. He may die of fatigue or in battle. The threat of assassination has succeeded so well, or what is nearly the same thing, appears to have succeeded so well, that it will be repeated. Nothing is more dangerous than to have yielded, or to be supposed to have yielded, to such a motive. When he gets to Milan can he, a despot, create a Milanese Republic to be connected with the Republics of Rome, Florence, and Naples ? If he does not, will not the Mazzinists say, 'You are still a false *Carbonaro;* we do not intend your success to turn to the profit of Monarchy or of aristocracy.' This war may obtain for him a respite, but may ultimately increase the danger of assassination.

Senior.—Do you think that the Republicans are right in expecting to gain by his death ?

Dumon.—I think that they are right in believing that his death would give them a chance of power for a time, long enough to rob us or to cut our throats. Perhaps they would be more likely to obtain one or both of those objects if, instead of being killed, he were beaten by the Austrians, and were to throw himself, as he probably would do, on the Socialists for support.

I spent the evening at Thiers'. The Bill authorising a loan of twenty millions was discussed in the Corps Législatif to-day and passed unanimously. M. Plichon, a member, came in, and was congratulated on his speech, which was opposed to the Bill, though he voted for it.

Plichon.—I thought my speech very moderate, and so did those to whom I communicated its substance before I rose, but it excited a perfect storm.

Senior.—What were the opinions that roused the storm ?

Plichon.—Those in which I said that France had nothing to gain by the war and much to lose; that what I most feared was 'l'inconnu qu'elle recèle dans son sein—qu'on ne saurait être révolutionnaire en Italie, et rester conservateur en France et à Rome.' But the really bold speech was that of Jules Favre. Baroche had said that the war was a defensive war; that France had declared it because Austria had attacked her in the person of Piedmont. Favre denied this. 'The war,' he said, 'was the Emperor's war. He resolved to have it; he prepared it in profound peace more than a year ago; its whole responsibility falls on him, and I honour him for it. Its object must be the independence of Italy; for no other purpose will France fight. Still I have a painful remembrance of 1849, when, under the same guidance and after similar professions, we sent an expedition to Rome; and we know what followed. I am anxious therefore to know whether I am wrong on either of these points. I ask M. Baroche to tell me whether this is not a war 'provoquée par l'Empereur pour libérer l'Italie.' His answer or his silence may decide my vote. He is silent. Then I vote for raising the money, 'sauf à demander compte après la victoire de l'usage que les triomphateurs en feront.' I do not expect either of our speeches to be fully reported.

Target, Duvergier's son-in-law, was sitting next to me. I said that the earnest wish to be delivered from this tyranny seemed to prevail even over the desire for the triumph of the arms of France.

Target.—It does so. Our military fame rests on foundations which cannot be shaken, and the blow must be tremendous, far severer than any that Austria can give, that would really weaken our strength. But a victory by Celui-ci might consolidate a tyranny which is producing a moral degradation worse than even the loss of reputation or of power.

As I was going, Thiers followed me into the ante-room,

and we walked up and down for half an hour. I said to him what I had said to Target.

Thiers.—It is quite true. Ten years ago, if any one had prophesied that a time would come when I should look with any feelings but those of the bitterest grief at a reverse undergone by France, how angrily I should have resented such an imputation, and yet the time *has* come.

Senior.—I am told that the last move of Austria has had a great influence on public opinion; that France is supposed to have been attacked, and that the war has become almost popular.

Thiers.—That is not true as to the higher and middle classes, or as to any classes except the most ignorant and stupid of the *canaille*. The war is as unpopular as ever. You must cross the Channel to find people who affect to believe that the attack came from Austria. I have been reading Palmerston's 'incroyable' speech. Admitting that it was meant only for the hustings, it shows what falsehoods your public men will utter when they address an uniuformed audience. If Mr. Bright or Mr. Packington, who know nothing of the affairs of the Continent, had used such language one would have only smiled; but from Palmerston it shows what is much worse than ignorance. He must know as well as I do that Louis Napoleon has planned this war for years; that for years he has forced Austria to keep up establishments far beyond her means; that she is bleeding to death; that the Congress was a trick; that as soon as *he* was prepared, and *she* was exhausted, he would spring on her; and because she would not wait for his spring he calls her an aggressor. All your parties seem to combine against Austria; all your intervention has been disastrous to her. It has prevented her being at the foot of the passes of the Alps on the 1st of April. If she had been there, as she ought to have been, this war would now have been over.

Tell me what you expect to be the conduct of England if Celui-ci succeeds?—if he gets, as he intends to do, to the Tagliamento? Will you allow him to do whatever he likes?

Senior.—Yes, in Italy.

Thiers.—And in Savoy?

Senior.—Yes.

Thiers.—And when he goes to the East and to the North, when he takes the Bavarian Palatinate, and Bonn, and Cologne?

Senior.—I think that the moment he gets beyond Italy and Savoy we shall interfere.

Thiers.—Even if his friend Palmerston is your minister?

Senior.—I do not believe that Palmerston's friendship for him or for any one else would affect his public conduct. Palmerston has been accused of many faults, but never of sacrificing the interests of England to his affections or his fears. What do you believe of this Russian alliance?

Thiers.—That there is an understanding that Russia will attack Austria if Germany attacks France. The object is to interest Austria herself in the neutrality of Germany. The attack however, if any is made, is more likely to come from France. The frontier between the German and Italian dominions of Austria is intermixed, and not always clearly defined. Our soldiers are bad geographers, and not very scrupulous; they may commit a trespass ignorantly or carelessly, and then France becomes the aggressor, and the *casus fœderis* does not arise. I fear however that it may have been bought by horrible concessions to Russia.

Senior.—If those concessions respect Turkey we may be brought into the field, for we have guaranteed the integrity of Turkey.

Thiers.—So you have that of the German Confederation.

Senior.—I believe not, unless you consider the treaties of 1814 and 1815 as guarantees.

Thiers.—Now is the time for you to settle your fishery

questions and your African coast question. You will find him souple comme un gant. When this war is over, if it ever is over, he will be stiffer than ever.

We talked of Madame d'Harcourt's memoir of the Duchess of Orleans.

Thiers.—It is charmingly done; but one whole part of the Duchess' conduct is not alluded to, her resistance to the fusion. What has passed since shows its wisdom. Now that the fusion is abandoned, the branche ainée is forgotten.

Monday, May 2nd.—Prince Napoleon sent to ask me to call on him; so I went this morning to the Palais Royal.*

Tuesday, May 3rd.—I called on Mérimée, who gave me the Oriental hospitality of a chibouque. We talked of the war. I alluded to its general unpopularity.

Mérimée.—It is unpopular in the salons, as everything done by the Emperor is. He has long made up his mind that their hatred is implacable, and he despises it. It is unpopular too with the priests, and with those whose sons are affected by the conscription; but the bulk of the people approve it, and even like it. The last three weeks have produced an enormous change in public opinion, that is, in the public opinion of the ' bourgeoisie' and ' peuple de Paris.' I have been absent for a fortnight. When I left Paris they dreaded the war. On my return a week ago I found them reconciled to it, partly from the tendency of the French to accept and make the best of what is unavoidable, and partly from their belief that Austria is the aggressor.

Senior.—From the 1st of January I believed it to be unavoidable. The Emperor would not have made his speech to Hübner if he had not resolved on it.

---

* This conversation is not published.—ED.

Mérimée.—I believe that he much prefers war, but that yet, if Austria had offered concessions, which would have given him a triumph, he would have submitted to peace. Austria, if she really wished for peace, was wrong in making difficulties about the Congress. If she had accepted it he must have been taken at his word. He could not have refused to abide by its decisions, and the Emperor of Austria himself, if he had any sense, ought to have seen that he would have been a gainer by what was proposed. The misgovernment of Lombardy does more harm to Austria than to anybody else; but the selfish interests and stupid prejudices of the Court of Vienna and of the German population of Austria perpetuate it, just as the prejudices of the English people oblige you to misgovern Ireland. When a Congress or some other external pressure forces you to give religious equality to Ireland you will be great gainers, though you cannot do it until you are forced. If Louis Napoleon had been absolutely resolved on war he would have been better prepared for it.

Senior.—But why, if he was not resolved, did he make that speech to Hübner? Why did he give warning of what he intended?

Mérimée.—Because he wished to prepare men's minds for what was to come. Under this régime, where nobody cares for what is published in the newspapers, or is said in the Chambers, only what falls from the Emperor is attended to. And he is not sorry that such should be the case. One of the strongest opponents of the war was Thiers. At last I begged him to write his objections to it. He did so, and with great freedom and force. The Emperor read the paper, and said that some of it was true, but that on the whole it was 'bourgeois.'

Senior.—But if he had remained at peace after obtaining a diplomatic triumph, enough to gratify his vanity and that of France, would not the danger of assassination by the Italian Republicans have continued?

Mérimée.—I do not believe that the fear of assassination was among his motives. He and the Empress are both of them fatalists. The strange events of their lives have *created* this feeling in *her* and *strengthened* it in him. What, after all, is fatalism? It is merely the belief, logically carried out and acted on, of a special Providence, which is common among devout people. And if there be such a thing as a special Providence, if the world is not arranged, like the planetary system, to go on without interference, the lives of Sovereigns, at least of the Sovereigns whose existence affects the interest of nations, are likely to be its peculiar objects. You know that more than a year ago I tried to persuade the Emperor to wear a light cuirass. I made another attempt not long ago. I was laughed at by him and by her. The day before yesterday at the reception I had a long conversation with her, quite unreserved, as it was in Spanish. She expressed no alarm at the dangers to which the campaign may expose him. 'I am happier,' she said, 'than I have been for, months. Our cause is good, our army is excellent, and *he* is full of confidence and energy. The suspense of the last three months affected his health and spirits; now he is as happy as I am.'

Senior.—What do you suppose to have been his real motive for the war, if it were not the fear of the *Carbonari?*

Mérimée.—The motives were three. First and foremost was his hatred of Austria and of the Roman Government. He hates them both with the intensity of a conspirator. Such feelings must be his earliest recollections. When, after the insurrection in which his brother died, he was carried a prisoner to the Roman frontier, and then pardoned and driven out, he said that he would pay another visit to the Cardinals.

Senior.—I can understand his hating the Cardinals; but what quarrel has he with Austria?

Mérimée.—Every Italian, and he is an Italian by education, hates Austria. Then he has to revenge her conduct during the Crimean war.

Senior.—So have we, and yet you see that we bear no malice.

Mérimée.—A nation may forget her rancunes; an individual, at least the individual of whom we are speaking, does not.

Senior.—Has he any real sympathy with the Italian people?

Mérimée.—Sympathy with them as the enemies of Austria, but he cares little about their real happiness. After he had written his letter to Ney* in 1850 he never thought more about Papal misgovernment. It affects him as the misgovernment of the Bosnians or of the Mongols affects us. We say, 'It is very atrocious,' and forget it. His second motive is the desire of military glory, first for himself, next for us. He hopes to add a brilliant page to French history, with his name at the beginning. His third motive is that he believes that military success will establish his dynasty.

Senior.—In none of these motives is France interested; she does not hate Austria; she has more military glory than she wants, and she would be as happy under an Orleans dynasty as under a Bonaparte one.

Mérimée.—Thence the Emperor's anxiety to make out Austria to be the aggressor, in which, by his own dexterity, by the mismanagement of Austria, and by your assistance, he has in a great degree succeeded.

Senior.—Will he be satisfied with a victory over Austria?

---

* A private letter approving highly of the Roman expedition.—ED.

Mérimée.—I believe that there is only one person who knows anything as to his intentions, the Empress, and I doubt whether she knows much; she looks with fear at the chance of the war extending beyond Italy. I said to her the day before yesterday that I only feared the Emperor's having too many allies; allies not only in Italy but Hungary. 'That,' said the Empress, ' is what *I* fear. I should be exceedingly alarmed by an Hungarian insurrection, which by giving Hungary to Russia, might make her our neighbour and a Mediterranean power.' In fact, the danger is great. Austria, with her usual stupidity and brutality, has made enemies not only of the Magyars but of the Croats, who rendered her such services in the late insurrection. Most of them belong to the Greek Church, and she has been fool enough to trouble them about their religion. The Russians too, when they entered Hungary, behaved with the utmost moderation; paid liberally for all that they wanted, and when they had beaten the Hungarians, protected them against the Austrians. I hear that Klapka has already gone to Hungary, and that Kossuth is going. If a Russian army were to enter Hungary the people would be on their knees before it.

Senior.—How came Russia to join Austria in putting down the Hungarian insurrection?

Mérimée.—It was a folly of Nicholas. He fancied himself the champion of order; he said that he should have come hither and set France in order, if there had not been forty millions of Germans between him and us. When Schwartzenberg threatened to be ungrateful he knew well that Nicholas had ceased to be friendly.

Senior.—Do you believe in the Franco-Russian alliance?

Mérimée.—Only that Russia is engaged to prevent the Confederation from attacking France. I believe that the army which Russia is assembling is directed against Turkey, and that she will, some fine day when we are otherwise engaged, re-enter the Principalities. The great evil of this war is the opportunity which it gives to Russian aggrandizement. It may give her a port on the Adriatic, for which all that we can get in Italy would be a poor compensation.

Tuesday, May 3rd.—I called at Guizot's, and found there his son-in-law, De Witt. I inquired into the state of feeling in the provinces.

De Witt.—I came on Saturday from Val Richer. The portion of the peasantry who care about politics are Socialists. Most of them are members of secret societies; they delight in the war because it is made, they say, contre monsieur le curé; and they see in war the chances of revolution. The others may be divided into those who have sons, those who have horses, and those who have neither. Those who have sons grieve, as they fear to lose them by the conscription; those who have horses are delighted, as they will sell them at double their value; those who have neither sons nor horses are utterly indifferent. The 'bourgeoisie' are 'tristes;' until the last movement of Austria they were furious against the Emperor, as driving them into war; they thought that he must be a rascal or a fool; they now believe Austria to be in fault, and are reconciled to him.

Senior.—And what is the feeling of the higher classes?

De Witt.—There are none, or almost none, near us. Debt, extravagance—though on an humble scale, and borrowing at five per cent. to invest in land at two and a half per cent.—have ruined them. Three neighbouring families have sold their land in lots and disappeared during the six years that I have lived at Val Richer. Rents have risen little, while commodities and services have become much dearer, and habits of ostentation have grown up which require a larger consumption of these dearer things. We feel this in Paris. Some years ago there were three thousand people in Paris, who kept a sort of open house for their friends: one dined on the ordinary fare of the family. One dines out now only by invitation, and to a sort of banquet. Very few people allow one to see how they live when alone.

I spent the evening at the Princess Belgiojoso's.*

Princess Belgiojoso.—I can scarcely believe that what is going on can be real. I think that I must be in a delightful dream. Only two things remind me that even the happiest events have some alloy of pain; one is that I am anxious for my brother in Milan; he is too infirm to have taken part actively against the Government, but they may have seized him as a hostage for the conduct of his relations. I have not heard from him for a week. My other grief is that I am not at Turin. I might have been useful; at all events I should have known what is going on. This darkness and silence are terrible. Five days have passed since the Austrians crossed the Ticino, and we know nothing.

Senior.—We are spectators; we are in the pit. The spectators always think the delay before the curtain rises intolerable.

Thursday, May 5th.—I called on the Duc de Broglie, and found him calm but melancholy.

Duc de Broglie.—Whose fault all this is, is now mere

---

* The Princess Belgiojoso was remarkable for her beauty and her talent, and above all, for her patriotism. She took a prominent part in the Italian revolutionary movement in 1848, and raised a battalion of volunteers. After the failure of the Italian cause she lived in Paris, published several books, and wrote frequently in reviews. Most of the eminent men in Paris frequented her salon.—ED.

matter of history. I do not trouble myself with that question. 'Le vin est versé, il faut le boire.' When once we are at war I can wish only the success of my country. The results of that success are 'dans l'inconnu.' All that we know is, that the war for Italian freedom opens by the destruction of the liberties of Piedmont.

We talked of the acceptance by the Duc de Chartres of the post of aide-de-camp to the King of Sardinia.

Duc de Broglie.—I think that, in the very difficult circumstances in which he was placed, he has done right. I am told that his letter to his brother, in which, after regretting that he cannot fight under the French flag, he rejoices that he fights by its side, is admirable. Of course there are objections to the course which he has taken, as there are objections to everything. People say that if the French and Sardinian armies unite, he may be commanded by the usurper, and may have Garibaldi for his companion. And the fear of this would perhaps have been a sufficient reason for his not going from England to Piedmont *after* the breaking out of the war. But the war finds him there; he is a soldier; he has 'une occasion de faire ses épreuves dans la cause de la France,' and to make himself known to the French army, which loves and honours his House. He was right in not letting mere scruples of 'convenance' overrule these motives.

Friday, May 6th.—Guizot, Ampère, Corcelle, and Lanjuinais breakfasted with us. Ampère talked of biographical prejudices.

Ampère.—Posterity will believe, in fact we who are now posterity believe, that Josephine was a delightful person, *un peu légère* perhaps, but full of grace, intelligence, and charm. The fact is, she was a trifling ill-educated creole, good-natured, but with little intellect and no tastes except for dress and expenditure.

We talked of the Emperor.

Senior.—It is remarkable that Louis Napoleon, with his name and his excellent manners, should have made such little way in London society.

Guizot.—In fact he contributes nothing to society. He has no invention, no originality. You see in all that he does, and in all that he says, and in all that he writes, that he is a copyist. Look at his proclamation, a paper obviously written by himself and without advice or assistance. It is full of the commonplaces and exaggerations of the worst times of the Empire. He threatens to drive Austria to the Adriatic, as his uncle threatened to efface Prussia from the map. When all France, however opposed to his dynasty, is giving him her sons, he calls those who disapprove of his war, 'fauteurs de désordre, hommes incorrigibles, pactiseurs avec nos ennemis.' He commits his wife and son to the patriotism of the National Guard, and to the devotion of the people; phrases which he knows to be as empty as all the rest. He intends his battle to be fought at Marengo, and does not seem to recollect that in 1800 it was the Austrians who were surprised, and now it is the French. He calls himself the friend of order, when we well know that for the last six months his agents have been traversing Hungary and Italy exciting and, I fear, preparing a series of frightful revolutions.

The conversation passed, I forget how, to Cardinal Mezzofanti. Corcelle knew him well and described him as almost a saint.

Corcelle.—He did not leave enough to bury him; all was given away. One day a phrenologist called on him, and after some circumlocutions, which the delicacy of the negotiation required, said that in fact the object of his visit was to purchase the reversion of the Cardinal's skull, as illustrative of the organs of language. Mezzofanti was no phrenologist, and dismissed the negotiator rather roughly. Immediately afterwards a woman came to him, as everybody in want used to do, to beg. He had not a farthing. But he recollected the proposal which he had just refused, called back the phrenologist, and said, 'On second thoughts I am inclined to treat with you for my skull, but it will be dear. I am not sure that there is such another in the world.' The bargain was made, the money was given to the woman.

Senior.—And where is the skull now?

Corcelle.—In Rome with the rest of his bones. Mezzofanti got tired of carrying on his shoulders a head belonging to another person and repurchased it.

Saturday, May 7th.—I dined *tête-à-tête* with A.*

A.—Persigny is going to London. He is most anxious for peace and for the renewal of the English alliance, and I believe that if you are able and firm you may have them both in two months. Celui-ci must have a success. 'Il est condamné à être brillant.' And he *will* have one. We shall beat Austria, not as we did at Austerlitz, but still sufficiently to show her that if the contest go on, she will be ruined. Celui-ci's great object will have been attained. He will have gained military fame.

Senior.—But will he have satisfied the Italian conspirators?

A.—Of course not, for it is impossible. But if peace is made on the terms which I hope and expect, he will

---

* A friend of Louis Napoleon's up to the coup d'état. He has long since been dead.—Ed.

have done much for them. Italy will not be oppressed by German administrators, or tax-gatherers, or soldiers. The better class of Republicans will accept this as an instalment.

Senior.—And what are your terms?

A.—The obvious ones, of erecting the Milanese and Venetia into a kingdom, or an independent principality, perhaps under an Austrian Archduke, but with its own Italian administration, army, and policy, and the relinquishment by Austria of her claim to interfere in the rest of Italy.

Senior.—What do you do with the Papal territories?

A.—Let the Pope keep Rome and the Ager Romanus, and secularize the remainder of his territories. They might be erected into a principality under a native Prince, with the Pope for Suzerain—as Moldavia and Wallachia are, or were, under the Sultan. If they were neutralized under the protection of Europe, they would require no army or navy, merely a police, and might give the Pope a considerable revenue; enough to enable him to keep the monuments of Rome in repair and to live splendidly. Another plan is to give them to the young Duke of Parma, in exchange for the Duchy of Parma, which Piedmont ought to have. It will be a poor compensation for her sufferings in this war. It is said that the Emperor has written to the Duchess to propose this arrangement.

Senior.—At the same time that he has written to the Pope to promise to him the integrity of his dominions?

A.—I see nothing in all this to which England need object. If you propose it, and insist on it, he will accept it. He has already, indeed, prepared for it, by saying that he shall astonish the world by his moderation. You have to deal with a man who with all his blustering is 'faible.'

Senior.—What do you mean by 'faible?' He seems to me to be bold up to rashness and pertinacious up to obstinacy.

A.—He tries to appear so, but he is not so. He is an impostor. He is bold when he is alone and merely planning. His schemes are audacious. But he is timid, vacillating, and irresolute in execution. He has not courage enough to dismiss a minister.

Senior.—He has just dismissed three.

A.—That was done by others. His selfishness is beyond all description, beyond all imagination. Do you know why our army was allowed to waste a second winter in the Crimea? It was because he had resolved to finish the war in person. Sebastopol might have been taken in the spring of 1855. But he was not able to leave Paris at that time, and ordered his generals to do nothing decisive until he came. The objections to his journey kept multiplying and at last he gave it up, and allowed the war to be finished. But the delay cost *us* fifty thousand men and the Russians two hundred thousand.

Before the coup d'état all Louis Napoleon's friends were convinced *qu'il fallait en finir avec l'Assemblée*, and so was he. But with him it did not go beyond a vague intention. Persigny and Fleury planned it. They gained the colonels of four or five regiments. But they wanted a commander. Fleury had heard of St. Arnaud, then in Algeria, as a man bold, intelligent, and unscrupulous; convicted of embezzling the pay of his own men, and ready to do any act that might retrieve his fortunes. It was agreed that he should go to Algiers and secure St. Arnaud. But money was wanting. Neither of the conspirators had a farthing, nor had Louis Napoleon; he offered to give bills for sixty thousand francs payable out of his salary. But no one would discount them. They were offered to Fould and refused by him. At length the bills were sold to some Jews for very little, but enough to send Fleury to Algiers. St. Arnaud promised his services, but he was then only general of the brigade. A *razzia* on some poor Cabyle tribes was ordered, he was put in command of it, and a pretext was afforded for making him general of division, recalling him to Paris, and giving him the command of the garrison. It was not until towards the end of November that Persigny and Fleury informed Louis Napoleon that their plot was mature. They were afraid of his raising objections or interfering to delay it.

Senior.—When you talk of our making a proposal, and insisting on it, how do you intend us to insist?

A.—By declaring that if your proposal be accepted by one party, and not by the other, you will make war on the party who rejects it.

Senior.—We are anxious to restore peace to Europe, but not by making war. We must not threaten what we cannot perform, and I am sure that Parliament would not allow such a threat to be executed.

A.—But will you declare that you will interfere if the war goes beyond Italy? If *he* marches on Vienna and *Russia* into Hungary? Will you preserve your impartial neutrality while Austria is dismembered, Russia extends herself to the Adriatic and the Dardanelles, and France to the Rhine?

Senior.—I have no doubt that we shall interfere if the war goes beyond Italy.

A.—Then say so, say so immediately, say so peremptorily, and it will not so extend. But you must first get rid of your blundering, timid Tories. With Palmerston for your Premier, and Clarendon Foreign Secretary, or, if you must have Lord John to carry the Reform, with Palmerston for Foreign Secretary, you will be believed. Here when Malmesbury shows his teeth everybody laughs, for they know that he does not bite. There is nothing that Celui-ci fears like a war with England. I am sorry to confess that it would be popular at first among the masses, but in a short time it would be hated even by them. And *then* it would be fatal to him. He knows this and will never voluntarily encounter it. He may drift into it, if you let him go too far before you declare yourselves. He may have so engaged the national vanity in a war for our natural boundaries as to be unable to retreat. Stop him therefore at the onset. If Palmerston had been in power this war would never have broken out. As for his ministers, they are all with you. Walewski has always protested against the war. But for him the offensive and defensive alliance with Russia, of which your papers talk, would have been made, or at least attempted. Celui-ci sent to propose it. Walewski heard of it, urged on him that it would be the beginning of a general war, and orders were sent by the telegraph to erase that portion of the proposal and reduce it to the terms which are actually agreed on, namely, that Russia is to interfere only in the case of an aggression in France by the Confederation. But whatever you do, do not trust *him*; he was well described by one of your diplomatists; *Je ne conçois pas cet homme ; il ne parle jamais, et il ment toujours.* Not one of them trusts any one of the others. The other day Persigny said to the Emperor, 'Si votre majesté laisse l'Impératrice entre Fould et Magnan, elle sera comme le Christ entre les deux larrons.' 'Peut-être,' answered the Emperor.

Senior.—Who were present?

A.—Only three persons—the Emperor, the Empress, and Persigny.

Senior.—Then how do you know that the story is true?

A.—Because Persigny told it to me the same evening.

Senior.—But which is the 'bon larron?'

A.—We do not know that yet; it will be the one who repents. Let us hope that it will be the Christian. I will tell you something not generally known, but which I know as a matter of absolute certainty. The atrocious addresses of the colonels after the attentat were actually dictated, not perhaps in words, but in substance, by the Emperor, and the scene with Morny was a comedy. Morny complained bitterly to a friend of mine that he had been snubbed in public for repeating an address which the Emperor himself had prepared. He then was meditating war for the Rhine. It seems that afterwards he thought it best to begin by Italy; but depend on it the Rhine or London is his next object.

Senior.—What then shall we get by imposing peace?

A.—You will get this: that Austria will not have been previously ruined, as she will be if she has to contend single-handed against France; and you may be sure that a long war, ending successfully, will make us only the more able and the more willing to begin another, especially with you. Under the new principle that to succour oppressed nationalities is our mission, we shall never want a pretext while the Roman Catholic Church of Ireland is deprived of her endowments. A war in such a cause would unite all parties, clerical as well as lay. Every day of war makes us less peaceful. You may perceive that in the change in public opinion during the four weeks that you have been here. From detesting the war we have come to acquiesce in it; in three months we shall like it. His object is to repeat the old Empire by attacking the different Continental powers one by one until he has rendered each of them subservient and can turn his whole strength on you. Your preparations ought to be such as to render the attempt to invade you, the only war that you fear, hopeless. He is nearly mad, but not enough to venture an obvious impossibility.

I met in the evening M. Lafitte, who belongs to the party of the despotic Republicans, and is a follower of Comte.*

Lafitte.—This reign is one of transition. Louis Napoleon does not believe, nor does any one else, in his dynasty, or in any dynasty whatever, but it is an approach to the only form of government that suits us. Its defects, or rather its mischievous excrescences, are its Senate, its Corps Législatif, its Conseil d'Etat, its great officers of State, its Court, and its pomp. What we want for the present is a 'Dictature Progressive;' one person, or one small body of persons, combining legislative and executive power, and removing all obstacles to improvement.

Senior.—A Government which need do nothing illegal, since if a law stands in its way it can repeal it.

Lafitte.—Exactly so; and so far as this Government approaches that model it is good. It is the best that we have ever had; it gives us tranquillity; it allows liberty of thought, and speech, and writing.

Senior.—Not if you wish to attack an act of the Government, or to say that M. Fould is a rogue, or M. Arrighi an imbecile.

Lafitte.—That sort of freedom we have not, and in general it does more harm than good. The freedom that we have is the really important one, the power to discuss freely every social question; the power to contribute to the enlightenment of mankind. The glorious eighteenth century did no more. It worked for sixty years under a despotic Government without thinking of improving it. You will not find in Voltaire even a wish for a constitution. But it dispersed some of the darkness, and prepared us for better things than constitutions. Let mankind be once

---

* I have retained this conversation, as it expresses the political faith of the Comtists.—ED.

thoroughly enlightened, and there will be no misgovernment. No ruler will venture to misgovern an enlightened nation.

Senior.—How is he to be restrained?

Lafitte.—By public opinion.

Senior.—But that opinion must exhibit itself in some physical form. As there can be no lawful resistance to a Dictator, recourse must be had to unlawful resistance. Your Government is a ' despotisme tempéré par l'émeute.'

Lafitte.—Rather a ' despotisme tempéré par la révolution.'

Senior.—A revolution presupposes an émeute; a revolution is merely a successful émeute.

Lafitte.—It never would be necessary to recur to that remedy. The Dictator of an enlightened nation would be enlightened himself.

Senior.—You approve of this Government?

Lafitte.—I do.

Senior.—Do you approve of its sending ten thousand people last year to Cayenne and Lambressa?

Lafitte.—He had lost his head; he was going rapidly on his way to London; but public opinion, even in the present state of enlightenment, was strong enough to stop him.

Senior.—How long is it to last?

Lafitte.—Probably until his death, and that I hope may be distant. Then comes the Republic.

Senior.—In the form of an Assembly?

Lafitte.—No; of a Provisional Government which will name, or cause to be elected, the Dictator. What is called Parliamentary Government is dead, is burned, is covered by a mass of ruins, from which it never can rise. Of all forms, that which we most hate and despise is constitutional Monarchy. What we want is progress. A constitutional Government does nothing. Its checks and counterchecks reduce it to inaction; if it moves it is by one aid—of corruption. The ' bourgeois lettrés,' such as Guizot and

Thiers, deplored the loss of the constitution because it gave them power and importance. Every one else was delighted by 1848.

Senior.—Then the Bourbons have no chance?

Lafitte.—The branche ainée have absolutely none. As for the Orleans Princes, as they are a distinguished family, the Republicans may take one of them and make him Dictator, but it would be their doing, not his. We shall not allow that he has any claim beyond that of fitness. Next to this, the best Government that we have had was that of the Restoration. Louis XVIII. really governed, and the aristocracy took part in his Government. It was a Government of progress. Louis Philippe rested solely on the bourgeoisie, the most narrow-minded, selfish, ignorant, obstinate portion of the community. It was they that governed, not the King, or Guizot, or Thiers. This man depends on the Prolétaires, who are excellent people, honest, diligent, good in their family relations, and above all open to reasoning and anxious for truth.

Senior.—What is the exact meaning of the word prolétaire?

Lafitte.—It means, not etymologically but by use, a working man; a man who lives by his hands, not by his capital.

Senior.—Who will make the next revolution?

Lafitte.—The Rouges; they have the most energy.

Senior.—And what are the Rouges?

Lafitte.—Practically Communists.

Senior.—And what are Communists?

Lafitte.—Communism depends on two principles. First: that all the commodities are mainly the produce of anterior labour, and that the labour which has been expended on a thing by a man's predecessors gives him no claim to that thing. Secondly: that those who bestow the immediate labour which fits a commodity for use ought to have in it a larger interest than they now have. 'We build palaces,' say the masons, 'but we live in cellars or garrets.' 'We furnish them,' say the carpenters, 'but we can scarcely get a chair or a table.' 'We make coats,' say the tailors, 'yet we are clad in rags.' In fact they deny that the right which we call that of property ought to exist.

Senior.—What do they want, then? A general scramble.

Lafitte.—No. They wish the share of each individual in the whole mass of production to be assigned to him by a constituted authority, and as far as is possible to be in proportion to the services which he renders to society. I do not defend all the doctrines of the Communists. I admit that the abolition of the right of property is absurd and impracticable. But they are an important sect; they must be taken into account by all who attempt to govern France.

Senior.—Is the war popular?

Lafitte.—No. We are already wise enough to hate war; but when both our own Government and yours tell us that Austria is the aggressor, we think that we cannot help ourselves.

Senior.—Has the opposition of the priests contributed to its unpopularity?

Lafitte.—Not in the least. They have absolutely no political influence. In Paris there is no religion among the working classes. You see the churches filled, but it is only by the bourgeois, who fancy religion is conservative. In the provinces the priest is respected because he is useful. His father was a peasant; he knows their ways of thinking, he is raised above them by knowledge and education, but not too high. He advises them, he makes up their quarrels, he rebukes evil-doers, but he never talks dogma to them except from the pulpit, and then the few who are present

go to sleep. He never attempts to influence them by extra-
terrestrial motives; he does not say, 'If you steal you will
not go to heaven.' There is not a peasant who believes in
the Paradis, or who would not sell his chance of it for
twenty sous. The priest's argument is, ' You will be despised, you will be hated, or you will be imprisoned.' Still
the profession is not popular. The people say, ' Dominus
vobiscum a toujours le pain.' Yet they do not like to take
orders. The seminaries are not full, and I know dioceses
in which many of the cures are not filled. On the whole,
the peasants, who form three-fourths of the population of
France, are prosperous. There are whole districts in which
you will not find a single family in indigence. When
people describe the Emperor as establishing freedom in
Italy and tyranny in France, they talk nonsense. Compared to that of Lombardy or Naples, this tyranny is freedom. The utmost aspirations of a Venetian or of a Sicilian
would be satisfied if he had the degree of liberty which is
now enjoyed by every Frenchman.

I went afterwards to Madame de Circourt's and met
there a man whose name I did not catch, a Legitimist, a
brother-in-law of Villemain's. We talked upon elections,
which led the conversation to Parliamentary Government.

Legitimist.—It is good for you, who have an aristocracy
of birth and fortune, who have local institutions and
religious belief; but for us who have none of those requi-
sites it is the Government of a corrupt, ignorant, talking,
jobbing, selfish bourgeoisie; *you* can have a House of
Commons because you have municipal institutions.

Senior.—On the contrary, we have municipal institutions
because we have a House of Commons. An absolute
Government would centralise us, as it has centralised you.

Legitimist.—You must admit that Parliamentary Government dethrones the Sovereign; he may enjoy the splendour of Monarchy, but he cannot perform its duties; he cannot govern.

Senior.—What form of Government do you wish for? Do you like what you have?

Legitimist.—Much better than any that we have had since 1814. What is really fit for us is the old régime—a King unfettered by law, but controlled by custom and by constituted bodies who act independently of him.

Senior.—But who are liable to be sent to the Bastille or to a provincial town, or to be abolished if they offend him.

Other people came in and we separated. The Legitimists and the ultra-Republicans have much in common.

Sunday, May 8th.—I called on Madame Cornu and gave her an outline of my interview with Prince Napoleon.

Madame Cornu.—When the Prince thinks that the great object of the war is to terminate the preponderance of Austria to the south of Italy, he gives his cousin too much credit for statesmanship. That may be *one* of its objects, but it is a subordinate one.

Senior.—Subordinate to his fears of assassination, or to his hope of military fame?

Madame Cornu.—Those also are subordinate motives. My own conviction is, that if he had not made this war he would have been assassinated, but I doubt whether *he* thinks so. He has recovered from the shock of the attentat; and resumed his fatalism. His real motive, which towers high above all others, is his hatred of Austria, a hatred bred in his very bones—a hatred which began in his early infancy, which was fostered during all his childhood and youth, which made him a conspirator and a carbonaro, when most boys are thinking of their games or of their lessons. On the 24th of December, 1848, a fortnight after he had been elected President, I waited on him at the request of the Italians in Paris, to ask what he intended to do for Italy? 'Tell them,' he said, 'that my name is Bonaparte, and that I feel the responsibilities which that name implies. Italy is dear to me, as dear almost as France, but my duties to France ' passent avant tout.' I must watch for an opportunity. For the present I am controlled by the Assembly, which will not give me money and men for a war of sentiment, in which France has no direct immediate interest. But tell them that my feelings are now what they were in 1830, and repeat to them that my name is Bonaparte.

Senior.—Can he wish to give free institutions to Italy?

Madame Cornu.—I believe that he does. I believe that he has a sympathy for freedom, though where he himself is concerned it is overruled by his desire for power. He likes to be absolute himself, but wishes all who are not his subjects to be free. Then he desires most eagerly everything that he thinks will give him posthumous fame. Imagination is his predominant faculty. I have often said that nature meant him to be a poet. He would have been a great one. Like most men of imagination he lives in the future; as a child, his desire was to become an historical character. He has no moral sense, he does not care about ' le bien ou le mal, ça lui est égal, ou plutôt il n'en conçoit pas la différence,' nor does he care much about present reputation, except as an instrument. He begins now to hope to fill as many pages in history as his uncle has done, and he hopes that they will be brighter, at least that they will be darkened by fewer shadows; and if he believes, as I have reason to think that he does, that the man who founds free institutions in Italy will be praised a thousand years hence, he will do it. He will do it if he hopes that history will accept it as a sort of compensation for his having destroyed such institutions in France.

I spent the evening at Duchâtel's. His opinions as to the dangers of a Russian irruption coincide with those of the party at Vuitry's,* but he is less sanguine as to our power of averting it.

Duchâtel.—The Château talks of finishing the war by two battles and a siege; but my military friends expect two campaigns. They think that we shall get to Milan this year, and perhaps to Piacenza, but that we shall not begin the siege of Verona till next year. Our army will pass the unhealthy season in an unhealthy country. Our loss in a couple of years may be equal to a year's conscription. We shall have to borrow another five hundred millions. Austria will suffer still more, both in men and money. Before the peace is made Russia will have had ample time to make her 'coup.' Unless she is entangled by the serf question or has abandoned under the new Emperor her traditionary ambition, she may be mistress of Constantinople a year hence. Who is there to stop her? You cannot do it; Prussia cannot do it. France and Austria could, but they will be otherwise engaged. Her old enemies, France and Sardinia, may perhaps have made her mistress of all Eastern Europe.

All the streets leading to the places in which subscriptions for the loan are received are crowded by intending subscribers, almost all in blouses or cotton gowns; they are ranged in lines three deep, and let in by batches of two dozen at a time. It is said that three times the amount wanted has already been asked for. The Government papers treat this as a proof of the popularity of the war and of the Emperor; it only shows that the Minister of Finance has made a bad

---

* As I believe most of the party are still alive, I have not published that conversation.—ED.

bargain. The three per cents are at 61·50. The loan, considering that it is to be paid in by instalments running over eighteen months, and that interest runs on the whole from Christmas, is really given out at 57·50—that is to say, at five per cent. below its value. The Government might have got twenty-one millions for the price which it pays for twenty millions. I am delighted to see that it is taken by Frenchmen, and by the lower classes. A large public debt held by hundreds of thousands will not easily be repudiated, and will interest those hundreds of thousands in the restoration of peace.

Tuesday, May 10*th.*—Duvergier, Lanjuinais, and Chrzanowski breakfasted with us. We begged Chrzanowski to tell us what is to happen.

Chrzanowski.—Nothing for the next week, unless one side or the other should commit some great ' bêtise.' The French are not yet ready to attack; their troops have come up in haste by different routes, and are not fully equipped or concentrated, and, I believe, have orders to do nothing decisive until the Emperor's arrival. As for the Austrians, no general voluntarily attacks unless he thinks himself superior morally or numerically. The Austrian army has by this time little numerical superiority, and it must be morally inferior. An invading army is discouraged as soon as it ceases to make progress. The Austrian has made none after the first two or three days; it must have lost its 'élan,' and it must have lost its confidence, if it ever possessed any, in its commander. All its marches and countermarches, its crossing and recrossing the rivers, its ' tâtonnements,' its fruitless cannonades, and its expeditions for mere plunder show the absence of Hesse and the presence of Giulay, a man who never before was at the head of ten thousand men. I suspect, too, the interference of the Emperor, Francis Joseph, which cannot but be mischievous.

Senior.—We are told that the movements of the Austrians have been stopped by the rains, by the melting of the Alpine snows, which have swelled the rivers, and by the inundations made by the Piedmontese.

Chrzanowski.—That is nonsense. These are the excuses of persons who did not know what to do, or were afraid to do it: none of these obstacles would have stopped men of decision. The inundations are trifling. If, indeed, the banks of the Po were cut lower in its course beyond Mantua, where its bed is thirty or forty feet above the plain, the country would become impassable; but no serious inundations can take place in the Piedmontese plain.

Senior.—And what ought the Austrians to do now?

Chrzanowski.—Retreat to their position between Peschiera and Verona, which they had better not have quitted. Whether they can do so without great loss will depend on the generalship on each side. If the Austrians are well managed they will retire in a compact body, turning from time to time when they are in a strong position, and beating by their superior numbers the advanced parties who may attempt to press on their flanks, and they may reach their strong position without serious loss. If the French are well commanded they may follow the Austrians vigorously, and try every opportunity to bring on a general action, and may perhaps obtain a considerable success. Either party who commits a fault may be severely punished, if the other does not neutralize it by committing another. I expect nothing but blunders on each side. If one makes fewer than the other he will win; if both blunder equally I think that the French troops being better than the Austrians, good as the Austrians are, will succeed. But the presence of Louis Napoleon is a tower of strength to his enemies; he is much worse than Giulay, bad as Giulay is; he is intoxicated by the success of his Châlons campaigns; he ranged his men there à la Vauban, in curtains and bastions, and believes now that it was a great military invention. It is no slight affair to range one hundred and fifty thousand men in order of battle, to protect them against the enemy's fire by the inclinations of the ground, and to give them the advantage of every eminence and of every cover. It is no slight thing to move them, to keep the different corps separate while they advance, and to unite them in order to fight. And the greatest difficulty of all, especially in an enemy's country, a country already laid waste by the retreating army, is to feed them. Napoleon has seen nothing except a review; his lieutenants have seen nothing except a razzia. If it is possible to lose the game he will lose it. Pelissier was offered a command in the army of the Alps; he refused if the Emperor was to be present.

Senior.—Will the new arms much change the art of war?

Chrzanowski.—Not much, unless a musket can be invented with a long point-blank range. A musket whose precision depends on calculation of distance is of little value. A man appears to be nearer, or more distant, according to the state of the atmosphere, according to the brightness or the darkness of his dress, according to his being in light or in shadow. A hair's-breadth difference of elevation will send the ball above his head or before his feet. Then as to the new cannon. It proposes to hit an object five miles off. Under the old system, when we fired at nothing much more than half a mile off, we obtained the range by seeing what the first balls did, whether they went over the enemy or fell short of him. But at five miles, or even at two or three miles' distance, the result cannot be seen. A battery may fire a whole day without discovering that it is firing in vain.

Lanjuinais.—It is odd that Louis Napoleon's best friends should have been Lord Derby, who certainly does not like him, and Francis Joseph, who is his bitter enemy. The silly, hopeless interference of Lord Derby caused Austria to lose three weeks; the mismanagement of Francis Joseph, or of the 'imbéciles' to whom Francis Joseph has trusted the fate of his army, perhaps of the Empire, has turned the loss of those three weeks into the loss of the campaign.

Duvergier.—Lord Derby has done still worse than that; he has given to Louis Napoleon the support of the French people; he has made the war, which was most unpopular, national. The people are told, on Lord Derby's authority, that Austria is not only an aggressor but a criminal. These words have run through France like wildfire.

Lanjuinais.—The only excuse for them is that they were made after dinner. But what can we think of a statesman who can make an after-dinner speech on such a subject, who can allow the destinies of Europe to be affected by an extra bottle of champagne?

Duvergier.—Would you like to hear the story of Vaillant's dismissal? It was related to me by one of the actors in it. The Emperor had long been told of Vaillant's incompetence, but with his usual indolence and procrastination he took no steps; he has a fellow-feeling for idle men. At last the utter unpreparedness of the army, which Vaillant has represented as fit for service, astonished and irritated him. He hates a discussion, and cannot bear to wound a man who is before him, though he does not care what he does to a man who is absent. So, without preparing Vaillant or giving him an opportunity of defending himself, he ordered M. de Cadore, one of his aides-de-camp, to communicate to Vaillant his dismissal. No one likes now to act on verbal instructions from Louis Napoleon; a hundred times, on the least change of circumstances or of his own humour, he has disavowed his agents. So Cadore asked for a written paper and got one. He found Vaillant in consultation with several officers. Vaillant took the note, laid it aside, and continued the discussion. Cadore reminded him that it came from the Emperor, and might require an immediate answer. Vaillant opened it and read it half-aloud. It was in these words: 'J'ai toléré votre négligence pendant la paix; je ne dois pas la tolérer en guerre. J'ai nommé le Maréchal Randon votre successeur.' Vaillant got up, sent away the officers, and hurried to the Château. 'I am disgraced,' he said, 'by a dismissal in such terms.' Louis Napoleon was astonished. These Bonapartes do not suppose that anybody else has any feelings, or that anything coming from them can be resented. 'I had not the least intention,' he said, 'to annoy you. It is too late to keep you as Minister of War, so you shall be my major-general.' This is the most important post in the whole army.

We talked of the deference paid in France to official rank.

Lanjuinais.—It is becoming our aristocracy. Birth has lost its prestige, except among the remains of the old noblesse, and wealth, when unconnected with power, excites envy rather than respect. A man in office has always something to give. A Minister is a demi-god, for he may have a thousand things to give. Under Louis Philippe a Deputy was a great man. Every one made way for him. Now he is nothing. His vote is not worth having; he is merely a man elected by the people to do nothing for a comfortable salary, and ranks far below the lowest nominee of the Crown. A friend of mine, who, after sitting in the Chamber of Deputies, the Assemblée Nationale, and the

Constituente, is now a member of the Corps Législatif, called the other day on a Minister. He had been accustomed to find every door open to him. He was walking into the well-known cabinet when the huissier stopped him. His Excellency was engaged. 'When can I see him?' said the member. 'I do not know,' said the huissier. 'But I am a member of the Corps Législatif.' 'I have no orders,' said the huissier, 'as to the Corps Législatif.' My friend was going away in despair when the compassion of the huissier, who had known him as Deputy, was moved. 'If,' he said, 'Monsieur held any office?' 'I am Maire,' said my friend, 'of my parish.' 'Ah,' said the huissier, 'passez, Monsieur le Maire.'

Sunday, May 15*th.*—I went with Mohl and the young Princess Belgiojoso to spend the day at Bûcheron, the country seat of M. de Tourgénieff,* separated by a wall only from Malmaison.

Tourgénieff is a Liberal. He was high in office under the Emperor Alexander, though not actually a Minister. He was travelling at the time of Alexander's death, was accused of being cognisant of the conspiracy which broke out immediately after, and was required to return to take his trial. He offered to do so, on condition that his trial should be a regular one, and not by a military tribunal, or a special commission. This was refused, he was tried in his absence and condemned to death. His property was given over to his brother, who gradually sold it, and carried on his own person to Tourgénieff the bills which represented its price; Tourgénieff invested it in the French and English funds, and is rich. The present Emperor pardoned

---

* A distant relation of the well-known novelist. He endeavoured by every means in his power to assist the emancipation of the serfs. He died in 1872.—ED.

him, and an aunt left him an estate of about three hundred souls, so that he is again a Russian proprietor. A soul in Russian enumeration signifies a male. So that his serfs are about six hundred, or one hundred and twenty families, which supposes six square miles of land. I mentioned the general dread in Paris of a Russian invasion of Turkey.

Tourgénieff.—You need not fear it for the present. The frightful mortality of the late war reduced the Russian army below its peace establishment. Nothing is so dreaded in Russia as a recruitment. Those whom it takes from their homes nominally for twenty years, are never seen there again. Alexander on his accession promised that there should not be another until the country had recovered itself, which it is far from having done. And a further difficulty is occasioned by the serf question. Under the existing law the recruits are selected by the proprietor, or, as he is usually called, the lord. It is proposed that they should be selected by the Mir, the local authority, the Court Baron of the Manor. In the present excitement it would be dangerous to employ either of those modes.

Senior.—What are now the limits of the lord's power over his serfs?

Tourgénieff.—Scarcely any, except those imposed by custom, or by opinion. It is not usual, there is a doubt whether it is legal, to sell serfs, except as attached to land, or to separate families on sale. It is not legal to inflict on them more than forty blows at one punishment, nor can the lord maim or kill them, but he has every other power. He can banish them to Siberia. He can require from them whatever labour he chooses, their property is his, they cannot marry or contract, or quit their villages without his permission. On the other hand, he is bound to support them, and to administer justice among them, and he is responsible for the poll-tax, which amounts to about seven francs a head. A Russian province consists of an aggregate of manors which are indivisible, can be owned only by nobles, and are inhabited only by the lord and his villeins. A portion, perhaps at an average. of two-fifths, is held by the lord as his demesne, the rest is divided among the villeins, who pay for it a rent in money or in days of labour. The Mir, or Court Baron appointed by the lord, distributes the land among the villeins, endeavouring to give to each family enough to live on and pay its tax, and as the population of the manor increases or diminishes, the distribution is varied, the tenants being jointly and severally responsible to the lord for the aggregate rent.

Senior.—This resembles the Irish rundale system. When an estate is in rundale, the tenants divide it among themselves, endeavouring to make the different tenancies about equal in value, and as the distribution is permanent, a man who has improved his land may find that he has done so for the benefit of his successor.

Tourgénieff.—So it is in Russia. You may see the fertile part of an estate divided into narrow strips where a plough can scarcely turn, while the inferior part is in comparatively large farms. The Mir, which, being supported by the lord is omnipotent, forces the tenants sometimes to take more land than they wish, in order to throw on them a higher rent, sometimes to give up land which they have improved, because it is wanted by some idle neighbour. The necessary consequences are, the want of agricultural capital, the want of diligence, of skill, and a population distributed not according to the extent or the capabilities of the soil, but to the good or bad management, or to the caprice of the lord. Some estates are over-peopled, others are under-peopled. So miserable is their cultivation, returning at an average about four for one, that about twenty-two acres and a half are supposed to be required for a family. To convert into

men and women who have to provide for themselves, a
population which for centuries have been treated as domestic
animals, or, at the best as children, would be no easy task,
even if there were full time and good agents. But there
are neither. Nothing can be worse, more narrow-minded,
more corrupt or more perverse than the Russian bureaucracy, nothing more frivolous or more ignorant than the
Russian nobles, and these are the instruments. Nearly a
year and a half has passed since committees of the nobles
of each province were formed and were required to report
within six months on the means by which the emancipation
of the serfs could be best effected. That subject, previously
prohibited, was allowed to be discussed by the press. A
whole literature has been published on it. There are newspapers exclusively devoted to it. The one hundred thousand
noble families who own all the land that does not belong to
the Crown expect ruin. Their twenty-two millions of serfs
have vague hopes of some enormous good. The suspense of
one party, and the impatience of the other may soon become
dangerous. Well or ill, the thing must be done quickly.
The basis of the plan, or rather of the suggestion of the
Government are, to give to the serf personal liberty and
about one-half of the land of each manor, to be paid for by
him in rent or in labour. This scheme throws the whole
loss on the lord. He has now a legal title to all the land,
and also to all the labour, and to all the property of the
serf. He is to give up half his land, and receive in exchange
for it only a part of the serf's labour or money. The lord
who has only serfs, or whose income is principally derived
from their services as artisans or tradesmen, loses everything. This scheme therefore is generally reprobated. The
only equitable plan is, to diffuse the loss over the whole
Empire, by paying by the State the indemnity due to the
lord. But the amount of this indemnity is rated at sums

the lowest of which, sixty millions sterling, is a heavy burthen, and the highest, four hundred and thirty millions, would be insupportable.

Senior.—What occasions the discrepancy between these estimates?

Tourgénieff.—One cause is the admitting or not admitting the claim of the lord to be repaid for the loss of the personal services of the serfs. The general opinion is, that this right is an abuse, and that if in exceptional circumstances the lord is to be paid for surrendering it, it must be an act of grace, not of justice. Another source of discrepancy is, the admitting or not admitting that the serfs are to repay to the State, wholly or in part, the indemnity which it advances to the lord. Another is difference of opinion as to the amount of land to be given up to the peasants, and as to the rent which they ought to pay for it. The committee of the Government of St. Petersburg proposes that each peasant family should have nine 'desiatines' (about twenty-two acres and a half) and pay for it annually to the lord twenty days of labour per desiatine, or in all one hundred and eighty days of labour; that is nearly two-thirds of their labour during the year. Under such an arrangement how are they to cultivate their own land? Another of the suggestions of the Government is, that the serfs are to be obliged to take the land whether they wish for it or not, that they are not to be allowed to sell any portion of it without the permission of the lord and the Mir (Court of the Manor), and that they are not, without such permission, to quit their villages during the first twelve years. This would be, in fact, retaining serfage for twelve years. It resembles your West Indian apprenticeship, which, as we know, failed. On the whole I can only repeat that the subject is one of enormous difficulty, that neither our statesmen nor our administrators are capable of treating it well, even if they had time to do so, and they have not that time.

Senior.—And you think that until that question has been disposed of, Russia cannot act powerfully beyond her own frontier?

Tourgénieff.—I think that the external action of Russia is suspended until the Serf question has been disposed of, and perhaps for some years afterwards. The ultimate result will, I trust, be the increase of her power by the increase of her population in numbers, in industry, and in wealth. But that will not be perceptible in our time.

Wednesday, May 18*th.* — Drouyn de Lhuys, Count Arrivabene, the Marquis Capranica and his wife, Ristori, breakfasted with us. She gave her name at the door, not as Marchioness Capranica, but as Madame Ristori. We all agreed that she is still handsomer in a room than on the stage. On the stage the action both of her face and body is, at least to our northern taste, excessive; nothing can be more simple or more charming than her manners in society. The Marquis is of a great Roman family; she is from the Terra Firma. They are strong Italian Liberals.

Madame Ristori.—Until now I detested Louis Napoleon. I never would be presented to him or to the Countess Montijo, who tried to become acquainted with me. Now I worship him. If I were a man, I would join the French army to-morrow.

Senior.—Do you think the liberties of Italy are safe with him?

Madame Ristori.—The liberties—perhaps no; but the independence—yes. Before the end of the war we shall have 300,000 Italians in arms. So armed, and warned by our long experience of French treachery, we shall not be subdued or deceived.

Senior.—Would the Terra Firma like to be reunited to Venice, if the old Republic can be resuscitated?

Madame Ristori.—It would be delighted. With all its faults the old aristocracy has left grateful recollections. Perhaps our ancestors in the last century were more tolerant than we are of arbitrary rule; perhaps the Governments, keeping up much smaller establishments, were less exacting. They meddled perhaps more, and taxed less. And if the Venetian Republic were reanimated, it would not be with the golden book, or the Council of Ten, or the Piombi.

Arrivabene.—The Piombi, if I may judge from the one which the Austrian Government did me the honour of putting at my disposition, were very tolerable residences. I had a splendid view over the Grand Canal, the Lido, and the Adriatic. Below me was the Bridge of Sighs. It was in early spring, however; they may be unbearable in summer.

I fear that if Lombardy and Venetia are completely separated from Austria she will always be endeavouring to regain them. I had rather place them under a member of the House of Hapsburg; but of course with Italian administration. The Bourbons of Naples were not under the influence of the Bourbons of France.

Madame Ristori.—I saw Victor Emmanuel when I was in Turin some years ago. I thought him pleasing, and, above all, simple and very natural. Naturalness is the greatest of charms, perhaps because it is so rare. 'Il me paraît que tout le monde joue la comédie autant que moi.' The lawyers do it; the deputies do it; and, above all, the priests do it. I once followed a crowd into a church at Palermo, the attraction was a man lying before the altar extended on a cross. He was absolutely motionless, and seemed unconscious of the crowd around him, absorbed as he was in devout meditation. One of my servants recognised him next day in a wine-shop. He complained bitterly of the priests. 'They pay me,' he said, 'only one or two lire for lying for hours on a piece of wood, without daring to brush the flies from my face; and they charge five times as much for saying a single mass, which does not take a man half an hour.' I went yesterday to say my prayers at St. Roch. I had scarcely knelt down before a priest came to me, rattling his box. 'Ton-ton pour la fabrique.' Then came another; 'ton-ton pour les pauvres.' Then another; 'ton-ton pour les âmes en purgatoire.' Then another; 'ton-ton pour l'autel.' Then the woman; 'deux sous, madame, pour la chaise.'

Drouyn de Lhuys.—' Passe pour la chaise.' It is worth paying two sous, and even being interrupted, to escape the discomforts of a pew. Massillon was once asked what compliment had pleased him most. 'One day,' he said, 'I had just entered the pulpit when I heard a conversation below me. A man was bargaining for a chair. He offered two sous; the woman asked a petit écu. 'Croyez-vous,' she said, ' qu'on entende Massillon pour moins?'

Madame Ristori.—I thought it a comédie when they prevented in England my playing Mirrha. There is no piece that I have studied more deeply; there is not a syllable that can offend the purest ears. I ventured to remark that ' Don Juan' was permitted. 'Yes,' they said, ' but ' Don Juan' is only sung, ' people don't know what it means '—as if every girl did not read the libretto.

I asked the Marquis, who is a Roman, what was to become of the Pope?

Capranica.—I do not wish him to be a subject; I think that he must be a Sovereign, but there is no necessity for his being an absolute Sovereign. He was not so formerly; even his election as Sovereign required the ratification of the people. His great difficulty, if he is forced to secularise his Administration, will be the providing for the swarm of ecclesiastics who now live on the public revenue.

Senior.—This would be only a temporary difficulty, as they are all unmarried.

Arrivabene.—I am inclined to hope that the Pope is not so Austrian as he is supposed to be. I had a conversation just before I left Brussels last week with the Nuncio, a respectable man, but narrow-minded, and until now violently Austrian. I found him changed into a Progressista, anxious for Italian freedom and Italian unity in the federal form, with the Pope at its head. 'Why,' he said, 'should it be assumed that the Papal troops are not to fight? The Pope is a temporal Sovereign, and a temporal Sovereign must sometimes have military duties.'

Drouyn de Lhuys.—I know that in 1847 proposals were made to him that he should put himself at the head of an Italian confederacy. I will not say that he accepted them, but I will say that he did not reject them.

Madame Ristori was anxious, as all Italians are, to know what hope their cause had of English assistance.

Senior.—We cannot interfere until one party has obtained a decided success. We cannot assist France against Austria, for though we lament the treatment of her Italian subjects by Austria, and are anxious that it should be put an end to, we cannot sanction a principle of intervention which would be the source of eternal war. What peace could there be if every nation made war on every nation, which in its opinion misgoverned a portion of its subjects? We cannot assist Austria against France, because that would help to perpetuate the misgovernment which we deplore. But if Austria beats France, or, what I expect, if France beats Austria, we may then interpose and suggest terms of peace.

Drouyn de Lhuys.—The great mistake of England and of France was that they did not interfere in 1848. Palmerston committed a fatal error when he refused to support or even to communicate to the Piedmontese Austria's offer to grant independence to Lombardy. Cavaignac was as short-sighted or as timid. I urged him in vain to co-operate with England in arranging the Italian question. I hope even now that it will be settled by England and France. But what misery has been undergone and will be undergone before that is done, and how great are the dangers that it may not be done.

Cousin drank tea with us. His great wish is to see Palmerston Premier.

Cousin.—We think that on the Italian question he agrees with us more than Lord John does. We think that he takes a stronger interest in foreign politics, and that from his long experience he understands better their details. When Lord Lansdowne brought him to Paris several years ago he was our ' bête-noire,' but before he left he was popular. He is a thorough Englishman, looks at everything from the English point of view, would close the Mediterranean, as he keeps the Isthmus of Suez uncut, if he thought that he could increase in the slightest degree the commerce or the power of England. But I do not complain of this; a statesman ought to be selfish as respects his own country. Much more harm than good is done by those who affect to sympathise with foreign countries and oppressed nationalities. He is above such hypocrisy; he delighted us by his frankness, by his sagacity, and above all by his decision. He knows what he wants and what he intends. If he had been in your Foreign Office this war would not have broken out, and if he return to your Foreign Office he will put an end to it. Celui-ci could not have deceived or bullied him, as he has your present men, and will again. He has turned to his own account their hopes, their fears, and even their dislike of him. He will not attempt to make a tool of Palmerston. One of Palmerston's great advantages is his perfect French. I do not know twenty persons in France who speak it as well, and not more than two in England. They are Lord and Lady Stanhope; but I tell Lady Stanhope that if she intends to continue a perfect French-woman, she must not neglect Paris.

I ended the evening at Thiers'.

Thiers.—The military events of the last week appear to show that Giulay has made way for Hesse. Instead of wasting time in useless marches and countermarches, and crossing and recrossing rivers, the Austrians are concentrating themselves in the square bounded by the Sesia to the west, the Po to the south, the mountainous country to the north, and the Ticino to the east. There they await their 6th corps, which is coming to them from Verona.

Senior.—Why do not they fall back to meet it?

Thiers.—Because they cannot, after having made their invasion of Piedmont, retreat without some apparent cause. It would be a confession of weakness which would demoralise their army. If they had been twenty days earlier, which they would have been if they had not been arrested by your silly mediation, or even ten days earlier, as they would have been if Buol had not waited for the return of his courier from Turin, instead of acting as he ought to have done, on the telegraphic dispatch of his minister; or if, late as they were, they had been aware of the unprepared state in which the French had come up, without cavalry, artillery, or even ammunition, they might have crushed the Piedmontese, broken up the railway, and laid a contribution on Turin. But having lost all these opportunities, they will remain until the country is eaten up, and then retire as the French advance. Such is the carelessness of our headquarters, that they have entered on a campaign in a country intersected by rivers without pontoons. Our army will be delayed a week while pontoon trains are sent from Vincennes. Our troops are so much better than the Austrians that it will take an enormous amount of blundering to seriously compromise them. But such an amount is possible, and would not surprise me. I fear much, too, from the difficulties of feeding so large an army, and from the unhealthiness of the country. Altogether I expect a long war.

Madame Dosne.—In which England will have to take part unless Austria prove a match for France. A war with England, a revenge for Waterloo, is Celui-ci's ultimate object. This war is merely a prelude to it. When one or two years of war have trained his army and shown who are his good generals, and the military spirit of France is fully awakened, he will satiate on you his long-deferred vengeance.

Thiers listened, but said nothing.

Friday, May 20th.—We dined at the Mohls, and met the Marquis Capranica and his wife (Ristori), Villemain, Cousin, and Mignet. Villemain was late, but we waited for him.

Madame Mohl.—Now that Tocqueville is gone, Villemain is the president of the republic of letters. He bears his honours meekly, but he expects them to be acknowledged.

We asked Madame Ristori why she played Cassandra in a yellow wig instead of her own fine black hair.

Madame Ristori.—It is not a wig; it is my own hair,

powdered yellow. Somma is somewhat of a pedant. He tells me that Cassandra had yellow hair. It is very disagreeable, does not suit my complexion, and takes me hours which I can ill spare, to wash out. But I must keep to it while he is in Paris. As soon as he goes I shall give up the yellow powder.

Mignet said that there was no part in which he liked her better than that of Maria Stuarda.

Madame Ristori.—Perhaps it is because I love Marie Stuart: I represent her with far more feeling than I do Elizabeth, whom I abhor.

Mignet.—Elizabeth was not amiable, but Marie Stuart was not reproachless.

Madame Ristori.—I will not believe that she murdered Darnley; it was all Bothwell's doing. The murder of Marie Stuart herself by Elizabeth was a much more atrocious crime, for it was unprovoked. Elizabeth was a fit daughter of Henry VIII.

Mignet.—Henry VIII. murdered no one. His wives were unfaithful, and he let the law take its course. *We* call him a tyrant, but he was popular.

Cousin.—So was Nero, although in consequence, according to Gibbon, of the perverseness of the Christians, ' il s'est permis d'user envers eux des procédés regrettables.'

Villemain talked to me for some time about England.

Villemain.—I cannot understand your policy abroad or at home. You guarantee the integrity of the Turkish Empire; an empire which no exertions of yours or of anybody's else can prevent falling to pieces. If you do not interfere with the processes of nature its provinces will gradually detach themselves from one another and crystallize into separate independent principalities, as Egypt and Greece have already done. But if you keep together that corrupt, ill-joined mass for a few years longer it will become the subject of partition. Russia and Austria will take the lion's share, and France will not choose to be altogether left out. She may pounce on Egypt, or seek an indemnity on the Rhine, and the war which you dread will be the result of your own conduct.

Senior.—What would you do with Constantinople? Would you make it the capital of the new Greek Empire?

Villemain.—No; I would not have a Greek Empire which would be a dependency of Russia. I would make Constantinople a free commercial Republic. Then as to your home policy. Your constituency is already too Democratic. It is so Democratic that it gives you a House of Commons more unmanageable, more eager to govern, and less fit to do so, after every dissolution; and you propose to extend your franchise, to lower what is already far too low. You propose to do it wantonly, when there is no demand for it; you are on the road to universal suffrage. When your political men select reform as a battlefield they seem to me to be fighting in a powder magazine.

[Mr. Senior left Paris on the 23rd.—ED.]

1860.

[THE war in Italy had been decisive and glorious. The battle of Magenta, in which the Austrians were defeated, was fought on the 4th of June, and was followed by the victory of Solferino on the 24th. After these two victories, Louis Napoleon, seeing dangers ahead, agreed to an armistice, and forgetting a promise with which he had opened the war, 'to free Italy from the Alps to the Adriatic,' patched up a hasty peace at Villa Franca on the 11th of July, by which Austria surrendered Lombardy to Louis Napoleon, through whom it was transferred to Sardinia.

Cavour was indignant at this check in the full tide of conquest. He immediately resigned, and Ratazzi became Prime Minister. But the spirit of Italian patriotism was far from contenting itself with the terms of Villa Franca. The duchies of Parma, Modena, and Tuscany, which Louis Napoleon had agreed to restore to their former rulers, one and all chose Victor Emmanuel for their King, and their example was followed by Bologna and the Æmilia, which threw off the Papal Government. This movement was secretly supported by Cavour, who continued to sway the destinies of Italy from his country-house at Leri. Louis Napoleon insisted upon receiving the provinces of Nice and Savoy as the condition of his assent to the aggrandisement of Victor Emmanuel, and Cavour was recalled to the Premiership in January, 1860, to give his official support. The cession of these provinces was never forgotten by Garibaldi, a hero who was now to attract the attention of Europe, and whose character proved a marked contrast to that of his rival, Cavour. Unable to endure the slow progress of events, and neither discouraged nor openly supported by the Government, in the following May Garibaldi set out on an expedition to Sicily at the head of a small band of devoted followers. In three months he had conquered the island, and on the 18th of August crossed over to Calabria. Everywhere he was welcomed by an enthusiastic population; Francis II. fled before him to his army at Gaeta, and on the 7th of September Garibaldi entered Naples without opposition.

These revolutionary proceedings greatly alarmed Pius IX., who, fourteen years previously, had been a leading champion of Italian liberty, but, under the influence of his minister, Cardinal Antonelli, had now become one of its strongest opponents. He placed General Lamoricière at the head of an army collected from all countries, ready to fight for the Papacy, and to support Francis II., who threatened an invasion of his former dominions from Gaeta, while Austria from Mantua and Verona was preparing to join their cause. Cavour hesitated no longer; he determined at once to take possession of the Papal States in Umbria and the Marches, already in open revolt, push forward the army to Naples and Sicily, and wrest from Garibaldi the leadership of the nation. The deputations from these provinces demanding immediate annexation were favourably listened to, Cardinal Antonelli was summoned in the name of Italy to disband his mercenaries, the Sardinian army crossed the frontier, and the fleet set sail for the Adriatic. The Sardinians defeated the Papal troops at Castelfidardo on the 18th of September, besieged and took Ancona (29th of September, 1860), and entered the Kingdom of Naples, under Victor Emmanuel, on the 15th of October, having taken Lamoricière prisoner, and scattered his army to the winds.

Garibaldi had meanwhile defeated the Neapolitan troops in the battle of Volturno, and driven them under the guns of Gaeta. The two victorious armies met at Capua, and Garibaldi was the first to salute Victor Emmanuel with the title of King of Italy.

Mr. Senior visited France in May, and again in August and September.—ED.]

Sunday, May 6th.—We reached Paris yesterday evening. Dussard, a Republican of 1832, breakfasted with us. He bought some years ago an extensive estate in the Pyrenees, near Perpignan. I asked him how his purchase had turned out.

Dussard.—Badly. My neighbours, all peasant proprietors, treat me as a common prey, as a thing to be eaten. They destroy my fences; they turn their cattle into my inclosures; they cut down my young plantations to heat their ovens; they dispute my boundaries, and the tribunals give me no redress when I am plaintiff, and always decide against me when I am defendant. I am a large proprietor, and I am a stranger. In the provinces either of these predicates excludes a man from justice. If the judges, like your justices of assize, were itinerant, or, like your county-court judges, were sent from the capital, or, like your justices of quarter-sessions, were gentlemen, they would be impartial. But they are the people of the country, ill-born, ill-educated, and ill-paid. I do not know whether they are open to bribery, but they certainly are open to solicitation; in fact, they invite it. My opponents, however, need not bribe or solicit. Both the law and the facts are always on the side of the peasant against the great landowner, of the native against the Parisian, of the ignorant against the educated man. I must sell my property for half its intrinsic value, and cheap as it will appear to be, the buyer will find it dear unless he be a native, and unless he breaks it up and re-sells it in lots.

We talked of Louis Napoleon.

Dussard.—His last war has seated him firmly on the throne. No one cared about Sebastopol. It was too far; the siege lasted too long. Celui-ci took no part in it. We got nothing by it that we cared for. But this war was made under our eyes, it was short and successful, and it has extended our frontier. Chauvinism, glory, and conquest are irresistible to a Frenchman. Popular opinion, which the massacres of 1851 and the deportations of 1852 and 1858 had made hostile to him, turned in his favour as soon as he took the command of the army. I saw him pass through the Boulevards on his way; the enthusiasm was universal and sincere. Robespierre said that if he could ride he should have no rival. What he meant to express was the admiration of the 'peuple' for a man of action, for a man who uses his body as well as his mind, who shares with them the only fatigues and dangers to which they are accustomed. On the few occasions on which they have had a military Sovereign he has been omnipotent.

Senior.—I am told that Louis Napoleon's management of the campaign was deplorable.

Dussard.—So it was, as respects his military skill. The generals talk of it with unreserved contempt; but he showed courage and self-reliance, and *he succeeded*—that is all that the mass of the army or the mass of the people know about it. Even his follies make him popular. He borrows at an extravagant interest. All who have little hoards to invest, and there is scarcely a peasant or a petty shopkeeper who has not, tried to get a bit of the loan. He is wasting millions after millions in pulling down and rebuilding Paris. This produces a high rate of wages in the Faubourgs of St. Antoine and St. Jacques. In the old sources and centres of émeutes not a barricade would be raised against him. I see only two dangers in his path. One of course is assassination; but that he shares with all Sovereigns—even your Queen was shot at—the other is an unsuccessful war. But that would take time. A first or a second defeat would not upset him; and the present state of the Continent offers many reasons for believing that his next war will be successful.

Senior.—You expect another war?

Dussard.—Certainly, I expect one. A Bonaparte dynasty exists only on the condition of successful war; and until we have recovered what we lost in 1814 and 1815 the French nation will expect one. To regain our national frontier is now our passion; that desire was not extinct when it seemed asleep. The unpopularity of the Restoration and the unpopularity of Louis Philippe, the Revolution of 1830 and the Revolution of 1848, the election of Cavaignac and the election of Louis Napoleon, were all expressions of it.

Senior.—Would a war for the Rhine be popular?

Dussard.—Not perhaps for the first three weeks; but, unless it were a failure, it soon would become so.

Senior.—And if it involved a war with England?

Dussard.—That would, I fear, tend to its popularity. We should think that it added still more to the reward than to the danger. I expect war, too, from what I know about him and about his plans. General Jomini was sent by the Emperor Nicholas to talk to him in the beginning of 1852. He told the story of their interview the day after it had taken place to the Piedmontese Minister, who told it to a friend of mine, who told it to me. So I had it third hand, but through a good channel. They sat up the whole night with the map of Europe before them; Jomini was frightened at the *remaniement* which he proposed; none of the results of 1814 and 1815 were to remain.

Senior.—Did you see much of Louis Napoleon when you were both exiles in England?

Dussard.—Not so much as of some of the other Bonapartes. My great friend was King Joseph. I used to dine with him every Saturday. That family you know, though combined against the rest of the world, were always quarrelling. Joseph never submitted to the senatus consultum which gave the succession to a younger branch. He looked on his nephew as a usurper. Still Louis Napoleon used to dine at the Saturday parties, but said little. Once, however, he spoke long and even eloquently. Some of 'us had said that if Napoleon had lived and reigned he would in time have given to France constitutional freedom. This Louis Napoleon strongly, almost fiercely, denied. He maintained that his uncle never intended to give to the French more freedom than they then enjoyed, and that if he had given it to them, they would have used it to no good purpose, that they were incapable of permanent self-government.

'Do you not see,' he continued, 'that this Constitutional Government is leading us straight to a Republic, that is to anarchy? Besides, under the rule of the bourgeoisie, France cannot take her proper place in Europe. To do so, she must act as one man, and therefore be governed by one will. When that takes place, when she has burst the fetters of the 'Pays légal,' and the Chambers, when the whole people rest their whole destiny on the one man whom they trust, you will see how quickly, and how high France will mount.'

I have often thought over these words. I look back to them now as prophetic. One of the worst signs, indeed, one of the worst causes of evil, is the military spirit which has infected the young men of the higher classes. It was always difficult to find 'carrières' for them. They despise what you call the learned professions, the bar, the Church, and medicine, but the judicial career, and the civil service could be entered *sans déroger* and were full of them. Now these are closed to all, except to the very few who choose to ask favours from the Government. The army remains and they crowd into it. They call it serving their country, while they call the others serving the Government. A young man who serves the Government is despised as a renegade. One who engages in no profession is a fainéant. 'Péquin' (Pekin) has again become a word of reproach. Thousands of Orleanist and Legitimist families have sons in the Emperor's armies, and begin to sympathize in the thirst for war, which a soldier feels, indeed ought to feel. All means too are tried to make the service popular with the bourgeoisie. The soldiers are a privileged class; they are not tried even for civil offences by the civil tribunals; they may insult, and they may murder a civilian with impunity. Orders are given to the prefects and to all the distributors of Government patronage and promotion, to prefer in every case the man who has served. The military fever is spreading. In a year or two it will be as difficult to keep us at peace, as it would have been before the coup d'état to rouse us into making war.

I called on Madame Mohl. We talked of Madame Récamier.

Madame Mohl.—For about eighteen years I saw her every day. For four years I lived under the same roof. My mother and I had, among our small circle of friends, some who belonged to Madame Récamier's society. She always liked to know where her friends had spent their day, our names therefore were well known to her. She heard that we wanted an apartment, and offered us the large rooms on the first floor, next to the apartments which she then inhabited:

she had left the third floor about ten years previous to my knowing her. Their full value was above our means, but she let us have them at our own price : here we lived for seven years. She took a fancy to us, often came with a few of her friends, and spent the evening in our room, and when she did not I went to hers. The party generally broke up before eleven, when the convent door closed. I often stayed till twelve, and so did Ampère. I recollect those hours as among the pleasantest of my life. She used to relate to us her early life, and to talk over her guests and the occurrences of the evening with infinite humour and finesse. No one told a story better, or so well, but she was lazy, and often begged Ampère to do it for her.

When I first knew her in 1831 she was fifty-three. Her complexion was still fair, but her colour, which had been brilliant, was gone. Her hair had been dark, but turned grey very early. Her eyes were black and both bright and soft. Her figure, fine in youth, but never slim, was dignified, though not tall. She was still pretty rather than handsome, though I have known women keep their youthful looks much later. She was anxious to please, and had as much frankness as is compatible with that anxiety. With great softness and attractiveness of manner, she had something about her which repelled familiarity. No one ever took a liberty with her. A clever little girl of seven years old whom I took to see her, asked me if she was related to the Queen. 'Why,' I said, ' do you ask?' 'Because,' she answered, ' she looks like a Queen.'

She read much, and contrived to do so by having regular hours on which no one intruded. Her door was not open till half-past two, and then only to Châteaubriand. At about four came other intimate friends, and later in the evening the general circle. It was one of the few houses in which you could hear a subject sifted. She liked discussion, not indeed to take much part in it, but to hear it. In modern conversation you get to the bottom of nothing, the most interesting questions are taken up, and thrown down again not half-examined. At Madame Récamier's any subject that deserved it was gone into, and at times it would be taken up again the next day. She would put forward opinions which she had heard or remembered to have heard on the same subject which she had recollected in the night.

I liked Châteaubriand; his vanity, his ambition, his jealousy, his susceptibility, were rarely exhibited in society. He kept them under control, and showed them most in his letters. This has enabled Madame Lenormant to leave on the reader's mind an impression far less amiable and agreeable than the reality. He was generally ' bon enfant,' and only sarcastic where the Government was in question. He liked a droll story beyond measure, and Madame Récamier always made much of whoever had the luck to amuse him. Madame Récamier had early imbibed religious sentiments at her convent, which she always retained, but certainly was not at all a professed dévote. She has been represented as a cold-hearted coquette, so fond of the possession of a royal slave, that though her own mind was made up in 1807, she allowed Prince Augustus of Prussia to pass miserable years of deferred hope and uncertainty, before she at last in 1812 communicated to him her decision to remain Madame Récamier. Her treatment of the Prince certainly was not blameless, but he was not the faithful anxious lover that some people have described him. I knew very well his daughters, the Countesses of Waldenberg; they must have been born, one of them about 1808, the other about 1810 or 1811. During his years of uncertainty, therefore, he had found consolations, and she well knew it.

Senior.—Do you believe that she was Récamier's daughter?

Madame Mohl.—It was the general opinion. I heard it from childhood, and long before I entered the Parisian world. It is the only explanation of the strange relations between them, which began, and that is the strangest part, on the very day of the marriage. They were parental, not conjugal. Her mother left M. Bernard very soon after the marriage, and lived and died in M. Récamier's house. You must remember what strange times those were. M. Récamier used to go every day to see the people guillotined. He said that as he was rich he was sure his time would come soon, and he wanted to prepare himself. Everybody knew that he was Madame Bernard's lover, and possibly the father of her daughter. She was anxious to provide for her child's safety in case of her death, and therefore married her before she was fifteen to M. Récamier, to give her a legal protector. Marriage in those days was a merely civil ceremony—it was arranged in a few words by a notary. What was odd was that M. Bernard always considered her as his own daughter, though no one else did. I never, however, heard Madame Récamier allude to anything against her mother; she cherished her memory very tenderly; but as I said before, we must remember that in those strange times strange things were the commonest. When M. Récamier died, people ceased to think about him, and the mystery of the marriage was forgotten. I never heard of any proof of the suspicion. It rested on general belief, which you can find out if you will inquire, and can estimate as well as I can.

One of the most wonderful of Madame Récamier's powers was the devotion which she excited among her friends; a devotion which did not end with herself, but could be turned by her at will towards third persons. Ampère was her slave—that was little—but she made him the slave of M. de Châteaubriand, whom he disliked. For love of Madame Récamier he visited his own rival and his preferred rival, M. de Châteaubriand, at his own hôtel every day, wrote articles for him in the papers, and learned stories to amuse him. Paul David, her husband's nephew, dined with her every day for thirty years. During the last four years of her life her eyes would not permit her to read. David was a bad reader at the best, and loss of teeth—for he was of about her own age—had not improved him. David read to her every day for hours, and when he found that his bad reading annoyed her he took lessons. It was to him that she confided the letters which she wished to be burned.

She kept a collection of letters of peculiar interest, and let her favourites read them in a little back room. They were not to be taken out of the house. I read them all; those of Benjamin Constant were charming. She had them copied and bound. She intended them to be printed after her death, and gave them to Madame Collet for that purpose. Madame Collet printed three in a feuilleton. Madame Lenormant saw them, and with the concurrence of Benjamin Constant's heirs, proceeded against Madame Collet at law, and obtained a decree, which for the first time had established the principle that the heirs of a deceased person can prevent the publication of his letters; a decision unfortunate for the public, whom it will deprive of much amusing gossip; and unfortunate for Madame Lenormant herself, who has heaps of letters addressed to Madame Récamier, which the heirs of the writers will not allow her to publish. I should like to tell you a story of Ampère, only I am afraid that you will put it into your journal.

Senior.—I daresay that I shall.

Madame Mohl.—Well, I will run my chance. When Ampère was twenty-one and Madlle. A—— was about eighteen, he used to come every day to the abbaye. Some one suggested to Madame Récamier that something might be growing up between the two young people. Madame Récamier one evening hinted to M. Ampère this suggestion. He hid his face in his hands and burst into tears. At last he said, 'Ce n'est pas *elle*.' Madame Récamier told me the story; she was then forty-four years old.

M. de Rémusat came in and was followed by M. Mohl, and the conversation became political.

Rémusat.—The war and the annexation have produced vast results, especially the annexation. It has been giving the first taste of blood to a tiger whelp. For many years, in fact from 1812 until last spring, we had been accustomed to consider war as an unmixed evil. It brought with it a doubled conscription, an increase of debt and of taxes, and gave no results except a little military glory, of which we had more than enough before. Now, for the first time since Tilsit it has become productive. We are again growing; we again find that a war can be short, decisive, and profitable. Hopes which a year ago seemed extravagant have now become possibilities. The state of the Continent is more favourable to a war of ambition than it has been since 1812. Russia is looking eastward; he will allow us to do what we like in the west and the south. Austria is falling to pieces; Prussia is quarrelling with Denmark, and talking of indemnities. The smaller German Princes, in their fear of Prussian annexation, cling to Austria; their subjects are tired of them, and look rather to France than to Prussia.

Madame Mohl.—And we are *travaillant* them. The Government publishes in German a revolutionary paper called 'Le Correspondant de Strasbourg,' and sends 15,000 copies into Baden and Würtemburg. I know a poor German who was sent to all the Germans in Paris to propose to them to subscribe. He was to receive four francs for every 'abonné' that he could procure. He was abused and 'mis à la porte' by all of them but one.

Mohl.—Similar journals are sent into Belgium, Rhenish Bavaria, and Rhenish Prussia. Within the last two years a French party has been created all along the Rhine and the Scheldt.

Rémusat.—No pains are taken to conceal this; it is rather paraded. Celui-ci is trying to familiarize our minds to a war of aggrandizement. He wishes us to believe that it must come; that we cannot prevent it; that even if we dislike it, it is our business to make the best of it; and that glory and the Rhine will pay us richly for the loss of 300,000 men and an addition of a milliard to the debt. And he is succeeding. Even a war with England, the most dangerous and the most destructive of all wars, a war of which the mere fear was enough to turn out a Ministry in Louis Philippe's time, is now desired by many, and acquiesced in by all, as a necessity.

Madame Mohl.—The prestige of England has been sadly shaken by the commercial treaty.* With our general ignorance of political economy we believe that you are to gain enormously by it, and that we are to lose. It has made all the fabricants and proprietors of forests and mines your bitter enemies, and even your best friends are angry with you, for having become parties to a trick which has enabled Celui-ci to change our whole commercial system without consulting us.

Senior.—I doubt whether the treaty can have much increased your dislike of us.

Madame Mohl.—Still there was a party, the most intelligent and liberal in France, by whom you were respected,

---

* The Commercial Treaty with England, negotiated by Michel Chevalier and Cobden. Signed on January 23, 1860.—ED.

who admired your institutions, and thought your foreign policy proud perhaps, and overbearing, but honest. Now these are the persons who accuse you of having sold Savoy for commerce, of having been bribed by the treaty into submission to the annexation.

Senior.—The accusation is utterly false; the treaty is no bribe. The alteration of our tariff in your favour, that is, our receiving your produce at a less duty, is the only real advantage that it is to give us, and of course we could have made, and probably should have made, that alteration without a treaty. We consented to do it by treaty for your sake, not for ours. As for the annexation, you cannot accuse us of acquiescing in it, though we do not choose to go to war about it.

Madame Mohl.—Still you must admit that the transaction is open to suspicion. I wish that if you were to have a treaty you had taken another opportunity for it. Nor do we like to be treated as children, to be told by you and by our master that we do not know what is good for us or bad for us.

Senior.—What effect has all this on Louis Napoleon's position?

Rémusat.—Decidedly to strengthen it. Though the generals despise his military talents, the army looks only to his success; it is delighted at being promoted and petted. The people care nothing for liberty; they have forgotten Louis Philippe; they are better off than they were during the Republic, and are satisfied. The fabricants hate the treaty; but though they were powerful in the Chambers, and are so even in the Corps Législatif and the Senate, they count for little in the nation. The salons of Paris hate him as they did before, but they are nothing. They have no more influence than the 'frondeurs' of Bonaparte's time, whom he used to call 'idéologues.'

Senior.—I am told that he is anxious to follow public opinion.

Madame Mohl.—There is some truth in this; but the public opinion which he wishes to follow is always the lowest and the most vulgar, for it is the only one that he understands. Being destitute of the feeling of right and wrong, he does not attribute it to others. He cultivates the low propensities of the nation, not so much from calculation as from sympathy.

Senior.—What is the disposition of the clergy?

Rémusat.—The clergy rather suspect than hate him; they certainly do not wish to change him. They prefer him to a Republic; to an Orleanist, or even to a Legitimist Sovereign. He can afford, which the other Governments could not, to favour the clergy without being accused of being priest-ridden; he has done more for them than any Sovereign since Louis Quatorze. They care more, perhaps, for the Pope than they do for France, but they care for themselves much more than they do for the Pope. They sprang from the people; they sympathize with the people; they like the Socialist tendencies of this Government; they enjoy the degradation of the higher classes. Louis Napoleon has nothing to fear from them.

Senior.—It seems to me that he has nothing to fear from anybody except himself.

This seemed to be the general opinion.

I called on General Chrzanowski.

Chrzanowski.—The Italian war has shown that our long peace has destroyed military skill. The soldiers did their duty. The Austrians fought well, much better than the Russians did in the Crimea; the French fought as well as troops could fight; but the generals did absolutely nothing. At Solferino there was no command on either side. The

French line was five leagues long; the Austrian line was seven. How can there be any real command at such distances? How can a general know what is going on to his right and to his left ten miles off? The troops on each side ran at one another, and that was all. Lichtenstein, with 30,000 men, holding two leagues of ground beyond the French line, had no one in front of him. His 30,000 men constituted the excess of the Austrian numbers over those of the French. He might have operated on the French flank and rear with decisive effect. He stood quiet, never fired a gun, looked on at the battle, and retreated as soon as he saw that the Austrians were beaten. He had no orders; this was a good technical excuse. A subordinate officer who acts without orders may compromise the whole army; but what is to be said of the commander-in-chief who left 30,000 men without orders?

Senior.—How do you account for Hesse's failures?

Chrzanowski.—Hesse, while he retained his faculties, was a skilful general, perhaps one of the best in Europe; but he is seventy-five. He lately married a young wife; his mind is gone.

Senior.—How did Louis Napoleon manage?

Chrzanowski.—Worse than even Giulay; worse than any of them. He fought the battle of Magenta with only 40,000 men against 100,000, although he had 100,000 men more ten miles in his rear. Nothing but the wonderful courage and discipline of his men and the incapacity of his enemy saved him. The French army says with truth that the battles were won ' par le Général Soldat.'

Senior.—Is it true that the French army was surprised at Solferino?

Chrzanowski.—It was so far surprised that they did not know that the Austrians were within a few miles of them. They had no avant garde, and the people of the country served the Austrians best, and gave the French no information. What saved the French from actual surprise was that in consequence of the heat they began their advance two hours before their usual time. When they came in front of the Austrians' position they found to their astonishment the hills occupied by the Austrian army; so they attacked it without any regular plan of battle, without any attempt to turn one of its wings, or to concentrate their force in order to break through its weakest point, but merely by brute force. The Austrians used no more generalship, and the two armies fought it out. This occasioned the enormous slaughter.

When battles are fought scientifically each commander tries to save his own men. There may be a violent struggle and a great carnage at the particular point which is the key of the position that is attacked, without much fighting along the rest of the line. Here everybody was fighting everywhere. One blunder, however, of the Austrians diminished the French loss. They made little use of their artillery. There is not a more established rule than that artillery should be used as profusely as possible at the beginning of the battle while the enemy is advancing. As soon as they are close at hand you cannot fire on them without endangering your own men. At Solferino the Austrians kept back their artillery, and in fact scarcely used it at all.

Senior.—What sort of an army will Victor Emmanuel get together?

Chrzanowski.—A very bad one. The Savoyard Brigade, which was the best portion of it, is gone, and even that was not very good. It was spoilt by the others, and got into a habit of saying, 'If the Piedmontese don't fight, we will not fight for them.' At Magenta the Piedmontese were not engaged. At Solferino 40,000 of them were disgracefully beaten by 25,000 Austrians. The men are good, or if well led might be made good; but the officers are worth nothing. They are ignorant, conceited, undisciplined, and careless. As for the Tuscan, Modenese, and Parmesan troops, they are a canaille. Those Sovereigns, especially the Grand Duke of Tuscany, have long been trying to destroy the military spirit in their countries. They thought it safer to have defenceless subjects and to rely on Austrian protection than to give them arms and habits which might render them less submissive; and they have succeeded. The Grand Duchies will not furnish 10,000 good soldiers. The Romagnese are a braver population, but they have no military experience. It is said that Victor Emmanuel intends to raise an army of 150,000 men. If the French leave him it will be beaten and dispersed by 60,000 Austrians.

I asked him if he had read Prince Dolgoroukow's book 'La Verité sur la Russie.'

Chrzanowski.—Of course I have. There is some exaggeration in it, as there is in every book in which a man attacks the institutions of his own country, but it is substantially true. He is a man of high rank and connexions, and knows the real state of Russia as well as it can be known.

Senior.—Do you join then in his hopes or in his fears of a revolution in Russia?

Chrzanowski.—I do. The Romanoff family are a worn-out race, and I should not be surprised at seeing them turned out and replaced by one of the old Russian families. Another possible revolution is one of which the object should be a constitution. The oppression and mismanagement of the last reign, the general corruption, judicial as well as administrative, and the disastrous war, which has ruined the army, the finances, and the military reputation of the nation, have convinced all thinking people that this blind stupid tyranny must not be allowed to continue. If I were a Sovereign at war with Russia, with an army of 60,000 men I would overturn this Government. I would take it by sea to the neighbourhood of Riga, establish myself there, and proclaim that I came as a friend, to give to Russia a constitution, the emancipation of the serfs, and religious toleration. The country would join me in a few weeks.

Senior.—Is there not now religious toleration?

Chrzanowski.—Half the Muscovites detest the church which calls itself the national church, and has taken the Czar for its head. Some adhere to the patriarch of Constantinople, some to the Pope, and there are many sects besides. One of the most numerous sects is that which calls itself the Old Believers. About nine millions of Russians belong to it. The schism was occasioned by a new translation of the Bible. The Old Believers adhere to the old version; they make the sign of the cross with two fingers instead of three. These distinctions are enough to occasion them to be objects of persecution, and ready to endure it. Sclavs are excellent inquisitors and excellent martyrs. They are patient, obstinate, and ignorant. Their religion is a matter of tradition, not of reason. They take it as a whole, and neither the persecutors nor the victims inquire into the relative importance of a mere form and an essential doctrine. All dissenters are persecuted, and all submit rather than abandon the trifling peculiarities which separate them from the orthodox church. A dissident village is surrounded by soldiers, and the inhabitants are driven by force into the Government church. Others are punished for going to their own churches by blows, by exile, or by forced enlistment. In Russia every action of the Government is violent and brutal. You may easily conceive that when it takes to religious persecutions it is not mild.

He looked at the map of La Savoie Neutralisée.

Chrzanowski.—The dispute is an absurd one. No French army could ever invade Switzerland on the south side of the lake of Geneva. It would take the high road by Bâle or by Nyon. The neutralization of Chablais and Faucigny was useful only as against Piedmont. To insist on it as against France is applying an old routine to a new state of circumstances.

I dined with the Bourkes, and met Madame Gonfalonieri, M. de Bourke's sister. We talked of the Austrian prisons. I said that General Zucchi, who was kept by the Austrians in solitary confinement for eighteen years told me that he did not wish for a companion.

Madame Gonfalonieri.—That was the feeling of my husband; for the last seven years he was alone, and he much preferred it. He said that if you were shut up with your best friend *tête-à-tête* for seven years, you would come to hate him. At first the State prisoners at Spielberg were coupled with the ordinary convicts; but the convicts complained that the treatment was too severe, and were removed. My husband, deprived of books and of writing materials, employed himself in trying to recollect all that he had read. He recovered so much that at the end of his imprisonment his memory was better stored than at the beginning; but he had so much assisted it by his invention, that he frequently mistook his own alterations for original passages.

M. de Bourke.—I hear that Lamoricière has a hard time of it. Antonelli objects to all reforms, and Lamoricière can do nothing without them. Then he is beset by young

French Legitimists who have never learned anything except to ride and to fence, who cannot even speak Italian, and all want high employments. No one thinks that in a Papal army he ought to be less than a colonel. I shall not be surprised if we soon see him back in France. I am a Catholic, and I hope a good Catholic—at least I try to be one—but I do not see the necessary connexion between the spiritual and temporal power of the Pope. I am not sure that they do not do harm to one another. He never was better obeyed or more revered than when he was at Gaeta.

I went in the evening to Thouvenel's and Marshal-Randon's receptions. At the Hotel des Affaires Etrangères I found in the most magnificent private rooms in the world about fifteen persons. Among them was General Kalergi, the author of the Greek Revolution of 1843, now Minister from Greece. I asked if my acquaintance, R—— was still Minister of Foreign Affairs?

Kalergi.—Certainly not, or I should not be here. We have had a change of Ministry.

Senior.—And of system?

Kalergi.—There will be no change of system until we have a change of King. We are under a 'pensée immuable.'

We talked of Garibaldi.

Kalergi.—If Garibaldi were a Frenchman I should call him a pirate. His attempt would be that of Walker or any other American filibuster. It would be a case of private war, which I take to be the definition of piracy. But as he is an Italian, assisting an Italian insurrection against an Italian tyrant, I consider him as a soldier. The King of Naples has a right to hang him. The instant he touches Sicily he owes a temporary allegiance to the Sovereign, and is as much a rebel as any of the Sicilians are. But as against all other persons he is neither pirate nor rebel.

They may stop him, but they have no right to hang him. If he establishes himself for a few weeks he will succeed, not by the aid of the Sicilians, who are a feeble race, but by that of Italians, Frenchmen, and perhaps Germans, who will flock to join so distinguished a partisan and so attractive a cause. In that case the Sicilian revolution will resemble ours. The real Greeks would never have driven out the Turks. They were too degraded even to wish for liberty. For many years after we had achieved our own independence they called the times of Turkish rule 'the good times.' It was the Albanians and Macedonians and foreigners who fought the Turks.

I went to Marshal Randon's. There I found the Maréchale and four ladies sitting, and above one hundred men in uniform, standing about. From time to time somebody stood opposite to the Maréchale to speak to her. The general tone was stiff, not from the fault of the hosts, for the Randons are people of simple, cordial manners, but from the very nature, I believe, of a ministerial reception.

Friday, May 11th.—I spent the evening at Montalembert's, and visited him again the next morning. I will throw together the two conversations, or rather his two monologues, for I was quite satisfied to listen without interrupting him.*

---

* I sent my report of these conversations to M. de Montalembert, who returned it with a note, from which the following is an extract:—

'I have attentively perused, revised, and completed the accompanying pages. And I can but thank you most cordially for the opportunity which you afford me, of letting some few friends know what a man who prides himself on having been the most ardent friend and advocate of England on the Continent, is reduced to think and to say on her present policy.'

As his additions and alterations were made in English, there is nothing to distinguish them from my original report. As a general

Montalembert.—I do not ask you for English news, for you can tell me nothing but what is painful. I always detested your treatment of other nations; but as respects your home affairs you were the one green spot in the European desert, the one asylum of honesty, of freedom, of good sense; the one country governed by those who were morally and intellectually fit to govern. *Now* your domestic policy seems to be as blind and as irrational as your foreign policy. Without any pressure, without any hope, without any motive, well knowing that there is a precipice at its end, you are calmly and deliberately sliding down the slope of democracy, which can end in nothing but French centralization and autocracy. But I need not tell you this; you know it better than I do. The intolerable part of the matter is that all your public men know it, that with their eyes open they are combining to ruin or to abandon a Constitution better than any that ever was made, a Constitution which has grown up with the aid of hundreds of noble heads and hearts, and thousands of happy accidents. And not one of your public men dares to say the truth, the whole truth, and show the British nation to what an abyss of debasement Mr. Bright and Lord John Russell are leading you. They all seem to be just as much gagged by the fear of the popular prejudices of their electors or of the *Times* as we are by the refusal of our printers to print what we write and say, because they know that immediate ruin by the suppression of their *brevets d'imprimerie* would be the consequence. But what, people may ask, is the use of parliamentary government and political freedom if the ultimate result is the same with regard to the character and authority of public men as under the degradation of despotism?

---

rule, every very violent expression, and every very vituperative epithet, may be held to have been inserted by him. Subsequent reflection seems to have warmed, not calmed him.—N. W. SENIOR.

I had rather talk to you of your foreign policy, for as to that I can·hope to give you some information, both as to the judgment which we, the friends of England, pass on it, and the results which we expect from it. I will not go back to your conduct before the Italian war broke out; we discussed that last year. I then believed, and I believe now, that you might have prevented it. You thought, and I daresay you think now, that it was unavoidable. Well, peace was made on reasonable terms. Austria gave up Lombardy; Piedmont accepted it. The Duchies were to be replaced under their dukes, the Legations under the Pope, and an Italian Confederacy was to be formed, of which the King of Sardinia would have been the most powerful member, and the Pope the most eminent and revered. This arrangement gave to the Italians the only unity for which they are fit, the unity of a confederacy under their former princes, without any violation of the public law of Europe. If you interfered at all, it was your interest and your duty to support it. It was the best solution of the difficulties which Celui-ci's selfish—he is no fool, far from it —ambition and vanity had created. You used all your influence to upset it. You sanctioned its being attacked and destroyed by a weapon new in Europe, the most dangerous that democracy has ever forged, the use of universal suffrage to determine international relations; that is to say, the appealing to the uneducated portion of the people to decide whether their country shall stand independent or shall form a part of any other, and in that case of what larger political aggregate. This curse has been desolating South America for the last fifty years. The old Spanish provinces break up into smaller political units, reunite, and break up again, according to the passions or the caprices of the lower classes, until cohesion is gone and all are relapsing into barbarism.

This dissolvent principle has now with your sanction begun its work in Europe. Have you thought what are to be its limits? If the numerical majority of the Tuscans a year or two hence wish to separate from Sardinia, are they to be allowed to do so? If Sienna, or Pisa, or Lucca, declares by universal suffrage that it wishes to quit Tuscany, is it to do so? Are the Ionians or the Irish to separate from England as soon as separation appears to be the will of the majority? If so, who can attempt to deny that the numerical majority of the Irish people, if entrusted with universal suffrage, and duly instructed by French agents and French writers and orators (as the Italians have been by the English), would prefer any Government in the world, and more particularly the Napoleonic régime, to Queen Victoria's rule? And if one of the provinces of the Irish Republic wishes to leave the others, and to become an independent Ulster, is it to do so? Will Antrim have a right to break off its connection with Ulster, and Belfast that with Antrim?

The ceding, selling, buying, and exchanging subjects like flocks of sheep; the transferring them from Sovereign to Sovereign, as the Congress of Vienna did in 1814, is shocking; but it is far less dangerous and less repugnant to common sense and common morality than this principle of spontaneous disunion under the pressure of foreign interference. Such transactions as the former are solemn acts, carefully considered; they are planned and effected by statesmen responsible to public opinion and to history. They may be injudicious and oppressive, but they are not the results of blind popular prejudice or of caprice. The people—that is to say, the uneducated portion of a nation—never take in more than one, or at most two, ideas at a time. Sometimes it is a religious fancy, sometimes a political one, sometimes a social one. It sways them absolutely, because it has no counterpoise. Under its influence they might break old connexions or make new ones, without reference to their own permanent interests, or even to what are their own permanent feelings. Until now, at least in Europe, democracy disturbed by its follies only the internal affairs of a country; now it is to affect its foreign relations, and even the coherence of its parts. *These* results of the conduct which you have been sanctioning and exciting affect every civilized nation; others of its mischiefs will fall peculiarly on you. You have put Northern and Central Italy into the hands of a French prefect.

Senior.—Do you estimate highly the sagacity of Drouyn de Lhuys?

Montalembert.—*Highly* is a strong word. I think him very intelligent.

Senior.—He thinks that the creation of a strong kingdom in Northern and Central Italy is injurious to the power of France.

Montalembert.—So do *I* think; but what you are creating is not a strong kingdom; it is only a large one. The discordant, disjointed, and generally unmilitary populations which have elected Victor Emmanuel can oppose no real resistance to France or to Austria. *Our* assistance only can support him against external attack or internal revolution. If it were possible that upper and central Italy, or all Italy, could consolidate itself into one State of 25,000,000, and remain united for fifty years, such a State would alter the balance of power to our disadvantage, if the power to meddle, to tease, and to oppress be an advantage. But if all Italy were now, as you are trying to make it, Sardinian, it would still be a French prefecture, governed by French laws and a Frenchified bureaucracy. Again, you have deprived the Pope of one-third of his territory, and are trying to strip him of the rest. You are doing this at the expense of exciting the permanent indignation and hatred of 150,000,000 of Catholics, 10,000,000 of whom are your own subjects.

And this you are doing out of *mere Protestant bigotry*, as blind and as stupid as that of the Puritans two hundred years ago, but without their sincerity and their undaunted courage. The author of the celebrated Durham letter having been invested with the seals of the Foreign Office, the foreign policy of England has naturally and most appropriately been remodelled on its pattern. Instead of being a beacon and a refuge for the friends and victims of freedom throughout the world, and particularly in Catholic countries, the power and influence of England are narrowed down into the miserable precincts of sectarian hatred to the Pope and everything Popish. All her conservative alliances with Austria, &c., and her really liberal and glorious precedents of resistance to Napoleonism and piracy, have been sacrificed to this one object. If you could thus get rid of the Pope and all the 100,000,000 of Papists throughout the world, such narrow-minded wickedness might be intelligible, if not excusable; but you know very well you *can't* and you *wont* get rid of them. They *will* live on, notwithstanding Russell, Shaftesbury, Newdegate and Co., and therefore it is the rankest folly to identify the British name with every greedy demagogue or every 'astucieux' potentate who attempts to undermine or to overthrow the Papacy.

What are you to get by turning the Pope into a French archbishop? Pio Nono is a Christian; you have nothing to fear from his resentment, however just; but what will be the conduct of his successor, the tool as he will be, and as you are doing your best to make him, of your enemy? Then you have sent Garibaldi to set Sicily on fire, and to put a Murat on the throne of Naples.

Senior.—We have nothing to do with Garibaldi's piracies.

Montalembert.—Look at your blue-book on the affairs of Naples. Garibaldi has done nothing more than put in action the language of Lord John Russell, the language which Mr. Elliot, the Envoy, keeps repeating, and the Secretary of State keeps re-echoing, that there is neither law, nor justice, nor prudence, nor common humanity, in the Neapolitan Government; that its follies, its vices, and its crimes are driving it to rapid and merited ruin. You print all this, and your agents, or Garibaldi's, or Victor Emmanuel's, spread it through Italy. Garibaldi's piracy is one of its first and most natural consequences. Your excuse, I suppose, is that you could not remain silent spectators of the atrocities of the Neapolitan Government. How came you to be silent spectators of the atrocities of the French Government in 1852 and 1858? If Lord Normanby and Lord Cowley reported as fully and as faithfully as Mr. Elliot has done, they told quite as frightful a story. Why did no one think of printing and re-echoing in Parliament their accounts?

But your sympathies are only with Italians. You think any Government good enough for us. It may imprison, 'interné,' exilé, and 'déporté' without exciting even your attention, and without any of your political chiefs daring to open his mouth about it. But let it do something for the aggrandizement of France, and your Parliament and your press are in arms, and your foreign minister threatens that you will seek new alliances. I disapprove of the annexation of Savoy. I dislike all increase of territory. France is already too large to be well-governed, and too powerful to be just or even prudent. And I disapprove still more of appeals in such matters to universal suffrage, or indeed to any suffrage whatever. I think it a bad thing done in a worse way.

But it is absurd to talk of it as a real increase of French power.

Senior.—Our objection to it is as a precedent.

Montalembert.—Your objection is very just. It is a precedent, and a precedent which will be very soon followed at your expense. But of all Europe, no one has less right to complain of it than the English Government and Parliament, who have really forced the Emperor to make this annexation by the egregious folly which destroyed the work of Villa Franca, and insisted on the annexation of Romagna and Tuscany to Piedmont.

Senior.—You believe that Louis Napoleon intends to attack Rhenish Prussia and Belgium?

Montalembert.—I am not sure that they will need to be attacked. One of your eminent Liberals maintains that patriotism is folly, that if a man can increase his income by changing his allegiance, it is his duty to his family to do so. Such opinions are contagious. I know that in the manufacturing districts of Belgium there is a strong affinity for France. When once allegiance is a matter of pounds, shillings, and pence, the attraction of the great markets is irresistible. The priests indeed *now* distrust, or rather dislike Louis Napoleon, but that is a new feeling and a new language among the votaries of Veuillot and the *Univers*. The people say to them, 'M. le Curé, you have been telling us for seven or eight years that the French Emperor is an excellent Sovereign, much better than our parliamentary institutions. We trust more to your old opinions than to your new ones.'

As for the Rhenish provinces, a friend of mine has paid two visits to Aix-la-Chapelle and Cologne during the last six weeks. At the first, when Savoy had just been laid hold of, and when the idea of annexation was new, everybody was opposed to it. They said that they would remain Germans, hold out against the Imperial policy, and beat down this resurrection of Napoleonism. Six weeks after the whole tone was changed. 'Si ça doit-être,' they said, 'il faut le subir sans les malheurs de la guerre. D'ailleurs, l'Europe ne dit rien, à quoi bon nous sacrifier pour elle. Après tout, la France est une grande nation, et nous donnera de grandes débouchées.' The doctrine of your Government that questions of allegiance ought to be decided by universal suffrage, and that of Mr. Bright, that what a man thinks his interest is therefore his duty, will be applied, and we may get Belgium as quietly as we got Savoy. But whether quietly or not, we shall get it. Louis Napoleon has resuscitated the thirst for material greatness instead of interior freedom, which even he cannot resist. Nor does he wish to resist it. He is encouraging it with all his might. How soon he will publicly announce que la France 'revendique ses frontières naturelles,' no one can tell, not he himself. Perhaps it may be six months hence, perhaps on the 1st of January, 1861.

I am inclined to think that you had better submit to it, for you will not be able to prevent it. By your shameful sympathy with his domestic policy, and by your blind complicity with his Italian tactics, you have placed this man in a position which makes his moderation your best hope. He is more powerful than his uncle ever was, he has twice as much money and quite as good, if not better, soldiers, war has become far more a question of money, and his opponents are poor and disunited. I do not believe that the independence of Europe ever had so formidable an enemy, or was so ill-fitted to resist one. Russia is powerful only for mischief, and only against Turkey. Prussia is separating herself from Austria, and preparing another feud. The smaller Sovereigns, on the other hand, are quitting Prussia, which they think too liberal. Both they and their subjects are willing to sell themselves to France—the Princes, if France will patronise despotism, the people, if she will introduce Socialism. Louis Napoleon is equally ready to give either of them. His habits are despotic, but his instincts are Socialist. He can do what he likes, and with all his ambition, he has moderation sufficient to save him from his uncle's fate. Besides which, he has passed 'l'âge des passions.' When his uncle fell, he was but forty-five years old. Louis Napoleon is in his fifty-third year, he has always possessed a *sang-froid* which his uncle never had, and he has now sobered down into a most wily politician, who will very easily out-do and undo such politicians as the old Whigs and Lord John Russell's new reform will be able to produce against him.

Saturday, May 12*th.*—I spent the evening at Mr. Steiner's. He is an ardent free-trader, and this was a party in honour of the commercial treaty. I found there Cobden, Michel Chevalier, Perreire, Dussard, Circourt, and some fifty other free-traders, almost as many as Paris can furnish. Passy was invited, but he said to me yesterday, ' Je crains d'y trouver Baroche, Rouher, Fould, et toute cette canaille.' So he did not go.

I asked Chevalier to tell me the history of the treaty.

Chevalier.—Cobden and I had long been in correspondence as to the means of improving the commercial relations of our countries. I always told them that it could be effected only by a treaty, as the Legislature is ultra-protectionist. He met me at the railway terminus when I reached London last October to attend the Bradford meeting, told me that this was the time to make the attempt, that the long annuities had just fallen in and that he had seen Gladstone, who said that he was resolved that the money thereby saved should not fall into the gulf of a constantly increasing expenditure. He introduced me to Bright and to Gladstone, both of whom I found earnest in the cause.

On my return to Paris I consulted Rouher, Fould, and Baroche. I found them ready to co-operate with me. Cobden came to Paris, and it was agreed that on the 24th of October I should see the Emperor at eleven o'clock, and open the matter to him, and that Cobden should see him at three the same day.

I related to the Emperor the substance of my conversation with Gladstone. I said that I had had no previous communication on the subject with any of the ministers, that mine was a totally unauthorized proceeding, and would fall to the ground without inconvenience if his Majesty disapproved it.

The Emperor received the proposal favourably, and it was determined that, on this side of the water, no one should be admitted to the secret except the Emperor, Rouher, Fould, Baroche, myself, Cobden, and Lord Cowley. Walewski was peculiarly excluded from it. When we had settled the articles of the treaty, of course it became necessary to tell Walewski, but it was then too late for him to interfere.

Senior.—It is not true then, as we have been told, that the Emperor proposed to us the treaty, in the hope of reconciling us to the annexation of Savoy?

Chevalier.—Utterly false. The Emperor never thought on the subject until Cobden and I suggested it to him. Perhaps he may have adopted our suggestion more readily because he thought that it would please England. But I am sure that he also thinks that it will be useful to France. Not having studied the subject he is naturally a free-trader, for free-trade is the obvious common-sense doctrine —protection is artificial.

Sunday, May 13th.—I called on Madame Cornu. She tells me all the gossip of the Imperial family.

Madame Cornu.—The Emperor's great ambition now is reputation as a historian and an archæologist. He is writing a life of Julius Cæsar, and spends in collecting materials for it every minute that he can spare.

Senior.—The materials lie in a comparatively small compass.

Madame Cornu.—Ay; but it is to contain an essay on the military organisation of the Romans, and a general view of its progress from the tomb of the Kings to that of the Emperors. He sent, a few days ago, for M. Maury, of the Institut, took him into his closet, showed him the materials which he had got together, made him read what he had written of an introduction, and asked for candid criticism. Maury says that it was well done, though incomplete, and that he frankly pointed out the parts requiring further attention.

Senior.—Can he read Latin?

Madame Cornu.—Fluently; and Greek not ill. He is far above par as a scholar.

Senior.—I supposed him to be idle. That is the character given him by all his ministers and secretaries whom I have known, and I have known several.

Madame Cornu.—He is idle in matters of Administration. He hates details and he hates discussion. But he is fond of study, and very fond of writing. His ministers complain that since he has taken to biography and antiquities they cannot get audiences or even signatures from him.

Monday, May 14th.—We breakfasted with the Mohls, and met M. de la Ville Marqué, a Breton. I asked Mohl if he had heard of Louis Napoleon's new studies.

Mohl.—Certainly I have. He sent for Michcland, the

librarian of the Bibliothèque Impériale, told him what he was about, and begged him to let him have all the documents inédits on Julius Cæsar, and on the military affairs of Rome. Micheland informed him that no unedited documents on those subjects existed. 'That is to say,' answered the Emperor, 'none that you know of. But I hear that you have rooms full of manuscripts of the time of Julius Cæsar and earlier, which your indolent academicians have not examined. The lost books of Livy's 'Tacitus' are probably among them.' Micheland gave him no hopes. 'At least,' he replied, 'you must have plans of Roman fortresses and specimens of Roman engines of war?' 'Your Majesty will find some,' answered Micheland, 'on ancient bas-reliefs and coins, but not in our library.' 'But,' said the Emperor, 'there must be some in your illuminated manuscripts.' 'Our manuscripts,' said Micheland, ' are of the middle ages; the earliest are eight or nine hundred years later than Julius Cæsar.' The result of the interview was not to raise the Emperor's archæologism in M. Micheland's eyes.

M. de la Ville Marqué was President of the Breton Archæological Society. It met last year at Quimper. It was a purely literary association.

Ville Marqué.—I received a letter from Paris to tell me that I was to be arrested in the President's chair, and that the society was to be dissolved. I went immediately to the prefect. He denied that he had any instructions respecting us. I showed him the letter, and asked him if he would pledge his word as a man of honour that there was no foundation for it. ' Est-ce qu'un préfet,' he said, ' dit ou fait ce qu'il veut.' He then admitted that he had orders to watch us. Soon after my return to Paris, Monsieur Delangle, then Minister of the Interior, sent for me. 'We require,' he said, 'your resignation of the presidentship of the Breton Archæological Society, as we are going to dissolve it.' 'What have we done?' I asked. 'We abstain most religiously from politics—necessarily—for we are constituted of men of every different opinion.' 'Vous êtes un abus,' he answered. 'Why an abus?' I said. 'Charles X. gave us twenty thousand francs a year; Louis Philippe, fifteen thousand; the Republic, five thousand. You give us nothing. We have maintained ourselves for eight years by voluntary subscriptions without Government aid.' 'And what do you do?' he asked, 'with all these subscriptions?' 'We publish,' I answered, 'our Transactions, and we pay the expense of copying monuments and inscriptions. You may see all our accounts.' 'C'est égal,' he replied. 'You are to be dissolved, vous n'avez pas acclamé l'Empereur.' 'We have had no opportunity,' I answered. 'We have nothing to do with politics.' 'I repeat,' he replied, 'my demand of your resignation.' 'I received my mandat,' I answered, 'from the Society. I cannot resign until they require me to do so.' So ended my conference with the minister. Three weeks afterwards I read in the *Moniteur*: 'Vue la démission de M. de la Ville Marqué, la Société Archéologique de Finisterre est dissoute.' As this statement was repeated in the local papers I wrote to deny that I had resigned. The prefect forbade it to insert my denial. 'Can a journal,' I asked, 'refuse to insert such a denial?' 'Not legally,' he answered, and the proof is that I brought an action against the journal for the refusal, and recovered damages. An editor is often sorely perplexed. If he refuses the insertion of such a denial he is liable to an action, if he refuses to obey the prefect his journal may be suppressed.

Mohl.—A poor editor friend of mine, a Monsieur Bonnetier, was threatened with ruin for merely copying from the *Moniteur* the paper war between the Pope and

Louis Napoleon last Christmas. His paper, his only subsistence, was seized, the Procureur-Général commenced an action against him, and laid his fine at fifteen thousand francs. Add to which a condemnation would have brought him within the 'loi de sûreté générale,' and rendered him liable to be sent without further trial to die of fever at Lambressa or Cayenne. He is a poor inoffensive old man; the only sign that he gives of life is that he is an ardent Bonapartist. His journal circulates among the provincial clergy; it has no politics, and he copied these documents merely as interesting to them. He would have been ruined if he had not been begged off by some strong friends among the devout.

We talked of Germany.

Mohl.—This permanent preparation is exhausting the country. Germany is poor, not merely because in many parts the soil is poor and the climate severe, but from the restrictions imposed on industry. A lad must waste years as an apprentice before he is allowed to exercise a trade which might be learned in six months, and he is confined to that trade. A wheelwright is punished if he drive a nail as a carpenter, a cartwright must not mend a wheel-barrow, no manufacture can be established without the consent of the Government. In short, every German is protected against every other German and against himself by a minute surveillance. It is a country of privileges. The princes believe that they preserve their own power by guarding the privileges of the nobles, the nobles support themselves by a privileged bourgeoisie, the bourgeois protects the monopolies and exclusive rights of the artisan. No one is allowed freedom of action. There is less of this in Prussia than elsewhere; but even Prussia is a vast trades union, with thousands of arbitrary and mischievous restrictions and regulations enforced by law, and therefore it is poor.

I asked if Chrzanowski's scheme of substitution for the enormous militia a smaller good army could be adopted.

Mohl.—I fear that while France continues armed and aggressive Prussia cannot reduce its army. Our long irregular frontier, with few naturally strong points, requires to be constantly watched by a large army. But the expense is enormous. When the landwehr is called out as it was before Solferino industry stops.

Friday, May 18*th.*—I called on Guizot. He disapproves, I think, as much as Montalembert, our conduct in the affairs of Italy.

Guizot.—By sanctioning the violation of treaties, the transfer of States wholly or partially from one allegiance to another at the will of an uneducated majority, the acceptance of the spoil by a Sovereign at peace with the Sovereign who is repudiated, and with the State which is dismembered—in short, by assisting intriguers, rebels, and robbers to trample on all public rights and public morality, you are helping to bring us back to the frightful times of the First Empire, when fraud and force had subverted international law.

Senior.—Could we have prevented all, or indeed any part of this?

Guizot.—At least you need not have done your best to promote it all; you need not have yourselves proposed that the several states and provinces of Central Italy should take on themselves to declare their wishes as to their future destiny. You knew well what in their present state of excitement their vote would be. This proposition on your part, and its acceptance on theirs, in fact decided the matter.

But I am not sure even that you could not have prevented it. As is always the case, you were more powerful for evil than for good; but I think that if you had held the Emperor to his promises at Villa Franca, instead of advising and assisting him to evade them, you might perhaps have saved from the Revolutionists all Central Italy. I think it highly probable that you might have saved Tuscany. Among the ruling principles in Louis Napoleon's mind are his wish to conciliate you and his fear to offend you. I do not mean that he is always guided by them. He is too impulsive and too short-sighted to be constantly guided by any principle whatever, even by his vanity or by his ambition; but they habitually govern him. He deserts them, but always returns. He estimates highly, perhaps exaggerates, your influence in France. He thinks, I will not say with what reason, that Louis Philippe's throne tottered as soon as he quarrelled with you, and that your opposition finally overturned it. The eagerness with which he caught at your fourth proposition, as a means of extricating him from his engagements, ought to have warned you that it was a mischievous one.

Senior.—You believe, then, that he was anxious to escape from those engagements?

Guizot.—I have no doubt about it.

Senior.—From what motives?

Guizot.—It is difficult to explain the motives of so irrational a being. Among them probably were hatred of Austria, a desire of popularity, a wish to leave as many and as deep traces as possible of his passage through Italy—and, above all, a fear of Cavour.

Senior.—Cavour has great reason to be afraid of *him*, but why should *he* fear Cavour?

Guizot.—Because behind Cavour are hundreds of Orsinists. Not that Cavour would employ them or sanction their employment, or even omit anything to prevent it, but because Cavour's ambitious schemes of Italian unity are shared by millions, of whom hundreds are ready to be Orsinists.

Senior.—Last year I was told that the fear of the Carbonaro dagger was one of his principal motives for undertaking the war, and I was inclined to believe it. But the peace of Villa Franca convinced me that I was mistaken. It was obvious that the danger, whatever it was, was much greater after Villa Franca than before he crossed the Alps. If those fears still beset him, how came he to make that peace?

Guizot.—Because the motive that is newest is always the strongest. He felt that he was engaged in a business for which he was unfit. At Magenta, and again at Solferino, he had escaped ruin only by a miracle. He is idle and dilatory. His body and mind were worn out by fatigues to which they were unaccustomed. He did not dare to surrender the command to any of his generals, and if he kept it some great disaster was to be apprehended. Then the weather was becoming oppressive and dangerous. The field of battle was frightful—fever, cholera, every form of pestilence was probable. He followed the impulse of the moment and made the peace. But as soon as he was extricated from his difficulties and enjoying his laurels, his couch, his cigar, and his other comforts in the Tuileries, the motives which had originally impelled him to the war revived. He let the negotiations at Zurich drag on month after month; and when the treaty was made, instead of the explicit stipulation of Villa Franca, 'the Grand Duke of Tuscany and the Duke of Modena return to their States,' the only provision made for them is 'that their rights are reserved.' He very soon intimated to the Tuscans that they might oppose him with impunity.

Senior.—I know that. Prince Corsini told me early in August, that as he passed through Paris he had seen the

Emperor, who assured him that he would not use force to compel the Tuscans to receive the Grand Duke, nor would he allow Austria to do so.

Guizot.—What was that but telling them, ' You may do as you like; that treaty is a farce' ?

Senior.—Does he think the aggrandisement of Piedmont useful to France ?

Guizot.—He cares nothing about France; he cares only about his own immediate interests and caprices. His selfishness is intense, but it is short-sighted. He catches at the object which is nearest to him, without seeing that its possession is inconsistent with that of some more important object further off.

Saturday, May 19th.—I spent the evening at Thiers', and found Duvergier, Roger du Nord, St. Hilaire, and three or four other persons round the tea-table. The conversation at first was general. They talked of the ' frontières naturelles,' and every one agreed that the fears which the idea would have created in France and in Belgium four months ago were disappearing. All parties, they said, were inclined to consider the annexation of Belgium and of Rhenish Prussia as a necessity, and to be prepared to make the best of it. No one present seemed to doubt that the attempt would be made, or that it would be successful. We passed on to the Italian campaign.

Thiers.—Louis Napoleon's presence was necessary to prevent the marshals and generals from quarrelling. He was modest, took advice, and scarcely ever ventured to act altogether on his own judgment.

Senior.—How came you then to commit such blunders? For it is admitted that there were enormous blunders, and that nothing saved you but the excellence of the troops and the still more enormous blunders of the enemy.

Thiers.—Because our commanders had little experience in war against a civilized enemy. Africa gave us excellent soldiers and, indeed, officers, but few generals. The men were admirable; I believe the Zouaves to be the best troops in the world—the best that there are or ever have been.

Senior.—Perhaps excepting Cromwell's Ironsides.

Thiers.—The parallel is curious, for the Ironsides were saints and the Zouaves are eminently sinners. We cannot keep many of them in Paris. I should be sorry to meet one of them in a solitary place, even by day. They have utterly broken with civil life. They never had wives and children, they never intend to have them. They do not, like the conscripts, sigh after the little gardens and fields and cottages in which they were born, or after the girls, their early playmates, whom they might hope to find still affectionate and true on their return. The Zouave never thinks of returning. The few years he can expect to live are to be spent in the camp or garrison. But if his civil virtues ' laissent à regretter,' his military ones are perfect. My friends who saw the Zouaves in the Crimea and in Italy describe with enthusiasm their intelligence, their courage, their coolness, and their calm. They do not require to be commanded; 150,000 such men would march over Europe.

Senior.—Then why have you not 150,000 such men, instead of your 600,000 conscripts?

Thiers.—A soldier, at least a French soldier, is at his best at twenty-six, after six years' service. At thirty, after ten years' service, he is an old soldier; he has lost his élan and his enthusiasm; he begins to take care of himself, and he deteriorates in every subsequent year. If we had 150,000 or even 100,000 Zouaves, we must renew them by 10,000 or 15,000 every year, in order to keep up their efficiency. What would become of the disbanded men? They are unfit for civil life; they would be the pests of society. In a few years there would be 150,000 of them at large.

Senior.—What becomes of those whom you disband now?

Thiers.—We disband none; they die in the field or in the hospitals. The Arabs, the climate, and the Emperor take care that a Zouave shall not serve till he is too old. I believe that our military system is now the best in the world; certainly the best on the Continent. The soldiers of the line are good; they will follow wherever their officers will lead them; but they require to be led. As they are enlisted for only seven years, and really serve only five, they are never too old. A certain number of veterans, however, are necessary to keep up the traditions of the service. The 'remplaçants' supply them. Formerly the 'remplaçants' were provided by the conscripts who wished to avoid serving, sometimes directly, sometimes by the companies whose trade it was to insure men against military service. They took the vilest rubbish because they were the cheapest. A 'remplaçant' entered the service under a stigma, and almost always deserved it. Now the unwilling conscript pays a fixed sum to the Government. Last year it was two thousand francs. The Government chooses the 'remplaçant' generally from the best men who are entitled to their discharge, pays well, and it is well served.

Our officers are admirable. In other services the officers conceal the marks of their rank; in ours they display them. We lose them, however, in a far greater proportion to their numbers than we do the men. I attributed our enormous loss of officers in the Italian campaign to the Tyrolese marksmen, but I was told that it was the result of their own reckless self-exposure. That we can bear this loss is owing to our possessing a military 'bourgeoisie.' We lost in the Crimea and in Italy 200,000 men, of whom perhaps 10,000 were officers. Such a loss would have put all your aristocracy into mourning; diffused over our 'bourgeoisie,' it was not felt.

Roger du Nord.—I am told that under the Prussian system the men belonging to one district are to serve together. This is well in time of peace, and has some advantages in war; but if any Prussian division should be peculiarly exposed; if, as sometimes happens, one or two regiments should be destroyed, a whole district will be depopulated. The loss and the terror will be concentrated.

Thiers.—I cannot understand the Prussian system. From 18,000,000 of population they are raising 500,000 soldiers. It is as if with our 36,000,000 we had 1,000,000 of soldiers. They are ruining their finances, ruining their industry, and their great army will be a bad one. I fear that Prussia is on the eve of a great disaster. We have made an important improvement in our military system. We have supplied every dépôt with clothes and shoes on the largest war footing, and they are to be constantly kept complete and ready. We never are in want of men, and we have accumulated military stores, such as arms and ammunition, for ten years of war; but we have always found the want of clothing and shoes interfere with the rapid development of our military force. In the late war our soldiers were sent across the Alps and to Genoa ill-provided, and were detained for weeks at Turin and Alexandria, waiting for equipments. Now we shall equip them as fast as they come to the dépôts. We may thus gain a week or a fortnight over the enemy, and that week or fortnight may decide the campaign.

As I was going he followed me into the outer room, and we walked up and down together for about half an hour. We talked of the commercial treaty.

Thiers.—No event in modern times has done you so much harm, not even your opposition to the Suez Canal.

All our 'industriels' are anxious to escape from it even by war. I believe myself that it will be mischievous to them; they expect ruin, and many will be ruined. The 'métallique' industry will be destroyed. I am, as you know, a protectionist. I believe that free trade suits *you*. You are enterprising and expansive; you trust yourselves on the wings of credit. We are timid and prudent; we like ready money and metallic money. French trade will never rest, as yours does, on bills, discounts, and paper-money. Our protectionist policy is not a theory suddenly carried into execution, like your free trade; it has gradually grown up, and it suits us. The error of the political economists is that they think only of the consumer; a real statesman thinks more of the producer. Nothing is so easy as to make consumers, nothing so difficult as to make producers. This treaty ignores the frugal, intelligent, slowly created producer, or treats him only as lawful prey. It is true that the producers are the minority, and that the tendency of the present age is always and everywhere to sacrifice everybody and everything to the numerical majority. Here we have a Monarchy on its knees before democracy; in England you have an aristocracy also on its knees before democracy. In America there is neither monarch nor aristocrat; democracy sits on her throne alone, and to the American type all Europe will have to conform.

If all this had been done regularly by laws voted by the legislative bodies we might have deplored it; but we should have been angry only with our own Government. Now we are still more angry with you. We think that you have joined with our despot in a conspiracy to ruin the industry of France by a fraudulent interpretation of the constitution. We look on you as the accomplice of a tyrant and a rogue.

I hear that the Lords are likely to continue the paper duty. Does that imply the resignation of Gladstone?

Senior.—I cannot form an opinion.

Thiers.—Like everybody else, I admire Gladstone's genius and lofty character, but his budget fills me with terror. You are on the eve of a struggle for life or death, and you wantonly throw away 3,000,000 of revenue, when every farthing that you can scrape together may be necessary to you. War is now mainly a question of money, and we are twice as rich as you are. After deducting the interest of your debt you have only 36,000,000 a year; we have 60,000,000. Your debt is 700,000,000; ours is not 400,000,000. We can borrow 30,000,000 a year for the next five years, and if we want it we shall do so. Our master cares nothing about his debts or his expenditure. You are in the hands of a House of Commons; you think of the future; Celui-ci thinks only of the present.

Senior.—Is he stronger than he was when I was in Paris in May last year?

Thiers.—On the whole he is. The treaty, indeed, has done him great mischief with the trading classes. It has taught them practically that under a despot, who is totally unrestrained by law or principle, who has no settled rule of conduct, and changes the political, the territorial, the manufacturing, and the commercial systems of France according to the whim of the moment—nothing is stable or safe. The quarrel with the Pope too has been mischievous. But these injuries have been more than compensated by his military success, and above all by the acquisition of Savoy. The worst humiliation of 1815 has been wiped out, and a portion at least of our natural frontier has been restored to us. Even I, who am among those who most disapprove his general conduct, feel grateful.

Senior.—Your last volume is perhaps the most interesting of the seventeen. It is an epic with a hero of the mould of Achilles and Satan; but do you really think that Napoleon had a chance of success?

Thiers.—No one with less genius would have had any chance; but I think that *he* had. The coalition was timid and incoherent; one really severe blow would have broken it up. Perhaps his best chance was at the very end. The Allies had committed a great fault in running headlong into Paris when such a man was within a march of them. It was a question, perhaps, whether Paris should be destroyed or France conquered. Had I been in Marmont's place I should not have chosen as he did. I should have sacrificed everything to the independence of my country.

Sunday, May 20th.—I called on the Duc de Broglie. We talked of Garibaldi.

Duc de Broglie.—It is impossible not to admire his courage and self-devotion; but I was astonished to find a British Minister comparing him to William III. William's was a well-considered and well-planned scheme for preserving the civil and religious freedom of a kingdom of which his own wife was the heir. Its consequences were well foreseen; they were expected to be, and they have been, the existence of the best form of civil government that the world has ever seen. Garibaldi's wild attempt aims at nothing beyond the overthrow of a despot and the dismemberment of an ancient monarchy, without a notion as to what may be its consequences. They may be anarchy; they may be a murderous civil war; they may be the subversion of the Papal authority in the provinces still faithful to him; they may be its restoration in the Legations; they may be the return of the Grand Duke to Tuscany, or the expulsion of Austria from Venice; they may be the aggrandisement of Piedmont, or her ruin. No one can foretell; scarcely any one ventures to guess.

What do you think of this Russian demonstration against Turkey? It cannot be spontaneous. Russia is too sick herself to wish to interfere with her sick neighbour. The impulse must have come from the Tuileries. The favourite plan of Celui-ci is to destroy all that was accomplished by the frightful sacrifices of the Russian war.

Senior.—What is he to get by it?

Duc de Broglie.—What is a madman to get by throwing himself out of a window? You must not reason as to this man's projects or motives as if he were sane. We, and you, and the rest of Europe, are at the mercy of a ' fou' who thinks it his interest, or makes it his amusement, to surprise us and to frighten us every six months; who is treating Europe as he is treating Paris, making its old maps as useless as its old almanacs; who has 75,000,000 sterling a year of revenue, and 400,000,000 more that he can borrow, and 600,000 ' diables incarnés' to throw at anybody's head.

Is your Budget popular in London?

Senior.—I do not think that as a whole it is popular in London, or in the House of Commons. It was carried triumphantly through the House by Gladstone's wonderful powers of debate, and by a pressure from without, derived principally from the manufacturing and commercial and mining interests. They looked on it as a great source of trade and as a security for peace.

Duc de Broglie.—I think that they were mistaken, at least as to its immediate effects. We shall take from you little more than we do now. How then will you be able to take much more from us?

Senior.—If the world consisted of only two countries it is clear that one country's power of buying from the other would depend on its power of selling to it, and *vice versâ*. But even if you prohibited every English commodity we might still drive with you a great trade indirectly, by sending, for instance, cottons to Germany and receiving payment in your wine. But there is one commodity for which your demand is insatiable, which you cannot prohibit or even tax, which we produce every year in an amount far exceeding our own wants, that, of course, is gold. But I agree with you that the increase of our trade with you is not likely to be very great.

Duc de Broglie.—Still less is it a security for peace, so far as peace depends on mutual goodwill. But what alarms me in your Budget is your substitution of direct for indirect taxation, which I hold to be a return to barbarism. In indirect taxation every man taxes himself. Those who make a good use of their money, and increase the capital of the country, pay the least; the wasteful and extravagant pay the most. Every man, too, pays at the time and to the extent that is most convenient to him. The great objections to direct taxation are: first, that it is unlimited while the taxpayer has any tangible property. Indirect taxation shows signs as soon as it is excessive, and, if persevered in, ceases to be productive. We all know that in the arithmetic of the Customs two and two sometimes make only three. You may go on adding a penny more and a penny more to the income-tax indefinitely. Then it affects only the richer minority. You are relieving the labourer and the artisan at the expense of the proprietor. You are doing this at the same time that you are giving additional power to the working classes. They are to dispose of the national revenue, and not to contribute to it. Again, it is far more painful than any other form of taxation. Who can say that his happiness is really interfered with by the duties on spirits or on tobacco? But the visit of the tax-gatherer is always a vexation. Some politicians may think this an advantage, they may think that public expenditure is excessive, and ought to be repressed by making the collection of the revenue more disagreeable. I know nothing of your civil expenses, nor do I know whether your military and naval expenditure is well-managed; but I do know that, while we are armed and arming as we are, you are doomed, you are mad, if you economise in your preparations for defence.

Senior.—I do not think that that will be the form which our economy will take. The country is too much frightened. The first reduction which the Government proposes is on the grant for primary education.

Duc de Broglie.—I did not expect that from Gladstone.

Prince Albert de Broglie.—Another objection is the contagiousness of the example. Nothing travels more quickly than modes of robbery. When England, the freest, the most aristocratic, and the most practical nation in the world, adopts as the basis of its financial system an income-tax on the richer classes, is it to be supposed that our master will not be tempted to follow your lead? An income-tax would make the payment of the rentes much easier. It might be made the basis of a system of loans.

Duc de Broglie.—I do not think that there is much danger of his having recourse to an income-tax, or to any new tax, while the resource of loans is so easy and so popular. The worse the bargain he makes, the more abundant, of course, will be the tenders, and, strange to say, the more popular the measure. Among the wicked inventions for the eventual ruin of France which he has devised, this system of loans, subscribed for individually by the people, is likely to be among the most effective. It popularises waste and war.

Monday, May 21st.—We went this morning to the wedding of a niece of Madame A. Chevalier. She is a Protestant, so they were married three times over; once yesterday at the Mairie, again this morning in a Protestant church, and afterwards at the Madeleine. We joined them at the Madeleine. The bride and bridegroom and their nearest relations sat on grand chairs in front of the high altar under Marochetti's graceful Virgin. We were placed behind. A long Mass with fine music was performed. The priest blessed the couple by placing his hands over their heads, and all was over without the persons principally concerned saying a word or rising from their chairs.

From thence I went to a very different scene, the funeral of the Countess Duchâtel, Duchâtel's mother, who died on Saturday last. We were summoned at twelve, and I was exact, but found nobody except M. de Flahault, Duchâtel, and his son and brother. Gradually the drawing-rooms in which we were received filled. Guizot, Cousin, Lavergne, Mallac, Pontoise, the Broglies, Circourt, Chrzanowski, d'Harcourt, and many others of literary and political eminence came, and by half-past one there were more than two hundred persons. We then walked in procession to the church of St. Thomas Aquinas, about half a mile off. Between the transepts a great catafalque covered with black velvet was erected, under which the coffin was placed, and a very long Mass was sung. The performers were unseen; large black curtains, hung before the high altar and before the western door, concealed them. The effect of the voices answering one another from the opposite ends of the great church was fine. At last the priest chanted *requiescat in pace*. The coffin was then taken from under the catafalque, and placed on a bier in one of the transepts, and we walked round the church in procession, each as he passed sprinkling it with holy water. It is not, however, to remain in Paris; it is to be ultimately buried in the family vault near Bordeaux.

I walked home with Mallac. He is very uneasy.

Mallac.—No two countries can do one another so much

harm as England and France, for they are very strong and very near, and I see the moment of their engaging in a deadly conflict every day approaching. The acquisition of Savoy has made us mad. We are resolved to have the Rhine. Even if the Emperor wished to abstain from it, the people would not let him; if the people would let him, the army would not. They too are mad. They burn for glory, honour, and, above all, promotion. The more bloody the conquest, the better it will please them, for the quicker it will push on the survivors. You must not suppose that the pacific policy of Louis Philippe was founded on any fear of defeat. What he was afraid of was victory. He feared that the military passions, once roused, would be irresistible. Nothing is so dangerous as a military democracy, and this is the most powerful military democracy that has ever existed.

I called on Madame Cornu. I told her that I had heard that Naples was intended for Prince Napoleon.

Madame Cornu.—I know nothing of it. What would England say?

Senior.—We cannot wish to see Bonaparte Viceroys substituted for legitimate Sovereigns—do you think that Louis Napoleon would make many sacrifices or run any great risks for such a purpose?

Madame Cornu.—I do not believe that at present he is willing to make sacrifices or to run risks for any purpose whatever. Things in Italy are going too fast for him. His policy is dilatory and expectative. He has often said to me, 'Il ne faut rien brusquer. A celui qui attend tout arrive; à qui va trop vite tout manque.'

Senior.—The malicious world would call that a sign of his Dutch blood.

Madame Cornu.—The world would talk nonsense. He

has not a drop of Dutch blood. He is the son of
Louis. In the beginning of July, 1807, Napoleon effected
a reconciliation between Hortense and Louis. They
met at Montpelier, and spent three or four days, as was
usually the case, in quarrelling. She went off in a pet
to Bordeaux, where the Emperor was, on his way to begin
the seizure of Spain. She passed a few days with him,
and then returned, at the end of July, to her husband at
Montpelier. He has many little bodily tricks resembling
those of Louis. Louis never looked you in the face; when
he bowed it was not like anybody else—it was an inclination of the body on one side. He kept his hands close to
his sides; Louis Napoleon has all these peculiarities. In
the April of the following year Hortense was frightened
and taken ill suddenly, and Louis Napoleon was born on
the 20th of April, twelve days before he was expected. On
this pretext Louis, in 1815, tried to get a divorce, but of
course failed. He was always jealous of Hortense, bribed
all her servants to watch her, and often said of Louis
Napoleon, 'ce n'est pas mon enfant.' But he was half-
mad, and, I believe, said so only to teaze his wife. At one
time he took possession of Louis Napoleon, and became
exceedingly fond of him, which would scarcely have been
the case if he had really doubted his legitimacy. Louis
Napoleon indeed was an attractive child. He was mild and
intelligent, but more like a girl than a boy. He is a year
older than I am; when we quarrelled he used to bite, not
to strike. He used to say to me, 'Je ne t'ai jamais battu.'
'Non,' I answered, 'mais tu m'as mordu.' He was shy,
and has continued to be so. He hates new faces; in old
times he could not bear to part with a servant, and I know
that he has kept ministers whom he disliked and disapproved
only because he did not like the 'embarras' of sending them
away. His great pleasures are riding, walking, and, above

all, fine scenery. I remember walking with him and Prince Napoleon one fine evening on Lansdowne Hill, near Bath. The view was enchanting; he sat down to admire it. 'Look,' he said, 'at Napoleon; he does not care a farthing for all this. I could sit here for hours.'

He employed me, some days ago, to make inquiries for him in Germany in connexion with his book. Moquard wrote me a letter of thanks. Louis Napoleon added to it, in his own hand, these words: 'Ceci me rappelle les bontés qu'avait Madame Cornu pour le prisonnier de Ham. Les extrêmes se touchent, car les Tuileries c'est encore une prison.' While the Duc de Reichstadt and his own brother lived, he used to rejoice that there were two lives between him and power. What he would have liked better than Empire would have been to be a rich country gentleman in a fine country, with nothing to do but to enjoy himself.

Senior.—You tell me that as a child he was gentle (doux). Is he so now?

Madame Cornu.—In appearance, for he has great self-command; but 'au fond' he is irritable. He is also very pertinacious, at least in his opinions. Hence he hates discussion; it annoys, and never convinces him. He cannot bear either to see people 'triste' or discontented.

Madame Cornu went upstairs, and returned with a quarto volume.

Madame Cornu.—This contains his letters to me, at least those that I have thought worth preserving. Here is the one which he wrote to me the evening before his escape. He tells me that he has sent to me all his remaining MSS. on artillery, and all the proof sheets of the printed portion, and begs me to keep them. I was then in Paris. The instant I read it I said to my husband, 'He is going to try to make his escape; he is making me his literary executrix.' My husband laughed at me. The next morning at breakfast the papers came in. I read aloud, 'Yesterday Louis Napoleon Bonaparte made his escape from Ham.' 'Bah!' said my husband, 'you are going back to the nonsense which you talked yesterday.' I repeated, 'Yesterday Louis Napoleon Bonaparte made his escape from Ham.' 'Don't talk stuff,' said my husband. 'Read it yourself,' I answered. The next day I got this letter from him in London. 'I need not,' he writes, 'tell you the details of my escape, as you have them in the papers. My measures were so well taken, that in eight hours I was in Belgium, and twelve hours after in London. It seems a dream. Take care of my MSS. and proofs; the first volume is finished, and may be printed from the proofs.'

Here is another worth hearing. It was written in London, in 1847, in consequence of a common friend having accused him of personal ambition. 'In all my adventures,' he says, 'I have been governed by one principle. I believe that from time to time men are created whom I will call providential, in whose hands the destinies of their countries are placed. I believe myself to be one of those men. If I am mistaken, I may perish uselessly; if I am right, Providence will enable me to fulfil my mission. But, right or wrong, I will persevere, whatever be the difficulties or the dangers. Living or dying, I will serve France.'

Here M. Trouvé Chauvel* came in. She closed the book, but the conversation on Louis Napoleon continued.

---

* M. Trouvé Chauvel began life in a counting-house at Havre. He founded the bank of La Sarthe, which gave a lively impulse to trade and contributed to the success of many commercial enterprises. He was elected Maire of Mans and gave offence to the Government of Louis Philippe by a too liberal speech. After the Revolution of February, 1848, he was at the head of the Municipal Administration. He was elected member of the Constituent Assembly, and became Prefect of the Seine in July, and Minister of Finance in October, 1848. He retired from politics when Louis Napoleon was elected President. —ED.

Trouvé Chauvel.—My first introduction to him was in 1848, when I was Prefect of the Seine. He was then Deputy, and remarkably shy. The first time that he 'demanda la parole,' he mounted slowly the steps of the tribune, looked round him for a minute or two, and then descended without having uttered a word. Some time after he made a second attempt, and actually spoke, but very badly. As Prefect of the Seine, I gave a reception to the whole Assembly. He negotiated with me about his coming to it; he did not wish to be announced, as his name would draw all eyes upon him. It was agreed that he should come early, and that I should meet him in the passage, and lead him in without his name being mentioned. But he never came.

Madame Cornu.—It has been thought that he was pretending to be stupid, as a candidate for the Papacy pretends to be dying. I was with him when the Bill of the 31st of May, 1850, for the restriction of the suffrage was in discussion. 'I hear,' I said to him, 'but I do not believe it, that you support this Bill.' 'I do,' he answered. 'What,' I said, 'you, the child of universal suffrage, do you support a limited suffrage?' 'You understand nothing about it,' he replied, 'je perds l'Assemblée.' 'But,' I said, 'you will perish with the Assembly.' 'Not in the least,' he answered. 'When the Assembly goes over the precipice, je coupe la corde.' In fact the relations between him and the Assembly were such that one or the other must have perished.

Senior.—It seems to me that if Cavaignac had been President, the Republic might have been saved.

Trouvé Chauvel.—So I thought at the time, and so I think now. Much depended on Thiers. In 1849 I was Minister of Finance—Blanqui, not the conspirator, but the political economist—came to ask me to call on Thiers and see whether we could come to an arrangement under which Thiers would support Cavaignac. I said that Thiers was in many respects a much greater man than I, but still, as he was a mere private person and I was a minister, he ought to call on me. Thiers is proud and punctilious; he would not visit me, but it was agreed that he should come to me on the ministerial bench, and that we should go out and discuss the matter in the corridors. We had a long conversation, but it ended in nothing.

Senior.—What caused the failure?

Trouvé Chauvel.—He imposed conditions which we could not accept.

Senior.—Of what kind?

Trouvé Chauvel.—Personal power for himself and his friends. I said that nothing could long exclude such a man as he is from power, if he wished for it, but that Cavaignac could make no promises until Thiers had shown his devotion to the Republic.

Madame Cornu.—I have strange letters from the Rhine. My friends there are in the utmost excitement. They abuse Celui-ci as the enemy of the peace of the world, and say that they will die sooner than become a province of France. Now, as no hostile or armatory demonstrations have been made here, no proposal either to attack them or to annex them, I suspect that their fury is raised by perceiving that a French spirit is working among their own lower orders. All the higher orders, including the higher 'bourgeoisie,' are Prussian in feeling, but the lower 'bourgeoisie,' the smaller shopkeepers and the labouring classes, are French. What they care about are taxes and conscription. Now the Prussian taxes are heavier than the French ones, and the Prussian liability to serve lasts longer. 'These preparations for war,' they say, 'are worse than war itself.'

Wednesday, May 23rd.—Thiers paid me a visit. I asked him whether he thought that if Parliamentary Government should revive he would find that disuse had impaired his facility.

Thiers.—I think not; but I did not like the trade of a public speaker, and as I get older the dislike increases. I cannot speak well against my opinion. I cannot say with apparent sincerity what I do not believe. A party man must do both of these things; I used to be ashamed of my own sophistry, and the only time that I really liked speaking was in the Constituent Assembly. The members of that Assembly were honest and intelligent, but ignorant. They came up from the provinces full of all sorts of prejudices, which I delighted in destroying.

They wanted, for instance, to issue paper money; I so convinced them of its mischief that only twenty voted for it. In parliamentary speaking you seldom hope to influence votes, at least by a single speech; every one, whatever be his convictions, votes with his party. The party-men in the Constituent were few. Few men had any personal interest to serve, they were not accustomed to public speaking, they did not know its hollowness, even the appearance of frankness and sincerity put on by second-rate orators carried them away. I was really sincere, and found it easy to express strongly what I felt strongly. So I ruled them, though they hated me as a Monarchist.

Senior.—I thought that the Monarchical party was strong in the Constituent?

Thiers.—There was much Monarchical feeling, but no Monarchical party—the majority believed in a Republic and were astonished at finding that it did not bring with it prosperity. They used to say to me, 'Cannot we do something for the working classes,' as if the working classes wanted anything done for them—as if the duties of a

Government were not preventive, the averting external and internal war, commercial changes and unnecessary expenditure.

My greatest moral quality is love of justice. It has always kept me impartial; it has made me just to my enemies as well as to my friends. Most people are unjust to both; they exaggerate the faults of their enemies and depreciate the merits of their friends. I may be vain, and I may be irritable, but I do not think that I ever was jealous.

I am delighted by your rejection of the Paper Duties Bill—it is a step in the right direction. I hope that more of Gladstone's absurd budget will be defeated. I wish that the errors of your foreign policy could be as effectually remedied. Having wedged yourselves into this 'ornière' of Revolutionism it is not easy to get out of it. It is a lane in which there are few places where carriages can turn. Your first business is, I think, to keep Turkey together. If Turkey is dismembered France will look for compensation to Egypt or to the Rhine.

Senior.—Can Turkey keep together?

Thiers.—For an indefinite time, if left to herself. Nations die slowly of internal diseases—the machine keeps cracking long before it breaks. The Byzantine Empire was dying for three hundred years.

Senior.—Do you believe in the supposed treaty between the two Emperors?

Thiers. —If there be one, the secret has been well kept, for no one knows anything about it. I would bet against a treaty, but there may be an understanding which would be as bad as a treaty. Nothing of the kind would have been done by Napoleon; he was a true Frenchman. No selfish feelings, not even his dynastic hopes, which were his strongest personal feelings, would have induced him to do anything which he thought hurtful to France. He would not have brought Russia to Constantinople, even to keep Joseph on the throne of Spain. This man has nothing French about him, not even his sympathies. He hates the Pope much more than he loves France. I doubt whether he has any love for her, except the love which a cab-driver has for his horse. He loves her as an instrument, and tries to feed her and take care of her that she may be a strong slave. But he would sell her, if he could gain by the bargain. He is an Italian by disposition, and an Englishman by tastes and habits. He is cleverer, however, than any of his ministers. But he is ignorant, dreamy, and, above all, indolent. These faults may expose him to some great disaster, or by keeping him quiet, may save him from one.

Monday, May 28th.—I breakfasted with Mérimée. We talked about the Emperor's attachment to his old friends, to all who had been kind to him in exile.

Senior.—He seems to be good in private life, bad as he is in political life.

Mérimée.—He certainly is affectionate and kind in private life, but I deny that we have as yet a right to say that he is a bad politician—we are too near—history must decide that.

Senior.—Has he not filled Europe with distress, confusion, and fear?

Mérimée.—That Europe is very sick, of course, I admit, but not that he is the cause of the illness.

Senior.—Until he disturbed us we were quiet.

Merimée.—You remind me of a friend of mine, on whose head the tester of his bed fell. 'I was sleeping so quietly,' he said, 'until this cursed tester fell down.' I looked at it and found that all that kept it up had been a rope by which it hung from the ceiling. 'How came you to trust to a mere rope?' I asked him. 'It had kept up the tester for forty years,' said he, 'and I saw no reason for its breaking.' I believe little in the influence over great events, supposed to be exercised by individuals. I believe that even if Guizot had never lived you would still have had the Revolution of 1848, and that if Celui-ci had never lived you would still have had an Italian Revolution. Austrian supremacy hung by a cord, which like that which supported my friend's tester had become rotten. Europe, I repeat, is sick. This man did not create the sickness, he is treating it. I will not venture to say whether his treatment is or is not judicious. I admit that it is bold; he is an allopath, not a homœopath, rather an English than a French doctor. He bleeds and amputates freely. Ten years hence, we shall be able, by the state in which the patient then is, to estimate his skill.

I dined with the Mohls, and met the Marquis and Marchioness Capranica del Grillo (Ristori), Cousin, Mignet, and the Montalemberts. Montalembert talked to me about Turkey.

Montalembert.—Your statesmen ought to be prepared with a policy, to be used as soon as she falls to pieces. If you continue to strive to support her you will fail, and you will be injured in her fall. Your diplomacy, ultra-revolutionary in Italy and Sicily, seems to be ultra-conservative when you have to do with Mussulman power. You forbid Spain to conquer Morocco. The ground on which you forbid that conquest, though conquest is the only mode by which North-western Africa can be civilized, is, that it will increase the expense of feeding the garrison of Gibraltar. Never was the policy of an independent nation, in a matter of importance not only to herself but to all Europe, so wantonly interfered with. I do not believe that Spain can conquer Morocco, or hold the country if she did. Morocco is another Algeria, and we all know what waste of men and money Algeria has cost and is still costing France. You may really have done her good by stopping her; but no nation likes to be treated as a child and interfered with, even for her good, by another. And as to the supplying Gibraltar, the saying to Spain 'You shall not civilize Morocco because it would cost us £100,000 a year more to provision Gibraltar from England' is too monstrous a piece of selfishness. The Spaniards have a right to say, and do say, 'If you wish to remain friends with us do not aggravate the mischief and the humiliation inflicted on us by your occupation of Gibraltar. It is a matter that you should keep out of sight; it degrades us; it ruins our revenue by the smuggling which you organise and protect there, and now you make this very injury a pretext for another injury.' Lord John has travelled in Spain to little purpose. No one with any knowledge of Spanish feelings would have written those despatches.

Madame Ristori is going to Holland. She is very fond of the Dutch.

Madame Ristori.—The last time that I performed at the Hague they called me back to the stage seventeen times.

'Was not that fatiguing?' we asked.

Madame Ristori.—Not in the least; it was very pleasant. Applause is absolutely necessary to an artist. You can do nothing unless you sympathise with the audience and the audience with you. No one can act well to a silent pit. But what is still worse than silence is a 'claque.'

Senior.—What is a 'claque?'

Madame Ristori.—A 'claque' is a set of persons dispersed about the theatre and ordered to clap at particular passages. I always forbid the employment of 'claqueurs,' but an obstinate manager will sometimes introduce them without my knowing it. If I find it out, which my long practice generally enables me to do, I am spoilt. I well know the paid 'claque;' it begins too soon; it comes at once from different parts of the house; it distracts me, and, what is worse, it makes me distrust the real applause; and, as I said, unless I feel myself sincerely applauded I am cold and constrained. However carefully an actress may prepare herself still much must be improvised.

After dinner she read to us Dante's 'Francesca.' She reads, of course, admirably. As the audience was small and might be supposed to know that canto of the 'Inferno' by heart, she did not think it necessary to use the overabundance of gesture by which she tries to make herself intelligible on the stage.

Tuesday, May 29th.—Ristori took leave of the Parisian public to-day. The last acts of 'Maria Stuarda,' 'Elizabeth,' 'Macbeth,' and a little comedy called 'I Gelosi Fortunati' were the entertainment. I was in the balcony, a little too far to see her countenance. Her 'Elizabeth' is a most wonderful imitation of senility, the senility of a strong mind, body, and will, worn out by fatigue and passion. In the 'Gelosi Fortunati' I saw her for the first time in genteel comedy. I think that it is her forte. Her part was that of a young married woman who, as well as her husband, is half-mad with jealousy; throughout the whole play only two feelings, fondness and jealousy, were exhibited. She represented them with the utmost spirit and truth, though with no exaggeration. I am sure that in a part of more gaiety and variety she would be admirable. Lady Morley, an excellent judge, told me that she preferred her 'Lady Macbeth' to that of Mrs. Siddons. I do not. Nothing that Ristori or any one else can do equals the grandeur of Mrs. Siddons in the sleep-walking scene. It was the remorse of a mind too proud and too much under self-command to show repentance or regret in its waking hours.

Thursday, May 31st.—I breakfasted yesterday and to-day with Achmet Vefyc Effendi, the Turkish Minister. I have thrown the two conversations together. He complains of deranged liver.

Vefyc.—My illness followed four years and a half of what appeared to me to be perfect health: four of them were spent in Teheran, the last six months in Bagdad. The dryness of the air in Teheran was such that I found it necessary to surround myself with water. I lived in a kiosk in a garden between two fountains, in a room through which a stream ran; every tree in my garden had a rivulet reaching its roots, if the rivulet were cut off the tree died. My divans and little tables, which I put in new, fell to pieces. At night I could hear the wood shrinking and cracking with a report like that of a pistol-shot. I used, after a ride of three or four hours, to return bathed in perspiration, and sit to cool under a tree. The climate of Bagdad was nearly the same. Nothing could be more delightful; I always felt perfectly well, but when I returned to Rumeli Hissar, on the Bosphorus, I was fifteen years older than when I left it four years and a half before. Life in such a climate is vigorous, agreeable, and short.

Senior.—How does the climate of Paris agree with you?

Vefyc.—I have not had a fair experience of it, for the three months during which I have been here have been, I am told, exceptionally bad. But what I complain of is the mode of life. I am oppressed not by the official duties—they are easy, Turkey has few affairs—but by the social ones. I have had to write fifteen notes this morning, all about trifles. In Turkey life is 'sans gêne;' if a man calls on you he does not leave a card; if he sends you a nosegay he does not expect a letter of thanks; if he invites you he does not require an answer. There are no engagements to be remembered and fulfilled a fortnight afterwards. When you wish to see a friend you know that he dines at sunset; you get into your caique, and row down to him through the finest scenery in the world. You find him in his garden, smoke a chibouque, talk or remain silent as you like; dine, and return. If you wish to see a minister you go to his office; you are not interfered with or even announced; you lift the curtain of his audience-room, sit by him on his divan, smoke your pipe, tell your story, get his answer, and have finished your business in the time which it takes here to make an appointment—in half the time that you waste here in an antechamber. There is no dressing for dinners or for evening parties; evening parties, indeed, do not exist. There are no letters to receive or to answer. There is no post hour to be remembered and waited for, for there is no post. Life glides away without trouble. Here everything is troublesome. All enjoyment is destroyed by the forms and ceremonies and elaborate regulations which are intended, I suppose, to increase it or to protect it. My Liberal friends here complain of the want of political liberty. What I complain of is the want of social liberty; it is far the more important. Few people suffer from the despotism of a Government, and those suffer only occasionally. But this social despotism, this despotism of salons, this code of arbitrary little 'règlements,' observances, prohibitions, and exigencies, affects everybody, and every day, and every hour.

I am sorry that Rawlinson leaves Persia. He was one of the best English Ministers that I have known. But there are two circumstances attending his resignation that reconcile me to it. One is that I hear that he resigns because the Persian mission is now put under the Foreign Office, instead of the India Board. In my time the British Minister was the Minister not of the Queen, but of the East India Company, and his being so diminished his influence. The other is that he is succeeded by Alison. No one knows the East so well as Alison, and he is honest and intelligent. He will consult the interests of both Persia and England, and he will be trusted by the Persians; they are good judges of character.

Senior.—Do you like Bulwer?

Vefyc.—Yes. He is active and conciliatory, 'fin'—perhaps a little too much so—but certainly good. We prefer him to Lord Stratford. No one can deny Lord Stratford's ability, energy, or good intentions, or his knowledge of Turkey as Turkey was thirty years ago; but long habits of successful contest have made him proud and despotic. He does not like opposition; he hates not merely to have to combat arguments opposed to his own views, but even to listen to facts which are inconsistent with them. He retains therefore many opinions which were just when they were formed, but have ceased to be so. It was time that he should retire.

Senior.—What is the state of the Sultan's health?

Vefyc.—Bad. For some years past he has had a fever every autumn and spring, The attacks are not dangerous in themselves, but they undermine his constitution; and his habits are unfavourable to health. I fear that his life is not a good one. This Russian demonstration against us has passed off. You have been told, I daresay, that it came from France, but I have ascertained that it did not. Its origin was Russian; perhaps it was Gortschakoff's own invention. It has done us good. Russia has shown her ill-will and put us on our guard. On the whole I think that we are in less danger than we have been in for some time. The Christian interference in our affairs, which has been the ruin of Turkey, cannot now originate in the ambition, or bigotry, or caprice, of a single Power. For such a purpose you must all join, and we know how difficult it is to get five or six Cabinets to agree to act in common. All however depends on God. If it is His will we shall retain our European provinces; and all the symptoms of the case seem to indicate that it *is* His will. And you, do *you* feel safe?

Senior.—No one who sees the preparations of France and hears the language of French people can believe that we are safe from a war.

Vefyc.—From what I hear, I believe that there is only one way in which a war can be prevented—that is by your allowing the French to annex Belgium and the left bank of the Rhine. They are fully resolved to make the attempt, whether it cost a war with you or not. I am told by those who know well the Emperor that his passions are altogether dynastic, and that he believes that such an acquisition will establish his dynasty. As for the French people, they cannot stop him, nor do they wish to stop him. The French are like the Greeks; they care about nothing but foreign policy. They will bear anything at home from a man who flatters their vanity abroad. You did not find the Greeks much the better for their independence?

Senior.—I did not penetrate more than fifteen miles from Athens. The plain of Attica is desolate, without trees or cultivation.

Vefyc.—It had both under us; but Greece then had municipal freedom, it was lightly taxed, and it was free from the conscription. Its municipal liberties have now been swallowed up in the dreadful French system of centralisation. The taxes are heavy in their amount and oppressively levied, and there is a conscription, which is the more vexatious because it is fraudulently carried on, and because it is not wanted. They have no business with an army.

Senior.—Their commerce is rapidly increasing.

Vefyc.—It has increased, but I doubt whether it is increasing, and I am sure that unless they change their habits it will diminish. It is not an honest commerce; it is obtained by cheapness produced by badness. Their ships are cheaply, and therefore ill, built, and they are undermanned. The crews are ill-fed and ill-paid. They carry cheaply, but deliver their cargoes in a bad state. There are Greek houses in all the great manufacturing towns who make, or cause to be made, very bad goods at very low prices; goods such as no honest house would export—cottons full of clay; woollens made of refuse materials; pipes not bored. But they look like better articles, and the Greeks forge an impression from the well-known marks of good makers. They send them to a new market, undersell everybody else, get possession of the market, and keep it for a year or two until the fraud has been discovered. *That* market is then lost to them and they try another. The mischief which they do is enormous, not only to the importing country, which loses its money, but also to the exporting country, which loses its character. The English had a large trade with Persia; it once amounted to 4,000,000*l.* sterling a year. The Greeks got possession of it, deluged Persia with bad goods, and reduced it to 2,000,000*l.*, and now it is gone. They got possession of the export trade of Marseilles and ruined it. Wherever you see a Greek house of business you see a nest of robbers. Two-thirds of the Greek bankers and merchants of Galata and Pera have passed through the Bagnio in Stamboul.

Friday, June 1st.—Beaumont came to Paris to-day, and we went together to Mignet's.

We talked of Tocqueville's letters.

Tocqueville professed to dislike writing, but in fact wrote

much, and the beauty of his letters has occasioned them to be preserved. I have given Beaumont about seventy, beginning in 1833, and ending only a fortnight before his death. Beaumont himself has above three hundred. Madame de Tocqueville has perhaps a thousand—he wrote to her sometimes three or four times a day. She will not allow hers to be published during her lifetime, and Beaumont is puzzled to know what to do with the others. Almost all of them are more or less political, and as he was generally in opposition, the conduct of the persons in power is severely criticised. Now many, indeed almost all, of these men belong to the Liberal party; common misfortune has united them against the common tyrant.

Beaumont.—Perhaps Tocqueville's most valuable correspondence is that with Royer Collard. He made rough drafts of his letters to Royer Collard, and of them only.

Mignet.—And I know that when Royer Collard had to write to Tocqueville, he shut himself up, and allowed no one to come near him, so highly did each appreciate the critical powers of the other.

Senior.—In what state is the second volume of the 'Ancien Régime'?

Beaumont.—The whole is mapped out, even the heads of all the chapters are written, and the materials are prepared for them. Two chapters are ready for the press. I shall publish them, and if I were not restrained by my knowledge of what would be his wishes if he could be consulted, I should publish the whole. Imperfect as the work is, it still would be a most striking picture of the state of things which produced the Revolution. But I know that if he had foreseen his death, he would have prohibited the publication. He wished nothing to bear his name which was not as perfect as he could make it. I have known him re-cast a sentence twenty times over.

Senior.—Even his letters are full of erasures. It is strange that a man who talked so correctly and so fluently should have written so laboriously and fastidiously.

Beaumont.—I am not sure that, charming as his writings are, his conversation was not still more charming. Perhaps the elaboration of his written style is excessive; it is too condensed. You cannot safely forget a sentence which is not necessary to the reasoning or to the narrative.

Mignet.—It is important that your memoir of Tocqueville should appear before the reception of Lacordaire in the Academy. Lacordaire, as Tocqueville's successor, will have to pronounce his *éloge*. My fear is that he will try to make him out a dévot. Now we know that Tocqueville, though a Christian, was a philosophical Christian. He never practised the observances of the Church. His faith would have been very unsatisfactory to a confessor.

Beaumont.—The priest who attended his last moments was an excellent and liberal man. He asked for no profession except a general declaration that he was a Christian, and for no confession except a general admission of sinfulness, and a general expression of repentance.

Mignet.—Pray let this be known in time, or Lacordaire may exaggerate his reception of the sacraments into a profession of Ultramontane Catholicism and a renunciation of philosophy.

Beaumont.—I know well that he received the last Sacraments, not because he believed in their efficacy, but because it pleased Madame de Tocqueville, and because he wished to avoid giving any scandal. He believed Christianity to be the greatest blessing ever bestowed on man; he hated, as far as it was in his nature to feel hatred, its opponents; and though his opinions were, as you truly say, far from orthodox, he was most anxious to avoid wounding the faith of others. For that reason he avoided all religious discussion.

It was perhaps the only subject on which, during forty years of intimacy, we never conversed.

Saturday, June 2nd.—I breakfasted with Ampère and Beaumont. Ampère and I were together in Rome in 1851. He spent there the winter of 1858 and the spring and summer of 1859, and left it last October.

Ampère.—The change is not great, but as far as there is any it is for the worse. The Government is still more oppressive, and what accords ill with oppression, more childish. Except the repression of manifestations of opinion, and the collection of taxes, it does nothing. Its policy consists in always promising and never performing. It is shown even in trifles. A friend of mine is writing a book on ' Mæsian Antiquities.' The Vatican contains the most curious Aztec painted histories that exist. He asked permission to see them; Antonelli promised it. He went to the library; the librarian had received no orders. He went back to Antonelli, who said he had given them, and would reiterate. He went back to the librarian, who again said that he had received none; and so he was *balloté* from one to the other. There could be no objection to his seeing them; it was merely the traditional policy of evading everything.

Beaumont.—Lamoricière applied the other day to the Cardinal who is the Roman Minister of War for a plan of the fortress of Ancona. He was told every day that he should have one, but none was forthcoming. He got impatient, and went himself to hunt through the depositories of the Ministry. He found at last that there had been one, but that it had been sent, as those who promised it to him well knew, to Vienna.

Senior.—I hear that the French troops are certainly quitting Rome.

Ampère.—Then the Pope must go too. Lamoricière

cannot maintain himself against the population of Rome. He may take refuge in Ancona. The other day, when some of Garibaldi's people crossed the Roman frontier, Lamoricière went to drive them out. Half his troops deserted on the road. If the invaders had stood firm, Lamoricière must have retreated.

Beaumont.—Lamoricière is my relation and my intimate friend. It is a 'triste rôle' that he is playing there; he can get nothing done; his army will disgrace him—if such a man can be disgraced.

Senior.—What carried him there?

Beaumont.—Attachment to the Pope. Some time ago he lost a child whom he adored. His mind was shaken by it. His wife, too, is a strong Papist. Grief, disappointment, idleness, following a life of brilliant and constant exertion, and advancing infirmities—for his life has been a hard one—have thrown him into devotion. I have no doubt that his Confessor sent him to Rome.

The development of religious feeling among the higher classes is striking: it seems to take the place of political excitement. Among my own relations, three girls, young, handsome, and well connected, have become Sisters of Charity. My nephew, with what in France is a large fortune, about 800*l.* a year, has become a Jesuit. His father and I did all that we could to prevent him: I kept him with me three months in Paris, took him to balls and plays, which he enjoyed, for there is nothing austere about him, but he was unshaken. He told us that he felt a vocation. He is now in a seminary near Paris as a teacher, but he may be sent to-morrow to Japan. He may be refused permission even to take leave of his family. A Jesuit has no relations, no country, no friends, no will.

Senior.—What has become of his fortune?

Beaumont.—The Order behaved well, they allowed him to give it up to his sisters.

Ampère.—Religion may have gained in Paris: it has lost in Rome. The unpopularity of the Pope has extended to Popery. Revolutions exaggerate vices and virtues: they raise nations above their ordinary level, or sink them below it. How wonderful has been the conduct of the Italians during the last twelve months! They have been soberly enthusiastic. The Romans are ordered by the Liberal Committee to be quiet: the only demonstration which they permit themselves is to walk bareheaded before General Guyon's head-quarters. Sometimes a gamin cries 'Viva la Francia,' but a murmur of 'hush, hush,' quiets him instantly.

Beaumont.—So it was with us in 1848. Nothing could be better than the conduct of the people during the first six months of the Republic. But such impressions are transitory. The men who were heroes in 1848, are reptiles in 1860.

Senior.—What is the feeling in your province?

Beaumont.—Favourable to the Emperor. Prices are high, and the commercial treaty is popular. We expect to find a great market in England, and to get, what is wanting more than anything else to French agriculture—cheap iron. In Paris things are different. Every one is uneasy and dissatisfied: the Emperor is hated, the treaty is hated, and, above all, the English are hated. Mixed with that hatred is some contempt. I hear of nothing but 'la décadence de l'Angleterre.'

My answer is, that I see no symptoms of 'décadence' as yet. I shall believe her 'décadence' only in one event. Only if she submits quietly, or indeed submits at all, to our annexation of Belgium. Such an abandonment of all her traditional policy, such a temptation to France to injure her still more, and such an addition to our means of doing so, will prove that she has ceased to consider herself a great Power. And no country is greater than it believes itself to be.

June 3rd.—We left Paris.
[The interval was spent by Mr. Senior in London.—ED.]

Saturday, August 25th.—My daughter and I reached Paris at about one this morning. After breakfast I called on Cobden, and found him and Mrs. Cobden with the Countess Gigliucci (Clara Novello) just starting to pay a visit to Rossini at his pretty villa on the other side of the Bois de Boulogne. It was a present to him from the City of Paris. He is a pleasing old man of about ninety, or rather more. We talked of Venice, which he has lately visited.

Rossini.—Nothing can exceed its misery or its exasperation. Its trade is destroyed, its inhabitants are trying to fly from it, but they are refused passports, and if they escape, their relations are fined and ruined. Even their amusements are stopped: the coffee-houses on the Piazza of St. Mark, which used to be open almost all the night, are closed at nine o'clock. Bitterly as they hate the Austrians, they hate the French, or rather the French Emperor, still more. He promised them liberty—in seven hours they would have had it. Everything was ready for Admiral Bouet's attack, and its success was certain. He had more than forty steamers, more than half of which were coated with iron: he had three thousand infantry besides his crews. 'If,' they said to me, 'Louis Napoleon would have delayed his peace for only one day!' Now their cause is hopeless. Garibaldi can do them harm, he can exasperate the fears, suspicions, and cruelties of their tyrants, but he can do them no good. His Italians are no match for the Germans. The south always bends before the north.

The Grand Duke of Tuscany used to converse with me familiarly. I once said to him that I wondered why, when the Tuscan people themselves had restored him in 1849, he re-entered Florence surrounded by Austrian troops. 'I wish,' he said, 'that you had been in my place.' 'I should be very sorry,' I answered, 'to have been in your Royal Highness' place, but if I had been, I do not think that I should have chosen to commit such a bêtise as that.' 'I wish,' he repeated, 'that you were in my place, you would see that I have no choice in the matter. I am a dependent on Austria. I must wear the uniform, and use the troops, and hold the language that she pleases. I have no power, or policy, or will of my own.'

General Chrzanowski drank tea with us. We talked of Russia.

Chrzanowski.—Nothing is to be feared from her at present. The army has not been recruited for five years. An attempt to raise men was made about a year ago. The peasants said that if the Emperor wanted soldiers, he must send soldiers to take them. The mortality in the Russian army is frightful; of four men who enter a Russian hospital, three never quit it. I do not believe that Russia has now 300,000 soldiers. She cannot send a man across the frontier.

Senior.—What are they wanted for at home?

Chrzanowski.—They are wanted as police, they are wanted for the collection of the revenue, they are wanted as garrisons of the fortress, and above all they are wanted to prevent a servile war or a revolution.

Senior.—You think the danger of a revolution imminent?

Chrzanowski.—How can it be otherwise when the sovereign himself acts as a revolutionist? When he promises freedom to twenty-two millions of serfs, allows the promise to remain for four whole years unfulfilled, and throws the blame of its non-performance on the nobles? If the Russian peasants were not the most submissive of subjects they would have risen long ago. They are not without leaders. There are serfs who pay to their masters 10,000 or 15,000 francs a year; they are merchants, bankers, and shopkeepers; their children receive the best education that is to be had in Russia. The 'Seigneur' loses money at play; he tells his merchant-slave that he wants his son for a groom and his daughter for a kitchen-maid, and is bought off at some ruinous price. Such men, so educated and so oppressed, will be the revolutionary leaders. And who is there to resist them?

The conversation turned to the Italian campaign.

Chrzanowski.—The wisest thing that Louis Napoleon did was to make the peace. The battle of Solferino reduced his effective army to 80,000 men. Even a week after, when he had been joined by the fifth corps, under Prince Napoleon, it did not exceed 100,000. The Austrians, having fallen back on their reinforcements, amounted to 150,000. On the 6th of July, the day on which Louis Napoleon, having consulted no one except Vaillant, sent to Francis Joseph to propose an armistice, he expected to be attacked the next morning in front and in flank by superior forces. It is true that the Austrian army was discouraged by repeated failure, but the French army, though successful, was equally disheartened, for it felt that it was ill-commanded. The French soldier is eminently intelligent and inquisitive; he tries to discover all that has been done and all that is intended, reasons on it, criticises it, and if he finds that his leaders do not know their business he turns timid or sulky.

Again, Louis Napoleon committed the same fault as the Russians did at Sebastopol. He spoilt his troops of the line to make picked regiments, and then wasted those regiments prodigally. By the beginning of July he had spent three-fourths of his Zouaves; his uncle would have reserved them for critical occasions.

Even if he had repulsed the attack which he feared on the 7th of July he must have retreated. The weather was sultry, the country marshy and unhealthy. Verona, it is true, was ill-provided, but he could not have stayed in front of it. These I believe to have been the reasons—not the fear of Prussia—which induced Louis Napoleon to make his sudden ill-considered peace. The whole campaign shows how completely the long peace has destroyed military science. I am not now speaking of the Austrians—their blunders are too obvious to deserve comment—but of the French. The battle of Magenta was fought with only half the army, and but for the inconceivable folly of Hesse, who stopped for four hours the concentric movement of the Austrian army, it must have been a defeat. Though it was successful the French made no use of it; they allowed the beaten army to retire quietly from its wide position, through a country in insurrection, without loss of men or of material. At Solferino the French were not aware that Francis Joseph was in force only a couple of miles from them. They began their march in seven columns, and suddenly found the Austrian army in position. Fortunately for them that army was virtually without a commander. No one expected to be attacked; no one knew where to find the Austrian Emperor. The orders given to Hesse, the nominal commander, were overruled by Grün, the Emperor's favourite. The bulk of the army was collected to the left, and stood there inactive while the French attacked their centre. The right, under Benedek, was successful, and if the left had acted with even tolerable vigour the French attack on the centre would probably have failed disastrously. When the inconceivable folly of the enemy had given the French the victory, what did they do with it? Nothing. They allowed the Austrians quite unmolested to recross the Mincio, to concentrate themselves below Verona, and to receive their reinforcements, while the French army scattered itself in a line of twelve miles long from Castel Novo to Goito. Here they stayed three days, from the 30th of June to the 3rd of July, with a far superior army within a few miles. That they were not attacked and disgracefully beaten was owing only to the total absence of skill and enterprise on the part of the Austrians. In fact, the advance of the French after the battle of Solferino was a folly; they had nothing to gain by it; they were leaving their own resources and advancing into the terrible quadrilateral, the field which Austria had been for years preparing for the purposes of a defensive war. Everything was against them, the season, the country, and a superior enemy. Louis Napoleon's merit is that he discovered his situation in time to ask Francis Joseph's permission to retire. His good fortune is that he got that permission. His want of tenacity of purpose served him in good stead. Had he possessed his uncle's obstinacy he might have endured his uncle's fate—the sun of Venetia might have been as fatal as the frost of Russia.

The great superiority of the French over the Austrians was in their staff and in their generals of division and brigade. The men on each side were excellent; the commanders-in-chief on each side were detestable. Francis Joseph was the worst because he was the most presumptuous. Louis Napoleon knew his own ignorance and also knew the merits of others. Francis Joseph knew nothing about

himself or about anybody else; he trusted nobody except
the person whom he ought to have most mistrusted—himself.
When Giulay was in command Francis Joseph let Hesse
overrule him. When Hesse was in command he let Grün
overrule him. Hesse made Giulay lose the battle of Magenta.
Grün made Hesse lose the battle of Solferino; he ordered
away the artillery which was to have protected Hesse's
centre, and did so without telling Hesse what he had done.
It was not until it was wanted that Hesse knew that it
was gone. The commanders of each army being bad and
the men and regimental officers in each army being good,
the superiority of the French generals of division and
brigade turned the scale. Macmahon, Trochu, Canrobert,
and Niel may not be great generals, but they are far
superior to the aristocratic Austrian commanders who were
colonels at six months old and owe their advancement to
their pedigrees. If Macmahon, Trochu, Canrobert, and Niel
had commanded the Austrian divisions at Solferino, and
Clam Gallas, Zobel, Zedwitz, Lichtenstein, and Wimpffen
had commanded the French, Louis Napoleon, notwithstanding the excellence of his troops, would have been
utterly defeated.

Senior.—You think highly of the Austrian army?

Chrzanowski.—It is the best, after the English and the
French. Its great fault is its pedantry. Every detail is
pre-arranged. An Austrian general may be brought before
a court-martial for having deviated from the prescribed
rules as to the depth of his lines, or the use of his light
troops, or the position of his artillery, or the employment
of his reserves. While he obeys these rules he cannot be
censured, though he may be beaten; but if he breaks them
nothing but the most brilliant success can protect him.
When, as must often be the case, obedience to the rule and
success are incompatible, his only safe course is to stick to

the rule. A French general is governed, not by rules, but by something much better—by his own intelligence and by the circumstances of the case.

Sunday, August 26th.—Beaumont breakfasted with us. He says he can think and talk of nothing but his work on Tocqueville.* The first volume goes to the press to-day. It contains a short memoir of Tocqueville, a narrative of two tours which he made in the far west, and the two finished chapters of the second part of his 'Ancien Régime.' I tried to persuade Beaumont to publish the remainder, which is arranged and, to a considerable extent, written.

Beaumont.—Nothing shall force me to do so. I shall return it to Madame de Tocqueville and entreat her to burn it before her death. It would delight and instruct the public, but my duty is not to the public, but to Tocqueville, and my duty to him is to do what, if I could have consulted him in his last moments, he would have ordered me to do; that is, to publish nothing to which he has not given the very last finish. 'La forme' was his ruler, almost his tyrant. 'No idea,' he used to say, ' ought to be produced in déshabille. To be received it must be presented in the fewest words consistent with perfect clearness.' The chapters which I suppress have not this finish. A friend, who is writing on Mirabeau, asked me if Tocqueville had described him. 'Certainly,' I answered, ' he devoted almost a chapter to Mirabeau. There it is in that bundle of papers, but you cannot see it, nor will any one ever see it.'

There is a question on which I wish for your opinion; it must be decided to-day. Shall I group the letters, or arrange them chronologically?

---

* There is an English translation of this work, which was superintended by Mr. Senior, with large additions; published by Macmillan in 1861.—ED.

Senior.—I have no doubt on the subject: I should arrange them chronologically. Letters are often grouped in the first edition, but in the second edition they are always arranged chronologically. I was so annoyed by the grouped editions of Cicero's letters that I sent to Padua to get the chronological edition, and I found that I had never understood them before.

Beaumont.—That may be true with respect to letters which are chiefly political; but the political letters of Tocqueville cannot be published now. During almost all his political life he was in opposition. The men whom he opposed are now the heads of the Liberal party: his criticisms would weaken their authority. Some of those criticisms he would probably retract. Most of his letters to you, to Reeve, and to me, are full of politics. I lay them aside, to be edited by my son, and I shall advise him to arrange them chronologically; one letter throws light on another. But his unpolitical letters often derived a colour from the person to whom they were addressed; a different 'nuance' runs through a different correspondence. If I group the letters, the first volume will contain those to Kergorlay and to Stoffels. There is a marked difference between them and the others.

Senior.—Who were Kergorlay and Stoffels?

Beaumont.—Kergorlay is a cousin of your friend, a nephew of the man who refused allegiance to Louis Philippe. His Legitimist principles have prevented his taking any part in public life, but Tocqueville rated him very highly. 'Not one of us,' he said, 'has the intelligence or the cultivation of Kergorlay. If he had come forward he would have been the first in the very first rank.' Tocqueville's letters to him are chiefly intellectual and literary. Kergorlay treated democracy as an enemy to be resisted, and if possible beaten down; Tocqueville as a sovereign, to be feared, perhaps to be disliked, but to be obeyed. But their separation on politics seems to have tightened their union when they met on the common ground of philosophy and criticism. Stoffels is a man of whom, if Tocqueville had not lived, the world would never have heard. He is of humble birth and humble fortunes, a 'petit receveur' at Nancy. But Tocqueville and he were together at school, and the intimacy there contracted never cooled. They met whenever they could, but it was seldom, and the long intervals were filled by correspondence. If Tocqueville was unusually gay it was because he had received a letter from Stoffels; if anything interesting occurred he used to say, ' I must write all this to Stoffels.'

Senior.—Is Stoffels a man of remarkable talents?

Beaumont.—Of sound judgment and of considerable knowledge; but his moral qualities, his integrity, his fidelity, his delicacy, his sympathy, were what attracted Tocqueville. Intelligence predominates in the letters to Kergorlay; affection in those to Stoffels.

Lévy tells me that he is printing a translation of your Turkish journal.

Senior.—Yes; it is by Madame de Bury.

Beaumont.—She will do it well; her French style is admirable.

After breakfast I called on Thiers.

Senior.—When I was here three months ago you thought the preservation of peace doubtful.

Thiers.—Whatever depends on the will of an individual must be doubtful, especially if that individual be visionary, unscrupulous, capricious, and rash; but I see many indications that the desires, or rather the *velléités*, from which I feared a conduct that might drive you into war, if not extinguished, have become tepid. Our master's mind dwells constantly on his uncle's history; as a coalition was fatal to Napoleon, he fears that it might be fatal to himself. He wishes without doubt to restore the Rhine to France, but he wishes far more earnestly to remain Emperor; he believes that an unsuccessful war would dethrone him, and he puts lower than I do the chances of a war against united England and Germany. I think that he would have a fair chance of beating Prussia before Austria could assist her, beating Austria afterwards, and tiring out England. I do not believe that England is to be conquered. Were I War Minister, against England I would not attempt an invasion; it would be hazardous. But with the aid of Spain and the new artillery, Gibraltar might be taken; the gold-ships might be intercepted; your trade and commerce might be seriously injured. You would not think it worth while to fight for twenty years, or for ten years, or for five, for the mere purpose of preventing our keeping Rhenish Prussia.

As I said before, Louis Napoleon is less sanguine; his 'idée fixe' is the fear of a maritime war. He will take whatever he can get by cession or by bargain, but will do nothing which he believes you will make a casus belli. I attach great importance to his letter to Persigny. He has shown himself a good judge of French feeling. He must have known that its cajoling, apologetic tone would be unpopular here; that it would hurt, what it is most dangerous to hurt, our vanity. Yet in the hope of pleasing you he risked it.

I do not advise you to discontinue your preparations. His friendship for you depends on his fears, but you ought not to talk so much about them. You ought not always to be putting war, and invasion, and capture of gold-ships into our heads. Arm, but as far as it is possible for a constitutional country to do so, arm silently. It is *our* interest and *your* interest, and the interest of Europe, that he should remain quiet. Peace will give us liberty. If there be no foreign war to distract our attention and to inflame our passions, we shall use the power of controlling him which he has been forced to leave in our hands. There has been a considerable opposition this year in the Corps Législatif. After the next elections it will be much stronger; I expect to see a minority of sixty. After the last elections the minority was only four, and yet that small minority has been very troublesome. Nothing but war and military glory will induce so proud a nation as France to acquiesce in having no will of its own.

Senior.—What I fear is that he is of your opinion.

Thiers.—I daresay that he is; but he knows that the war which would compensate us for liberty must be a successful war; and, as I have already said, he does not expect a maritime war to be successful. He had rather be a despot than a constitutional King; but he would rather be a constitutional King than an exile. As a real friend of France I delight in the coalition which has been formed to restrain our aggression. The coalition will force us to be peaceful, and if we remain peaceful we shall become free.

You in England believe that the annexation of Savoy was a scheme long ago formed, and constantly persevered in. I do not. He may indeed have formed it two years ago; but I know that he had given it up. The accusation against Palmerston and Russell, that by favouring the Piedmontese annexations they brought on that of Savoy, is well founded. There can be no doubt that Louis Napoleon had gained enormously by Magenta and Solferino. The details were not known, there was great apparent success: but the peace disappointed every one. He did not choose to confess that his rash advance had put the army into a situation of great danger, from which he could extricate himself only by asking for an armistice. He assigned as the ground of the peace his fears of Prussia—a motive offensive to our pride.

Then Piedmont, which had been his slave, took the bit into her mouth; began to annex without consulting him; persevered in opposition to his orders, his threats, and at last his entreaties; and raised on our south-western frontier a formidable power which threatens to increase. He could not control the movement which he had set in action. It did in one direction much less and in another much more than he intended. He could not perform either the promises he had made at Genoa or those which he had made at Villa Franca. I know that his ministers told him that he was losing his prestige, that he was suffering France to be humiliated in his person, and suggested the acquisition of Savoy as a compensation to us for the affronts which we were suffering in Central Italy.

I am very glad that he has taken Savoy; glad because it rounds our frontier towards Italy, glad because it gives us 500,000 more fellow-citizens belonging to us by their interests, their sympathies, and their language; and I am still more glad because, while it has done *us* good, it has done *him* harm, not in France, for it is popular, but in his external relations; because it has created the coalition which will keep him quiet. I believe that his failure at Baden has decided him, at least for the present: that he intends to spend the rest of his life, which is not likely to be long, in fêtes and tours and amusements. I know that what he saw of actual war disgusted and alarmed him. He has not had experience enough to be callous to its horrors : scenes frightened him to which his uncle would have been indifferent. A young officer who served in the campaign of 1815 published an account of it, and described the appearance of Ligny, where 10,000 lay dead and dying in a small space, as 'affreuse.' The book was read by Napoleon at St. Helena; he made this note in the margin, 'Affreux, affreux; joli mot pour un jeune homme qui voit un champ de bataille pour la première fois.' He talks modestly of the campaign, admits that he began too late to be fit to command 200,000 men, and yet he would be afraid to remain at home while a great war was going on on our frontier.

The conversation passed to Italy.

Thiers.—The enemies of Italy are not Francis Joseph or Francis II., but Mazzini, Garibaldi, and Cavour. The first is mad, the second presumptuous, the third is weak.* Garibaldi may perhaps hope for a united Italian kingdom. Mazzini intends to have a dozen democracies, each governed or ungoverned by its own mob. Cavour is carried away by the torrent which he has let flow. He has too much sense to believe that three towns with histories like those of Rome, Venice, and Florence will submit to be the subjects of a Piedmontese; he knows too well the feelings of the Catholic world to suppose that it will allow the Pope to be a fugitive; he knows too well the strength of the quadrilateral and of Venice to believe that Garibaldi can conquer Venetia.

Senior.—I am told that Bouet did not estimate highly the strength of Venice.

Thiers.—That is a mistake. Bouet is my intimate friend. I have talked the matter over with him. He believes Venice to be impregnable towards the land; towards the sea it is protected by the long strip of the Littoral, which has only three entrances, narrow and shallow, all well for-

---

* In power is meant.—N. W. S.

tified. Bouet, with enormous means and complete command of the sea, thought his success very doubtful, and he is one of the boldest men that I know. It is absurd to suppose that Garibaldi, with no means at all except what he may acquire by getting possession of the Neapolitan fleet, can succeed where even France was in danger of failing. I know that only two days ago the Emperor assured Metternich that if Garibaldi alone, or Garibaldi and Piedmont together, attacked Austria, he would leave them to their fate. I do not think that he would allow Lombardy to return to Austria; that would be too complete an abandonment of the programme of Genoa; but he would see with pleasure the return of Tuscany, Modena, and Parma to their old Sovereigns—in fact, the carrying out the Treaty of Villa Franca. I know too that the French garrison in Rome has been reinforced. The utmost that Garibaldi will be allowed to do is to conquer Naples. But if he were a really patriotic Italian, if he really wished for the good government of the Italian people, he would be satisfied with the freedom of Sicily, and leave the new constitutional Government of Naples to consolidate itself. Austria would not then attempt to interfere. The Neapolitans have shown themselves anxious for freedom, and with no foreigners to beat them down, and with Sicily to assist them, they will preserve it. I do not blame Mazzini. I do not blame Garibaldi; but I bitterly blame Cavour if, for the selfish purpose of retaining his power or his popularity, he allows Garibaldi and Mazzini to destroy the only chance of constitutional Government that Southern Italy has ever had or is ever likely to have.

Val Richer, Tuesday, August 28th.—We left Paris this morning for M. Guizot's place, Val Richer, in Normandy, about seven miles from Lisieux. Our road ran through a pretty, well-peopled country. The only considerable town that we passed was Evreux; the cathedral, as seen from the station, looked fine.

Val Richer stands on a small plateau in a park, surrounded by forests partially cleared. The population of the district is thin, and diminishing; there are seldom more than two, or at most three, children to a marriage. All the peasants are small proprietors; their cottages and generally an enclosure of eight or nine acres, enough to feed a couple of cows, belong to them. About fifteen acres are supposed to be necessary to support a family; and as few have so much, the proportion of persons who work as day-labourers for the larger occupiers is considerable. The ordinary wages are forty sous a day, in harvest fifty sous.

The whole population is about 360, of whom ninety are electors—that is to say, males above twenty years of age. The conscription hits from two to three every year, but few serve. Every family tries to set aside annually a sum to produce the 'rachat' when the son attains twenty years of age. At present that is 2000 francs; during the war it rose to 2600. Of the children who attain twenty, more than half are unfit for service, so that it is very rarely that the same family can have to buy off more than one son. They live well, eat meat once a day, and inhabit cottages quite as good as those in the best parts of England—cottages costing from 80*l.* to 100*l.* to build. Some built by M. Guizot cost more.

The plan of this house is simple, but uncommon. The garden front is about 150 feet long; the hall is in the centre, on one side the dining-room and orangery, on the other the library and drawing-room. Each of these last rooms has thorough lights, and occupies the whole breadth of the house, the library being a passage-room to the drawing-room. On the first floor a corridor runs the whole length into which the bedrooms open; they all look west except those at each end, which look north and south. The library and drawing-room, the corridor, and most of the bedrooms, are full of books. M. Guizot's sitting-room and bedroom are over the orangery. On the east or garden front stands in the summer and autumn a range of finé orange trees, about three hundred years old, presented to M. Guizot by the purchaser of the Château de Rosny, the residence of Sully. They cannot stand the winter out of doors, and if the temperature falls below 28° Fahrenheit, the orangery must be warmed.

The farm consists of about six hundred acres, of which about half are in wood. The park contains about twenty acres, prettily tossed about. When M. Guizot purchased it twenty-four years ago it contained only three trees; now it is well wooded. He planted a straight chestnut avenue to walk and read in.

In the 'vacherie,' a large and airy room, we saw fourteen cows. They leave it only during the nights of summer, but are perfectly healthy.

The family consists of Guizot's two daughters, Henriette and Pauline, their husbands Conrad and Cornelius de Witt and their children, and M. and Madame Guillaume Guizot. Conrad manages the farm and lives here with his wife during the whole year. The others spend eight months here and four in Paris.

We have coffee at eight, breakfast at half-past eleven, walk out at half-past three, dine at seven, drink tea at half-past nine, and separate at a quarter after ten. M. Guizot rises between half-past five and six. The children, remarkably nice and well-behaved, breakfast and dine with us, leaving the drawing-room at about nine.

Wednesday, Aug. 29th.—I walked with Guizot over the park and the farm. He asked me if I had seen Thiers, and what were his views. I explained them.

Guizot.—I agree with Thiers that Louis Napoleon now wishes for peace; but I do not think that he would dislike war if he thought, as he did when he began his Russian and his Austrian wars, that the chances were greatly in his favour. He certainly made proposals to the Prince Regent of Prussia which would have led to war with you. Perhaps he was not sorry that they were rejected, and that he could say to himself and to us that a Continental war was impossible, and that he had nothing to do but to enjoy himself in peace. I hear that his visit to Baden was a failure, socially as well as politically; that the Sovereigns thought him dull and uninteresting. I do not wonder at it. I have seen him seldom, but on one occasion he detained me for some time. His mind seemed to me to be neither full nor inventive, to have few acquired ideas, and to be incapable of originating any. His manners are exceedingly good; simple and kind, and yet dignified.

I differ also from Thiers as respects Savoy. I believe that Louis Napoleon never intended to release Victor Emmanuel from the engagement made at Plombières in 1858 to give Savoy in exchange for Lombardy. But he cannot do anything frankly and directly. If the bargain had been avowed at the beginning of the war, or even if it had not been disavowed, Europe would have taken it more quietly. In itself the thing is good; it gives us a frontier which separates us completely from Italy, and prevents our having any pretence to interfere in the affairs of the Peninsula.

Italy will never be really united. If Garibaldi attack Venetia, what is called the Italian cause is lost. He will be beaten, the old Sovereigns will be restored, and Austria will recover her influence. If Garibaldi does not attack Austria, and Italy is left to herself, she will fall in pieces. I know how difficult it is to make a new King, for I have helped to make one. It is ten times as difficult to make a new kingdom. All Europe tried to make a new kingdom of the Netherlands. All was in its favour, a common origin, rich and well-instructed populations, contiguity and common interests; yet in fifteen years it split up. The very configuration of Italy is opposed to unity.

I cannot excuse Palmerston and Lord John Russell for countenancing the deciding by universal suffrage what shall be the political relations of the States of Central Italy. Direct universal suffrage is one of the most mischievous legacies of 1848. Even in the wildest times of our first Revolution it never was employed. If a nation has to choose its Sovereign, surely the decision ought to rest with its educated classes. The return of the Dukes with constitutions, guaranteed if necessary by England and France, and the imposing reform on the Pope was the only useful solution of the Italian question. True wisdom almost always employs compromises and half-measures. Revolutions are relentlessly logical, and Palmerston's politics, though Conservative at home, are revolutionary abroad.

Thursday, Aug. 30th.—We took a long walk with M. Guizot and M. and Madame de Witt among the woods, towards the little church and parsonage of La Roque, and returned by its old feudal château.

At about a mile from home, on the outskirts of M. Guizot's property, we passed a plateau partially cleared, on which were scattered several houses, most of them miserable and almost roofless.

Guizot.—That is a colony which fixed itself there many years ago, when much less of the forest was cleared. The land is poor, and they got it cheap. Whence they came we do not know, their names are unlike those of their neighbours; it is only among one another that they intermarry, or rather consort, for they seldom contract regular marriages. They never frequent the church, and seldom are baptised. They have large families and live wretchedly on the produce of their little farms, and on what they can steal. Sometimes they will work for wages and labour vigorously, but it is only for two or three days. They are recruited from the bad characters of the neighbourhood. It is a sort of Alsatia, or Asylum of Romulus.

We found the curé in a neat little house. He is the son of a peasant, a man of simple, easy manners, but with no pretensions to the rank of a gentleman. I was struck by the absence of books.

De Witt.—Probably he has only his Breviary, and perhaps the Vulgate; though it is not certain that he has *that*. I was in a priest's house the other day and wished to look at his Vulgate, but he had lent it five years before to a neighbouring priest, and had not got it back.

Senior.—How, then, does he spend his evenings? He must not smoke, and he must not go to the cabaret, and he must not play at cards.

De Witt.—He has an aunt who lives with him. He gets up early; he works in his garden and in his little field; he visits his people, for he is an excellent priest, and in the evening he reads his Breviary and dozes.

Madame de Witt.—Besides that, he shells beans, perhaps makes nets. By six or seven o'clock in winter he is in bed.

Senior.—And when does he get up?

Madame de Witt.—In winter as soon as it is light, which it is by seven.

Senior.—So that he is twelve hours in bed.

Madame de Witt.—That is the life of most of our peasants. They light no candles. They talk or meditate or smoke by fire-light for an hour after sunset, but pass the bulk of the dark hours in bed.

Senior.—Does the curé ever dine with you?

Guizot.—Once a year. If you were here in October you would be present at a dinner which I give to my two curés and my two maires.

Senior.—At Tocqueville M. and Madame de Tocqueville dined once a year with their curé.

Guizot.—Our curé gives no dinners, at least in that sense of the word, though I know that he has given away his own dinner to a poor traveller. His whole income consists of this house, garden, and paddock, and about 80*l.* a-year; but it is quite equal to his wants.

Senior.—Has he to give much in charity?

Guizot.—Little in money, something in kind—bread or other victuals. There is little destitution here. Out of a population of three hundred and sixty, not above four or five require assistance.

We looked into the church. It is pewed, as all the country churches are.

Guizot.—In this department the sale of the Bible is prohibited. The prohibition is illegal, but no one thinks it worth while to resist.

Senior.—I know several persons who are anxious for martyrdom. I will try to get one of them to come here and hawk Bibles.

Guizot.—Pray do. Send us Borrow if you can. The prefect will certainly put him into prison. I will appeal, carry the question, if necessary, from court to court, and bring him out, not only a martyr, but triumphant. I should like to see 'The Bible in France.'

The Gallican Church committed a great mistake, I may almost say a great crime, when it persecuted and destroyed the Jansenists. If they had been tolerated, they would have rendered in France, to a certain extent, the service rendered in England by the Dissenters. They would have kept the Established Church awake. The hierarchy would not have become mere men of fashion, and the curés ignorant. They would not have lost their hold on the higher classes. They would not, indeed, have done to us all the good which the Puritans did to you, for they would not have given us liberty. It is possible that if it had not been for the Puritans, Charles I. would have triumphed. It seems to me almost certain that the general relaxation of morals and depravation of opinions under Charles II. would have destroyed or corrupted your free institutions, if the Puritans had not been there to preserve the traditions of morality and freedom.'

Senior.—How came your Church, once so independent, to become Ultramontane?

Guizot.—It was the effect partly of the first Revolution, and partly of the Concordat. During the Republic and the Directory, the clergy, attacked by the Government and by the mob, fell back on Rome for consolation and support. 'The world was not their friend, nor the world's law.' In their own country they were persecuted and hated or despised. They transferred their allegiance to the Pope. Napoleon, by the Concordat, by making the Pope, by his own power, without the consent of the bishops, dethrone bishops and suppress sees, gave the sanction of the temporal power to the Pope's autocracy. Napoleon was the destroyer of the Gallican liberties, and the real re-creator of Ultramontanism.

Senior.—Could it not be checked by a proper selection of bishops? The Government is omnipotent. The Pope consecrates whomever it chooses. Could it not appoint only men of Gallican opinions?

Guizot.—Up to the present time the Government has not considered whether its candidates were Gallican or Ultramontane. It has looked out only for its friends, or for quiet men who would not give it trouble. I hope that in time it will correct this neglect, and give us Gallican bishops. It will not be easy however to find good candidates. But the people care little about the question. If we had many Dissenters, many Protestants, or even Jansenists, we should have zeal and belief. There are both at Nismes and in the other Protestant districts. But in this country the peasants, unexcited by dissent, are indifferent. They are not unbelievers, but they are not believers. They do not think about religion. If you were to ask them about any of the details of their faith, you would find them ignorant. The subject never occurs to them. They go to church from habit, for they do not understand the service; they respect the curé, and ask his advice in their difficulties, and would resent any injury or disrespect of which he was the object. But their faith, such as it is, influences little their conduct.

The little château of La Roque is moated, defended by towers and by a barbacan, and seems to be in the state in which it was five hundred years ago. The lords of La Roque and the abbés of Val Richer were generally at war. M. Guizot has a pardon granted by Henry IV. to the Seigneur of La Roque for having treacherously killed the abbé. The château was bought some years ago by a rich Rouen manufacturer, who uses it as a shooting box for three or four weeks in the year. Six châteaux have been bought in this country during the last ten years. Two have been bought by Protestants, one by a Jew, and one by a Greek, a Fanariote.

Thursday, August 31*st.*—It rained all day. After dinner we had a fire. Guizot stood before it, and talked of some of the eminent men whom he had known. He began by the English, and put Lord Aberdeen as a diplomatist at the top.

Guizot.—The great fault of the English statesmen is that they speak only with reference to their English hearers, and act only with reference to English interests or English opinions. Lord John Russell favours the expulsion of the Italian Sovereigns because they are under Austrian influence, and Austria is unpopular in England. Peel called our conduct in Otaheite an outrage, in order to please the missionary public, without reflecting that the use of such language by the leader of the House of Commons was a much greater outrage than the dismissal of an English missionary from an island under French protection. Now, Aberdeen never fell into this fault. He was a citizen of the world. He knew the interests and the feelings of foreign nations, and consulted them. He never cut knots; he untied them. He never lost his temper. Though he could not bear contradiction in the House of Lords, he was tolerant in his Cabinet. He has often said to me, ' We had better talk no more on this question to-day, or we may render it insoluble. A week hence, when we have both thought it over, we will recur to it.' Three times during his Ministry there were questions which menaced a quarrel. They were Otaheite, the right of search, and Morocco. If Peel had been then Minister of Foreign Affairs, they would have led to war. On the other hand, if I had had to negotiate in 1840 with Aberdeen, the Eastern question would have been amicably arranged. Syria would have been quiet under Mehemet Ali, and Mehemet Ali and his successors would have been put under restrictions which would have prevented the misgovernment of Egypt, and the calamities which followed the rupture of the 'entente cordiale' would have been averted.

De Witt.—A great improvement has recently been made in the management of international quarrels. Instead of going to war, we make preparations. If we offend you, you build ships. If you annoy us, we arm Cherbourg, or we case with steel some frigates. 'L'honneur est satisfait,' not by killing some hundred thousand men, but by wasting some millions of money. It is expensive, but far less expensive than war.

Guizot.—In my time this expedient had not been thought of. Nor were we able to silence the tribune. There was always a danger, therefore, that the violent language of your Chamber, meeting the violent language of ours, might produce an explosion. Peel, as leader of the House, gave us great trouble. If he had been Foreign Minister, I doubt whether peace would have been preserved, in the state of French feeling and of French liberty which existed from 1841 to 1846.

Other nations hate war, and treat it as a calamity to be avoided as long as it is avoidable. France actually likes it. It is an amusement which she is sometimes forced to refuse to herself, but it is always with regret. She submits to peace with the reluctance with which you submit to war. This renders the situation of a French minister who has any sense exceedingly difficult. In proportion as his policy is peaceful it is unpopular. It is called, and in one sense it *is*, anti-national.

No one can doubt Palmerston's talents or knowledge. He is admirable in discussion. He sees with the utmost clearness the point that is before him. He seizes with sagacity the best means for carrying it; but he sees only one thing at a time. His policy, therefore, is narrow and insulated, and sometimes inconsistent. His mind wants keeping. In this respect he is the opposite of Talleyrand. Talleyrand saw with admirable sagacity what were the great interests of his Government; he pursued them with vigour, and adhered to them with obstinate tenacity; but he sacrificed to them, with a facility which was almost ostentatious, all triumphs of mere vanity, and even all interests which, though real, were subordinate. He was always ready to exchange pawns for pieces. If Palmerston has set his heart on taking a pawn, he will sacrifice a rook for it. Another fault of his policy is its irritability. He picks up every straw of offence that lies in his path. If a man did so in private life, he would quarrel with his wife once a week and with his valet once a day. He resents a fillip as if it were a stab, and fires a ninety-eight pounder against a wasp's nest. If the house of a Gibraltar Jew who never possessed 1000*l*. is plundered, he asks for 30,000*l*. of indemnity, and blockades the Piræus to extort it.

Senior.—I must defend Lord Palmerston as to the Pacifico and Finlay affair. A mob, headed by the son of a Greek minister, had plundered Pacifico; the King himself had robbed Finlay. Otho, with childish obstinacy, refused any reparation whatever. He would not let the claims made against him be even inquired into. What was Lord Palmerston to do? He was forced to take Pacifico's story because the King would not discuss the matter. He was forced to employ force because the King would not hear argument. And he sent an overwhelming force in order to save the King's honour by rendering resistance impossible.

Guizot.—Well, I am not enough acquainted with the details to discuss with you the Greek affair; but you must admit that Palmerston is generally blamed for it.

Senior.—Yes; for the very reason that makes *you* blame him, that the details are not known.

Guizot.—You will not defend Palmerston's revolutionary foreign policy ?

Senior.—The conduct of many foreign Governments has been such that nothing short of a revolution can reform them. I do not see how Palmerston could avoid feeling this, or feeling it, and knowing that it was felt by all the Liberal party in England, how he could avoid expressing it. And he has done no more. I am inclined to think that France has favoured revolutions among her neighbours quite as much as England has.

Guizot.—That is true as respects the French people. With the exception of that of the 18th Fructidor, which was the beginning of military despotism, all our early revolutions were useful. They did enormous harm, but it was over-balanced by still greater good. In our minds, at least until 1848, revolution was associated with reform, with liberty, and with progress, and above all, with the downfall of what we most hate, aristocracy. We expect every insurrection among our neighbours to produce justice and liberty and equality. We are exposed, too, far more than you are, to the influence of refugees. They are generally harmless with you. They do not speak your language or understand your feelings or your institutions, they cannot enter your public service. You are ' penitus toto divisi orbe Britanni.' They find England dear, foggy, unsympathetic, and quit it. With us they are almost at home. We adopt them and we employ them.

Senior.—You do much more, you naturalize them, they go home, and you allow them to claim your protection, as if they were natural-born Frenchmen, against their own Governments.

Guizot.—That was a great abuse, but we are scarcely responsible for the acts of the ' Gouvernement Provisoire.' The question of asylum, however, is a grave one. The right to give it is noble and useful, useful to all parties. It is often a bridge of gold for a flying enemy. But it is so abused that I sometimes fear that it may be lost. Paris is now full of Italians and Hungarians openly conspiring against Austria. London is the centre of an avowed conspiracy against Louis Napoleon. Turin and Genoa have been the head-quarters of the Sicilian and Neapolitan conspirators.

The Governments whose laws authorize them to send away conspirators are inexcusable; you, who have no such laws, ought to make them.

Senior.—We think that an alien act would be inconvenient. That, in general, it would be difficult to act on it, or to refuse to do so.

Guizot.—What are Governments meant for, except to deal with difficulties?

Senior.—How do you account for the insertion in the *Moniteur* of the addresses of the colonels in 1858?

Guizot.—Louis Napoleon meant to intimidate you. It was a strange blunder for a man who had lived in England. But the effects were excellent, it opened your eyes. If he had said nothing, you would have passed the Conspiracy Bill, and have still trusted him as your faithful ally.

In 1830 Spain encouraged the Legitimist conspirators. Bourmont was just within the frontier. The Duchesse de Berri was to join him. I brought the Spanish Government to its senses by giving to the Spanish refugees, Mina, Valdez, Isturiz and their party, full liberty to conspire against it. Ferdinand was alarmed. He knew that he was hated, despised, and, what is worse than all for a Sovereign, distrusted. He implored us to discountenance all conspiracies in France against him, promising to repress all in Spain against Louis Philippe.

Friday, September 1st.—We talked this morning at breakfast of Lamartine.

Guizot.—Never was nature more prodigal, and never were her gifts more abused. He began with eloquence, imagination, courage, beauty, birth, fortune; all have been destroyed by the want of self-command. He never can resist the immediate gratification of his vanity. He has wasted his fortune in ostentatious hospitality and almsgiving, he boasts that he is 'la Providence' of all his neighbours. He falsifies the facts of his history in order to introduce claptraps and theatrical effects, he falsifies its spirit to please, to influence, and to deceive the ignorant mob of readers. His policy, when a member of the Provisional Government, was all vanity. He hoped that the Republicans and the bourgeoisie would unite to make him President. I cannot read his Girondins.

De Witt.—When Lamartine was in power, he used to jot down indiscriminately hints for his poems and hints for his Administration. In a paper containing, among other things, a list of prefects, was found the word 'David.' M. David appeared, therefore, in the *Moniteur* as prefect, and Lamartine's secretary came to him to ask M. David's address. Lamartine was sorely puzzled. The name certainly was there, but he could not tell why. At last he recollected that he had put it down as a memorandum of some allusion to King David, to be introduced into a 'meditation.' So a notice appeared in the *Moniteur*, nominating A.B. a prefect in the place of M. David, 'appelé à d'autres fonctions.'

Madame de Witt.—Has Lamartine any children?

Guizot.—None. The paucity of children to a marriage in the higher classes is such that it very much diminishes the chances, at all times small, of seeing an eminent man succeeded by an eminent son. Scarcely any of the great men of the Revolution left sons of any merit, Lanjuinais is the best that occurs to me. He is a man of sense and integrity, but would not be distinguished if he were not the son of the Conventionist. Carnot's son is nothing. Thibaudeau's son was clever, but a 'mauvais sujet.' The Regicide Thibaudeau was one of the most respectable members of the Convention.

Senior.—I knew him and liked him. He was proud of his English, and once said to me, 'It is nonsense to say that Frenchmen cannot pronounce th. I can say 'dat' as well as you can.'

Guizot.—This paucity would facilitate the reconstruction of an aristocracy. The rich families remain rich, or rather increase in riches, for their numbers diminish, and the value of their properties increases.

Senior.—You will obtain, indeed, you have, a rich upper class; but a real aristocracy, that is, a body of men, uniting political importance to hereditary fortune is scarcely compatible with the reign of universal suffrage.

Guizot.—That is true, though *you* have as yet escaped universal suffrage, the lowering the suffrage by your reform has destroyed the aristocratic character of your Government. You could not now, as you did from 1793 to 1815, hold on through military failures, financial difficulties, and commercial distress, until the long-deferred success arrived. You could not, as we did from Henri IV. until Louis XIV. pursue for one hundred years our undeviating policy. Your reformed House would not stand more than a very few years of ill-success. I have no doubt that your home Government is better than it was under Pitt, or under Pitt's followers. An unreformed Parliament would not have given you poor-law reform, or municipal reform, or free-trade. But it would have given you greater statesmen, and a firmer and a wiser foreign policy.

Your next fall will be into what will be virtually universal suffrage; for it will place power in the hands of the uneducated majority, and it signifies little whether they are sixty per cent. or ninety-nine per cent. of the electors. And a Parliament elected by universal suffrage will never be moderate. It will always oscillate between servility and revolution. With us it is servile; with you it will be revolutionary.

Your present semi-Radical House has already forced you to break down the two great Conservative powers in Europe —Russia and Austria. I admit that there was much to disapprove in both of them, and, from Russia, much to fear. Her people are in the semi-barbarous state which renders them the blind instruments of their Sovereigns, and their Sovereigns have often been semi-barbarians, violent, aggressive, and despotic. Under Nicholas, she was the consistent enemy of all Liberal institutions and Liberal opinions. So is Austria, and, though not covetous of territory, she is covetous of influence, and her influence is exerted in favour of despotism and against improvement. If you had weakened only one of them, you might have done well; or, if there had been no such country as France in the world, it might have been well to destroy the power of both of them. But France is a standing danger, sometimes to the freedom, sometimes to the good government of Europe. And what bulwark have you now against her? Not Prussia. Her army, out of all proportion to her population, or her wealth, is a militia. Our military men treat it with contempt. Sardinia, or by whatever name the new Kingdom of Italy is to be called, is, at least for the present, powerful only for mischief.

The Netherlands and Belgium could bring into the field two hundred thousand men—a force not to be despised; but they have no military reputation. Russia is 'hors de combat.' Our troops have returned from Italy with a great respect for the Austrian soldiers. But they have enough to do to keep down Hungary and Venetia. Austria, while intact, supported by Belgium and Holland, and, in case of need, by Prussia, was a check to the ambition of a French despot, or to the madness of a French Republic, which was useful, I might say indispensable, to you and to ourselves. And you have done, and are doing, all that you can, without actual war, to break her up.

I asked M. Guizot, if he had read the 'Revue Rétrospective.'

Guizot.—Certainly, and speaking as I think that I can do at this distance of time, of the Royal family, my colleagues, and myself, as mere historical persons, I venture to say that we have a right to be proud of it. All our papers of every kind, our most private notes, even our memoranda for our own use, were in the hands of our enemies, men perfectly unrestrained by any scruples, or by any feeling of the reserve due to us or even to themselves. They published everything; at least everything which they thought would sell. And what is there that we have to be ashamed of—that any one of us has to be ashamed of? I know of no letters that do more honour to their writers than those of Louis Philippe and his family.

Senior.—The editors were not utterly unscrupulous, for they did not falsify.

Guizot.—They did not falsify for two reasons. First, because we were alive; and, secondly, because a suspicion of falsification would have spoiled the sale. The 'Revue Rétrospective' was more a commercial than a political speculation.

Sunday, September 2nd.—Before breakfast Guizot read to

us a sermon of Bourdaloue's, and Pauline de Witt a prayer. They both read admirably. Later in the day there was another service for the servants, most of whom are Swiss Protestants.

Guizot.—The same sermons, or even the same prayers, are not fit for us and for our servants and children. What interests us is only partially intelligible to them; what they can understand we think commonplace. Bourdaloue is the first of our preachers. Massillon has too much ornament. The ornament is good, but a sermon deals with interests of such overwhelming importance that the preacher ought not to appear to think of his style.

Senior.—Nor ought any other speaker or author to appear to do so.

Guizot.—Without doubt, the less he shows that he does so the better. But when period after period is perfect; when every idea is presented clearly, vividly, and concisely; when, after it has been exhibited at full length in a long sentence, it is repeated in miniature in a short one, no one can fancy that the author was not thinking of his style. No one can believe that Tocqueville or Macaulay thought only of his subject and nothing of himself. Now, one might believe that Bourdaloue did this; at least a person not of the 'métier;' a person who did not know from experience how difficult it is to write simply and naturally, might believe it.

The 'Ami de la Religion' was on the table.

Guizot.—It is the best of the Catholic journals. I take it in because it contains excellent articles on English politics, written under the signature of Audley.

Senior.—It seems that little attention is paid to the law requiring real signatures.

Guizot.—Not the least. The Imperialist papers began to publish with false signatures; the others have followed the example, and no one is interfered with. It appears that M. Billault and his master think that the system of 'avertissements' is a sufficient gag to the Liberal press.

C. de Witt.—The change from Delangle to Billault as Minister of the Interior is a misfortune. Delangle was liberal, at least for an Imperialist; Billault is worse than even Espinasse. Espinasse had some reserves. Louis Napoleon, when the coup d'état was imminent, asked Espinasse if he might rely on his obedience in all circumstances whatever. 'I am ready,' said Espinasse, 'to throw all the Deputies into the Seine, and to shoot every one who looks as if he intended to raise a barricade; but you must not put me where I may meet the Duc d'Aumale. He saved my life in Africa. Si je le rencontre, je brise mon épée.'

Guizot.—Our best, our most trusted, and our most trustworthy journalist, was Bertin de Vaux. I always talked to him freely, both in office and in opposition, and he never made any use of my conversation to which I could object.

M. Guizot talked at breakfast of the royal personages whom he had known.

Guizot.—Louis XVIII. has the reputation of Constitutionalism, but it was not because he liked, or even approved, Parliamentary Government. He hated the charter, but he believed it to be necessary, and he submitted to it with a good grace; with better, indeed, than Louis Philippe, principally because he took less interest in public affairs. Louis Philippe's spirit was broken by the Revolution. He worshipped Republicanism as some Asiatic nations do the devil, as a maleficent principle, to be flattered and propitiated, but not to be resisted. Among his ministers, those whom he caressed most, such as Lafitte, and afterwards Thiers, were not those whom he trusted most or liked most. He used to call them by their simple surnames; he never did so to Casimir Périer, or to the Duc de Broglie, or even to me. He was not familiar with those whom he respected; or rather he ceased to respect those who appeared to wish for his familiarity. He has been called false, but I never found him so. Though personally brave, he was politically timid; he preferred address to force; he always wished to turn an obstacle instead of attacking it in front. He has been called avaricious; that is another calumny. He did not like to waste his money, but he devoted it liberally to public purposes. Though never confident as to the future, he made no private purse. In 1848 he lost his head. When he went down into the Carrousel and found the National Guard crying 'La réforme!' his presence of mind deserted him. He answered, 'Vous avez la réforme; Barrot est chargé de la préparer,' went back, and abdicated. If he had let Bugeaud act for him all would have been saved.

Thiers was not a good counsellor in extremity. I do not believe that he wants courage, but his imagination disturbs his judgment. His real place is in the tribune. In the streets he loses his presence of mind; in the Cabinet he always preferred 'une politique de vanité à une politique de raison.' I was forced to return to France in 1840 to prevent his engaging us in a war in order to give Syria to Mehemet Ali, a thing quite right and useful, but not useful peculiarly to France; not more worth a war than the giving Lombardy to Piedmont was. And even in the tribune, although a first-rate debater—clear, simple, ingenious, and persuasive—he had two great faults. First, he was too long; he repeated himself too often. Every speaker must repeat himself, since in every assembly some attend at one time and some at another; but Thiers abused this privilege, or this necessity. His other fault was the want of order. There was no principle of arrangement in his speeches; the end might have been at the beginning, and the beginning at the end. This made it difficult to answer him, because it was difficult to remember him. In order to recollect his speech it was necessary to reconstruct it.

Senior.—Was Madame Adelaïde a superior woman?

Guizot.—Morally, not intellectually. She had good sense, but it was commonplace good sense. Such too was the character of Louis Philippe's mind. He had sagacity and knowledge of mankind, but he was better fitted to decide between different counsels than to suggest. This similarity led to the opinion that Madame Adelaïde had great influence over him. She appeared to have influence because they generally took the same view of a question. He was an admirable causeur; perhaps too good, for his pleasure in talking often made him lose time, and sometimes made him indiscreet. He did not, like most royal persons, assume to lead the conversation; he let it take its course. You might suggest topics; you might even ask him questions. Queen Christina was one of the cleverest Sovereigns that I have known. No one taught me so much about Spain. She judged persons and things with great intelligence and impartiality. Another very able man is the King of Würtemburg.

Senior.—Twenty years ago Prince Woronzoff told me that he considered him the best general that Germany then possessed.

Guizot.—He is quite as remarkable as a statesman, at least as a theoretical statesman. He used to complain to me of his nullity in practice. 'You,' he said, 'because you are a subject, can be a minister; you can affect the destinies of France, and through France, those of the world. What can a poor little King of Würtemburg do? He cannot be a minister, and if he were to affect to play the independent Sovereign he would be laughed at. The Bund will not allow him to have a foreign policy, or even a domestic policy. Of all institutions for *mis*government, the Bund is one of the worst. It renders the German Sovereigns powerless for good and irresistible for evil.'

Senior.—You knew Metternich and you knew the Duke of Wellington. Which do you put the higher as a statesman?

Guizot.—The Duke of Wellington, beyond all comparison. Metternich was dexterous; he was skilful in his dealings with other diplomatists; but he knew nothing of the people. The explosion of 1848 found him not only unprepared, but unsuspicious.

Senior.—A few days before the Austrian revolution of 1848, Lord Hardinge, on his return from India, spent some days with him at Vienna. 'See,' he said, 'the results of my policy. While the other thrones of Europe are tottering, Austria is not even threatened.' One of the first persons whom Lord Hardinge met on his arrival in London was Metternich, who in his flight had preceded him.

Guizot.—He told me in 1847 that he was not aware that he had ever made a political mistake.

'Illi mori gravis incidit
Qui notus nimis omnibus
Ignotus moritur sibi.'

His wit was chiefly antithetical. He said of you, 'Les Anglais ont plus de bon sens qu'aucune autre nation. Et ils sont fous.'

Senior.—That was like Talleyrand's praise of English education: 'C'est la meilleure en Europe, et elle est détestable.'

Guizot.—What struck me most in the Duke of Wellington was his wonderful good sense and sagacity. He had not a spark of imagination, but he did not want it. It was not necessary to him as it is to other men, in order to supply the defects of perception. He was not forced to conjecture; he could see every part of his subject.

Senior.—Whom do you consider your best general?

Guizot.—Trochu. Lamoricière, MacMahon, and Changarnier are all good. But Lamoricière has never been tried against civilized soldiers. He has encountered only Arabs, Cabyles, and 'émeutiers.' MacMahon is an admirable general of division, but those who have served with him doubt his fitness to command 150,000 men, and, unhappily, that may now be considered as the normal force of an army. Changarnier is like Harpagon's cook, he wants large appliances. He requires 100,000 men to do what Napoleon would have done with 50,000. Trochu was the favourite scholar and aide de camp of Bugeaud. When he was only a captain, and a very young one, Bugeaud wrote to me to propose to raise him over the heads of hundreds, his seniors, to the rank of chef de bataillon. It is the most important step in the service. 'I should not ask it,' he said, 'if I were not sure that I am preparing a Maréchal for you.'

Senior.—Why were *you* consulted? You were not Minister of War.

Guizot.—No; but I was leader of the house. The nomination was sure to be attacked, and I had to defend it.

After breakfast we begged Madame de Witt to show us some of her father's orders. She brought down three —the Golden Fleece, the Elephant, and a Chinese order. The last, it seems, is the greatest; the owner of it wears a blue button, and ranks after the Emperor. It consists of a collar of amber beads, with a sort of brooch of jasper, and a jasper tassel.

Guizot's collar of the Golden Fleece is the one which was worn by Philip II. of Spain. It is of gold and enamel, and finely worked. It confers grandeeship, but whether hereditary or not, Guizot does not know. Queen Isabella wished to make him Duke of San Antonio. When he refused the dukedom, she sent to him the Murillo which ornaments his apartment in Paris.

Guizot's pictures at Val Richer are modern. His mother, by Ary Scheffer, and the Queen of the French, by Winterhalter, are the best, and are both very good. A remarkable one is an equestrian portrait of Mehemet Ali. He had not the common Mussulman objection to being painted, and sent this picture to Guizot after the Syrian affair in 1840.

We walked in the afternoon over the wooded hills overlooking the Abbey. We talked of Hebrew poetry.

Guizot.—Verse is not essential to poetry in Hebrew; what distinguishes it from prose is that every thought is repeated with a slight modification—

> 'Thinkest thou that I will eat bull's flesh,
> Or drink the blood of goats?
> All the beasts of the forest are mine,
> And so are the cattle on a thousand hills.

The first people who wrote sensibly were the Hebrews; all other Asiatic literature is childish. From them common sense passed to the Greeks.

Senior.—I have always considered Egypt as the parent of civilization.

Guizot.—Yes, in point of time. But the Egyptians, though rich, refined, and civilized, while all the rest of the world was barbarous, do not appear to have had any valuable literature. Their characters were too cumbrous to be much used in books. They are essentially lapidary. Their cosmogony was as wild as that of the Hindoos. Their worship was still worse; it was the most degraded Fetichism. I do not think that we owe much to the wisdom of the Egyptians, though Moses is said to have studied it. There are no Coptic words in Greek; it is a branch of Sanscrit. Greek language and art came from the Assyrians and the Phœnicians.

Some of the Basques appear to be Phœnicians. They use words which are to be found in the 'Penulus' of Plautus.

The use of characters easily written and easily read seems to be necessary to a high degree of literary cultivation. The want of such characters has kept stationary the Chinese. The complexity of their characters probably was one of the causes which arrested the progress of the Arabs, an exceedingly intelligent race, who yet have contributed little to literature. The Carthaginians, great as they were in commerce and in arms, and using Greek characters, must have had poets and historians. The irrecoverable loss of their language is a great misfortune.

The conversation went from Hebrew to Italian.

Guizot.—There is much modern Italian poetry of great merit, of which you know nothing. Even Macaulay, who knew everything, was little acquainted with it.

Senior.—Was his knowledge of French literature great?

Guizot.—Greater than that of almost any Frenchman. He told me once that he knew only three perfect works— Madame de Sévigné's Letters, the Lettres Provinciales, and Molière's great plays. Have you read Gladstone's Homer?

Senior.—Of course I have.

Guizot.—I thoroughly sympathise with his admiration of Homer, and with his belief in the individuality of Homer; but his geography and his mythology are too deep for me, and his love for Helen puts me in mind of Cousin's passion for Madame de Longueville.

Senior.—It is wonderful that beauty, never seen, known to us only by description, should so affect us.

Guizot.—Nay, Helen's beauty is not known to us, even by description. For all that we know she may have been blonde or brunette, she may have had blue eyes, or hazel eyes, or black eyes. Homer only tells us that it was no wonder that for such a woman nations should fight for years. Gladstone is not her only conquest; she turned the head of Goethe.

Senior.—I never read the second part of 'Faust.'

Guizot.—It is not worth reading. The meaning is not easily made out, and is seldom worth making out. Goethe, like many other Germans, fell in love with his own creations and his own ideas, and dwelt on them till he wore them out. The second part of his 'Wilhelm Meister' and the latter part of his 'Wahl-verwandschaften' are scarcely readable. The best German poems are the ballads. I am a great novel reader, but I seldom read German or French novels. The characters are too artificial. There are too many forced situations, and the morality is generally detestable. My delight is to read English novels, particularly those written by women. 'C'est toute une école de morale.' Miss Austen, Miss Ferrier, Charlotte Brontë, George Eliot, Mrs. Gaskell, and many others almost as remarkable, form a school which in the excellence, the profusion, and the contemporaneousness of its productions, resembles the cloud of dramatic poets of the great Athenian age. It is remarkable that while you are great in some of the imitative arts, you fail in others which are closely connected with those in which you excel. Your painters are good; your architects, with a few great exceptions, are detestable.

Your dramatic writers are not first-rate, but they are respectable. Your actors do not approach mediocrity. Young Kean is very bad. Macready was worse, and yet he has a high reputation. The greatest living tragedian is Madame Viardot. Her acting in Glück's Orfeo is perfect. She has more real passion than even Rachel. And yet Rachel was very great. Rachel's exquisite tact and powers of imitation showed themselves by her conduct in society.

She was ill-educated, she was ill-conditioned, she was already grown-up, and, as one would suppose, with manners not only formed but fixed, when she was first introduced into good company. She must have known that she was not respected, that she was tolerated only as a show. One can scarcely imagine greater disadvantages. And yet her manners were perfect. They were dignified and graceful, yet unrestrained.

I much preferred her to Ristori, particularly as a reciter. Ristori is too vehement. She rages and gesticulates before it is proper, and more than it is proper. Rachel began quietly and slowly, and gradually rose to passion as the audience became 'passionnée.' In the evenings, too, on which she was to recite, she was composed, almost reserved, from the time she entered the room. She did not jump, as Ristori does, from gay badinage, or fierce politics, to passionate declamation.

We study Molière rather less than we used to do; less than you do Shakspeare. I do not think that three or four lines from Shakspeare could be quoted in the House of Commons without being detected. But when I quoted in the Chambers of Deputies these lines—

> 'Je hais tous les hommes;
> Les uns parcequ'ils sont méchants et malfaisants,
> Et les autres pour être aux méchants complaisants'

the House did not find out that it was Molière, or even that it was verse. They accused me of abusing the House, and I doubt whether I appeased them by telling them that it was a quotation from the 'Misanthrope.'

In the evening, nonobstant Sunday, the children danced.

Monday, September 3rd.—We went before breakfast to

see the school. It is mixed, and contains, when full, about sixty children; but as this was the first meeting after the vacation, not above twenty were present. The boys read well, better than in any English school that I have visited, except Mr. Rogers' Charterhouse Schools, and the school at Loughborough. Their writing, consisting of tasks slowly copied during the vacation, was admirable. The subject of one was Tobit, that of another a history of the First Revolution. The lines

'Ça ira, ça ira, ça ira,
Tous les aristocrats à la lanterne'

formed part of it, but with proper reprobation. I desired a boy to sketch on the blackboard a map of France. He made a fair outline and put in all the towns which I mentioned to him.

Guizot.—We pay more attention to the geography of France than to that of Palestine, to French history than to Jewish history, and to modern French history than to that of Clovis or Pepin. Your practice I believe is different.

The schoolmaster is a pleasing, intelligent young man. He has a neat house, built, as was the school, by M. Guizot, and an income of about 60*l.* a year. With this he is content. His chief want is that of society. There is no medical man or notaire in the village. He is far more cultivated than the farmers or even the curés, but they must be his associates. The children looked healthy.

Guizot.—We have no manufactures. The difference in health between our agricultural and our manufacturing villages is striking. There are two communes between me and Pont l'Evêque, which adjoin. They differ little in soil or in air or in the number of their inhabitants; but one is purely agricultural, the other is chiefly manufacturing. Each furnishes in time of peace, every year, fourteen conscripts.

In order to get fourteen youths fit for service twenty-eight ballots are necessary in the agricultural commune and sixty-four in the manufacturing one. Of those who draw the lot of service among the manufacturers fifty are rejected as unfit, for fourteen among the agriculturists.

Senior.—Even the rejection of fourteen out of twenty-eight seems a large proportion.

Guizot.—It is not large for France. The majority of the young men, who as entering their twenty-first year become subject to the ballot, are unfit for service. And if our wars continue that proportion will increase. The mere occupation of Algiers is a drain on our able-bodied population. For many years it required a garrison of 100,000 men; it now requires 60,000. If, as is probable, we take in Tunis, it will again require 100,000. We are always in danger too of having to conquer Morocco. Even our present African empire is almost as great a burden to us as India is to you. If we are forced, as you were forced, to make further conquests, it may become a still greater burden. Avarice, or rather cupidity, created the germ of *your* distant empire, vanity created ours; and the ignorance and perverseness of semi-barbarous neighbours may oblige us, as they obliged you, to extend it. Africa has given us good soldiers and India has given you good generals. There the advantages to the dominant countries end, though I hope that the conquered countries will be better governed under Christians than they were under Mussulmans.

Senior.—You expect to see Tunis French? What is Constantinople to be?

Guizot.—It cannot remain Turkish. The attempt to preserve the integrity of the rotten Turkish Empire is an attempt to resist nature. Such an attempt, when made by two such nations as France and England, may be persevered in for years. The longer it lasts the greater will be the waste of men and money and diplomacy; but it must eventually fail. The Turks must be driven across the Bosphorus. We cannot occupy Constantinople, nor can you; we are both resolved not to let Russia have it, and all Europe would refuse to put it under Austria, even if Austria were mad enough to wish for it. It cannot be independent; it must therefore be Greek, the capital of a Greek Empire, to which you will be wise enough to cede your troublesome and useless protectorate of the Ionian Islands.

Senior.—The Ionians will not be gainers by such a cession.

Guizot.—Of course they will be worse governed by the Greeks than they are by you; but a people had rather be ill-governed by its fellow-countrymen than well-governed by foreigners. In Algeria we have put an end to the civil wars of the tribes; we have made the country safe; we distribute impartial justice; its produce has enormously increased in quantity and also in price. Never was a conquered country more benefited by its conquest; yet it requires the constant presence of a French army, and the constant vigilance of the 'Bureaux Arabes' to prevent an insurrection more extensive than your Indian mutiny, and quite as vindictive.

On the evening of the 3rd of September we left Val Richer, after a most agreeable and instructive visit. M. Guizot is never greater or more amiable than in his own family.

THE END.

www.ingramcontent.com/pod-product-compliance
Lightning Source LLC
Chambersburg PA
CBHW032141010526
44111CB00035B/745